In Search of the
Indo-
Europeans

In Search of the
Indo-Europeans

Language, Archaeology and Myth

J.P. Mallory

With 175 illustrations

THAMES AND HUDSON

For Deirdre, Conall and Eimear

© 1989 Thames and Hudson Ltd, London

First published in the United States in 1989 by
Thames and Hudson Inc., 500 Fifth Avenue,
New York, New York 10110

Library of Congress Catalog Card Number 88-50232

Printed and bound in the German Democratic Republic

Contents

Foreword

By the first century AD historical records reveal peoples settled from the shores of the Atlantic to India all speaking languages closely related to one another. These are the Indo-European languages whose origins can be traced back to a common ancestor that was spoken in Eurasia some 6,000 years ago. We call the people who spoke this ancestral language the Indo-Europeans or Proto-Indo-Europeans. But although we can give them a name, they are unlike almost any other ancient people we are likely to encounter. As the linguistic ancestors of nearly half this planet's population they are one of the most important entities in the prehistoric record – and yet they are also one of the most elusive. No Proto-Indo-European text exists; their physical remains and material culture cannot be identified without extensive argument; and their geographical location has been the subject of a century and a half of intense yet inconclusive debate.

To attempt to survey the origins of *all* the different Indo-Europeans and then track each of them to their original homeland and discuss their common culture is a task to daunt any single writer and certainly outrun the competence of any single scholar. Out in the academic world neither of these problems has ever been a serious deterrent, and in the past century there have been at least seventy volumes published as general surveys of the Indo-Europeans and their origins. Yet, other than sporadic attempts to resolve the problem of Indo-European origins with cursory reference to the different Indo-European peoples, there has not been a full general survey of the Indo-Europeans in English for at least a half century. This has encouraged me to produce this volume to fill the gap.

During the course of writing this book, the authors of two recently published works on the Indo-Europeans were gracious enough to send me copies of their own books: Tomas Gamkrelidze and Vyachislav Ivanov's massive two-volume study *Indo-European Language and Indo-Europeans* (in Russian), and Colin Renfrew's more popular *Archaeology and Language: The puzzle of Indo-European origins*. I disagree rather fundamentally with both works which in some ways seem to have strayed light-years away from whatever consensus the general run of Indo-European studies has managed to achieve. Nevertheless, I have profited greatly from the vast accumulation of data offered by the two Soviet linguists and, while I am unconvinced of their solution to the problem of Indo-European origins, they will see in other discussions throughout this book the debt I owe their work.

Colin Renfrew's book provided a stimulus of another kind. Although I had largely anticipated his conclusions on Indo-European origins in my original draft, my publishers encouraged me to make some additions to the basic text to take into account Professor Renfrew's most recent exposition of his theories. His latest work is very much a challenge to the conventional wisdom. While I regard my own work to be in the general mainstream of this 'conventional wisdom', I thought it out of place to reduce this book to an interminable counter-attack on a colleague's opinions. Consequently, I have examined Renfrew's main theories primarily in one part of my own text (Chapter Six), while reserving some more detailed argument for the notes. I should emphasize that I have not written this book simply to propose yet another solution to the Indo-European homeland problem; rather, I have also attempted to provide a general but, I hope, useful survey of the current state of our knowledge about the earliest Indo-Europeans.

I believe that a discussion of the Indo-Europeans without the evidence of their languages would be like statistics without mathematics. For this reason, a number of linguistic 'figures' have been included in my belief that the general reader is far more interested in seeing what a line of Sanskrit or Gothic looked like than what pot the speakers of these languages may have cooked in or what device held their clothes together. Throughout this work I have always tried to keep in sight the fact that Indo-European is fundamentally a linguistic concept and that any cultural (pre)historian has certain obligations to the evidence of comparative linguistics. Nevertheless, I must plead guilty to both generalization and simplification. A certain graphic simplicity for linguistic forms is necessitated because too many diacritical marks, necessary though they may be for the proper articulation and analysis of the forms, have a way of terrifying a general reader. Those linguists who will immediately know what is missing from my forms will, I am sure, restore the vowel lengths, accents, and other necessary diacritics. I might add that any reference to Indo-Europeans in general, or to more specific Indo-European groups such as Greeks or Slavs, should be construed merely as short-hand for 'Indo-European-speaking' or 'Greek-speaking' or 'Indo-European who occupied an area and later developed into a Greek-speaker', and no necessary reference to a specific physical type or material culture is intended.

Although Indo-European is fundamentally a linguistic construct, I have written this book primarily from the perspective of an archaeologist who has been subjected to a certain number of the methods of the historical linguist. I have tried, as far as possible, to strike a balance between the evidence of the two disciplines, although I know only too well that the competing arguments for the 'primacy' of archaeological or linguistic evidence will not satisfy everyone. Even with extended treatment, much of the archaeological discussion must, like the linguistic, be severely abbreviated to avoid losing both author and reader in incredible detail. As for the prehistoric (BC) dates cited in the text, these are all approximations based on the tree-ring-calibrated radiocarbon chronology, that is, BC = Cal. BC, or, for the reader unacquainted with these terms, BC dates are in ordinary calendar years.

CHAPTER ONE

The Discovery of the Indo-Europeans

> My leisure hours, for some time past, have been
> employed in considering the striking affinity of
> the languages of *Europe*; and finding, every day,
> new and most engaging entertainment in this
> pursuit, I was insensibly led on to attempt
> following them to their source.
>
> JAMES PARSONS, 1767

That James Parsons approached his subject as a dilettante is obvious. Certainly his earlier studies on the human bladder, the structure of seeds, and hermaphroditism do not form the academic prelude that one might expect from someone seeking to trace the origins of the ancient peoples of Europe. But in fact, James Parsons, physician and fellow of both the Royal Society and the Society of Antiquaries, was probably no less well equipped to pursue such a study than any of his eighteenth-century contemporaries. The primary evidence for such an investigation was then limited to the more speculative efforts of ancient historians coupled with both pious and politically motivated fabrications of medieval monks, all of which was then constrained by a literal interpretation of the Book of Genesis. This confined all discussion to no earlier than 2350 BC (or about 1,656 years after the Creation) when the families of Noah and his sons disembarked from the Ark and set out to populate the world. The marriage of such diverse sources often required the eighteenth-century historian to find or forge correlations between the Bible and the Classical world resulting in such mammoth compendia as *The Universal History from the earliest account of time to the present* (1736–65). If Parsons had confined his investigations to these sources alone, his work could be justly dismissed as merely another academic curiosity presently disintegrating on a handful of library shelves. But Parsons recognized that there was a largely untapped source of evidence bearing on the most ancient peoples of Europe and Asia – a comparison of their different languages offered a guide to their relative affinity with one another and their distant origins.

The close relationships between some European languages had already been clearly remarked upon by the beginning of the seventeenth century. Joseph Scaliger (1540–1609), for example, attempted to divide the languages of Europe into four major groups, each labelled after their word for 'god'. The transparent relationship of what we today call the Romance languages was recognized in the *deus* group (for example, Latin *deus*, Italian *dio*, Spanish *dio*, French *dieu*), and contrasted with the Germanic *gott* (English *god*, Dutch *god*, Swedish *gud*, and so on); Greek *theos*; and Slavic *bog* (such as Russian *bog*, Polish *bog* and Czech *buh*). Beyond this grouping Scaliger would not go, and he specifically denied any relationship between these different groups. However, during the course of the next century it became increasingly apparent to some that both the ancient languages and the peoples of Europe were more closely related than Scaliger had imagined. To those who preferred to take their historical evidence from the classical world, a wildly injudicious use of the term Scythian or Thracian came to be applied to most of those Europeans who had been situated north of the Greeks and Romans and who seemed to share some natural affinity. To those who preferred their history from the Bible, the label for these vaguely related Europeans was also easily obtained. Genesis had made it explicitly clear that the Semites (Jews, Arabs) and Hamites (Egyptians, Cushites) had derived from Shem and Ham respectively. It was then left to Noah's third son Japhet to father much of the remaining human race and hence it was not uncommon to lump the early peoples and languages of Europe under the name Japhetic.

In 1767 Parsons published his study *The Remains of Japhet, being historical enquiries into the affinity and origins of the European languages*. Had this work been much shorter, its author might be better remembered. Unfortunately for Parsons, this rather tedious book ensured his obscurity and subsequent neglect in histories of Indo-European studies, a neglect not entirely deserved.

Parsons began his linguistic survey by demonstrating the clear affinity between Irish and Welsh with an extensive (1,000 word) comparison of their vocabularies. This led him to the conclusion that Irish and Welsh 'were originally the same'. He then expanded his attention to the other languages of Eurasia by comparing their words for the basic numerals under the perfectly sound linguistic principle that 'numbers being convenient to every nation, their names were most likely to continue nearly the same, even though other parts of languages might be liable to change and alteration'. The comparisons were extensive and included Celtic (Irish, Welsh), Greek, Italic (Latin, Italian, Spanish, French), Germanic (German, Dutch, Swedish, Danish, Old English, English), Slavic (Polish, Russian), Indic (Bengali) and Iranian (Persian). No one, no matter how untutored in the techniques of comparative philology, could fail to see similarities between the different languages in his list. In addition, in an exemplary instance of sound methodology, Parsons also listed the same numerals in Turkish, Hebrew, Malay and Chinese all of which failed to show any outstanding similarities either with the previous list of Eurasian languages or with one another. Parsons therefore concluded that the first group, the languages of Europe, Iran and India, were all derived from a common ancestor, the language of Japhet and his offspring, who had migrated out of Armenia, the final resting place of the Ark.

In both proposing and demonstrating that the languages of Europe, Iran and India had all derived from a common ancestor, James Parsons could well be credited with having independently discovered what we now call the Indo-European language family. But Parsons shrouded his theory in a mass of biblical references, a gullible acceptance of the histories and chronicles of

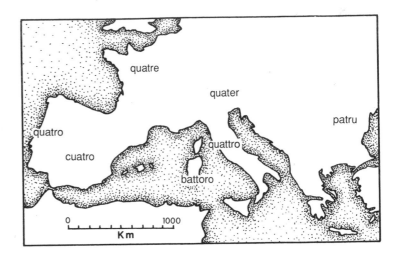

1 The outcome of Latin quattuor *'four' in various Romance languages shows how words for numerals tend to remain relatively stable although they experience phonetic change through time.*

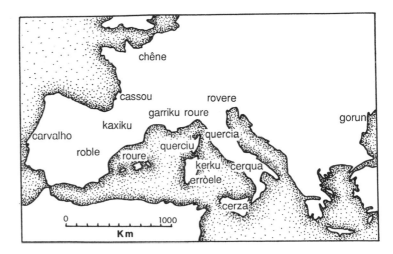

2 Unlike numerals and other items of 'basic' vocabulary, most words are not so stable as can be seen in the various ways the Romance languages express the word for 'oak'. Some drew their word from Latin quercus *'oak', specifically* Quercus robur, *others from the more general Latin* robur *'oak, hard tree', while French retained an older Celtic form* kassanos, *parts of Iberia preserved a local word* *kaxiku *and Romanian adopted an old Balkan word* gorun.

medieval Irish monks, the mistaken inclusion of Hungarian among the related Japhetic languages as well as the assertion that North American Indian languages showed clear Japhetic characteristics. Finally, Parsons was guilty of the bizarre fallacy of Goropianism (after Goropius Becanus who had traced *all* languages back to Dutch) by assuming the pristine nature of Magogian (Irish) from whence all other Japhetic languages might be linguistically derived. Whether these mistakes coupled with the author's quite unrelated works on plant and human physiology sufficed to ensure his linguistic obscurity it is difficult to say, for the place of honour for the discovery of both the Indo-European family and comparative philology is traditionally assigned to Sir William Jones.[1]

In 1796 Jones, Chief Justice of India, founder of the Royal Asiatic Society, and, unlike Parsons, a scholar whose eminence in linguistic matters guaranteed the attention of the academic world, presented his famous discourse on Indian culture. During the course of the lecture, in what amounted to but little more than an aside, Jones made his famous pronouncement on the affinities of the

	Irish	Welsh	Greek	Latin	Italian
1	aon	un	hen	unus	uno
2	do	dau	duo	duo	due
3	tri	tri	treis	tres	tre
4	ceathair	pedwar	tettares	quattuor	quattro
5	cuig	pump	pente	quinque	cinque
6	se	chwech	hex	sex	sei
7	seacht	saith	hepta	septem	sette
8	ocht	wyth	okto	octo	otto
9	naoi	naw	ennea	novem	nove
10	deich	deg	deka	decem	dieci
100	cead	cant	hekaton	centum	cento

	Danish	Old English	Polish	Russian	Bengali
1	en	an	jeden	odin	ek
2	to	twa	dwie	dva	dvi
3	tre	thrie	trzy	tri	tri
4	fire	feowre	cztery	chetyre	car
5	fem	fif	piec	pyat	pac
6	seks	siex	szesc	shesht	chay
7	syv	seofon	siedem	sem	sat
8	otte	eahta	osiem	vosem	at
9	ni	nigon	dziewiec	devyat	nay
10	ti	tien	dziesiec	desyat	das
100	hundrede	hund	sto	sto	sa

3   The 'Japhetic' numerals abridged from James Parsons' list and expanded to include Lithuanian, Albanian, Armenian and Tocharian.

ancient language of India – Sanskrit – which I fear no historian of linguistics can resist quoting:

The Sanskrit language, whatever may be its antiquity, is of wonderful structure; more perfect than the Greek, more copious than the Latin, and more exquisitely refined than either; yet bearing to both of them a stronger affinity, both in the roots of verbs and in the forms of grammar, than could have been produced by accident; so strong that no philologer could examine all the three without believing them to have sprung from some common source, which, perhaps, no longer exists. There is a similar reason, though not quite so forcible, for supposing that both the Gothic and Celtic, though blended with a different idiom, had the same origin with the Sanskrit; and the old Persian might be added to the same family.

This model advanced by Jones suggesting a common and extinct ancestral language for the majority of the peoples of Europe, Iran and India has been seen by many as the first essentially modern exposition of the Indo-European theory. But perhaps this really places far too much credit on what Jones failed to convey to his audience in his brief lecture; we need only look to one of his later discourses to the same society to see how little Jones differed from Parsons.

Spanish	French	German	Dutch	Swedish
uno	un	einz	een	en
dos	deux	zwei	twee	tva
tres	trois	drei	drie	tre
cuatro	quatre	vier	vier	fyra
cinco	cinq	fünf	vijf	fem
seis	six	sechs	zes	sex
siete	sept	sieben	zeven	sju
ocho	huit	acht	acht	atta
nueve	neuf	neun	negen	nio
diez	dix	zehn	tien	tio
ciento	cent	hundert	honderd	hundra

Persian	Lithuanian	Albanian	Armenian	Tocharian A
yak	vienas	një	mi	sas
do	du	dy	erku	wu
se	trys	tre	erek'	tre
cahar	keturi	katër	cork'	stwar
panj	penkti	pesë	hing	pän
shesh	sesi	gjashtë	vec	säk
haft	septyni	shtatë	ewt'n	spät
hasht	astuoni	tetë	ut	okät
noh	devyni	nëntë	inn	nu
dah	desimt	dhjetë	tasn	säk
sad	simtas	qind	hariwr	känt

When engaging the problem of the 'common source' of these languages, Jones was content to follow the trail again back to the Ark whence issued the three great branches of humanity whose sons 'proceeded from Iran where they migrated at first in great colonies'.

It is only in the first half of the nineteenth century that we see the actual development of a recognizable comparative philology and the growth of a concept of linguistic affinity unfathered by Noah. Rasmus Rask (1787–1832), for example, showed that it was not enough to allude to the intuitive linguistic similarity between various languages as was the practice of the earlier linguistic antiquarian; he argued that these similarities must be demonstrated systematically. The affinity between the Greek word for 'oak', *phegos*, and English *beech* was founded on more than Japhetic intuition since it was predicated on a systematic correspondence of Greek *ph* = Germanic *b*; for example, Greek *phero* 'I carry' and English *bear*, or Greek *phrater* 'clan member' and English *brother*. Similarly, one could demonstrate the regular relationship between Greek *g* and Germanic *k*: Greek *gyne*, Old Norse *kona* 'woman'; Greek *genos*, Old Norse *kyn* 'family'; or Greek *agros*, Old Norse *akr* 'field'.

In addition, it was not merely the similarities of sounds that were striking but the structure of the languages as well. The Sanskrit and Latin words for fire,

	Turkish	Hebrew	Malay	Chinese
1	bir	'ehad	satu	yi
2	iki	s(ə)nayim	dua	er
3	üc	səlosa	tiga	san
4	dört	'arba'a	empat	si
5	bes	hamissa	lima	wu
6	alti	sissa	enam	liu
7	yedi	sib'a	tujoh	qi
8	sekiz	səmona	(de) lapan	ba
9	dokuz	tis'a	sembilan	jiu
10	on	'asara	su-puloh	shi

4   The basic numerals from Parsons' four 'non-Japhetic' languages.

agnis and *ignis* respectively, are not only similar in sound but display similar changes in different grammatical cases:

	Sanskrit	Latin
Nominative Singular	agnis	ignis
Accusative Singular	agnim	ignem
Dative/Ablative Plural	agnibhyas	ignibus

Such grammatical comparisons became the subject of major syntheses, the more famous of which were produced by Rask (1818) and Franz Bopp (1816, 1833). Rask continued the eighteenth-century tradition of ascribing to the ancestral speech an ethnic designation, in his case Thracian, but Bopp was content to leave the ancestral speech under the vague heading *Stammsprache* ('original' or 'source' language), and the Book of Genesis began to evaporate from most linguistic discussion.[2] Indeed, as early as 1813 that remarkable polymath, Thomas Young, coined the term Indo-European in a review of Adelung's *Mithridates*, a multi-volume attempt to discern the linguistic affinities of the world's languages by comparing translation texts of the Lord's Prayer.

August Schleicher

By the mid-nineteenth century Indo-European studies were firmly established and major compendia of comparative philology were published. An excellent marker of the advances made by linguists of the time is the work of August Schleicher (1821–1868) who provides a convenient point of departure for a number of topics. Schleicher was not only interested in systematizing the comparative evidence but also in elucidating the fundamental form of the Indo-European languages by working back through the linguistic history of each individual language. In short, Schleicher set out to reconstruct the earliest Indo-European form of the words being compared. For example, before

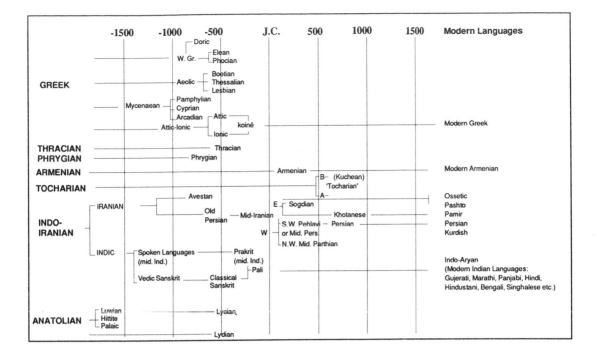

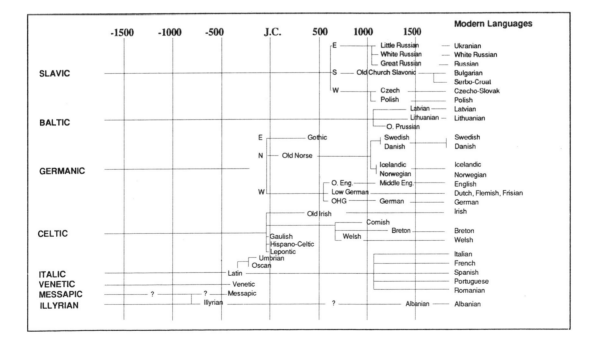

5   *The major Indo-European languages.*

Schleicher one might have only remarked the correspondence evident in the following list of words for 'field':

Sanskrit	ajras
Greek	agros
Latin	ager
Gothic	akrs

But Schleicher could argue that in comparison with other Indo-European languages, it was clear that Gothic had regularly replaced a *g* with a *k* and that the vowel in the final syllable before *s* had been lost. The earlier Germanic form of Gothic *akrs*, therefore, must have been **agras*. Similarly, in the mistaken belief that the Sanskrit language better preserved the Indo-European vowels, the underlying earlier form of Greek *agros* must have been **agras*. Ultimately, a fundamental form **agras* was postulated for the original Indo-European language and its outcome in each individual Indo-European language could be predicted according to each language's historical development. The reconstructed form of the word is marked with an asterisk to indicate that the word is not actually attested in any written source but is the product of linguistic reconstruction.

The question as to what extent the reconstructions, or as some might prefer, linguistic triangulations, represent the 'original' language has always been a source of debate. There have been those who would argue that the reconstructed forms are founded on reasonably substantiated linguistic observations and that a linguist, projected back into the past, could make him or herself understood among the earlier speakers of a language. Others prefer to view the reconstructions as merely convenient formulas that express the linguistic histories of the various languages in the briefest possible manner. Their reality is not a subject of concern or interest. For those sceptical of claims to a practical reality for linguistic reconstructions, Schleicher's greatest folly was his attempt to write a folk tale in the reconstructed Indo-European language. He titled his tale '*Avis akvasas ka* (The sheep and the horses).

Schleicher's reconstructed forms were heavily influenced by a legacy that overvalued the utility of the early Sanskrit grammarians' description of their own language. By the twentieth century, comparative linguists had progressively altered the forms of their reconstructions and in the 1930s we find an updated rendition of the same tale, now *Owis ek'woses-kʷe* by Herman Hirt. Today Hirt's reconstruction can be regarded as slightly archaic in light of more recent linguistic theory coupled with the evidence of the Indo-European languages of Anatolia, such as Hittite. As a gauge of the more recent changes some now prefer to reconstruct our unfortunate sheep as *$*H_3owis$* or **Oewis*, but as we are not concerned here with Indo-European phonology, the more traditional (and pronounceable) reconstructions of the early twentieth century will be employed throughout this work.[3]

Another of Schleicher's legacies was his model of the linguistic development of the Indo-European languages. Schleicher had always had a profound interest

August Schleicher's version of 1868
Avis akvasas ka
Avis, jasmin varna na a ast, dadarka akvams, tam, vagham garum vaghantam, tam, bharam magham, tam manum aku bharantam. Avis akvabhjams a vavakat: kard aghnutai mai vidanti manum akvams agantam.

Akvasas a vavakant: krudhi avai, kard aghnutai vividvant- svas: manus patis varnam avisams karnauti svabhjam gharmam vastram avibhjams ka varna na asti.

Tat kukruvants avis agram a bhugat.

Herman Hirt's revised translation published in 1939
Owis ek'woses-kʷe
Owis, jesmin wᵉləna ne est, dedork'e ek'wons, tom, woghom gʷᵉrum weghontm, tom, bhorom megam, tom, gh'ᵉmonm ok'u bhertontm. Owis ek'womos ewᵉwekʷet: kerd aghnutai moi widontei gh'ᵉmonm ek'wons ag'ontm.

Ek'woses ewᵉwekʷont: k'ludhi, owei! k'erd aghnutai vidontmos: gh'ᵉmo, potis, wᵉlənam owjom kʷrneuti sebhoi ghʷermom westrom; owimos-kʷe wᵉləna ne esti.

Tod k'ek'ruwos owis ag'rom ebhuget.

In 1979 Winfred Lehmann and Ladislav Zgusta published yet a third version with slight elaborations
Ōwis ekwoskʷe
(Gʷərei) owis, kʷesyo wlhna ne est, ekwons espeket, oinom ghe gʷrum woghom weghontm, oinomkʷe megam bhorom, oinomkʷe ghmenm oku bherontm.

Owis nu ekwobh(y)os ewewkʷet: Ker aghnutoi moi ekwons agontm nerm widntei.

Ekwos tu ewewkʷont: Kludhi, owei, ker aghnutoi nsmei widntbh(y)os: ner, potis, owiom r wlhnam sebhi gʷhermom westrom kʷrneuti. Neghi owiom wlhna esti.

Tod kekluwos owis agrom ebhuget.

A quite literal translation might run:
[The] Sheep and [the] Horses
[On a hill] [a] sheep, on which wool not was, saw horses, one, [a] wagon heavy pulling, [another] one, [a] load great, [another] one, [a] man swiftly carrying. [The] sheep to the horses said: heart pains me seeing [a] man horses driving.

[The] horses to the sheep said: listen sheep, hearts pain us seeing: man, [the] master, wool of the sheep makes for himself [a] warm garment and to the sheep wool not is.

That having heard, [the] sheep to the plain fled.

A freer translation runs:
The Sheep and the Horses
[On a hill] a sheep that had no wool saw horses – one pulling a heavy wagon, another one a great load, and another swiftly carrying a man. The sheep said to the horses: it hurts me seeing a man driving horses.

The horses said to the sheep: listen sheep! it hurts us seeing man, the master, making a warm garment for himself from the wool of a sheep when the sheep has no wool for itself.

On hearing this the sheep fled into the plain.

6 *Three versions of Schleicher's Proto-Indo-European tale. Each version employs a different Indo-European word for the man who is abusing sheep and horses alike. Schleicher reconstructed his from the series: Sanskrit* manus, *Gothic* manna, *English* man, *Russian* muz; *Hirt drew his from the Proto-Indo-European* *ghmon *'human', e.g., Latin* homo, *Gothic* guma, *Tocharian B* saumo, *Lithuanian* zmuo; *and the most recent version prefers* *ner *'man', cf. Sanskrit* nar-, *Avestan* nar-, *Greek* aner, *Old Irish* nert, *etc. A fourth term,* *wiros, *means 'he-man'.*

in biology, and he employed the model of the genetic tree to describe the differentiation of the Indo-European languages. The Indo-European hypothesis presupposed that the great similarity between the various Indo-European languages could only be explained by assuming that they had all derived from a common language. This original language we would call Proto-Indo-European (or PIE) today. Over the area in which it was spoken, different regions began to diverge, branching off into various major language groups, or 'fundamentals', as Schleicher called them. Examples of the 'fundamentals' would be Celtic, Germanic or Slavic. By the same gradual process of divergence, these fundamentals split up into different languages, for example, Celtic (Irish, Welsh, Manx, Breton, and so on) or Slavic (such as Russian, Ukrainian and Polish), and these further branched into dialects or sub-dialects. In order to depict this historical process Schleicher resorted to the biological model of the family tree to describe the differentiation of the Indo-European languages. The length of the branches indicated the duration of time that various 'fundamentals' had remained closely associated and the distances between branches indicated the degree of relationship. Thus, from Schleicher's diagram it was clear that the North European languages embraced by the Germanic, Baltic and Slavic languages were more closely related to one another than the South and West European languages. It could also be seen that the Germanic language had diverged from the northern branch long before Baltic and Slavic had separated.

It is immediately apparent that the genetic model could not help but affect all discussion of the individual histories of the Indo-European languages and peoples. The model constrained one to frame questions such as when did the Germanic languages separate from the Balto-Slavic? And this was easily translated into the questions: When did the Germanic *peoples* move off from the Balto-Slavic peoples? When did the Celts separate from the Italic peoples? The Indians from the Iranians? And such historical questions demand a specific type of answer, not far removed from chasing after the offspring of Noah.

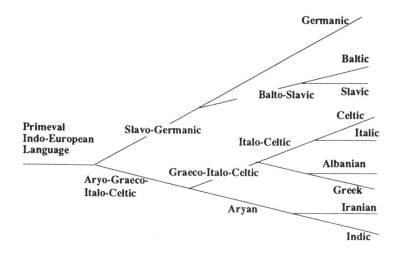

7   *August Schleicher's tree of the Indo-European languages.*

The overschematism of Schleicher's model of a family tree provoked a reaction. First, Schleicher's model had adopted the implicit premise that languages branch away from one another and remain isolated from contacts with other languages. But this was surely contradicted by historical experience. Medieval French and Latin (Italic) has had an enormous impact on the English (Germanic) language. More importantly, Schleicher's model failed to explain many linguistic relations that were transparent even to a nineteenth-century linguist. For example, cutting across Schleicher's three main branches is the famous division between *centum* and *satem* languages. This refers to the Proto-Indo-European sound *$\check{k}$* which has markedly different outcomes in different languages. The word for a hundred, *$\check{k}mtom$*, yields the *k* sound in Latin *centum*, Old Irish *cét*, Greek *hekaton*, Gothic *hund* (from *$\check{k}unt$*), but changes to a sibilant (s-sound) in Indic *sata*, Iranian *satəm*, Lithuanian *simtas*, and so on. Schleicher's tree demanded an intensely close relationship between Germanic and Balto-Slavic, yet here Balto-Slavic were more closely allied with the Asian languages. For every readjustment of the branches, another linguistic isogloss (similarity) could be found to contradict it.

Johannes Schmidt's (1843–1901) resolution of this problem was to go beyond a model of genetic development via ramification to one that imagined a broad band of Indo-European speakers in whose respective areas innovations developed and spread like waves to some, but seldom to all, other languages. The resulting image was therefore not a tree but a series of interlocked or encompassing circles that expressed specific similarities between one language and another. Schleicher's Balto-Slavic languages might share the same outcome of Proto-Indo-European *$\check{k}$*, but similarities with the Germanic languages were also depicted in the overlapping circle. This provided a somewhat more realistic presentation of the linguistic relationships between languages but it also rested on a major premise: the positionings of the languages in the diagram portrayed geographical realities without specifying the *time* at which anything occurred. The model, in short, was a synchronic

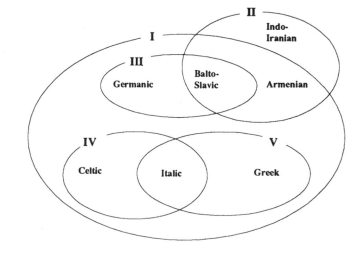

8 *Johannes Schmidt's wave model of the Indo-European languages. Those languages encompassed under I all share an* e *where Indo-Iranian has an* a, *e.g., Latin* est *but Sanskrit* asti. *Those in II change* *k *to an s-sound (centum versus satem), while those in group III form some case endings in* m *rather than* bh.

description of the Indo-European languages but offered little or no historical perspective. The Celts were simply people who spoke a language that seemed to share certain similarities with the Italic languages. That some of these similarities may have been inherited from the original Proto-Indo-European at one period, and that others were only acquired perhaps thousands of years later, could not be discerned in Schmidt's diagram. To be fair to Schmidt, it was not his intention to replace Schleicher's model but rather to provide another (synchronic) dimension to the interrelationships of the Indo-European languages. A more subtle tool than Schleicher's, Schmidt's wave model still failed to convey the historical development of the languages.

While we might wish to turn now to a universally accepted model of the development of the Indo-European languages, unfortunately, all subsequent attempts to depict the interrelationships of the Indo-European languages invariably collapse into the two dimensionality of Schleicher or Schmidt, albeit updated with far more information and vastly more complex articulations. The modern historical linguist will still find it hard to escape from the use of the 'fundamentals' of Schleicher or separate out the complex stratigraphy of Indo-European isoglosses that make up a wave model. There is, to be sure, unequivocal agreement on some matters, for example, that the Indians and Iranians were extremely closely related (linguistically) before their emergence into the historical record; yet Indo-European dialectology still remains a fruitful and frightful area of research and debate.

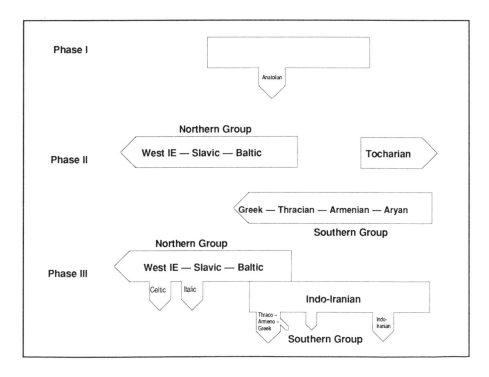

9   The development of the Indo-European languages according to Francesco Adrados (1982).

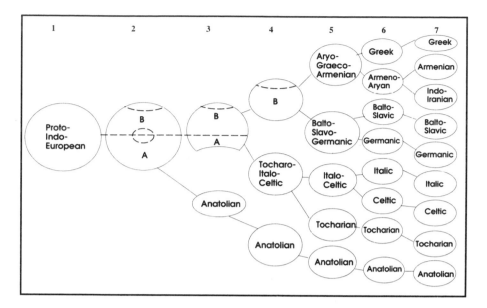

10   The development of the Indo-European languages according to Tomas Gamkrelidze and Vyacheslav Ivanov (1985).

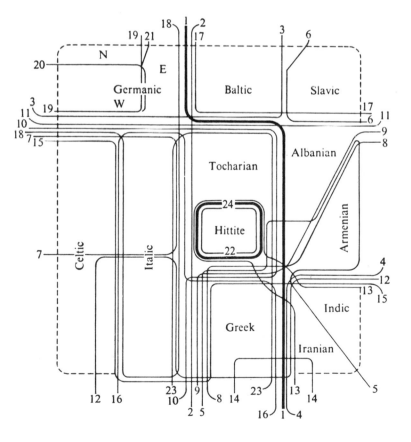

11   A modern 'wave model' of the Indo-European languages according to Raimo Anttila (1972). The numbers indicate 24 isoglosses (similarities) shared among different Indo-European languages. Isogloss 1 indicates the centum:satem split (Schmidt's wave II). A number of isoglosses, generally interpreted as innovations, appear to link Greek-Iranian-Indic-Armenian; similarly, Germanic-Baltic-Slavic share a number of similarities, while a large isogloss 'bundle' divides Italic from Greek. Hittite and Tocharian tend to be on the conservative side of most dialect developments in accordance with their peripheral positions with respect to the other Indo-European languages.

The Indo-European hypothesis

If details are still a matter of controversy, the Indo-European hypothesis is most certainly not. It is the only explanation that can convincingly account for why approximately half the earth's population speaks in languages clearly related to one another. This requires the assumption that at some time and some place in Eurasia there existed a population which spoke a language directly ancestral to all of those we now recognize as Indo-European. The usual label for such a language, Proto-Indo-European, is also applied to speakers of this language who are the subject of this book. Furthermore, it is assumed that they once occupied an area considerably more circumscribed than that where we find them when they first enter the historical record. Unfortunately, this conclusion has all too often rested on a form of latent Japhetism – a tendency of nineteenth- and even twentieth-century writers to portray the Proto-Indo-Europeans as a single people constrained within their homeland, perfecting their language and then bursting out all over the earth waving swords and spreading paradigms. This metaphor haunts much of what has been written about the Indo-Europeans as a people. But its failure wholly to convince, or worse, its ability to attract derision rather than critical appraisal, has little to do with the validity of our concept of a confined homeland and people. Since this element of our perception of the Indo-Europeans is fundamental to much of our investigations here, we need to consider this aspect more closely.

The one constancy of language is that it is always changing; it is stasis that is unnatural since this would require numerous individuals over a period of generations to reproduce precisely the same sounds and replicate the same idiom, a task which is contrary both to the nature of human behaviour and to the necessity for language to accommodate continual change in culture. The complex reasons for language change – for example, social class, phonetic drift, analogy, contact with other languages – cannot concern us here. We merely

Modern English
Yahweh is my shepherd, I lack nothing.
In meadows of green grass he lets me lie.
To the waters of repose he leads me.

Early Modern English
The Lord is my shepherd, I shall not want.
He maketh me to lie down in green pastures.
He leadeth me beside the still waters.

Middle English
Our Lord gouerneth me, and nothyng shal defailen to me.
In the sted of pasture he sett me ther.
He norissed me upon water of fyllyng.

Old English
Drihten me raet, ne byth me nanes godes wan.
And he me geset on swythe good feohland.
And fedde me be waetera stathum.

12 Translations of the 23rd Psalm illustrate how the English language has changed over the past 1,000 years.

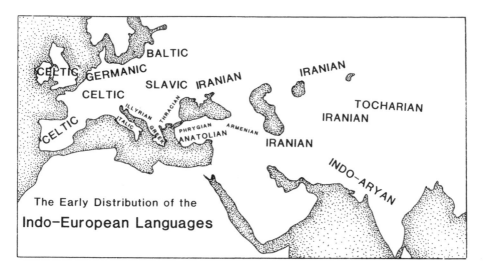

13   The early historical distribution of the major Indo-European linguistic groups.

need contemplate that the English language spoken by Chaucer would be on the outer reaches of intelligibility to a speaker of twentieth-century English. And when confronted with the Old English language, the modern English speaker swiftly bids goodbye to comprehension in the same way that a Frenchman, Spaniard or Romanian would despair of carrying on a conversation with an ancient Roman. If continuity of language can be ascribed it is not because of stasis but rather because its speakers, over time and in a specific region, have maintained a course of relatively similar linguistic change.

It should be clear then that several factors severely affect linguistic continuity, or parallel language change. We may expect that the amount of change will be partly dependent on the extent of time that has elapsed in the linguistic continuum. Also, it will be affected by the size and nature of the geographical area occupied. In the absence of mass media or a written standard, people speaking originally the same language but separated by large distances are unlikely to maintain parallel changes. Where we find great similarity of speech over a large area we can normally assume a recent expansion since the factors of time and distance will normally reduce a single language into a continuum of mutually related but increasingly different languages. This being so, the similarity of the Indo-European languages when we first encounter them historically, stretching from the Atlantic to India, all speak for their relatively recent spread from a more confined area. To ascribe to such a dispersion a very great antiquity would be to attribute to the Proto-Indo-European language properties wholly contrary not only to all the evidence from the world's other languages but also to human behaviour itself. In short, the Indo-European hypothesis presupposes a Proto-Indo-European language spoken by a population in some area of Eurasia severely more confined than their earliest historical distribution. How confined, when and where will be problems for later chapters.

CHAPTER TWO

The Indo-Europeans in Asia

Asia is called the cradle of mankind. The times
change. People change. But the belief in the
Asiatic cradle has not changed.

HANS VON WOLZOGEN, 1875

The Indo-Europeans did not burst into history; they straggled in over a period
of 3,500 years, announcing their arrival in the historical record in as varied
media as clay tablets in Anatolia and Greece, inscriptions carved on the face of
an Iranian cliff, a dedicatory inscription on a German helmet or a Lutheran
catechism for pagan Lithuanians. But no matter when or how we first
encounter the language of Indo-European speakers, they all have one thing in
common: they invariably speak an already differentiated Indo-European
language, never Proto-Indo-European. As this work seeks to trace the origins of
the earliest Indo-Europeans, we must confine our attention to that brief
moment when each Indo-European group first emerges in the historical record,
and then seek its more immediate linguistic and archaeological origins. In so
doing, we hope to draw nearer to the ancestral Indo-European community
whence they all originated.

We cannot, however, pursue this course without making reference to some
fundamental archaeological terms. These will include 'cultures', which are
traditionally defined as the recurrence of similar ceramics, tools, architecture
and burial rites over a limited area, for example, the Gandhara Grave culture of
the Swat Valley in Pakistan. It should be emphasized that such cultures are the
constructs of modern archaeologists and their correspondence with actual
prehistoric social groups is a constantly debated topic. The evidence for these
cultures is to be found in archaeological sites which may contain various levels
dating to different periods, each designated with a numeral, such as Troy V (the
fifth major phase of the site of Troy). Events such as the destructions of sites, or
the appearance of a particular item of culture, may be found across various
cultures at apparently the same time and constitute an 'horizon'.

Since the historical record itself begins in Asia, this is where we will first take
up their trail.

The Anatolians

The earliest Indo-European-speaking peoples to enter the historical record
were the Anatolians who are first attested by about the nineteenth century BC.
By this time Assyrian merchants had penetrated into south central Anatolia and

established their *karum* or 'trading office' at Kanes, the modern Kültepe. Excavations at this site, and at several other Assyrian trading posts, have uncovered clay tablets in Assyrian cuneiform that record the daily business of the Assyrian tradesmen. In addition, they also mention personal names and places which are recognizably Indo-European.[4] By about the mid-seventeenth century BC the Indo-European speakers are declaring themselves in several different Anatolian languages. By far the best attested of these is Hittite. With their capital at Hattusa (modern Bogazköy), the Hittites have left us over 25,000 clay tablets spanning the period from about 1650 to 1200 BC. In addition, their archives contain tablets in two other Indo-European languages, Luwian and Palaic. They present us with a picture of Anatolia where the Hittites are masters of the central region, the Palaic speakers subservient to their north, and the Luwians occupying the role of traditional rival in much of western and southern Anatolia. After the collapse of the Hittites about 1200 BC, Luwian seems to have prevailed widely over southern Anatolia and Luwian-related languages such as Lycian continued down into the last centuries BC, only to be finally engulfed by the expansion of Greek colonists.

It is most important for our purposes to inquire how autochthonous were the Anatolian languages in their respective regions. The general opinion of both linguists and archaeologists would almost universally deny them a role as natives to Anatolia but cast them rather in the part of Bronze Age intruders who assimilated the indigenous non-Indo-European populations. The Assyrian merchants of the nineteenth century BC not only record the names of Indo-European peoples in their texts but make it quite clear that there was also a great body of non-Indo-European-speaking peoples in the region. The existence of

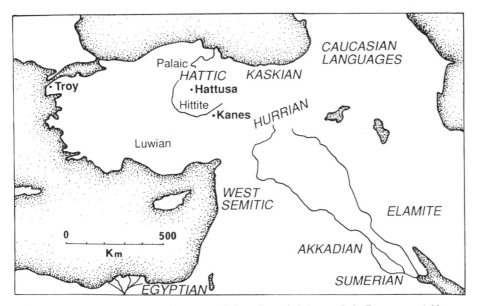

14   The earliest Indo-European languages of Anatolia and their non-Indo-European neighbours (in upper case).

these non-Indo-European peoples is undoubted since the Hittite archives themselves contain texts, translations of texts, and frequent borrowings from a language called Hattic. These Hatti are regarded as the predominant substratum, the aborigines if you will, of central Anatolia over whom the Hittites and Palaic speakers superimposed themselves. From the Hatti the Hittites borrowed not only many words,[5] but also much of their culture, certainly much of their religion, and even the name Hittite derives from Hatti (the Hittites called themselves *nes* and their language *nesili*). Linguistically, Hattic is a non-Indo-European language with no certain close relationships, although there are some grounds (absence of grammatical gender, use of prefixes) to link it with the northwest Caucasian group of languages (Abkhaz) or perhaps Kartvelian, the major south Caucasian linguistic group.

Further to the east, on the fringes of Anatolia and north Syria, lay another major non-Indo-European people, the Hurrians. Hurrian texts maintained in the Hittite archives, coupled with Hurrian loan words in Luwian and the Hurrians' own inscriptions and texts in north Mesopotamia which date as early as the twenty-third century BC, all speak for an additional non-Indo-European presence on the eastern borders of the Indo-Europeans of Anatolia. To their south were the lands of the Semites and (formerly) Sumerians, again non-Indo-European speakers. The natural conclusion to be drawn from all of this is that the Indo-European-speaking Anatolians were intrusive into central Anatolia and were unlikely to have emigrated from directly east or southeast of this region where major non-Indo-European populations are historically attested. It is also clear from the abundance of mixed texts, foreign loanwords in Hittite and Luwian, and the entire cultural picture that emerges from the content of the texts, that the Indo-European Anatolians had already undergone considerable assimilation to the culture of the non-Indo-European Anatolians before they appear in history. Now what do linguistics and archaeology tell us about their origins?

For the linguist, the existence of three Indo-European languages in Anatolia by the seventeenth century BC generates two issues of considerable historical importance. The first is their relationship with the other Indo-European languages. Here there is fairly universal agreement among historical linguists that the Anatolian branch offers us some of the most extreme examples of archaism among all the Indo-European languages. By this is meant that they

Hittite	Hattic	
n = asta assu	malhip = hu	Then goodness
anda tarneskiddu	te-ta-h-sul	should he let in,
idalu = ma = kan	asah = pi	But evil
anda le tarnai	tas-tu-ta-sula	should he not let in.
ᴰSulinkattis-san	ᴰSulinkatti	(The god) Sulinkatte,
LUGAL-us	katti	the king,
anda eszi.	a-ta-niua_as	sits within.

15 A bilingual religious text in Hittite and Hattic. The Hittite text contains Indo-European words, e.g., assu 'good' is related to Sanskrit su, Greek eu 'good'; Hittite anda 'within' is cognate with Latin endo; and eszi 'sits' is to be compared with Sanskrit aste and Greek asti. Sulinkattis, however, is a Hattic name which the Hattic text reveals to be made from Sulin + katti 'king'. LUGAL indicates the Sumerian sign for 'king'. Structurally Hittite and Hattic are very different languages. The Hittites borrowed much of their religion from the indigenous Hatti.

16 Some basic numerals and kinship terms indicate the fundamental differences between Hurrian and Indo-European.

		Hurrian	Proto-Indo-European
2		sin	*duwo
3		kik	*treyes
4		tumni	*kʷetwores
6		sinta	*s(w)eks
9		nis	*newn
10		eman	*dekmt
brother		sena	*bhrater
sister		sala	*dhugəter

retain grammatical forms and constructions that disappeared very early on in the other languages.[6] Some would go further and argue that the Anatolian branch appears to lack some grammatical forms that developed in all the other Indo-European languages. This, they maintain, indicates that the Anatolian branch diverged from the rest of the Indo-European continuum before it had even evolved into the form of Proto-Indo-European that gave rise to all the other Indo-European languages. This view is not universally accepted, especially since most linguists admit that the Anatolian languages had already undergone vast changes under the influence of non-Indo-European native populations before they emerged into history. Although there is much finely argued controversy about the details of these linguistic issues, there would be few to argue against the conclusion that the Anatolian languages represent a very early separation or divergence from the common Proto-Indo-European continuum of dialects.

The second major issue is the internal relationship among the Anatolian languages. With our evidence for both Luwian and Palaic so meagre compared with Hittite, it is difficult to ascertain fully how divergent the three languages were. That differences did exist can easily be seen in comparing some of their vocabulary:

	Hittite	Luwian	Palaic
father	attas	tati	papa
sun/day	siwat	tiwaz	tiyaz
honey	melit	mallit-	malit-
countryside	kimmara-	immara-	
hand	kessera-	issari	

But despite these differences, and some are more thoroughgoing than these, the three languages are vastly more similar to one another than they are to any of the other Indo-European languages, even those other languages which are also attested as early as the Bronze Age. They give all the appearance of being the result of linguistic differentiation across a broad band of common Anatolian dialects. Their divergence from one another must obviously have occurred before their earliest historical attestation, but not too long before or we would expect yet greater differences. Linguists normally provide a broad estimate that the ancestors of the different Anatolian languages penetrated into their respective territories some time during the third millennium BC, or possibly as early as the later fourth millennium. Where does all this leave the archaeologist?

First, the Indo-European-speaking Anatolians are difficult to distinguish from their non-Indo-European neighbours or predecessors. They appear to have embraced thoroughly the local Anatolian Bronze Age cultures and they display no obvious cultural traits that mark them off as *distinctly* Indo-European. This is hardly surprising, as the basic social picture of Bronze Age Anatolia is of a series of city-states comprised of linguistically diverse populations sharing the same material culture. It has even been suggested that Hittite itself was not the language of the dominant group but rather a lingua franca, developed out of the close association of the earlier Hittites of Kanes with the Assyrian merchants, who were the first literate population in Anatolia and who used Kanes as a trading base.[7]

We must also remember that our knowledge of Anatolian archaeology is still quite inferior to many other areas of Eurasia and so any arguments for ethnic intrusions are generally built on admittedly meagre evidence. This is more than compounded by the length of rope with which the linguist has provided the optimistic archaeologist, because with a 1,500-year time span to seek intrusions, few archaeologists who believe that such phenomena are traceable in the archaeological record can resist discovering several possible invaders – from both the west and the east.

Probably the most widely accepted case for intrusion falls at the end of Early Bronze Age II, about 2700–2600 BC, when the evidence for population movement is coupled with destruction and abandonment. Beginning in western Anatolia we see destruction phases on every major site and the abandonment of smaller sites. The Konya Plain is offered as the most convincing example since field surveys here have indicated a collapse from 100 Early Bronze Age II sites to a mere four in the following period. Some suggest that an infiltration by nomads who profoundly altered the sedentary economy of the region may be credited with this change. In addition, new ceramic elements which take their origin from northwest Anatolia (Troy V) spread rapidly eastward as also does

17   Principal sites associated with theories of Anatolian invasions.

the classic form of status or ritual architecture – the megaron which was common at Troy and Beycesultan – which now begins to appear in central Anatolia at such sites as Kanes-Kültepe.

The arguments for a west to east movement of intruders in the mid-third millennium BC accords well with some linguistic theories concerning the dispersion of the Anatolian languages. Essentially, the new horizon embraces the subsequent historical lands of the Luwians who maintained a west to east pressure throughout their existence. This crisis at the end of Early Bronze Age II may have been either the manifestation of the earliest Luwians or even the earliest Anatolian speakers, including the ancestors of the Hittites, who underwent subsequent linguistic differentiation. The abandonment and destructions may nevertheless have simply been the result of climatic or internal calamities while the spread of yet another ceramic style or architectural form may not have required a new people with a new language.

The original nucleus of these proposed expansions is northwest Anatolia, which naturally includes Troy itself. Links between this region and Southeast Europe, especially in ceramics – including figurines – and architecture, have long been known, and until the past few decades generally attributed to an expansion of Near Eastern high culture to European barbarians. More recently there has been a recognition by some archaeologists that the direction of influence may require reversing, at least during the transition from the Chalcolithic to the Early Bronze Age. This can be seen, for example, in the ceramics, metallurgy and architecture exhibited at Bulgarian sites such as Ezero which only appear later at Troy. These similarities are seen by some to be little more than a general cultural horizon embracing both sides of the Sea of Marmara while others argue for actual folk movements, possibly refugees, who abandoned the Balkans for northwest Anatolia about 3500–3000 BC under either the pressure or leadership of the Indo-Europeans. The remains of horse – whether wild or domestic is not certain – at Anatolian sites such as Demirci Hüyük is also cited as evidence for intrusions from Southeast Europe where the domestic horse antedates the Anatolian evidence and is a known possession of the earliest Indo-Europeans. We are not yet prepared to follow such a trail so early in our enquiry since this concerns too closely the problem of the Indo-European homeland itself. Rather, we must briefly turn our attention to those who prefer to seek the origins of the Indo-European-speaking Anatolians to the northeast.

Most arguments for an Indo-European invasion from the northeast concern the appearance of a new burial rite at the end of the fourth and through the third millennium BC. At this time, both north of the Black Sea and the Caucasus, burials on the Russian-Ukrainian steppe were typically placed in an underground shaft and covered with a mound (*kurgan* in Russian). Before 3000 BC there begin to appear in the territory of the indigenous Transcaucasian (Kuro-Araxes) culture somewhat similar burials such as the royal tomb of Uch-Tepe on the Milska steppe. As tumulus burials are previously unknown in this region, some would explain their appearance by an intrusion of steppe pastoralists who migrated through the Caucasus and subjugated the local Early Bronze Age culture. More importantly, a status burial inserted into a mound at the site of Korucu Tepe in eastern Anatolia has been compared with somewhat similar burials both in the Caucasus and the Russian steppe. The discovery of horse bones on several sites of east Anatolia such as Norsun Tepe and Tepecik are seen to confirm a steppe intrusion since, as mentioned earlier, the horse, long known in the Ukraine and south Russia, is not attested in Anatolia prior to the Bronze Age.[8] Continuing contacts or migrations are employed to explain subsequent similarities between the royal tombs of north-central Anatolia, such as the thirteen graves of Alaca Hüyük, with tombs formally similar or possessing related grave goods known north of the Caucasus.

At present, a northeastern intrusion does not make quite so good a linguistic 'fit' as does the northwestern hypothesis. The evidence for intrusion is either confined to eastern Anatolia – lands historically attributed to Hurrian or Caucasian languages – or north-central Anatolia where we might expect Hattic or Kaskian, another apparently non-Indo-European linguistic group. The evidence of kurgan-related burials is generally absent from those territories where we find the major Indo-European peoples of our search, especially the Luwians of southern and western Anatolia. And even if our kurgan-entombed overlords are proximate to the Hittite's traditional territory, linguists adamantly oppose an eastern entry for the Hittites and a separate western entry for the Luwians. The languages seem too closely related, too similar to have experienced the degree of separation implied by each having taken an opposing course around the Black Sea. Furthermore, what similarity exists between royal burials both north and south of the Caucasus may have far more to do with the need to develop more impressive forms of entombment for the hierarchies that developed in both regions during the Early Bronze Age, and which participated in mutual exchange networks of prestigious goods. At present, the scales are tipped in favour of a western entry.

The Phrygians

With the collapse of the Hittite empire about 1200 BC, the configuration of Indo-European languages in Anatolia changes. Luwian speakers continued to dominate southern Anatolia and parts of north Syria and were so successful at adopting the mantle of the Hittites that they retained this ethnic designation, at least in the Bible. These Luwians employed a hieroglyphic script which due to its discovery in the Hittite capital formerly bore the mistaken name of 'Hieroglyphic Hittite'; now it is more commonly called Hieroglyphic Luwian. As we have seen, in western Anatolia other late Anatolian languages such as the Luwian-derived Lycian continued until its speakers were assimilated by Greek colonists. But in central Anatolia itself, in the heartland of the Hittite empire, there appeared a new Indo-European language, Phrygian, which stands outside the Anatolian group and cannot be derived from any of the former Indo-European languages of Anatolia.

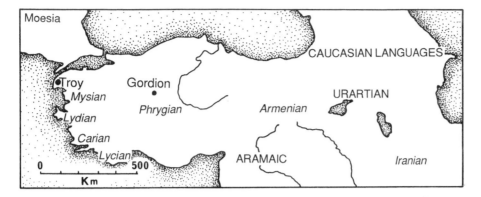

18   Anatolia after the collapse of the Hittites. Indo-European languages are indicated in italics; non-Indo-European languages are in upper case.

From 1200 BC to 800 BC the Phrygians are commonly associated with other intruders who swept across central Anatolia from the west, participating in the destruction of the major Hittite cities and plunging Anatolia into its 'Dark Age'. The archaeological evidence for these invaders is not yet secure, especially since there is an embarrassing gap between their occupation of Troy VIIb in the twelfth century and the earliest emergence of distinctive Phrygian pottery in central Anatolia during the eighth century BC. Their handmade black ware is known from numerous sites, including the ancient Hittite capital at Hattusa and the Phrygian's own capital of Gordion. As a power they dominated central Anatolia for several centuries and produced a number of figures of both Greek legend and Anatolian history, who all bore the name of Midas.

The historic King Midas ruled from the eighth century BC, and in his contest with the Assyrians and his attempt to expand the frontiers of Phrygian power, he brought the state to its apex, only to see it collapse under the pressure of Kimmerian invaders from the north (who drove Midas into committing suicide by drinking ox-blood). More famous, naturally, is the legendary Midas whose story is variously set in both Macedonia and Phrygia, a confusion which we will soon see dovetails neatly with the whole problem of Phrygian origins. Having captured a silenus – an older, wiser but even more besotted version of the classical satyr – by spiking a spring with wine, Midas returned him to Dionysus and was rewarded with his fondest wish – the golden touch. When the starving Midas discovered that even his food and drink turned to gold on touch, he repented his folly to the god and was instructed to wash himself in the river Pactolus. This river instantly became a major source of gold and provided the economic foundation for that other great symbol of wealth, Croesus. The wealth of the Phrygians was not purely legend since one of the relicts attributed to them are their large and rich tumulus burials.

Linguistically, we are severely limited by the sparse remains of the Phrygian language. The earlier inscriptions number only about twenty-five and date to the period 800–600 BC, while about 100 much later inscriptions, generally

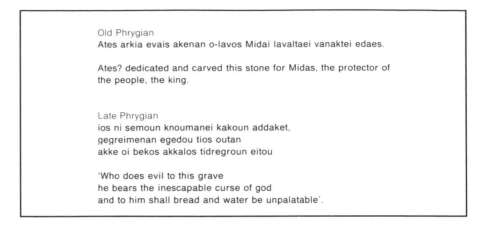

Old Phrygian
Ates arkia evais akenan o-lavos Midai lavaltaei vanaktei edaes.

Ates? dedicated and carved this stone for Midas, the protector of the people, the king.

Late Phrygian
ios ni semoun knoumanei kakoun addaket,
gegreimenan egedou tios outan
akke oi bekos akkalos tidregroun eitou

'Who does evil to this grave
he bears the inescapable curse of god
and to him shall bread and water be unpalatable'.

19   Two Phrygian inscriptions. The later inscription contains the word kakoun *'evil' which may be compared with Greek* kakos *'bad', lent into English in words like cacophony. The word would appear to derive from a Proto-Indo-European child's word* *kakka *which should not require translation, cf. Armenian* kakor *'excrement', Greek* kakkao, *Latin* caco, *Middle Irish* caccaim, *etc. At the other end of the spectrum is* tios *which some have attempted to relate to Sanskrit* dyaus, *Greek* Zeus *and similar words for the Indo-European sky-god. Note also that the later inscription employs* bekos *which we know from Herodotus to mean 'bread'.*

unsuccessful interdictions against tomb plundering, are recorded from the first centuries AD. In addition, we have the customary evidence of early place names and personal names and a few glosses (marginal comments in manuscripts providing definitions for otherwise obscure words). One of these comes to us in an entertaining story by Herodotus, who relates how the Egyptian king Psammetichus (663–609 BC) once attempted to discover the oldest language in the world. This was accomplished by ensuring that two infants heard no human speech until they had uttered their first words, under the assumption that these would be from the primeval language. The children's first word was *bekos* which Herodotus informs us was the Phrygian word for bread, and hence Phrygian was reputed to be the oldest language in the world. This fantastic story may do little to encourage us to accept Herodotus as a thoroughly reliable source when he also tells us how the Phrygians originally lived in Macedonia and migrated into northwest Anatolia, perhaps about the time of the Trojan War, where they changed their name from Bryges to Phrygians. Nevertheless, consensus does derive the Phrygians from Southeast Europe.

Although the sparseness of the linguistic evidence makes it difficult to assess the dialectal position of Phrygian within the Indo-European languages, there is certainly no convincing evidence that it was specifically an Anatolian language closely related to Hittite, Luwian or Palaic, and hence there are sound linguistic grounds to regard it as a later intruder. There have been a number of attempts to link Phrygian closely with Thracian and Illyrian, two major Indo-European languages of the Balkans which offer even more appallingly sparse linguistic remains, and many handbooks speak of the Thraco-Phrygian group of languages. Today such a close relationship is still unproven, although Phrygian has more affinities with the Balkan languages than with any others.

Consequently, it is from that direction that the linguist seeks the original Phrygians and defers to Herodotus's account as at least more plausible than any alternative hypothesis.[9]

The historical and archaeological evidence is much too meagre to erect a convincing case for Phrygian origins. It is perhaps ironic that the best archaeological evidence for an intrusion, the abrupt break between Troy VIIa and VIIb with its introduction of Southeast European Knobbed Ware about 1200 BC, although fitting remarkably well with Herodotus's account, gets us no further than northwest Anatolia. Consequently, it is difficult to employ this evidence to support the late Hittite records of a King Midash (an early Phrygian Midas?) on its northern frontier prior to the destruction of Hattusa. It is only in the eighth century BC, when the inscriptional evidence and a distinctive pottery style cojoin to provide us with an unambiguous Phrygian presence, that we can safely mark their existence in Anatolia. The one clearly intrusive item of their culture is the tumulus burial, especially prominent at Gordion. Large tumuli are well known in the Balkans and have a much longer ancestry there, consequently, a link between the two regions on these grounds has long been suggested. But since such tumuli only appear in Phrygian territory from the eighth century onwards, the link between a Balkan homeland and Phrygia can only be entertained if we detach the Phrygians from the destruction horizon associated with Troy VII and Hattusa. Before attempting any conclusions here, we should first look at one more group of intrusive Indo-Europeans, the Armenians.

The Armenians

In his enumeration of the great army of the Persian king Xerxes (519–465 BC), Herodotus includes the Armenians, whom he informs us were 'Phrygian colonists'. On the basis of this statement, coupled with the linguistic position of Armenian within the Indo-European family, it is generally accepted that the Armenians, like the Phrygians, emigrated from the Balkans into Asia Minor.[10] However, unlike the Phrygians whose language has long been extinct, Armenian is still spoken today by approximately five million people. Its earliest texts, largely religious, are traditionally ascribed to the fifth century AD but are probably more recent. Nevertheless, there are no grounds whatsoever to believe that they took up their historical position so late. In their native tradition the Armenians trace their own existence in Armenia back until the eighth century BC, and references to them by their Iranian neighbours indicate an Armenian presence by at least the second century BC. The name Armenia (*Arminiya*) itself occurs in inscriptions as early as about 600 BC although one should always be wary of equating the name of a country with a people sharing that name. For the actual origins of the Armenian people we must rely on the evidence of their language, the historical testimony of their neighbours and predecessors, and archaeology. While all these approaches have not led to total consensus, there is broad agreement on the outline of the origins of the Armenians.

Old Armenian
Hayr mer or erkins: surb elici anun k'o. Ekesce ark'ayut'iwn k'o.
Elicin kamk' k'o orpes erkins ew erki.

'Father our which in-heaven: holy become name thy. Come
kingdom thy.
Become will thy as in-heaven and on-earth.'

20   *The opening lines of the Lord's Prayer in Classical Armenian. The first word* hayr *is the Armenian reflex of Proto-Indo-European* *pəter *where* *p *either changed to* h, *e.g., Proto-Indo-European* *penk^{w}e *'five' but Armenian* hing, *or was usually lost, e.g., Sanskrit* pad-, *Greek* pous, *Latin* pes *and English* foot *but Armenian* otn *'foot'.*

Although Armenian is clearly an Indo-European language, like Phrygian it shows no especially close relationship with the Anatolian languages other than borrowings. These are important since they indicate that proto-Armenians were in contact with both Luwian speakers and, more importantly, with Hittites. As Hittite was replaced by Luwian by 1200 BC, we may expect that proto-Armenians were passing through Anatolia before this time. The nearest linguistic neighbours to the Armenians were the Phrygians, Thracians and most especially the Greeks (some linguists even speak of Graeco-Armenian). All of this directs our attention towards the Balkans for their location prior to their migration through Anatolia. That the proto-Armenians were intrusive into their historical home is confirmed by the fact that they came to occupy the territory of the Urartians, the powerful kingdom of Van which flourished from the ninth to the sixth centuries BC and left abundant textual evidence that they were non-Indo-European speakers. Linguists today identify the Urartian language as closely related to Hurrian, the major non-Indo-European language of eastern Anatolia and northern Mesopotamia. Igor Diakonov has recently assembled evidence with indicates that the Armenians borrowed from the Hurro-Urartians words for slave, brick, seal, tin, local plant names (mint, pomegranate, plum, quince) and other items native to the region. The proto-Armenians apparently rose to power in the Armenian mountains after the collapse of the Urartian state and were certainly present there in the last half of the first millennium BC. The Armenian language then absorbed a vast quantity of foreign vocabulary from its neighbours, especially Iranian and Aramaic, the Semitic language spoken in north Mesopotamia, and the earliest of these loans appears to have taken place from the fifth to the first centuries BC. All of this suggests that the Armenians may have been part of the broad series of movements that also carried the Phrygians into Anatolia, and that by 500 BC they were establishing their pre-eminence in Armenia.

In the most closely argued study of Armenian origins, the eminent Russian linguist and historian Igor Diakonov suggests that they may be identified with the Muski and perhaps other tribes known in Assyrian sources to have occupied the Upper Euphrates and lower Aratsani by 1165 BC. These people appear to Diakonov to be in the right place at the right time, and their name offers tenuous links with both the Armenians themselves and with the Balkans. Muski is compared with the Georgian name for the Armenians, *(Sa)mekhi*, and with the ethnic formative found in both Mysia in Asia Minor and the Thracian province of Moesia. Diakonov envisions that the Muski (proto-Armenians) drifted eastward absorbing both the Luwians of southern Anatolia and the Urartians in eastern Anatolia to form ultimately the Armenian people of today.

The linkage of the Phrygians and Armenians to the same broad wave of migrations tangles their origins almost hopelessly. The Muski, identified by Diakonov in twelfth-century Assyrian texts as proto-Armenians, are just as probably assigned a Phrygian or Thracian identity by others, and without inscriptional evidence it is impossible to resolve the issue. It is useful to step back from the details and examine the broader patterns.

It seems probable that a second wave of Indo-European migrations passed through Anatolia following that which produced the earlier Anatolian languages of Hittite and Luwian. Linguists do not find any cogent reasons for accepting an evolution of the earlier Hittite or Luwian languages into Phrygian or Armenian. Moreover, historical tradition such as that of Herodotus, coupled with the evidence of place names, for example, Thracian Moesia, Anatolian Mysia, and dialectal similarities with Greek, converge to suggest that these later Indo-European migrations derived from the Balkans. The evidence for these migrations in the archaeological record, other than the Balkan impact on northwest Anatolia, is not unequivocal, and we hardly need detail alternative explanations for the destruction horizons met in the twelfth century BC. But when Assyrian annals of the same century accuse the Muski of carrying out invasions with armies numbering 20,000 men, we have reason to accept the hypothesis that this was a period of migrating peoples. In two instances, we see clearly documented the linguistic replacement of one group by another – the Phrygians over the Hittites of central Anatolia, and the Armenians over the Urartians in eastern Anatolia. By the first centuries AD, all of these languages save Armenian have either long become extinct or are rapidly disappearing.

The Indo-Aryans

At first glance logic might seem to dictate that as we move east of Anatolia, the next Indo-European-speaking people we should encounter is the Iranians. It

Avestan	təm amavantəm yazatəm
Sanskrit	*tam amavantam yajatam*
	surəm damohu səvistəm
	suram dhamasu savistham
	mithrəm yazai zaothrabyo
	mitram yajai hotrabhyah
	This powerful strong god Mithra strongest in the world of creatures, I will worship with libations.

21   The concept of a common Indo-Iranian language is indicated by the close similarities between this Indic (Sanskrit) translation of an early Iranian hymn. The god Mitra/ Mithra was common to both Indians and Iranians.

will soon become apparent that this is not so and that we are compelled to examine the evidence for Indian or Indo-Aryan origins first. In addition, when considering Indian origins we must keep in mind the broader ramifications of Indo-European dialectology. Probably the least-contested observation concerning the various Indo-European dialects is that those languages grouped together as Indic and Iranian show such remarkable similarities with one another that we can confidently posit a period of Indo-Iranian unity between the earlier Proto-Indo-European language and the subsequent appearance of the individual Indic (or Indo-Aryan) and Iranian languages. To these languages we may add the Kafiri languages of the Hindukush. Although these are only attested in recent times, they exhibit certain features that suggest that they are neither a direct descendant of Proto-Indo-Aryan or Proto-Iranian but an independant third branch of the Indo-Iranian group.

Today Indic comprises the major languages of India and Pakistan, for example, Hindi-Urdu, Bengali, Panjabi, Marathi, and a host of others which total approximately 750 million speakers. These languages are essentially confined to the Indian subcontinent with the exception of more recent colonies that have expanded into Africa, the Pacific and Europe. The only exception to this is Romany, the language of the Gypsies, that was carried from northern India into Europe in the Middle Ages.

The earliest written evidence preserved for Indo-Aryan in India only occurs about 300 BC with such monuments as the Asoka inscriptions. These, however, represent what linguists term Middle Indic, specifically Prakrit, and they by no means can serve as a *terminus* for the arrival of the Indians in the subcontinent. A vast literature of Old Indic, known as Sanskrit, preceded the Middle Indic inscriptions and formed the medium of the earliest Indic literary and religious language known to us. These were initially preserved only in oral form, but

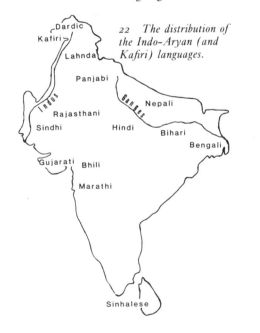

22 *The distribution of the Indo-Aryan (and Kafiri) languages.*

indrasya nu viryani pra vocam
yani cakara prathamani vajri
ahann ahim anu apas tatarda
pra vaksana abhinat parvatanam.

I shall proclaim now the heroic deeds of Indra,
the first ones which the club-wielder performed,
he slew the serpent, he made a breach for the waters,
he split open the bellies of the mountains.

23 *A short excerpt from the* Rig Veda *celebrates the warrior god Indra's victory over the evil Vrtra. The opening line contains a number of words with numerous cognates in the other Indo-European languages. For example,* nu *is the same as Greek, Old Irish, Lithuanian and Old English* nu 'now'. *Indra's heroic deeds* viryani *are 'manly deeds' from the root* vir- *which is also found in Latin* vir, *Old Irish* fer, *Lithuanian* vyras *and Old English* wer *where it still survives in the compound 'werewolf'. To proclaim, literally 'speak forth'* pra vocam *is cognate with Latin* pro 'forth' *and* voco 'I call'.

there is abundant circumstantial evidence to indicate that they were written down by the sixth century BC. The earliest representative of this Old Indic is to be found in the *Vedas*, the ancient religious literature of India. The language of the *Vedas* is very archaic, and the cultural and geographical world portrayed in these hymns suggests that they were composed in northwest India sometime before the first millennium BC with a notional date of around 1500–1200 BC.

Although in India itself we can go no earlier than the *Vedas*, we have not thoroughly exhausted our sources, because the earliest written evidence for an Indo-Aryan language is not to be found in India but rather in northern Syria. Here lay the empire of the Mitanni who, by the fifteenth-fourteenth centuries BC, had expanded their power from the shores of the Mediterranean to the Zagros mountains thus coming into conflict with both the Hittites to the west and Egyptian control of the Euphrates. The language of the Mitanni was Hurrian, which we have already met in eastern Anatolia and north Syria. Although the basic language of the Mitanni was non-Indo-European, there is, nevertheless, clear evidence of the use of an Indo-European vocabulary in the Mitanni documents. These derive from diplomatic correspondence in foreign archives such as Bogazköy (Hittite) and El Amarna (Egyptian), as the native Mitanni archives have not yet been discovered. But there can be little doubt that there was a distinctly Indo-Aryan element in the Mitanni kingdom.

In a treaty between the Hittites and the Mitanni, the king of the latter swears by a series of Hurrian gods and then adds a series of names that are transparently the names of major Indic deities – *Mi-it-ra* (Indic Mitra), *Aru-na* (Varuna), *In-da-ra* (Indra) and *Na-sa-at-tiya* (Nasatya). A Hittite text on horse-training and chariotry, whose author is identified as Kikkuli the Mitanni, employs the names of Indic numerals for the courses that the chariot makes about a track – *aika* (Indic *eka* 'one'), *tera* (*tri* 'three'), *panza* (*panca* 'five'), *satta*

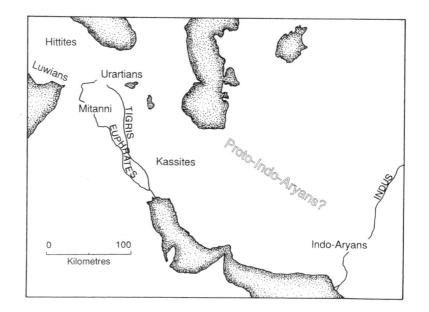

24 The Mitanni and their neighbours.

'Thus (speaks) Kikkuli, the *assussanni* (horse-trainer), from the land of Mitanni:

When he lets the horses onto the meadow in the autumn, he harnesses them. He lets them trot 3 miles, but he lets them gallop over 7 fields. But on the way back he has them gallop over 10 fields. Then he unharnesses them, provides for them, and they are watered. He brings them into the stable. Then he gives them mixed together 1 handful of wheat, 2 handfuls of barley and 1 handful of hay. They eat this up. As soon as they have finished their fodder, he binds them close to the post.'

25 *The opening instructions from the Hittite text on horse-training by Kikkuli the Mitanni. In order to describe Kikkuli's profession, the text employs the Indo-Aryan word* assussanni, *(Sanskrit* asvasani-*).*

(*sapta* 'seven') and *na* (*nava* 'nine'), while a Hurrian text from Yorgan Tepe employs Indo-Aryan words to describe the colour of horses, for example, *babru* (Indic *babhru* 'brown'), *parita* (*palita* 'grey') and *pinkara* (*pingala* 'reddish'). The Mitanni word *marya* is precisely the same as the Vedic *marya*, 'warrior'.

To these examples we may add a series of names for the Mitanni aristocracy and other names for divinities which associate the Indic element in the Mitanni language with the personal names and gods of the ruling dynasty. In addition, we naturally must include the special vocabulary of horsemanship for which the Mitanni were famous. These provide the clues that form the basis of the most widely accepted theory: an element of Indic-speaking chariot warriors superimposed themselves on a native Hurrian-speaking population to form a ruling dynasty that endured for several centuries. The precise mechanics by which this Indic element fused with the Hurrians to form the Mitanni is unknown, and scholars have employed everything from the model of an outright military conquest to the more benign analogy of the Varangian Norsemen who were 'invited' to establish the Old Russian state of Kiev.

The date of the appearance of an Indic element in north Syria bears on any discussion of the origins and expansion of the Indo-Iranians in Asia. Although we possess texts from Mesopotamia in the preceding eighteenth and seventeenth centuries, there is no evidence in them that conclusively points to an Indic presence in the region. By the fifteenth century, we do have evidence for Indic elements in the Mitanni kingdom and there are also possible (though disputed) Indic traces in the names of a few gods revered by the Kassites, the dynasty from the Zagros region that assumed control of the Babylonian empire. By the thirteenth century the Mitanni kingdom collapses which sees an end to the Indic presence in Southwestern Asia. All of this suggests that the Indic element ascribable to the Mitanni (and perhaps to the Kassites) did not enter until about the sixteenth-fifteenth centuries BC. Furthermore, it attests the existence of a very archaic form of the Indic language as early as 1600 BC. This indicates that a separate Indo-Aryan language had already diverged from Iranian by this time and that the putative period of proto-Indo-Iranian 'unity' must predate this, perhaps by as much as a half millennium or more. This accords well with the broad estimates of historical linguists who believe that a continuum of Indo-Iranian languages probably began to diverge by 2000 BC, if not somewhat earlier.

In tracing the origins of the Indic element in Western Asia we should begin with the obvious. The Indic presence is clearly not native but is intrusive to the Mitanni whose own language was Hurrian. The Kassites who apparently occupied the Zagros region before descending southwards into Babylonia also spoke a non-Indo-European language whose meagre textual remains do not permit clear association with any of the better-known languages of Asia. In either case, we are talking of intrusion, but one that is not so apparently thoroughgoing as among the Anatolians since it seems to have been limited to a small ruling dynasty which was otherwise assimilated by the native populations. A solution to this nearly impossible archaeological puzzle was argued at length by the late Roman Ghirshman.

Ghirshman observed that the area of Hurrian political power coincided with the distribution of a distinct ceramic type – Habur Ware. Within the territory of the Mitanni, and confined to the palaces of the aristocracy, there appeared this table ware, which included dark wares undecorated, impressed and white painted, none of which had a convincing local origin. Consequently, Ghirshman interpreted this pottery as the traditional ware of the Indic aristocracy in Mitanni and he found their closest parallels with wares from Shah Tepe in the Gorgan region southeast of the Caspian. We will see later that dark wares, specifically grey wares, have often been employed as an ethnic marker for other Indic and Iranian speakers. In addition, it is in the Gorgan region that the domestic horse first appears in the Near East about 3000–2250 BC. There is, for example, a cylinder seal depicting a horse-drawn vehicle from Hissar IIIB. As the association of horsemanship and chariotry with Indic elements among the Mitanni has already been clearly established, this evidence could indicate the route of Indic movements towards Mesopotamia. Ghirshman concluded that at the end of the fourth millennium BC, a people carrying black wares and familiar with both the domestic horse and wheeled vehicles had penetrated northeastern Iran from the north. Here they subsequently developed chariotry and trumpets, a technological necessity of chariot warfare. They then gradually pushed south along the shores of the Caspian where they encountered the Hurrians about 1800 BC at such sites as Tepe Giyan II/III. This was the period of symbiosis of the Indic and Hurrian elements in the Zagros. They then expanded as part of the Hurrian movement into northern Mesopotamia where we have already alluded to their subsequent history. If one accepts the hypothesis, then by the third millennium BC the southern borders of either Proto-Indic or Proto-Indo-Iranian had already extended to the southeast Caspian and could be discerned throughout this region in the gradual adoption of grey wares.

The primary ceramic evidence for migration of Indo-Aryans into the region of the Hurrians are the black and grey wares that appear abruptly in northern Mesopotamia and which Ghirshman derives ultimately from the southeast Caspian. This evidence has been challenged in two ways: either because grey

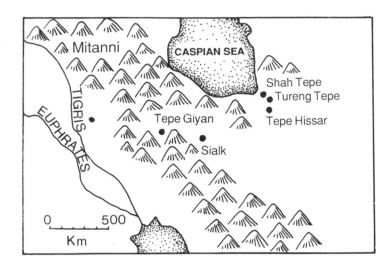

26 *Roman Ghirshman suggested that the Indo-Aryans migrated from southeast of the Caspian into the lands of the Mitanni.*

wares appear at Shah Tepe as early as 3000 BC, far too early to be assigned to the already differentiated Indo-Aryans; or else because grey wares in Iran itself expand too late and over too broad an area to be associated with anything other than the later Iranian migrations, not the earlier Indo-Aryans. Neither of these assertions, however, is wholly incompatible with Ghirshman's theory. It is theoretically possible that Proto-Indo-Iranian was spoken in the southeast Caspian about 3000 BC when grey ware first appears at Shah Tepe, but by the end of the next millennium, the language had gradually evolved into (Proto-) Indo-Aryan. The temporal crux of the argument is that migrations did begin when the urban centres of the Gorgan Grey Ware culture collapsed around 1800 BC. The abandonment of major sites such as Tepe Hissar IIIC, Shah Tepe and Tureng Tepe was, according to Ghirshman, the result of nomadic pressure from the north which is reflected in the deposition of treasures on Gorgan sites and destruction horizons. The Gorgan refugees were forced around the Caspian and into the Zagros where they mingled with the Hurrians to emerge several centuries later as the Mitanni. Unfortunately, the ceramic evidence does not really support this migration, and the derivation of Mitanni dark wares from Gorgan Grey Ware remains distant and as yet unbridged by intermediary stages. Nor, of course, is there any prima-facie case for assuming that the expansion of the dark wares indicates a population movement much less a specifically Indo-Aryan movement. Moreover, the mechanics by which the Indo-Aryan element retained its ceramic forms but abandoned most other aspects of their language and culture to the Hurrians invites more scepticism than belief.

Of Ghirshman's arguments, those pertaining to horse and chariot warfare demand our greatest attention, for here we find cultural elements that are inextricably associated with the specifically Indo-Aryan element in Mitanni and clearly set them apart from their non-Indo-European neighbours in the Near East. We have diplomatic correspondence between Egypt and Mitanni where the former requests both horses and chariots from the latter, indicating the Mitanni's reputation for horsemanship throughout the Near East. We have already seen in the linguistic evidence, such as Kikkuli's manual on horsemanship, that the terminology of chariotry included a distinctly Indo-Aryan vocabulary. Furthermore, the earliest evidence for the domestic horse is from the Pontic-Caspian region, and all present evidence suggests that it diffused from there through the Caucasus into Anatolia and perhaps around the eastern Caspian into northeast Iran. Hence, the appearance of both the horse and the chariot have frequently been attributed to an expansion of Indo-Europeans from the north into Western Asia. Specifically, Indo-Aryan charioteers are seen penetrating the kingdoms of Southwest Asia where, in the case of the Mitanni, they were able to dominate the local Hurrian substrate. Naturally, the evidence is anything but so certain.

We know that wheeled vehicles were employed in Mesopotamia by 3000 BC in early Sumer, and their presence in southern Mesopotamia has no obvious direct association with the Indo-Europeans. These vehicles were basically drawn by bovids, although there was a gradual increase in the use of equid draught in Western Asia. This, however, was primarily the onager or ass, and at no time prior to the second millennium BC can we regard Southwest Asia as practising the horse- and chariot-centred warfare that one finds among the Indo-Aryans. The earliest evidence for the horse in Western Asia is presently limited to Tal-i Iblis in south-central Iran (3500 BC) and Selenkahiyeh in Syria (2400–2000 BC), and its attestation in cuneiform texts appears to be similarly late and dates to the end of the third millennium BC. But from early in the second millennium BC we find unequivocal evidence for both the horse and the chariot, and by the seventeenth-sixteenth centuries this form of warfare is found from northern Anatolia south to Nubia, which illustrates the rapid spread of this revolutionary technology. J.H. Crouwel and M.A. Littauer have argued that this evidence suggests a perfectly logical evolution of the two-wheeled cart into the spoked-wheel chariot within Western Asia itself prior to the appearance of the Indo-Aryans whose presence in this region cannot be demonstrated before about 1600 BC. Some scholars such as Diakonov go on to argue that there is consequently no case for employing the earliest appearance of the domestic horse and chariot in the Near East as an ethnic marker for Indo-European migrations.

No easy solution presents itself since the problems here involve at least three issues which need not necessarily be linked – the origin of the domestic horse in Southwest Asia, the origins of the chariot, and the date of Indo-Aryan movements into the region. Current evidence provides little reason for seeing the domestic horse as anything but intrusive into Southwest Asia. The paucity of sites on which horse bones appear is in sharp contrast to the abundant evidence of the domestic horse during the fourth-third millennium across the Pontic-Caspian-Siberian steppe, and the most economical argument is to derive domestic horse populations from this direction during the third and early second millennia. The chariot, on the other hand, could possibly have been invented independently in the Near East as well as in the steppe. There is,

I think, much to be said for Stuart Piggott's suggestion that the Near Eastern war-chariot may have been the result of a symbiosis of the local needs and tradition of battle vehicles brought into contact with the dispersal of horse-drawn vehicles employing spoked wheels typical of the steppe. In any event, the horse-drawn war-chariot need not be regarded exclusively as an Indo-European ethnic marker, especially as it spread so rapidly over a vast area. But we should not be too quick to exclude the possibility that the earliest chariots were associated with Indo-Aryans because the Indo-Aryans are not attested in the Near East until several centuries after the appearance of chariots. Our dating of the Indo-Aryan element in the Mitanni texts is based purely and simply on written documents offering datable contexts. While we cannot with certainty push these dates back prior to the fifteenth century BC, it should not be forgotten that the Indic elements seem to be little more than the residue of a *dead* language in Hurrian, and that the symbiosis that produced the Mitanni may have taken place centuries earlier. On such an issue, where the discovery of a single datable text could advance the Indo-Aryans to greater antiquity in the Near East, it is not wise to rush to judgment on the issue of chariot warfare. We will return to the Mitanni problem when we have expanded our survey of the Indo-Iranians.

Before we turn to the Indian subcontinent, we must briefly tackle the obvious problem of the relationship with the Indo-Aryans of Western Asia and those of India itself. Of three possibilities, received opinion rejects two of them. It is highly improbable that the Indo-Aryans of Western Asia migrated eastwards, for example with the collapse of the Mitanni, and wandered into India, since there is not a shred of evidence – for example, names of non-Indic deities, personal names, loan words – that the Indo-Aryans of India ever had any contacts with their west Asian neighbours. The reverse possibility, that the main line of migration was into India and that a small group broke off and wandered from India into Western Asia is readily dismissed as an improbably long migration, again without the least bit of evidence. Having excluded the unlikely, we are left with the merely possible – either the Indo-Aryans divided south of an earlier staging area with some moving east and others far to the west, or they actually immigrated in mass forming a broad continuum across Western Asia to the Indus and were later divided by the incursion of Iranian-speaking peoples. The first explanation is still along those lines advanced by Ghirshman and others while the Indologist, Thomas Burrow, has argued for an initial Indo-Aryan settlement not only of north Mesopotamia but also of the Iranian plateau itself. The arguments are primarily linguistic and religious, among which the latter is the most intriguing.

Burrow sets out to explain why the Indic word for god, *deva*, should occur under its Iranian cognate *daeva* to mean 'demon'. The Iranian situation was the result of the great religious reformer Zarathustra's (or Zoroaster as he is known through Greek sources) influence on the Iranian religion which, according to Burrow, resulted in the relegation of those specifically Indo-Aryan gods such as Varuna and Indra to the role of demons, since they were the gods of the indigenous Indo-Aryan occupiers of Iran and were not recognized as gods in the new Iranian religion. This argument goes much further, because Zoroastrian religion employs a special class of words to describe demons. Some of these words are clearly formed pejoratives, but a small set of them appear to derive from an earlier Indo-Aryan substrate. Further evidence is found in the names of Iranian rivers which are seen to be borrowings from an earlier Indo-Aryan language and attested in India itself. In short, Zoroastrianism was a religious-based crusade against the remnant Indo-Aryan population which occupied Iran, and it was the success of this Iranian expansion that split the Indo-Aryans into western (Mitanni) and eastern (Indian) groups.

Burrow argues that the conventional dating of Zarathustra to about 600 BC is far too recent and that there are reasons for placing him half a millennium earlier at least. Hence, Burrow would argue that the Indo-Aryan continuum that spanned Southwest Asia and Iran was established before 1400 BC by which time the Iranians were already beginning to expand into northeastern Iran.

While a number of the specifics of Burrow's theory have already been dismissed by some linguists, his suggestion that there must have been an Indo-Aryan element in the substrate later subsumed by the expanding Iranians is still attractive. Unfortunately, the theory has been proposed almost exclusively on linguistic grounds and there has been little attempt to seek archaeological correlations for his scheme. This is not at all the problem, however, when we turn our attention to the intrusion of Indo-Aryan speakers into India itself.

As we have done with the other Indo-European peoples of Asia, we must preface our inquiry into the origins of the Indo-Aryans in India with the problem of their autochthony. Although the great majority of scholars insist that the Indo-Aryans were intrusive into northwest India, there have always been a few to claim that the Indus Valley civilization that flourished about 2500–1500 BC was Indo-Aryan and it must be admitted that direct written

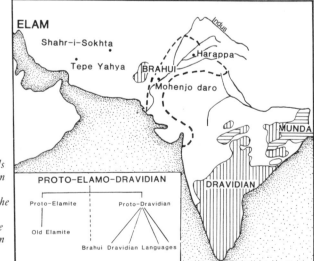

27 *The area of the Indus civilization (dotted line) falls within the general distribution of the Elamo-Dravidian language family. Note that the Dravidian languages are not only found to the south of the Indus but Brahui, a 'northern Dravidian' language, lies to its west.*

testimony is not so clear in India as it is in much of Southwest Asia. This is because the only written evidence left by the builders of the Indus towns – the Indus script – remains undeciphered despite periodic claims to the contrary. It is possible that the brevity of Indus texts, largely confined to seals, coupled with the absence of bilingual inscriptions will ensure our ignorance indefinitely. Nevertheless, linguists also recognize that there are some linguistic solutions to the problem of the Indus script that are far more likely than others.

It should be remembered that as well as Indo-Aryan languages, India also possesses two other major linguistic groups. By far the largest are the non-Indo-European Dravidian languages which dominate the southern third of India. The positioning of Indo-Aryan in the north, and the known historical expansion of Indic from north to both the east and the south, gives us every reason to deny the Indo-Aryans a prior home in those regions. Furthermore, there are still remnant northern Dravidian languages including Brahui to the west of the Indus and others to the southeast. The most obvious explanation of this situation is that the Dravidian languages once occupied nearly all of the Indian subcontinent and it is the intrusion of Indo-Aryans that engulfed them in northern India leaving but a few isolated enclaves. This is further supported by the fact that Dravidian loan words begin to appear in Sanskrit literature from its very beginning. This prior dominance of Dravidian in northern India makes it the most formidable candidate for the language of the Indus civilization. Much less likely is Munda, a non-Indo-European language now confined to central India but which once extended north to the Ganges. It appears to have been itself swamped by Dravidian languages and then further confined by the expansion of the Indo-Aryans.

Another candidate at least proximate to the Indus Valley is Elamite, the language of the major kingdom that occupied southern Iran. Here we are dealing with a literate society writing in a decipherable non-Indo-European language (related to Dravidian) which has left us intelligible texts from the late third millennium onwards. Within a number of Elamite sites there also occur pictographic tablets, related generically to the earliest Sumerian script, and dating as early as the late fourth millennium BC. They have been found on sites as far east as Tepe Yahya and Shahr-i Sokhta. These tablets are generally termed Proto-Elamite since they coincide with the location of later decipherable Elamite texts. For those requiring an exterior high culture to explain the origins of the Indus civilization (generally regarded today as unnecessary), Proto-Elamite can always serve as a popular candidate which offers yet another proximate linguistic identity for the Indus script. Whatever the merits of these arguments are, the existence of Elamite across southern Iran excludes this region as an earlier homeland of the Indo-Aryans.

Circumstantial evidence for identifying the language of the Indus Valley script with Elamite or Dravidian has been greatly strengthened by David McAlpin's work on the relationship between the Dravidian languages and Elamite. McAlpin has demonstrated that the two groups of languages derive from a common proto-language, Proto-Elamo-Dravidian, and that Brahui, traditionally assigned to the Northern Dravidian subgroup, would actually appear to be linguistically as well as geographically intermediate between the two major subgroups. McAlpin reconstructs to Proto-Elamo-Dravidian a common stockbreeding vocabulary (cattle, ovicaprid, goat, and so on), and traces special developments in the agricultural terminology of the Dravidian branch as it pushed southward into the Indian subcontinent. It is quite interesting that one may reconstruct a common word for 'brick' in Proto-Elamo-Dravidian as this was the ubiquitous building material of the Indus and other neighbouring civilizations. McAlpin dates the disintegration of Proto-Elamo-Dravidian to about the fifth millennium BC. All of this makes a good case for associating the early village farming economies that formed the foundation of the Indus civilization with Elamo-Dravidian languages – an hypothesis far more probable than Colin Renfrew's recent suggestion that the Indus Valley civilization was Indo-Aryan and that it was Indo-Europeans who introduced the farming economy to this region.[11]

Other than the Indus script, the very character of Indian society reflected in the earliest Vedic literature renders it highly unlikely that the Indus civilization was the product of Indo-Aryans. Although the earliest Vedic hymns are focused geographically on the Indus and its major tributaries in the Punjab, the culture represented in them bears little similarity to that of the urban society found at Harappa or Mohenjo-daro. It is illiterate, non-urban, non-maritime, basically uninterested in exchange other than that involving cattle, and lacking in any forms of political complexity beyond that of a king whose primary function seems to be concerned with warfare and ritual. Moreover, the *Vedas* recognize a dichotomy between the Indo-Aryans and their dark-skinned enemies, the *dasa*, who are on one occasion described as 'nose-less', which has generally been interpreted as a pejorative reference to Dravidian physical features. Vedic hymns commemorate or invoke divine support for the destruction of their enemies and the storming of their citadels. This is to be accomplished with the assistance of their horses and chariots, a technique of warfare apparently unknown to the Indus civilization. It is little surprising, then, that the Indo-Aryans have been viewed in the past as the probable destroyers of the Indus civilization about 1500 BC. Today, there is a tendency to seek internal causes for this collapse – climatic, hydraulic, environmental – rather than Indic warriors who are more often seen as a phenomenon of the post-Indus period. In either case, the only way that one may retain an Indo-Aryan identity for the Indus civilization is to assume that, after its collapse about 1500 BC, it receded into the type of world reflected in the Vedic hymns and that these are the product of the degenerate descendants of the Indus civilization. Given all the other objections, this solution would call for far more special pleading than anyone has reason to credit. All of our earliest evidence for the Indo-Aryans in India, therefore, indicates that they came from elsewhere and we should turn to the archaeological evidence to trace their migration.

A reasonable starting point is to assume that whatever culture occupied the lands depicted in early Indic literature in the first millennium BC has the most right to the label of Indo-Aryan. The Painted Grey Ware culture, centred from the eastern Punjab to the central Ganges, is at least one obvious candidate. The radiocarbon dates indicate that this culture flourished about 1300–400 BC, a time when we can be certain of the existence of Indic speakers in northern India without fear of over-extrapolating from the literary evidence. The culture, which takes its name from its fine grey ware painted with black or red decoration, meets some of the minimum requirements of an Indo-Aryan culture as seen through the earliest Indic literature. Settlements, where attested, tend to be of flimsy wattle and daub and bear no resemblance to the brick-built urban complexes known in the Harappan culture. The economy included the domestic horse, and although this animal has occasionally been recovered from Harappan sites, for example Surkotada and Kalibangan, no one would credit the earlier Harappan culture as exemplifying the horse-centred culture of the Vedic Aryans. Furthermore, there is an excellent correlation between the earliest Painted Grey Ware sites and historical sites mentioned in the great Indic epic, the *Mahabharata*, which according to tradition is set to an historical period of the early first millennium BC. That these sites also include what would later become major urban centres coincides well with their identity as early Indo-Aryan settlements which rapidly spread their language in northern India. The major problem with identifying them with the earliest intrusive Indo-Aryans is that the ceramics are without clear external as well as internal derivation and so it is difficult to postulate an invading culture. Furthermore, the remains largely date to the first millennium BC and are primarily concentrated to the east of where we would expect to find the earliest Indo-Aryan remains in India. For this we must look earlier and further west. There are just such candidates.

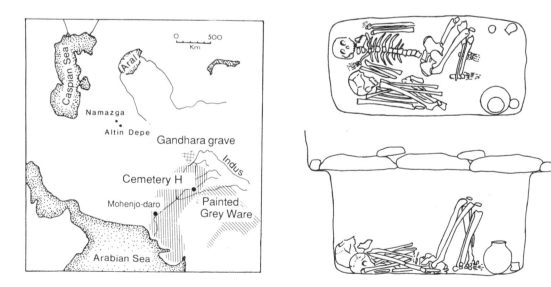

28, 29   The Gandhara Grave, Cemetery H and Painted Grey Ware cultures are traditional candidates for Indo-Aryan (or Kafiri) origins; seen here is a Gandhara Grave burial.

The Cemetery H culture of the middle Indus has been advanced as the possible archaeological manifestation of the Indo-Aryan invaders. Its temporal position is not entirely secure other than being post Harappan, and certainly some of the stratigraphic evidence of the Cemetery H remains suggests a significant interval between the fall of Harappa and this culture. This is not in itself a hindrance, since we have already seen that there really is no compelling reason to credit the Indo-Aryans with the destruction of the Indus civilization, although they have played out that role in a number of earlier archaeological models. It is their pottery with possible West Asiatic connections coupled with their fractional burial rite, that is, the collection of partial skeletal remains following exposure and their deposition in an urn, which has cast them as intruders. In addition, what little architectural remains exist also support the image of a less sedentary population than their Harappan predecessors. But their limited distribution and insecure foreign affinities do not encourage us to accept them as the whole solution to the Indo-Aryan problem.

One of the best candidates for intruding Indo-Aryans is to be found north of the Indus in the Swat Valley, which gives its name to the culture otherwise known as the Gandhara Grave culture. The Swat Valley occupies the position of a trip line, in that any intruder from the northwest is likely to pass through it first before arriving in either the Indus or Ganges Basin. Consequently, a major cultural change here at the appropriate time might signal the arrival of the Indo-Aryans. Just such a cultural break is argued to occur about 1800 BC with the introduction of a new burial rite and ceramics into the Swat Valley. The culture is known from cemeteries where we find both flexed inhumation in a pit (actually the sub-pit of an initial pit) and, more interestingly, cremation burial in an urn, often a face-urn. Such a rite attracts our attention not only because it is not found in contemporary cultures of the same region but also because early Vedic literature indicates that both inhumation and cremation burial were practised in early Indo-Aryan society. The goods found with the burials are not especially rich but do include copper, gold and silver in the earlier period, and iron is found by about 900 BC. The settlements indicate semi-subterranean huts in the initial phases with the later introduction of rubble-filled walls. The economy included a range of domestic plants and animals, among the latter the horse. It should be emphasized that the horse was not merely incidental to the faunal remains but we also have two horse burials as well as horse-trappings from the Gandhara Grave culture. Furthermore, the new ceramic style was a grey ware, approximately half of which was handmade and decorated with incisions. These ceramics show a similarity to grey wares of south Central Asia and northern Iran, precisely the direction from which we might expect the earliest Indo-Aryans. Moreover, the Swat region maintains its cultural continuity down to about 400 BC and, consequently, the Swat Valley culture offers itself as a most attractive candidate for early Indo-Aryans or Kafiri if we are correct in assuming that they must have migrated through this region. Finally, the area makes an excellent fit with the geographical scene depicted in the hymns of the *Rig Veda* and it does so at the expected time.

Naturally, our optimism at having identified a suitable archaeological expression of the Indo-Aryans must be tempered with some caution. It has not yet been possible to make a convincing association between the Swat Valley culture and any of the putative Indo-Aryan cultures that appear later in the Punjab or the Ganges Basin. The leap from the plain grey wares of the Swat Valley to the Painted Grey Ware culture of India, suggested by the Pakistani archaeologist Ahmad Hassan Dani, has not been accepted by Indian archaeologists. Moreover, the connection between the Swat Valley and the northern manifestations of the grey ware tradition is also in need of strengthening. We should also recall that it is out of this grey ware tradition that many also derive the Iranians, and it is specifically to their origins that we should now turn.

The Iranians

The Iranian languages, for example, Persian, Kurdish and Pashto, are today primarily confined to the modern states of Iran and Afghanistan, and to territories immediately adjacent, all of which comprise over seventy million speakers. The current distribution of Iranian, however, greatly belies its earlier expansion which included a vast portion of the Eurasian steppe. Reading from west to east we can include as Iranian speakers the major Iron Age nomads of the Pontic-Caspian steppe such as the Kimmerians (?), Scythians, Sarmatians and Alans. The incredible mobility of these horse-mounted nomads becomes all the more impressive when we recall their westward expansions through Europe. Sarmatian tribes not only settled in the Danube region but, during the second century AD, were conscripted to defend the borders of Roman Britain. The Alans travelled as far west as France and forced their way south through Spain, ultimately to establish a state in North Africa. Of these different peoples, only remnants of the Alans have survived to the present day in the modern guise

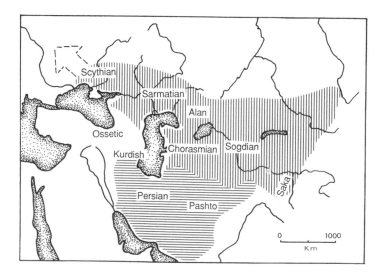

30 The historical distribution of the Iranian languages. The area of the northeastern languages is indicated with vertical hatching, the western Iranian languages are shown with horizontal hatching.

of the Ossetes who, retreating into the protection of the central Caucasus in the Middle Ages, still retain a population of nearly 600,000 speakers. Much further to the east were other Iranian-speaking peoples, such as those who have left us the remains of Sogdian, language of the ancient kingdom of Samarkand, first attested in the early Middle Ages and which still survives among the Yaghnobis of Tadzhikistan. Furthest to the east lay the bearers of Khotanese Saka, an Iranian language situated in Chinese Turkestan which was employed in religious texts of the seventh to tenth centuries and is preserved today among the Pamirs. This extremely broad group of steppe languages are all labelled Northeastern and Eastern Iranian by linguists, to contrast them with the more familiar Western Iranian language of Persian.

The earliest Western Iranian speakers emerge into history in northwestern Iran in the mid-ninth century BC. This is when Assyrian texts record the existence of the Medes (836 BC) in the vicinity of modern Isfahan and the Persians (Parsua) northwest of Kermanshah. At this time the twenty-seven kings of the Parsua are recorded delivering tribute to the Assyrian Shalmanesser III (858–824 BC). It is clear from the Assyrian narratives of both the Medes and the Persians that they are encountering already established peoples with whom they came into contact and conflict as the Assyrians pushed northeastwards to the Zagros. We may assume, therefore, that Iranian tribes were already settled by the beginning of the ninth century in the region north of the Zagros, and it is here that we can expect to pick up their trail.

The period in which we first encounter the Iranians in western Iran is designated Iron Age Period II (1000–800 BC). This in turn is seen as the direct and uninterrupted successor to Iron Age I which begins about 1400 BC. It is the initiation of Iron Age I that sees a major cultural break in this region. With its earliest appearance we find a shift from painted to plain grey wares, both in settlements and as grave accompaniments. The cemeteries themselves, such as Cemetery A at Sialk (V), mark a change from the intramural burials earlier encountered in the area. Iron is almost non-existent in the earliest phase but

---

Auramazda vazraka hya mathista baganam
hauv Darayavaum XSyam
ada hausaiy xsacam
frabara tya naibam
tya uratharam uvaspam umartiyam

Great Ahuramazda, the greatest of gods –
he created Darius the King,
he bestowed upon him the kingdom,
good,
possessed of good charioteers, of good horses, of good men.

---

31   A brief inscription of Darius in the Western Iranian Old Persian language. The last line contains three words with the prefix u 'good' followed by ratha 'chariot' (cf. Sanskrit ratha-, Latin rota, Irish roth, Lithuanian ratas 'wheel'; aspa 'horse' (Sanskrit asva-, Latin equus, Old Irish ech, Lithuanian asva); and martiya 'man' (Sanskrit marta-, Greek mortos, from the root *mer- 'to die', cf. mortal).

becomes increasingly abundant by Period II. Most importantly, the area in which the grey ware is found coincides in general with the later Assyrian evidence for Iranian tribes. On the basis of this evidence, T. Cuyler Young concluded that the Iron Age I culture north of the Zagros represents a sharp cultural break which should be associated with the emergence of the Iranians in western Iran. The continuity of this culture through Iron Age II sees trends towards greater regionalization and the absorption of foreign influences, which coincides well with the Iranians' contact with the Assyrian world. In short, some archaeologists argue that we have a relatively good association between an apparently intrusive culture and the historic distribution of an Indo-European people. It is when we try to trace the origins of the Western Iranians further back in time that our problems become much more difficult.

Since the Iranians are first encountered north or east of a chain of non-Indo-European Urartians, Assyrians, and Elamites, their approach most probably was from the north. We can readily exclude the northwest, that is, eastern Anatolia, as highly improbable given its prior identification with Hurrian populations. As we have seen, the possibility that the Western Iranians derived ultimately from the Pontic steppe was entertained by Ghirshman and others who argued for a migration across the Caucasus and down the western Caspian into northern Iran. The evidence offered to support such a migration is varied. There are linguists who note the occasional presence of Iranian loan words among the Caucasian languages along the proposed route. For their part, some archaeologists cite the appearance of steppe *kurgans*, dating to the centuries around 1000 BC, that appear in northern Azerbaijan. These, with their wooden burial structure, hearths and horse burials, are similar to those found in the Srubnaya (Timber-grave) culture north of the Caucasus as well as some burials in northwestern Iran. Moreover, the proposed migration route is precisely that which is historically attested for Iranian-speaking Scythians who penetrated from north of the Black Sea through the Caucasus and on into Southwest Asia. Nevertheless, many are still very sceptical that any secure link can be

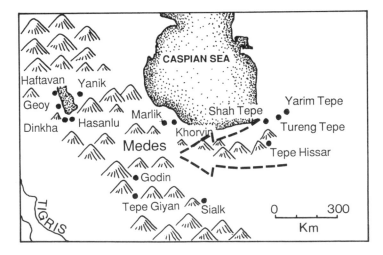

32 Grey-Ware sites are frequently associated with West Iranian migrations, possibly originating from the southeast Caspian. Note that the distribution of these sites exceeds the area of historically attested Iranians.

established between the Iron Age I culture of Iran and either the Caucasus or Pontic steppe, and they would dismiss outright any claim for a full-scale migration along this route about 1000 BC. This leaves but one other source – the northeast, a route which Diakonov argues is the most plausible since it involves passage between similar ecological regions (Central Asia and Iran), without major barriers.

We have already seen how the grey ware tradition had appeared in the Gorgan region before the end of the fourth millennium, and how it seems to terminate about 1800 BC (Hissar IIIC) coincidental with the abandonment of Bronze Age sites in the southeast Caspian. We have also reviewed how grey wares again begin to emerge about four centuries later in Iron Age I on sites further to the southwest, which coincides with the territory we would assign to the earliest historic Iranians. The most obvious and economical solution then would be to assume a progression – by migration or diffusion – of these wares from the Gorgan towards the Zagros. Some archaeologists, perhaps crediting radiocarbon dating with far greater precision than the technique usually delivers, have been troubled by the apparent 400 year hiatus between the final Gorgan material and earliest Iron Age I dates. Even if this hiatus is justified on the present evidence, some believe that it will be bridged in the course of future excavations. In any event, it is to the northeast that we naturally would seek the Iranians, since it is in this area that we subsequently find other major Iranian peoples such as the Parthians, Bactrians and Sogdians. Moreover, Diakonov argues that the absence of foreign words in the earliest Eastern Iranian language indicates its longer occupation of the area than Western Iranian which abounds in words drawn from its non-Iranian neighbours and substrates. Attractive as this solution might appear, we must admit that it does contain one major drawback – it sets the Iranians immediately on the heels of the Indo-Aryans.

We have seen how Ghirshman and others provided the Western Iranians with an origin in the Pontic-Caspian steppe while deriving the Indo-Aryans from Central Asia. Although we may be sceptical of the archaeological evi-

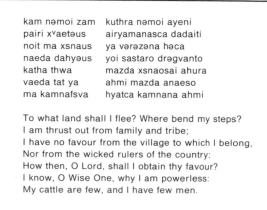

kam nəmoi zam   kuthra nəmoi ayeni
pairi xᵛaetəus   airyamanasca dadaiti
noit ma xsnaus   ya vərəzəna həca
naeda dahyəus   yoi sastaro drəgvanto
katha thwa   mazda xsnaosai ahura
vaeda tat ya   ahmi mazda anaeso
ma kamnafsva   hyatca kamnana ahmi

To what land shall I flee? Where bend my steps?
I am thrust out from family and tribe;
I have no favour from the village to which I belong,
Nor from the wicked rulers of the country:
How then, O Lord, shall I obtain thy favour?
I know, O Wise One, why I am powerless:
My cattle are few, and I have few men.

33 An excerpt from Zarathustra's Gathas, *the oldest part of the* Avesta.

dence adduced to demonstrate an Iranian migration across the Caucasus in the second millennium BC, it must be admitted that such a solution at least accommodates the linguistic divergence undergone by the Indo-Iranian languages. Derivation of both the Western Iranians and the Proto-Indo-Aryans from the Grey Ware tradition of the southeast Caspian offers little room for geographical separation between the two branches of Indo-Iranian. Only by detaching the Indo-Aryan element in Mitanni from a possible origin in the Gorgan culture can we avoid the linguistic implausibility of deriving both Indians and Iranians from precisely the same region at the same time. Or, of course, we can accept the Grey Ware identification with the Indo-Aryans and seek a different origin for the Iranians. For this, we must consider the origin of the Eastern Iranians.

It is unfortunate for us that the earliest native literature in an Iranian language is situated so far from those historical sources of the Near East that recount the earliest appearance of the Western Iranians. Avestan, the first attested Iranian language, takes its name from the great body of early Iranian religious literature. The earliest portion of the *Avesta* is the *Gathas*, which are credited to Zarathustra. This collection of hymns, localized geographically to Central Asia/northeastern Iran, displays much the same archaic nature as do the *Vedas*. It is this which has prompted linguists such as Burrow to reject the traditional dating of Zarathustra to the sixth century BC and to propose a much older date, possibly half a millennium or more. The nature of the dating controversy provides little room for compromise between the opposing forces, and from the archaeological perspective we can at least credit the earliest part of the *Avesta* to the Late Bronze Age-Early Iron Age, about 1000 BC.

The *Gathas* are fundamentally religious hymns and do not provide as rich a source for ethnographic inference as do either the later portions of the *Avesta* or the *Rig Veda*. What can be gleaned from the hymns is that they appear to be composed in an essentially rural milieu where stockbreeding, especially cattle-keeping, is held in esteem along with agriculture. Urbanism of any sort is not suggested although mention of citadels, irrigation canals, and the like, are met in other later Avestan hymns. The hints of political structure represented in the hymns are limited to family, village and tribe, or to district and country. Finally, it is commonly maintained that the *Gathas* reflect an opposition between the believer in Zarathustra's teachings and unbelievers, not between Iranians and foreigners.

If we search for an archaeological correlate for the world of the *Gathas*, then the area assigned by the few geographical references in the text fits well enough. By the mid-second millennium BC, most of the northern regions of Central Asia were occupied by pastoral societies deriving, either from the Timber-grave culture which was centred west on the Volga, or the Andronovo culture, a blanket term for a variety of steppe Bronze Age cultures that emerged in Central Asia and south Siberia. What is important for our purpose is that they are in sharp contrast to the proto-urban centres of southern Central Asia such as Namazga V or Altin Depe, whose sophisticated architecture including temples, technology, art and economy bear scant resemblance to that portrayed in the earliest Iranian literature. Moreover, the remains from these steppe Bronze Age sites provide us with some of the finest parallels with common reconstructions for Indo-Iranian culture. The settlement and cemetery of Sintashta, for example, although located far to the north on the Trans-Ural steppe, provides the type of Indo-Iranian archaeological evidence that would more than delight an archaeologist seeking their remains in Iran or India. Next to a small settlement occurs a cemetery of tumulus burials dating to the sixteenth century BC. These contain the remains of large quantities of sacrificed animals, especially horses and dogs which are noted in Indo-Aryan ritual, evidence of chariots, and an assortment of other Indo-Iranian ritual markers.

The identification of the Andronovo culture and at least the eastern outliers of the Timber-grave culture as Indo-Iranian is commonly accepted by scholars. It is out of this steppe region that we derive the Scythians who pushed westwards to the Pontic and then southwards through the Caucasus to ravage the Near East during the seventh century BC. This migration is traceable both in historical sources and archaeological remains such as burials and Scythian artefacts.

To the east of the Scythians emerged the Sarmatians, Massagetae, and Alans, all of whom can be derived from the Late Bronze and Early Iron Age of the Asiatic steppe. Parthians, Bactrians, Sogdians and other Iranian peoples known to us from Central Asia emerge out of the Iron Age cultures of their respective regions which seem to have involved the acculturation or evolution of earlier pastoralists to the increasingly urbanized or citadel-based settlements that emerged in the region in the first millennium BC. As the eastern limits of the Andronovo culture extended all the way to the Yenisey river, Kirghiziya and Tadzhikistan, one might even be able to provide a not too distant source for the easternmost Iranians, the Saka. Indeed, it is in the eastern Andronovo variants such as the Bishkent culture of south Tadzhikistan that one encounters again the probable expression of Indo-Iranian ritual in the archaeological record. At the cemetery of Tulkhar, male burials were provided with small rectangular hearths, reminiscent of the typical Ahavaniya, the rectangular fire-altar of early Indic priests, while females were provided round hearths, comparable to the Garhapatya, the female-associated hearth fire of the Indo-Aryan house.

Even if there is considerable disagreement as to detail, the identification of the steppe Bronze Age cultures as essentially Indo-Iranian seems fairly secure. This security, however, only remains if we are deliberately vague and do not specify whether we mean Indo-Iranian, Indo-Aryan or Iranian. It is often reasoned that since the steppe cultures date to the second millennium or later, it is most probable that they are (Proto-) Iranian rather than undifferentiated Indo-Iranians. Justification for this derives from our knowledge that Indo-Aryan had already emerged by the second millennium BC among the Mitanni. Having now come full circle, we must step outside the more specific arguments and briefly view this maze into which both linguists and archaeologists have got themselves.

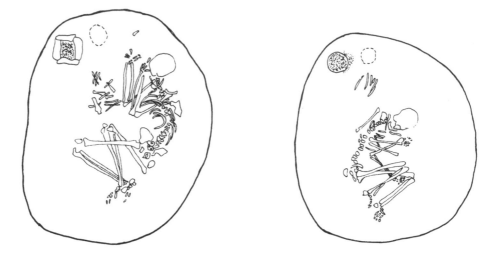

34, 35 A male and a female burial from Tulkhar. The male was buried with a rectangular hearth and with bones of a sheep, a dagger, pot, bead-amulet and a flint arrowhead; the female was buried with a round hearth, sheep bones and a pot.

All archaeological evidence adduced to indicate Indo-Iranian migrations derives broadly from two different sources – grey wares associated with proto-urban settlements extending from south of the Caspian across the southern border of Central Asia, and traces (often burials) of either mobile pastoralists or smaller villages, be they in the Eurasian steppe or in northwestern India. The evidence of the *Avesta* and the *Vedas* would clearly point to the second category of remains as the more probable archaeological expression of Indo-Iranian culture. Consequently, a number of Soviet scholars such as Edvin Grantovsky have rejected outright any ascription of grey ware cultures or any other evidence derived from the first category of sites to the Indo-Iranians as incompatible with their pastoral origins. But we should not forget that our cultural reconstructions are based primarily on an East Iranian text, the *Avesta*, and the *Vedas*, both of which were composed in regions remote from either the Indo-Aryans or western Iranians in the Near East. Here our literary evidence is very meagre. In short, we have no conclusive grounds to deny the Western Iranians or the Indo-Aryans of the Near East either an immediate urban past or at least a close association with urban societies. We cannot escape seriously entertaining all of those arguments that seek to trace population movements by the spread of essentially Central Asian ceramic styles, especially when alternative evidence deriving from pastoralists is as yet so poorly known in those areas of the Near East later occupied by Indic or Iranian speakers.

The use of grey wares to indicate migrations in Iran can, as we have seen, lead to apparent contradictions. It would seem improbable that the Indo-Aryans of Mitanni moved west with the same expansion of grey wares as the Western Iranians. Any increase in the antiquity of grey wares north of the Zagros will find us placing the putative ancestors of the Medes and Persians in their historical seats at the same time as the Indo-Aryans of Mitanni, a situation that would probably have been reflected in the historical record. For this reason, it has been suggested that the grey ware horizon should be seen as Indo-Aryan rather than Iranian and that for the ancestors of the Persians and Medes we must look to other evidence. This may be so, but I think we would do better to tie our star to the question of horses and chariots, the only Mitanni evidence that is demonstrably Indo-Aryan, rather than to ceramics. It must be admitted that at present we lack the necessary intermediary stages of the diffusion of horses or chariots from the steppe into northern Syria. We have only points on a map – the Trans-Ural steppe, the Pontic, the southern Caucasus, the seal from Hissar IIIB. These are not yet arranged into an interpretive framework from which we can trace movements, but future excavations are likely to help both fill in gaps of evidence and chronology. This, then, is a potentially resolvable problem which may provide us with sounder evidence on which to erect theories of Mitanni origins.

The grey wares of northern Iran that have been employed to substantiate a Western Iranian presence from the fourteenth century BC onwards have been linked genetically to the Gorgan. It will be recalled that about 1800 to 1600 BC the proto-urban settlements from Tepe Hissar IIIC eastwards to Namazga and Altin Depe witness an almost total collapse and restructuring. The causes of this collapse are unknown, although some Soviet scholars argue that steppe nomads were an important factor. In the intervening centuries before the resurgence of urbanisn in the Iron Age (about 1000 BC), it has been postulated that bearers of the grey ware ceramic tradition moved southwest into northern Iran. For those who assume a correlation between grey wares and Iranians, this spread may be interpreted as the movement of the Western Iranians into their earliest historical seats around 1400 BC. Alternatively, this may reflect the movement of non-Iranian refugees, especially as the distribution of grey wares exceeds the area of the historically attested Iranians and includes non-Iranian territories such as Hurrian or Urartian. We must never forget that the grey wares can only indicate a trajectory and are not inherently associated with Iranian ethnic identity. To reject their utility as markers for tracing Iranian movements because grey wares emerged in the Gorgan region as early as 3000 BC – far too early for an individual Iranian identity – is only compelling if one makes the unnecessary assumption that the Iranians had to invent grey wares in order to use them. In the southeast Caspian, the culture that emerges in the Iron Age, the Dahistan culture, is solidly regarded as Iranian (the land designated Varkana (Hyrcania) in early Iranian texts), and it is seen to have emerged out of the local Gorgan tradition possibly coupled with steppe influences. It takes no great imagination to suggest that these steppe influences may also have drifted southwestward with the expansion of grey wares in the preceding centuries. The plausibility of future explanations will depend to a great extent on much better chronological control of the evidence and a greater consideration of non-ceramic remains. What is clear is that our problem is not in discovering possible archaeological traces for Western Iranian migrations, but selecting the appropriate one. Naturally, by migrations we need not consider a single unique event but movements that may have continued for centuries.

The Eastern Iranians are comparatively secure in their association with many of the steppe Bronze Age cultures, although there is great room for dispute in selecting specific archaeological evidence to explain the ultimate appearance of any individual Iranian group.

Finally, the arrival of the Indo-Aryans in India itself remains a major problem. It is not alleviated by the fact that archaeological research has concentrated either in the areas adjacent to the Indus or in Central Asia; only now is work beginning in the intervening borderlands, and hence there is a plethora of solutions that involve tele-connections between ceramics or metal types separated by uncomfortably large distances. We can certainly talk about the possibilities of identifying a number of intrusive cultures that may help explain Indo-Aryan movements into northwest India although we are not yet prepared to erect the type of all-embracing archaeological model that explains their relationship with either the western Indo-Aryans or their Iranian cousins.

The Tocharians

Tocharian, the easternmost group of the Indo-European languages, is attested in Chinese Turkestan from manuscripts dating from the sixth to the eight centuries AD. These were recovered initially by the great archaeological explorers of the late nineteenth and early twentieth centuries who began to acquaint the West with the ancient ruins of this remote area of China. The manuscripts themselves were primarily the work of Buddhist monasteries and largely comprise translations from Sanskrit, tracts on magic and medicine, and occasionally the business transactions connected with the major caravan route that passed through the northern region of the Tarim Basin. The language of the manuscripts was identified as Indo-European (written in an Indic script they were quite easy to decipher) early in this century. The language was named Tocharian after the historical Tokharoi who were known to the Greeks to have emigrated from Turkestan to Bactria in the second century BC. The full arguments for the validity of this designation and other ethnic labels that have been pinned on the creators of the manuscripts has been hotly debated for decades and comprise a remarkably large percentage of Tocharian scholarship. This will not concern us here other than to conclude that there is not a shred of linguistic evidence to indicate that the people of historical Tokharistan spoke the same language found in the manuscripts of the Tarim Basin well over 1,000 kilometres to their east. Today few if any would accept that the proper designation for these people is Tocharian but as no alternative has ever achieved sufficiently wide approval, the earlier name, misnomer if you will, is still applied and will be used throughout this work.

Tocharian is divided into two major dialects. The easternmost is termed Tocharian A (or Turfanian or Karashahrian after the two major towns near which manuscripts of this dialect were recovered, or Agnean). Tocharian B, the

Tocharian

Ma ni cisa nos somo nem wnolme lare taka,
ma ra postam cisa lare mäsketär-n.
Cisse laraumne cisse artanye pelke kalttarr solämpa sse.
ma te stalle sol wärnai.
Taiysu pälskanoym: sanai saryompa sayau karttses saulu
wärnai snai tserekwa snai nane.
Yamornikte se cau ni palskane sarsa.
tusa ysaly ersate, cisy aras ni sälkate.
Waya ci lauke, tsyara nis wetke, lykautka-n pake po läklentas.
cise tsarwo sampate-n.

Earlier there was no person dearer to me than you,
and later too there was none dearer.
The love for you, the delight in you is breath together with life.
This should not change for life.
Thus I thought: with the one beloved will I live well
lifelong without deceit without pretense.
The god Karman alone knew this my thought.
Therefore, he caused dissension and tore from me the heart that belonged to you.
He led you away, separated me and had me partake of all sorrows.
The joy I had in you he took away from me.

Tocharian B	Latin	Old Irish	English
pacer	pater	athir	father
macer	mater	mathir	mother
tkacor	—	—	daughter
procer	frator	brathir	brother
ser	soror	siur	sister
ku	canis	cu	hound
yakwe	equus	ech	eoh (Old English 'horse')
ko	bos	bo	cow
suwo	sus	—	sow

36 A Tocharian love poem and a short comparison of some basic words in the Tocharian languages with those of other Indo-European groups.

western dialect, is also known as Kuchean after the prominent state of Kucha (Kuqa). These dialects are markedly different from one another in both vocabulary and grammar, so much so that they have been regarded as two separate languages that diverged from one another over a period of 500–1,000 years despite the fact that when we encounter them they are separated by only several hundred kilometres. In addition, there is evidence that Tocharian A may well have been on its way to becoming a dead language confined to liturgical works by the time of our earliest manuscripts. The evidence from Tocharian B, whose texts are found in both western and eastern areas, suggests a vigorous language which was at least the vernacular of the religious and civil administrative classes of the Kuchean state. If we wish to suggest a date for the existence of a common or Proto-Tocharian language, we might expect that it had been current in the first millennium BC. The problem becomes far more interesting when we turn to the question of *where* we might expect to have found Proto-Tocharian at this time.

One of the most striking and disarming aspects of the Tocharian languages is that their linguistic relationship with both their Indic and Iranian neighbours seems to date from a very late period and can generally be attributed to the influence of Buddhist missionaries as they pressed eastwards. Thus we find the Tocharians with Iranian-speaking Saka and other Iranians to their immediate south and west, possibly also to their north, all showing nothing more than a late impact on them. For closer linguistic connections we must look to Europe where uniquely similar items of vocabulary and grammar are shared with Baltic, Slavic, Greek, Armenian, Germanic and possibly Phrygian and other languages. Several features which may be of the utmost importance are shared with Hittite, Italic and Celtic, which so mesmerized one early scholar that he declared Tocharian to be a Celtic language. In Chapter 1 we encountered the famous division between the *centum* languages of Europe and *satem* languages of Eastern Europe (Baltic, Slavic) and Asia (Indo-Iranian). We can then imagine the astonishment that linguists experienced when the Tocharian words for hundred (A: *känt*, B: *kante*) showed it to be unequivocally a *centum* language. The implications of all this for determining the initial starting point for the Tocharians has been extraordinary. Here they were saddled with similar adjectival suffixes with Slavic, a medio-passive ending in *-r* which had been retained in Latin, Irish, Hittite and Phrygian and cognate words shared only with Greek. This meant that they must have proceeded from somewhere in Eastern Europe and were forced to trek over 4,000 kilometres to take up their historical seats. There were even some, obsessed by the fact that the Tocharian word for fish was the same as the Germanic, Baltic and Slavic words for salmon, who compelled the Tocharians to dine with their European brothers on the shores of the salmon-rich rivers of the Baltic before they set off to Turkestan.

37 The Tocharians of the Tarim Basin and some of their historic (largely Indo-Iranian) neighbours.

Forced to accommodate the linguistic evidence, archaeologists sought extra-ordinarily distant connections between Eastern Europe and the frontiers of China. The most serious attempt of this kind was by Robert Heine-Geldern who enumerated series of similarities between the metalwork of Europe and China about 800 BC upon which he predicated a 'Pontic Migration' from Europe across Asia. Before we should assume that the Tocharians are required to go to such heroic efforts to explain their presence, we might first seek more economical solutions.

Our knowledge of the Tocharians themselves is almost entirely founded on Chinese documents which trace the initial encounters between Han China and the barbarians of the western lands from 200 BC until the Tarim Basin became a Turkic-speaking region from about the eighth century AD. It should be emphasized that the area occupied by the Tocharians was not a desolate refuge but rather a series of profoundly important oases along the silk road that led from China to the West. The northern Tarim was a major centre for exchange and transit, rich in mineral resources, possessing a sound agricultural basis that also included horse-raising. The region attracted the constant interest of the Hsiung-nu nomads to the north and the Chinese to the east. The history of the region is a catalogue of diplomacy and wars between these competing forces with the Kucheans who were more successful than their eastern cousins at maintaining their autonomy. Tocharians were instrumental in spreading Buddhism to China, and the Chinese occasionally tell us something of their western neighbours.

The census for the Early Han (208 BC–8 AD) indicates that there were about 100,000 people in the Kuchean state, over one-fifth of which were military. Later documents describe the Kucheans as a sedentary population practising mixed agriculture, frequently dining on peacocks and, like good barbarians everywhere, given to excessive drinking. They practised skull deformation with a board to flatten an infant's head and wore their hair cut at the neck except for the king who wore his long and tied up with a band – a practice illustrated on a wall painting from the region. The Kucheans armed themselves with bows, swords, long spear and armour, and they cremated their dead. Their cultural practices were regarded as similar to their eastern cousins and we know of marriages between the royal families of the Tocharian A and B regions. On the other hand, the Chinese contrasted the culture of the Kucheans with both the Hsiung-nu and the Wu-Sun, their nomadic neighbours.

When we confine our attention to Chinese historical documents, our image of the people who produced the Tocharian manuscripts is geographically precise but it does have severe limitations. We have every reason to believe that Tocharian was not the only language spoken in these states, and we can only assume that its speakers comprised at least the monks and civil authorities, excepting, naturally, the Chinese. Secondly, the Chinese sources provide us with the political states of Kucha, Karashahr and Turfan but no larger ethnic entities. These have nevertheless been frequently proposed. The Wu-Sun, for example, occupied the territory immediately to the north of the Tocharians and are described in Chinese sources as having red hair, blue eyes and resembling monkeys. This pejorative, proudly seized upon by western scholars as indicating a Europoid population, does indicate a strong possibility that the Wu-Sun spoke either an Iranian or Tocharian language. The Tocharians themselves are depicted on wall paintings as having red hair and green eyes.

Another tribal confederacy, the Yueh-chih, plays an especially prominent role in the Tocharian problem. They first emerge in northwest China in the second century BC when they were defeated by the Hsiung-nu confederation of tribes (probably mixed racially and linguistically) who rendered the skull of the Yueh-chih king into a drinking cup. They fled westwards into the territory of the Wu-Sun only to be driven onwards again further to the west, ultimately to be identified with the tribes that settled historical Tokharistan. The territory of the Yueh-chih is seen by many also to have included the Tarim Basin and hence they have been credited as Tocharian speakers. This is a bit too much of the tail wagging the dog since we may well expect that the major tribal groups were very mixed and while Tocharian may have been once spoken by some members of the Yueh-chih, there is no reason to assume that the Yueh-chih were a Tocharian linguistic entity. In any event, in the first centuries AD the Chinese regularly differentiate the Tocharian-speaking states of the Tarim (Kucha, Karashahr, Turfan) from the Yueh-chih, Wu-Sun and Hsiung-nu. This was probably a distinction made on economic (nomads versus agriculturalists) and administrative principles and certainly not on linguistic ones. Hence the Wu-Sun or Yueh-chih – or at least some member of their tribes – cannot be demonstrated not to have spoken Tocharian, but despite occasional attempts to squeeze Tocharian etymologies out of their tribal names, there is really no convincing evidence one way or the other for what language they actually did speak during the first millennium BC, although Iranian and/or Tocharian would be fair assumptions.

Having indicated something of the scope of our ignorance, we can now see how far we can push towards a solution to the Tocharian problem. Our first unequivocal evidence for Tocharian speakers is no older than our earliest documents, about 600 AD. If we wish to assume that their presence in the Tarim Basin extends earlier, we must rely on indirect evidence. The close association of the documents with the Buddhist mission may permit us to assume that the Tocharians were present at least since the appearance of Buddhism in the region, variously dated from the second century BC to the first century AD. Moreover, Chinese accounts of the history of the Tarim Basin do not suggest that a new people had altered the ethnic identity of the Tarim states from the second century BC onwards. We must be cautious here, however, since there are ample instances of Hsiung-nu conquests, political usurpation, and intermarriage between the royal family of Kucha and its neighbours, all of which could disguise an ethnic intrusion. But there is certainly no compelling reason to assume that the Tocharians had not been present since at least the second century BC. Beyond this, historical testimony is totally silent, and the archaeological evidence for the Tarim Basin becomes exceedingly dim until the

Neolithic (4000–2000 BC), when we find evidence for the painted wares of the Yang-shao and the monochrome wares of the Longshan horizon. In both cases we are talking of cultures that later produced the distinctly Chinese societies of the Shang and Zhou periods. If the Tarim Basin was essentially a western extension of these Chinese cultures during the Neolithic, then it may be assumed that the Tocharians must have entered the region after this period. We may thus seek the earliest Tocharians in the very broad period of between 2500 and 200 BC.

To proceed any further we must return to the problem of the linguistic relationships of Tocharian. We have already seen how its close links with the European languages generated a model of a European homeland with a subsequent migration of over 4,000 kilometres. This migration seems to be set in general to the first millennium BC. On purely logistic grounds such a migration cannot be excluded since we have the historical examples of Huns, Alans and other steppe nomads. Yet it must also be admitted that any movement from the west to the east along the steppe would appear to be running counter to the general east-west current of steppe populations of the first millennium BC and later. In addition, the movements of the historical nomads involved an accretion of intermediate populations so that by the time the Huns, for example, burst into Central Europe they were an amalgam of Turkic, Iranian and Germanic-speaking peoples. Tocharians moving through thousands of kilometres of what we may expect to have been Indo-Iranian or more specifically Iranian territory should have emerged with a far greater accretion of Iranian influence than we find. In short, there are serious reasons to doubt that the Tocharians achieved their position on the eastern flank of the Iranians as late as the Iron Age.

An alternative model of Tocharian's relation to the European languages offers some hope of a solution. It weighs the similarities shared between Tocharian, Celtic, Italic and Hittite as essentially archaic features inherited from the Proto-Indo-European language at a very early period. These grammatical features were then replaced in later Proto-Indo-European by new forms that spread among the ancestors of Greek, Armenian and Indo-Iranian, but not to what had then become the outer periphery of the Proto-Indo-European continuum – the ancestors of Celtic and Italic on the west, Hittite and possibly Phrygian to the south, and Tocharian on the east.[12] In the eastward expansion of Indo-European languages, Tocharian preceded Iranian into Turkestan and was later engulfed by Iranian-speaking Saka to the south, Sogdian and others to the west, and, if Iranian river names in the Minusinsk Basin are included, also to their northeast. The occasional lexical similarities with some of the other European languages may then be dismissed as the chance occurrences that the historical linguist must expect of his material.

The archaeological evidence of the Tarim Basin is still far too poorly known to permit us to test our linguistic model archaeologically. Still, if we paint our narrative with an exceedingly broad brush, we may see something of a hint of an explanation. Earlier we saw how the Andronovo culture of the Asian steppe

38 The Tocharians may have found their immediate origins in the eastern Andronovo or Afanasievo cultures.

seemed to make an excellent correlation with the later appearance of Eastern Iranian peoples. But we need not be so perverse as to demand an exact correlation between an archaeological culture, especially one as vague as the Andronovans, and a single linguistic group, and it is entirely possible that the ancestors of the Tocharians lurked behind some of those Andronovo variants that appear in the southeastern area of its distribution. This would include Tadzhikistan and Kirghiziya to the west of the Tarim Basin where Andronovo-related sites begin to appear by at least 1400 BC. Although separated from the Tarim Basin by mountain ranges, these people were hardly strangers to high altitudes, especially those who occupied the Tien Shan region. One cemetery at Arpa, for example, is found at an altitude of 2,800 metres above sea level and is situated less than 500 kilometres west of demonstrably Tocharian-speaking territory. It may only be coincidental that this region does not practise the usual inhumation of the Andronovo cultures, but rather, like the Tocharians, cremation.

For those who require some form of symmetry between language and archaeological culture, there is yet another possibility. Prior to the Later Bronze Age appearance of the Andronovo culture across the Central Asian-west Siberian steppe, there appeared an Eneolithic culture whose boundaries were apparently confined to the Minusinsk-Altai region, 1,000 kilometres to the north of our Tocharians. This Afanasievo culture, dating to the third millennium BC, possesses many of the attributes that we often demand of any Indo-European culture – domestic horse, basic metallurgy, and possibly wheeled vehicles. What makes this culture so important is that it stands without any clear connection with the cultures to its north or east yet possesses clear analogues in ceramics, lithics, burial practices and physical type with the west, specifically with the Volga-Ural region. We will have very good cause to examine this culture in Chapter Eight; for now it suffices to observe that we have evidence of a possible eastward expansion from a territory producing other Indo-European speaking peoples at a date prior to the expected spread of the Indo-Iranians. It is possible that this represents the archaeological correlate for the eastward spread of the peripheral Indo-European languages among which Tocharian has fortuitously survived.

Conclusions

By virtue of its early development of writing, Asia offers us information about the early expansion of the Indo-Europeans that is much more difficult to acquire or substantiate elsewhere. We have seen that whenever we find decipherable Bronze Age documents, they attest to the intrusive character of the Indo-European presence in Asia. Hittite replaces Hattic (and Assyrian), Armenian absorbs the peoples and languages of the Indo-European-speaking Luwians and the non-Indo-European Urartians, Iranian expands over the earlier territory of Elam, and if we subscribe to the most acceptable approaches to the Indus script, Indo-Aryan made an impressive expansion over much of the vast non-Indo-European populations of India. It can hardly be doubted that from when we first acquire written documents in the Bronze Age, we find abundant evidence for migrations and linguistic replacement. In central Turkey alone, for example, the non-Indo-European Hattic is replaced by a series of Indo-European languages – first Hittite, then Luwian, then Phrygian, then a Celtic language that gives its name to the ancient province of Galatia, and finally Greek – only to be absorbed once again by the wholly different non-Indo-European language of the Turks who immigrated from the east. The history of the Near East also documents the expansion of Semites, Hurrians and others through the course of the Bronze and Iron Ages. All of these examples provide a salutary reminder to archaeologists that populations often shifted their boundaries no matter how poor our ability to trace such movements in the archaeological record or how much the model of migration conflicts with

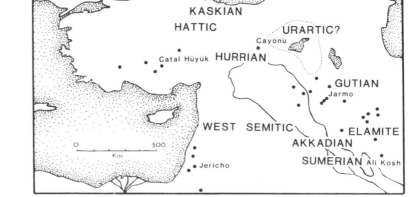

39 Early Neolithic sites of Southwest Asia and the distribution of non-Indo-European languages during the third millennium BC.

63

current approaches to culture change that stress local processes rather than folk-movement. It should be emphasized that such movements are in no way confined to state level societies (as anyone familiar, for example, with the distribution of the major aboriginal Indian languages in North America well knows – such as the Athapascans of northwest Canada and their southern linguistic relations, the Navaho and Apache, in the American Southwest). Folk movements may not have been exactly daily occurrences but they are amply in evidence and one need not stubbornly adhere to what Christopher Hawkes has recently termed the ideology of 'immobilism' to be interested in the processes of cultural change.

We may briefly reflect on the obvious demise of a number of the languages that here preceded the intrusion of the Indo-Europeans into Asia. The Indo-Europeans account largely for the total disappearance of at least three separate linguistic entities, perhaps language families – Hattic, Hurrian-Urartian and Elamite; the Semites must probably explain the ultimate disappearance of Sumerian. When we estimate the territory of each of these language families they approximate an area roughly equivalent to that of Germany or Poland or Japan. Naturally, some seem to occupy a much smaller area, such as the Sumerians, while others, such as the Semites, probably covered vast expanses during the Bronze Age. Whether or not these are fair estimates for the 'typical' territories of Bronze Age language families about 3000–2000 BC is difficult to say, especially as much of our sample derives from primarily urban populations which we will not encounter elsewhere. Nevertheless, the area traditionally defined as the Turkic homeland before their expansion in the early Middle Ages is of a similar order of magnitude. We may wish to keep the scale of these linguistic territories in mind when we begin to examine the Indo-European homeland itself.

As the evidence reviewed so far indicates the intrusive nature of the Indo-Europeans in most of Western Asia, this provides us with reasonable grounds for excluding these regions from the territory of the earliest Indo-Europeans. With the emergence of our earliest historical documents in the third millennium BC we find non-Indo-European populations occupying central and eastern Anatolia to the Caucasus and Caspian, the southern region of historical Palestine, and much of the Zagros region including all of Mesopotamia. These areas comprise the three main centres of incipient agriculture during the 'Neolithic Revolution' (9000–6000 BC) in Southwest Asia. Consequently, it would appear to be highly unlikely that we should associate the Indo-Europeans with these earliest farming communities in Southwest Asia and their immediate expansions. One might, of course, suggest some complicated reflux model where the earliest Indo-Europeans, for example, the Anatolians and Armenians, were driven from their homes by early Hattic or Hurrian expansions and then reclaimed these territories in the third to first millennia BC. This, I would think, not only requires special pleading but is inherently unlikely. We have too much evidence for unanalyzable place and personal names across Anatolia to suspect anything other than a non-Indo-European

and the compilation of the great Greek oral epics such as the *Iliad*. In the subsequent 2,500 years the Greek language has undergone marked changes to evolve into Modern Greek which is currently spoken by approximately eleven million people both in Greece and in a few of its remnant colonies.

The investigation of Greek origins has long been a subject of intense interest and there is a sufficient number of wholly contradictory theories concerning the 'coming of the Greeks' to banish any fantasies of universal agreement among either linguists or archaeologists. Nevertheless, there is a course we can steer that will at least follow the tack taken by the majority of scholars and we can note where others depart from this.

Why must the Greeks 'come' from elsewhere? In attempting an answer to this question we must admit that we lack the historical documentation that served us in Asia and, consequently, we cannot positively demonstrate a pre-Greek population on the evidence of contemporary testimony.[13] Yet it has long been argued that a pre-Greek population declares its existence loudly enough in the Greek language itself. There are two types of evidence.

Many would agree that a substantial portion of the Greek vocabulary pertaining to the specific environmental character of the Mediterranean cannot be explained as the Greek outcome of inherited Indo-European words. These include such plants as the vine, fig, olive, hyacinth, cypress, laurel, marjoram, chickpea, chestnut, cherry and parsnip. Among the animals are the ass, the wild ox and the beetle. Items of material culture are similarly non-Greek: metal, tin, bronze, lead, jar, pail, oil flask, sword, javelin, cornice, coping, chamber, bath tub and brick. Certain political or social concepts, basic to Greek society, are expressed with what are usually taken to be pre-Greek words. These include the word for king (*basileus*, Mycenaean *qa-si-re-u*), as well as slave (*doulos*, Mycenaean *do-e-ro*) and concubine. Neither do the most prominent heroes of Greek epic – Odysseus, Achilles, Theseus – nor many of the Greek divinities – Athene, Hera, Aphrodite, Hermes – bear obviously Indo-European Greek names.[14]

A second line of evidence derives from place names found in Greece. Many of the most important names cannot be explained by the Indo-European core of the Greek language. Either the roots of the names are meaningless in terms of Greek, or the names are constructed employing suffixes which signal that they

Linear B							
Transliteration	pu - ro	i - je - re - ja	do - e - ra	e - ne - ka	ku - ru - so - jo	i - je - ro - jo	woman14+
Greek	πύλος	ἱερείας	δοέλαι	ἕνεκα	χρυσοῖο	ἱεροῖο	woman 14+
Transliteration	Pylos	hiereias	doelai	heneka	khrysoio	hieroio	woman 14+
Translation	Pylos:	priestess'	slaves	on account of	gold	sacred	14+ women

40 An inscription in Linear B.

are not originally of Greek construction. These include major toponyms such as Corinth, Knossos, Salamis, Larisa, Samos and even Olympus and Mycenae. In an early interpretation of this evidence, Joseph Haley and Carl Blegen observed that many of the names and suffixes were also to be found in Anatolia and that it was probable that they expanded from that region into Greece during the Early Bronze Age (3000–2000 BC) when there was a general cultural uniformity over much of the Aegean. Whether all the details of this hypothesis can withstand the more critical scrutiny in current archaeological and linguistic circles is doubtful. Yet the linguistic evidence taken as a whole does indicate that the Greeks did borrow a considerable number of elements from a non-Greek language.[15] The vocabulary suggests that these borrowings were not wholly random, but rather tend to focus on words that a population intrusive into a new land might be expected to adopt from the previous inhabitants. At least some of the loan words borrowed into Greek would seem to have been derived from a culture familiar with a level of metallurgy (copper, bronze, tin) that existed no earlier than the end of the fourth millennium BC. The logical consequence of all this is that the Greeks are not native to Greece but were the product of Indo-European intruders who superimposed themselves on an earlier Bronze Age population. This, some would say, is further confirmed by the Greeks' own historical tradition which indicates that they had absorbed a number of earlier non-Greek populations, some of whom bear obvious non-Indo-European names.

The concept of a pre-Greek population is commonly agreed upon; the interpretation of the pre-Greek elements in the Greek language, however, is not. In identifying the nature of this pre-Greek element there are two major schools of thought with opinion scattered from one extreme to the other. One group terms the pre-Greek element 'Mediterranean' or 'Aegean' and sees it as the remnants of the non-Indo-European language(s) that were once spoken in Greece and perhaps more widely in the Mediterranean. The second school of thought admits that, while some of the words are indeed non-Indo-European, many others, nevertheless, are Indo-European. Some identify the Indo-European element as Luwian, especially on the basis of place names which occur both in Anatolia and Greece. Others opt for an otherwise unattested Indo-European language, closely related to some of the poorly attested Balkan languages, which is generally known by the name of Pelasgian, one of the

In earlier times there were two races living in Greece: the Pelasgians, who never left their original home, and the Hellenes (Greeks), who frequently migrated. . . . What language the Pelasgians spoke I cannot say exactly. If it is proper to judge from those of the Pelasgians who still survive, they spoke a non-Greek language. If that was true of the whole Pelasgic race, the Attic nation must have learnt Greek at the same time that they became Hellenized.

41   Herodotus's account of the Pelasgians reflects Greek historical tradition that the Greeks absorbed an earlier non-Greek population.

'autochthonous' peoples of Greek historical tradition. General linguistic opinion has neither been particularly impressed nor even kind to the Pelasganists, and most would still regard the pre-Greek vocabulary to be largely unanalyzable in terms of Indo-European with perhaps a grudging admission that some non-Greek words can pass muster as Indo-European, possibly Luwian or an anonymous Pre-Hellenic language, while others may be later Semitic loan words. Consequently, the linguistic evidence does seem to indicate that the Indo-Europeans who eventually emerged as the Greeks were essentially intrusive into Greece and that they mixed there with a non-Indo-European population and possibly with earlier Indo-European-speaking peoples as well.

Acceptance of the decipherment of Linear B as Greek leads us to the inescapable conclusion that Greeks must have been present in Greece by about 1300 BC when we find the earliest texts. These were discovered in the palace of Knossos on Crete and are generally interpreted as the product of an intrusive Mycenaean power which adopted the earlier Cretan writing system, known as Linear A, which was already flourishing by 1700 BC. Neither the language of the Linear A script nor the culture of Minoan Crete are regarded as Greek and its population is generally believed to have been thoroughly native at least from the Early Bronze Age, if not from the Neolithic. There is also sufficient evidence to indicate an intrusion of a Mycenaean warrior aristocracy into Crete about 1450 BC to permit archaeologists to postulate a genuine political take-over of the Minoans by the Greek-speaking Mycenaeans. The Mycenaeans appear to have adapted a near relative of the Minoans' Linear A script to suit their own language. The sheer clumsiness in expressing the Greek language by either the Linear A or Linear B syllabaries lends support that they were not originally invented by Greek speakers.[16] It is also clear from this that we cannot follow the trail of Greek origins on Crete but must look to southern Greece and the origins of the Mycenaeans.

The great Myceanaean citadels began about 1400 BC, and there is no reason to dissociate the people who built them from those who produced the Linear B texts. The Mycenaeans themselves are normally derived by way of a processual jump in social complexity from the earlier Middle Helladic culture whose roots extend back into Early Helladic III, about 2200 BC. There is, however, a sector of opinion which does not credit the sudden rise of Myceanaean chiefdoms to purely internal evolution but seeks an exterior stimulus. The stimulus is identified as a small body of warlike intruders who introduced the horse and chariot, new weaponry such as swords and the body shield, and status burials under a tumulus. These appear during the Middle Helladic period and culminate with the tumulus burials at Marathon which include rich burials that extend from the Middle Helladic into the Mycenaean period. Moreover, a horse burial in one of the Marathon tombs has been advanced as further evidence of Indo-European intruders. These tumulus burials are best known from western Greece and are held up in contrast to the exceedingly poor intramural graves that typify most Middle Helladic sites. A possible external

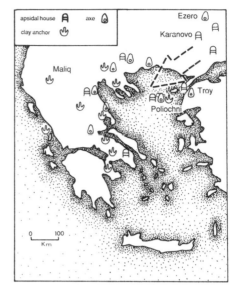

42 *The distribution of tumuli in Greece and Albania in the Early and Middle Bronze Ages.*

43 *The distribution of apsidal houses, clay anchors and stone battle-axes in Early Bronze Age Greece. Some suggest that these spread from Southeast Europe with the 'coming' of the Greeks.*

source for them is provided by roughly contemporary tumulus burials to the north, especially in Albania, for example, Pazhok and Vodhinë. Consequently, a few archaeologists see evidence for an intrusion from the north during the Middle Bronze Age, particularly associated with burials of a higher status than the native burials, and also directly linked with the emerging ranked society of the Mycenaeans. The evidence hangs to a large extent on what weight one attributes to the tumulus burial itself as an ethnic marker for there are really few other items associated with these burials that weld them together into an intrusive culture. The sword and body shield, for example, only begin to appear in number at the very end of the Middle Helladic period in the shaft graves at Mycenae. The only other element, perhaps, is the horse, which also makes an appearance on Albanian sites in the Middle Helladic period or earlier. There is some doubt regarding the Marathon horse sacrifice since it now seems, in fact, to have been an insertion from a much later period.

A far more widely accepted solution to the coming of the Greeks is the discontinuity that occurs between Early Helladic II and Early Helladic III, about 2200 BC. The relevant evidence includes the destruction and abandonment of Early Helladic II sites, changes in architecture especially with reference to the appearance of houses with an apsidal end, burials within settlements (although our evidence for this does not begin until the Middle Helladic period), perforated stone 'battle-axes', clay 'anchors' and the incessantly discussed Minyan ware. Following this break, mainland Greece appears to revert to a much simpler agricultural society, generally regarded as retarded compared with its neighbours on Crete who escaped the Early Helladic III destructions. Since all cultural development subsequent to the end of Early Helladic II appears to suggest almost monotonous continuity, it has been accepted by many that the new changes in culture are most likely to be attributed to those intrusive Indo-Europeans who later emerge as the earliest Greeks. Generally, the source of this intrusion is held to have been either from Anatolia or the Balkans. The former perhaps offers better ceramic parallels (which may ultimately be only the product of specialist craftsmen employing the fast wheel) while the Balkans, particularly the Ezero and Baden cultures, offer some of the earliest examples of apsidal houses. It is argued that these subsequently appear in western Anatolia and then slightly later in southern Greece. Stone battle axes and possibly a number of other traits are also tied to the Balkans.

Finally, one should mention the transition from the Late Neolithic to the Early Bronze Age itself since we have already seen that it is precisely in this period that some see movements from the Balkans into northwest Anatolia. The emergence of Early Helladic I about 3000 BC is still very poorly understood, and the degree of continuity from the Late Neolithic versus intrusion is by no means settled. This represents the earliest potential Indo-European invasion in the minds of most scholars, although at least one Pelasganist has opted for a Late Neolithic invasion to explain their presence in Greece.

Reconciliation of all these different theories seems out of the question, although acceptance of each hypothesis as evidence of an actual migration gives more than enough scope to slip Greeks, Luwians and anyone else in as well. The current state of our knowledge of the Greek dialects can accommodate Indo-Europeans entering Greece at any time between 2200 and 1600 BC to emerge later as Greek speakers. It is the archaeological evidence which really sits in the balance and must be more closely examined on a regional basis. The main evidence for Early Helladic II/III destruction, for example, is in southern Greece and the putative invaders are seen to derive from central Greece and not directly from outside Greece. Consequently, links between new cultural features in Greece and either the Balkans or northwestern Anatolia (other than some ceramic links and possibly apsidal houses) are yet to be built up in the necessary stepping-stone fashion that would ensure acceptance. Some archaeologists would argue that there are sufficient numbers of broad trends to see a pattern of intrusion and migration; others would dismiss the evidence and, even when granting some claims to immigrating populations, would see them as too few to have effected the linguistic change postulated by our model of the linguistic history of Greece. As we will see many times again, and have cause to examine more closely in a later chapter, there are no hard and fast rules for defining how much evidence is required to demonstrate an intrusive population resulting in the spread of a new language. For our present purpose, it is enough to note that there are plausible models of intrusions that are temporally congruent with our linguistic models; whether they are based soundly on the archaeological evidence is a different question.

The Thracians

The term 'balkanization', the breaking up of a territory into small hostile states, although of recent creation is also an apt description of the Indo-European groups which first emerged into history in the Balkans. These comprised the larger 'ethnic' units of the Thracians, Dacians, Getae and Illyrians, which were in turn subdivided into countless smaller tribes and tribal configurations. It is the precise geographical positioning of these tribes, their ascription to one of the larger ethnic groups and their possible association with peoples bearing the same names in neighbouring Anatolia that frequently occupy the attention of the modern scholar.

It is a sad irony that the people described by Herodotus as the greatest and most populous on earth (after the Indians), the Thracians who occupied the eastern half of the Balkans, have left no modern descendant of their language. Rather, we must content ourselves with but two inscriptions of disputed interpretation; glosses, especially on the names of plants since the ancient Greeks regarded the Thracians and Dacians as masters in healing herbs; and an abundance of onomastic data – the names of peoples and places. From the more reliable etymologies, a number that would not exceed fifty, and their grammatical endings, we can safely maintain that the Thracians spoke an Indo-European language and say something of its phonetic structure. The Dacian language, spoken by contemporary populations north of the Danube in present-day Romania, offers slightly less evidence, with some twenty-five words that can be given respectable Indo-European etymologies. With such meagre evidence it has been impossible to determine whether Dacian and Thracian represent two distinct languages or markedly different dialects of the same language. Certainly it is odd that the standard suffix in Dacian indicating a town, -*dava*, is not reflected in any of the three Thracian words for town, village or fort (-*bria*, -*para*, and -*diza*).

Both the Thracians and the Dacians achieved the status of impressive and powerful kingdoms before falling to the Romans. The Thracian Golden Age may be set to the flowering of the Odrysian state which began in the fourth century BC, while Dacia looks to the reign of Burebista in the first century BC, who achieved unity across much of the northeast Balkans. Our historical sources for these people, of course, run earlier, with the Thracians appearing as enemies of the Greeks by the mid-seventh century BC when they challenged their colony at Thasos, and still earlier they achieved their hostile reputation with the Greeks by siding with the Trojans in the *Iliad*. There are few if any who would contest the existence of the Thracians by the Iron Age. How much further back can we push them?

Attempts to seek the origins of Thracians, Dacians or Illyrians as we will see later, involve the concept of ethnogenesis among leading East European archaeologists and linguists. Adopting the term *ethnos*, a people with a common language and shared customs, most East European archaeologists argue that the creation of the various Balkan *ethnoi* involved a long complicated process. This included both local Balkan continuity and frequently intense interactions and influences from neighbouring peoples to produce the ethnic groups that one first encounters in the historical record. They argue that a basic continuity stretching from the Iron Age back into the Bronze Age cannot be denied and that this period sees the gradual evolution of a Thracian *ethnos*, including language, from earlier Indo-European components. This thread of basic continuity is normally extended back to the beginning of the Early Bronze Age, sometime prior to 3000 BC. Beyond this one encounters a major discontinuity in the archaeological record which many attribute to the earliest influx of Indo-European speakers into the Balkans.

We will examine the evidence for this invasion in Chapter Eight as any movement of putative Indo-European speakers in the fourth millennium BC concerns not only the origins of an individual Indo-European-speaking group but that of the Proto-Indo-European community itself. One important example of this discontinuity in the eastern Balkans will suffice for now.

Archaeologists can mark the gradual development of the earliest Neolithic settlement in the east Balkans by way of the large tell sites that were produced by generations of continuous settlement from the sixth millennium onwards. Such sites include Karanovo, the cultural yardstick of the east Balkans, which shows six major phases of evolution from the earliest Neolithic through the Eneolithic cultures of the late fifth millennium. Neighbouring sites also reflect similar sequences of local evolution. But following Karanovo VI there is widespread abandonment of these tell sites and only a few reveal evidence of a later Karanovo VII phase of resettlement. This last phase has little to do with any of the previous cultures of the tells and is regarded by many to have been the product of intrusive populations infiltrating the lower Danube region from the Pontic steppe. These intruders initiate the Early Bronze Age of the Balkans and, in the opinion of many, they also introduce a very early form of Indo-European language among the native populations of southeast Europe. After a fusion of native and Indo-European intruder in the Bronze Age, the major ethnic groups of the Balkans eventually began to crystallize in the Late Bronze Age to emerge in the early historical period as the Thracians.

The Illyrians

Next to Thracian the other great Balkan language was Illyrian which, like its eastern neighbours, comprised a series of tribes or tribal confederations whose linguistic identity is seldom entirely certain and which offers ample scope for historian, linguist and archaeologist to debate the problems of Illyrian ethnogenesis. There is, however, one major difference between the Illyrians of the west Balkans and the Thracians: it is at least possible that a modern descendant of one or more of the Illyrian languages is still spoken. Albanian, a language spoken today by approximately five million people, is situated in territory earlier attributed to the Illyrians. This permits many linguists to surmise that it is probably a descendant of the earlier Illyrian language although much affected by Latin, Greek, Slavic and Turkish. We must insist that this is a

Albanian
Në grurë kish rënë drapëri,
ish tharë bari nër ara,
pëlciste për ujë gjarpëri
dhe binin mullareve zjarre . . .

Upon wheat had fallen the sickle
was dried the hay within fields
sloughed off through water the serpent
and spring in haystacks fires . . .

*44 An Albanian poem. These lines contain basic words inherited from Proto-Indo-European. For example, the Albanian word for 'fire' zjarr is from Proto-Indo-European *g^wher- which yields Greek thermos, Latin formus, Armenian jer, all meaning 'warm', Old Irish gorn 'fire', and Russian gorn 'hearth'; uje 'water' is from Proto-Indo-European *wedor which yields Sanskrit udan, Greek hudor, Umbrian utur, Old Church Slavonic voda, and English water. There are also later loan words such as Northwest Greek drapanon 'sickle' borrowed into Albanian as draperi.*

surmise and not a certainty since there is little if anything to provide clear linguistic proof of the connection between Illyrian and Albanian: the modern language is known from written records only from the fifteenth century AD onwards, by which time it had undergone massive attrition in vocabulary to the above four languages. On the other hand, the linguistic evidence for Illyrian is pitifully small except for personal and place names. Otherwise the linguist must be satisfied with a few paltry glosses such as the Greek identification of *sabaia* as a type of beer, or that the Illyrian word for fog was *rhinos*, all of which provides scant basis for discussing its relationship with Albanian. Without actual Illyrian texts, we must content ourselves with regarding Albanian as an Illyrian language as merely a probable assumption.

Through a long series of wars the territory of the Illyrian tribes was finally incorporated into the Roman empire by the first century BC from which time onwards it became a truly integral part of the Roman state, a recruiting area for the Roman army and the home or birthplace of emperors such as Diocletian and Constantine as well as scholars such as Saint Jerome. As a major naval power of the Adriatic, dismissed as pirates by its Greek and Roman neighbours, the Illyrians could not fail to come into open conflict with those around them. Greek colonies had been established in the south of Illyrian territory as early as the seventh century BC and the names of tribes such as the Paeones and Dardani, later recorded in Illyrian territory, are mentioned by Homer as allies of the Trojans. They were also traditional opponents of the Macedonians and the immediate forefathers of Alexander the Great developed their military skills in their frequent conflicts with their Illyrian neighbours. The Illyrians also encountered the expansion of the Celts into southeast Europe during the fourth century BC.

Radoslav Katičić's study of personal and place names within the territory traditionally assigned to the Illyrians permits us to locate them in two major groups: a southeastern group which occupied Dalmatia as far south as Epirus, and a central group of names stretching from Dalmatia over western and southern Bosnia. This is the safest core region to label as Illyrian-speaking and it is the one with which we will concern ourselves.

Both Yugoslav and Albanian archaeologists are generally agreed that they can trace a fairly direct continuity of culture in this region back to the beginnings of the Early Bronze Age. The pivotal site of Albania, Maliq, offers a clear succession of cultural development, clearly influenced by foreign connections (especially with Bronze Age Greece) back to the Early Bronze Age levels of Maliq IIIa. Here, in marked contrast to the earlier Maliq IIb levels, there seems to be an abrupt break signalled by the appearance of a new culture with cruder ceramic types, frequently including double-handled vases and single-handled cups, with no connection with earlier Eneolithic levels. Furthermore, the appearance of tumulus burials in Bronze Age Albania is also regarded as intrusive and derived from the influx of steppe pastoralists of which we will speak later. Bosnia is similarly regarded by Yugoslav archaeologists as

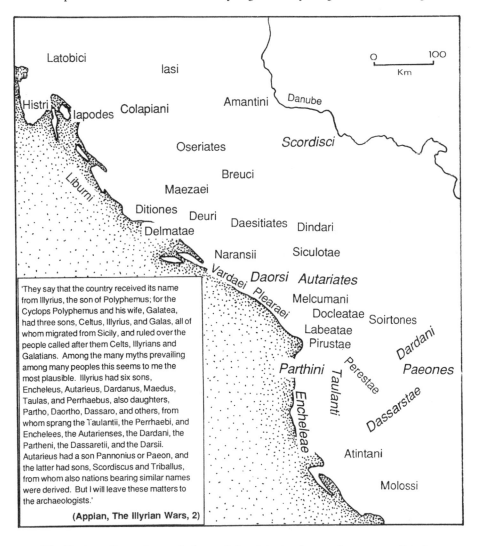

'They say that the country received its name from Illyrius, the son of Polyphemus; for the Cyclops Polyphemus and his wife, Galatea, had three sons, Celtus, Illyrius, and Galas, all of whom migrated from Sicily, and ruled over the people called after them Celts, Illyrians and Galatians. Among the many myths prevailing among many peoples this seems to me the most plausible. Illyrius had six sons, Encheleus, Autarieus, Dardanus, Maedus, Taulas, and Perrhaebus, also daughters, Partho, Daortho, Dassaro, and others, from whom sprang the Taulantii, the Perrhaebi, and Enchelees, the Autarienses, the Dardani, the Partheni, the Dassaretii, and the Darsii. Autarieus had a son Pannonius or Paeon, and the latter had sons, Scordiscus and Triballus, from whom also nations bearing similar names were derived. But I will leave these matters to the archaeologists.'

(Appian, The Illyrian Wars, 2)

45   *The Illyrian tribes and one solution to their origins by the second century AD historian Appian.*

offering an unbroken cultural succession from the Early Bronze Age to well into the Iron Age and the historical appearance of Illyrian tribes; this is seen especially in the great multiperiod tumulus cemetery of Glasinac. In Bosnia, too, there is frequent mention of this pre-Bronze Age culture break generated by intruding pastoralists who buried their dead under tumuli.

Although archaeologists identify this intrusion with the influx of Indo-European peoples, they and their colleagues in the field of linguistics are careful not to identify the invaders with the actual Illyrians. Rather, they view Illyrian origins, like Thracian, as an extremely complicated process involving an intrusive Indo-European-speaking component mixing with local populations and eventually, by the Iron Age, giving rise to linguistically related tribal groups which we must somewhat uncomfortably label as Illyrians.

The Slavs

The largest group of Indo-European-speaking peoples of Eastern Europe is the Slavs. Today there are about 430 million speakers of Slavic languages and with Russian as the lingua franca of both the European and Asiatic portions of the USSR, it is also one of the most rapidly expanding Indo-European groups. This expansion, as we will soon see, has been relatively recent when compared with most other Indo-European groups.

According to both historical tradition and the available written evidence the earliest Slavic texts date only to about the ninth century AD when the missionaries Constantine (Cyril) and Methodius devised the Cyrillic alphabet and translated portions of the Bible and the Eastern Orthodox liturgy into what we now term Old Church Slavonic. This is by no means our first historical acquaintance with the Slavs since the Sclavini, Antes and Veneti – all probable Slavic ethnic groups – were known several centuries or more before the earliest written Slavic texts. It was historians of the eastern Roman empire who recorded the explosion of Slavs into the Byzantine world from the sixth century AD onwards in a virtual litany of raids and invasions that carried the Slavs into the Balkans and Greece. Historians such as Procopius and Jordanes, writing

Old Church Slavonic:	Otice	nasi	ize	jesi	na	nebesichu:	da		svetitu	se	ime	tvoje.
Russian:	Otce	nas,	suscij		na	nebesach:	da		svjatitsja		imja	tvojë.
Czech:	Otce	nas,	kteryz	jsi	v	nebesich:			posvet	se	jmeno	tve.
Polish:	Ojcze	nasz,	ktorys	jest	w	niebiesiech:			swiec	sie	imie	twoje.
Serbo-Croat:	Oce	nas	koji	si	na	nebesima:	da se		sveti		ime	tvoje.
Bulgarian:	Otce	nas,	kojto	si	na	nebesata:	da se		sveti		tvoeto	ime.
	Father	our,	who	are	in	heaven:	be-hallowed				name	your.

46 *The opening line of the Lord's Prayer in Old Church Slavonic plus representative languages from the major modern Slavic groups indicates the type of close similarities one expects from a language that has differentiated in the not-too-distant past. The Slavic word for 'heaven' nebesa, nebo preserves the Proto-Indo-European word for 'cloud, mist, heaven' seen in Hittite nepis, Sanskrit nabhas, Greek nephos, Latin nebula, Old English nifol, and Irish neamh.*

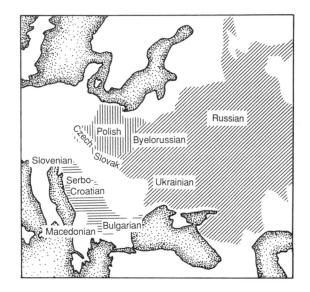

47 The distribution of the Slavic languages. The eastern group is indicated with diagonal hatching, the western with vertical and the southern group with horizontal hatching.

about the sixth to seventh centuries AD, locate the Slavic tribes of the Sclavini and Antes north of the Danube in a band stretching from the upper Vistula to the Dnieper. The earlier attested Veneti, known from the first to the second centuries AD, are more difficult to place, although this same general region would not be too far off most attempts to locate them more precisely.

Both linguists and archaeologists concerned with the origin of the Slavs see their borders as extremely dynamic from the fifth to the tenth centuries AD. This period is not only regarded as the primary time of Slavic expansions but also as the terminal period of proto- or Common Slavic. By this is meant that for the period AD 400–900 linguists recognize the collapse of Common Slavic and its fission into the different modern Slavic languages. Expansions to the east and northeast from AD 500 to 1000, for example, carried Slavic speakers into territories previously occupied by Balts and Finns. Today these eastern Slavs are represented by the Russians, Byelorussians (White Russians) and Ukrainians. The southern expansion across the Danube into the Byzantine empire, and subsequent divisions, account for the southern Slavs – Bulgarians, Macedonians, Serbs, Croats and Slovenians. In the west emerged the Poles, Czechs and Slovaks. This great fission of the Common Slavic language occurred very broadly at the same time as Latin was disintegrating into the various Romance languages, albeit under quite different social circumstances.

Linguistic evidence indicates that before the collapse of Common Slavic, that is, before the fifth century AD, the Slavs had been subjected to strong linguistic influences, primarily seen in loan words, from Germanic-(Gothic) and Iranian-(Sarmatian) speaking peoples. It is from the Sarmatians (or the Scythians), for example, that Slavicists derive the Common Slavic words for 'god', 'holy' and 'paradise' plus perhaps several score more terms. Even the names of the major rivers of the European steppe – the Don, Dnieper and Dniester – are all of Iranian origin. In addition, before the collapse of Common

Slavic there had been an extremely complicated (and controversial) relationship with speakers of the Baltic languages. This relationship has been seen by some as an intensely close genetic connection such that a common Balto-Slavic emerged out of late Proto-Indo-European (much like Indo-Iranian) before further dividing into Baltic and Slavic. Others prefer to see the similarities between them as contact relations between two adjacent languages that evolved independently from late Proto-Indo-European without an intermediary Balto-Slavic stage. It would be sheer folly to wade into the linguistic morass of Baltic-Slavic relations in a work such as this, and we will content ourselves with the minimal conclusions that both Balts and Slavs, at some time prior to the fifth century AD, lived in close proximity with one another, and indeed they would appear to have done so for much of their existence. The linguistic evidence positions the Slavs to the east or southeast of the Germans, south of the Balts and west of the Iranians.

The problem of the earlier location of the Slavs prior to their first entry into the historical records of the Byzantine state is a perennial occupation of Slavic linguists and archaeologists. While there is no total consensus, one can extract areas of relatively general agreement. Certainly it is not controversial to assert that about AD 500 the Slavs occupied some or all of the territory stretching in a wide band from the Elbe, Oder or upper Vistula on the west to at least the middle Dnieper on the east. Controversy only really begins when we try to identify the Slavs more specifically within this general region or at an earlier date. The Ukrainian archaeologist, Vladimir Baran, for example, initiates his study of the proto-Slavs with the historically attested peoples of the sixth to seventh centuries AD and assigns them to the Prague-Penkov-Kolochina complex that inhabited a very broad area from the Elbe on the west to beyond the Dnieper on the east. Throughout this area we find generally similiar ceramics coupled with semi-subterranean rectangular houses, hearths and cremation burials in urns. The general uniformity of the archaeological groups

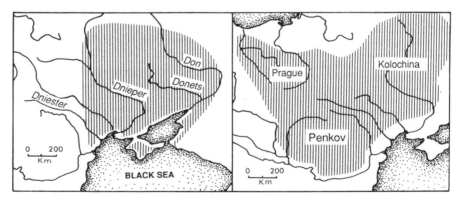

48, 49   The distribution of Iranian river names in Eastern Europe. These include the major rivers whose names are built from the Iranian word danu- *'river', whence the Don, the Dnieper (from* *danu apara *'river to the rear') and Dniester (**danu nazdya- *'river to the front'). The same Indo-European root underlies Celtic* Danuvius, Danube. *On the right is the Prague-Penkov-Kolochina complex.*

accords well with both our historical sources and our expectations based on the later appearance of Slavic peoples beyond the Byzantine frontier.

Attempts to push back beyond the fifth century AD and follow a trail of direct cultural continuity must somehow penetrate through the 'noise' produced by the Chernyakovo complex of the second to the fifth centuries AD. This culture, evidenced by more than a thousand sites, embraced most of the northwest Pontic region from the Danube northeast to the Seym. Its existence runs concurrent with the intrusions of the Goths from the northwest and Sarmatians from the east, all into an area with residual populations of Hellenized Scythians, Getae, Dacians and probably Slavs. Some argue that the Chernyakovo culture may be directly equated with the Goths while others deny the Goths any archaeological visibility and insist on interpreting this complex as a sort of *mélange* created among a number of very different local groups. A hint of the controversy can readily be seen when we recall that Marija Gimbutas regards this period as the time when Goths superimposed themselves politically on the Slavs and consequently passed on to Common Slavic a number of Germanic loan words such as 'bread', 'house', and 'stable'. Joachim Werner, on the other hand, regards the Chernyakovo culture as exclusively Germanic and places the Slavs further north in the forest, unable to push southwards until the Huns eliminated Gothic settlement and power in the forest steppe in the fourth century AD, while Valentin Sedov sees the northern region of the Chernyakovo culture as the area where Iranians and Slavs achieved their symbiosis. Basically, the Chernyakovo complex appears to have embraced a variety of different ethno-linguistic groups and we would assign only portions of it to Slav, Iranian, Goth or any another group.

Agreement is still more difficult to find when one retreats back further in time to the period of the Zarubinets-Przewor cultures of the second century BC–second century AD. The more easterly culture, the Zarubinets, is seen by many today as an unquestioned precursor to the later historically attested Slavic

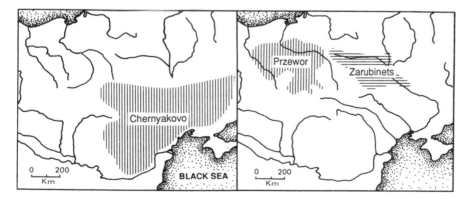

50, 51   The Chernyakovo cultural region which appears to have included Slavs, Goths and Iranian-speaking tribes. On the right is the Zarubinets-Przewor complex.

cultures. It is the more westerly situated Przewor culture of the Elbe-Vistula region, widely regarded as related to the Zarubinets, that provokes the most controversy. Its inclusion within the Slavic 'homeland' is in accord with the Polish hypothesis which sees cultural continuity in the Elbe-west Baltic region from the Bronze Age until the historical emergence of the Slavs. This continuity sufficed to justify the theory that the Slavs originated in this very region before expanding south and eastwards. In opposition to this theory is the frequently cited opinion of Germanicists that the Przewor region is more arguably within an early Germanic-speaking territory either of, or immediately adjacent to, the Elbe-Germanic tribes. Battle-lines drawn along a prehistoric border, one scholar jokingly observed that 'German scholars would like to drown all the Slavs in the Pripet swamps, and Slavic scholars all the Germans in the Dollart'. A resolution of these conflicting theories generally rests on inconclusive arguments for regional cultural continuity, the geographical deadreckoning generated from ambiguous historical sources such as Tacitus or Ptolemy, and Old Slavic river names.

There is a wide acceptance among both linguists and archaeologists that the study of river names can provide an important source of prehistoric information. The work of Oleg Trubachev, for example, provides a relatively well-defined zone of rivers retaining archaic Slavic names and neighboured by non-Slavic hydronymic systems. This archaic Slavic hydronomy is confined primarily to the region stretching from the upper Vistula basin to the middle Dnieper. Many archaeologists have accepted this as an important confirmation of their archaeological theories, although one cannot escape remarking that this common Slavic hydronomy is not an especially well-dated phenomenon and archaeologists can be rather cavalier in how they utilize it. Some, for example, apply the hydronymic map to the archaeology of the first centuries AD and see confirmation that the southeastern Przewor, part of the Chernyakovo and the Zarubinets cultures are all included as a Proto-Slavic homeland. Others see a

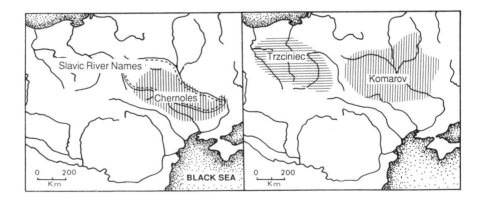

52. 53   The area of old Slavic river names (dotted line) plotted against the distribution of the Chernoles culture. On the right is the Komarov culture and its eastern neighbour, the Trzciniec culture; the latter has been variously assigned to both the earliest Slavs and the earliest Balts.

far better 'fit' by overlaying the river-name maps on the still older Chernoles culture of the period 750–200 BC. This area coincides with the territory attributed by Herodotus to Scythian-Farmers and a reasonable case can be made for seeing these Scythian-Farmers as Iron Age Slavs.

The earliest that Slavicists are generally willing to push the concept of a linguistically differentiated Proto-Slavic is 2000–1500 BC. The most widely accepted archaeological representative of this earliest Slavic period is the Komarov complex which dates to about 1500 BC and which occupies the region of the middle Dnieper to the upper Vistula. Again we confront the problem of a more westerly extension since both the Polish hypothesis as well as a number of Soviet scholars would also include the Trzciniec culture to its northwest as a related and hence Proto-Slavic culture. The Komarov culture itself is known especially from its burials which are primarily inhumation in a timber or stone-covered grave with a low tumulus.

The general course of investigations into Slavic origins may be laden with controversy but these differing opinions are normally confined to the western limits of early Slavic territory. It is difficult to deny that there existed a geographical centre weighted between the Vistula and Dnieper which is most commonly agreed to be Proto-Slavic and which appears to display a continuity of cultural development from about 1500 BC (or earlier) to the historical appearance of the earliest Slavic peoples. To derive the Slavs exclusively from a more westerly area such as the Elbe-Vistula region requires far less economy of explanation, not to speak of movement; moreover, the Iranian loans into Common Slavic make the case for a more easterly home for the early Slavs more attractive. It must be admitted that, throughout all of these arguments, we find ourselves engaging in the archaeologists' easiest pursuit – the demonstration of relative continuity and absence of intrusion. A long geographical stasis for the Slavs, however, is probably the model that would be most readily accepted by linguists who see in the Slavic language group little reason to assume that they have moved much since their development from Proto-Indo-European. Whether this can be employed as an anchor for yet earlier Indo-Europeans is, of course, another matter which we will have to investigate later.

The Balts

The course of expansion that carried the Slavic languages over much of Eastern Europe was also responsible for greatly reducing the area occupied by Baltic speakers. Today there are an estimated six million speakers of the two surviving east Baltic languages, Lithuanian and Latvian. The major representative of the western Baltic languages, Old Prussian, became extinct by about AD 1700. The pressure of Slavic expansions from the south and Germanic from the west has reduced the original Baltic-speaking territory to an estimated one-sixth of its previous area.

The earliest Baltic texts appear quite late when compared with most other Indo-European languages. In the sixteenth century we first encounter written

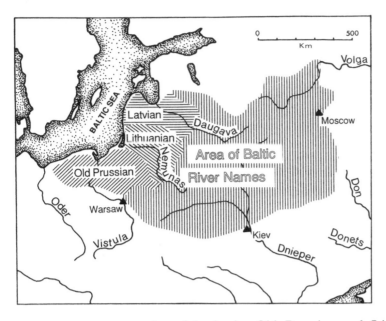

54 The maximum expansion of the Baltic languages.

examples of both the Old Prussian and Lithuanian languages generally emerging in the form of religious literature such as Lutheran catechisms. The texts, as indeed the modern Lithuanian language today, has always attracted the attention of linguists since, despite their recent date, they appear remarkably archaic in terms of Indo-European linguistics. To take a familiar example, the Lithuanian proverb 'God gave teeth; God will give bread' displays an almost incredible similarity to its translation into the much older Latin and Sanskrit:

Lithuanian	Dievas	dave	dantis;	Dievas	duos	duonos
Sanskrit	Devas	adadat	datas;	Devas	dat	dhanas
Latin	Deus	dedit	dentes;	Deus	dabit	panem

Because of this transparent conservatism, many linguists hold that the Baltic languages, like their Slavic neighbours, have probably moved but little since late Indo-European times.

Although the earliest written texts date to the sixteenth century, this is hardly a terminal point in our quest for Baltic origins. By this time much of Eastern Europe had already been encapsulated in a vast Lithuanian state, dating from the fourteenth century, which had witnessed the greatest expansion of Baltic political power in historical times. The Balts are also well attested in tribal and personal names as they confronted the Teutonic Order in the course of the thirteenth century. Before that we find them, especially in the form of the coastal Curonians, harrying the Baltic in the tenth and eleventh centuries, and they are mentioned by Scandinavians and the Anglo-Saxon Wulfstan from the seventh to the ninth centuries AD. Throughout all of these periods we find them in their historical homes centred on the Baltic Sea from the Vistula north to at least the Daugava. By this time, however, they have already undergone massive retraction in the east due to the pressure of East Slavic expansion, attested by finds typical of the Prague and other Slavic archaeological complexes.

Menuo sauluze vede	The Moon leads (home) the Sun,
Pirma pavasareli	In the first of spring,
Sauluze anksti keles	The Sun rose early,
Menuzis atsiskyre	The Moon left her.
Menuo viens vaikstinejo	The Moon alone wandered,
Ausrine pamylejo	With the Morning Star he fell in love.
Perkuns, didziai supykes	Perkunas, very angry,
Ji kardu perdalijo	With his sword he cut (him) to pieces.

55 An excerpt from a Lithuanian folksong which still reflects the pagan traditions of the ancient Balts. All of the celestial words here have good Indo-European origins: menuo 'moon' is cognate with a whole series of Indo-European words meaning moon and month, e.g., Sanskrit mas, Greek men, Latin mensis, Tocharian man and, of course, English moon. Saule 'sun' goes with Sanskrit suvar, Latin sol, Gothic sauil, etc., while ausrine is a diminutive of ausra 'dawn' and belongs with Sanskrit usas, Greek eos, Latin aurora, and English Easter all of which are similarly personified or deified. The verb vede is cognate with English wed and other Indo-European verbs derived from *wedh 'to lead home, to marry (from the groom's point of view)' which suggests that an early Indo-European bride moved to the home of her husband or his family. Perkunas is the archetypal thunder-god; his name is cognate with the Slavic god Perun and the same root furnishes us with the name of Fjörgyn, the mother of the Norse thunder-god Thor.

We can recede further into Baltic history via classical authors such as Ptolemy and Tacitus who list the names of Baltic tribes including the famed gatherers of amber, the Aisti – perhaps to be equated with western Balts – and tribes such as the Soudinoi and Galindai who emerge in the fourteenth century as the names of Prussian tribes. The only available historical reference beyond this period is Herodotus who speaks of a people known as the Neuri. Herodotus tells us little of the Neuri other than how they were driven from their country in the sixth century BC because of an enormous plague of snakes, and that for one or two days a year they transformed themselves into werewolves (a story that even Herodotus himself dismissed). Interestingly enough, the *žaltys*, the Lithuanian green snake, occupied an extraordinarily important role in pagan Lithuanian belief as well as folklore. We read how each household maintained its own snake, and contemporary accounts of the forced Christianization of the Balts by their German neighbours report how the Germans seized the snakes against great protest and burnt them in public bonfires in the middle of the Baltic villages.

Herodotus locates the Neuri north of the Scythian Farmers, the probable designation of the Slavs, and separated from the Scythian world by a lake, possibly the Pripet marshes. This locates the Balts in the territory assigned by archaeologists to the Milograd culture which occupied the northern Dnieper Basin, and it falls well within the Old Baltic hydronymic system.

Like Slavic river names, there has been a long tradition of research into the distribution of Baltic river names which clearly indicates that the Baltic linguistic area once included regions far to both the east and south of the coastal Balts, whom we encounter in most historical records from the Middle Ages onwards. The system is generally complementary to the Slavic river names, occupying the territory immediately to the north of the Slavs and bordered on the northeast by Finno-Ugric names. We naturally confront the same problem of their chronology which we encountered with Slavic river names. They must certainly predate the Slavic expansions of the fifth century AD and if truly coordinate with the Slavic area designated by Herodotus and the Chernoles culture, then we may place them to 500 BC. Wolfgang P. Schmid, however, would push them back into the greatest depths of Proto-Indo-European. Little is to be gained by overplaying the hydronymic card and asserting for one language that which cannot be demonstrated for any other. The minimal view would see the Balts, during the first millennium BC, occupying the area from west of the Vistula's mouth east to Moscow and the upper Volga (which itself carries a Baltic name), and south almost as far as Kiev. It may have been at this time or possibly earlier that a large number of Baltic words, especially those concerned with the technology of agriculture and stockbreeding, entered the Finnish language.

To recede any further into prehistory requires us to assume, as with the Slavs, direct continuity of culture and hence no evidence for movement of peoples within this region. This, so the argument goes, would carry us back to Middle Bronze Age cultures of about 1500 BC, including the Trzciniec culture of Poland which some have included as a Slavic culture. Although continuity can be argued to still earlier periods, it is useful to halt here, as we have done with other Indo-European groups, since we can only compound uncertainties by extrapolating further back into prehistory.

The Germans

The modern Germanic languages are traditionally divided into two major groups. The larger West Germanic group comprises English which is spoken by over 425 million speakers; German, spoken by approximately 120 million; and Dutch and its derivative Afrikaans which are spoken by about 30 million people. The smaller group consists of the North Germanic or Scandinavian languages which today embrace 20 million speakers of Danish, Swedish, Norwegian and Icelandic. Although many of these languages, especially English, German and Icelandic, offer abundant texts from the so-called Dark Ages and medieval period, our earliest substantial texts are in the extinct East Germanic Gothic language. The Goths had migrated from the north into the Black Sea region where they ruled until the arrival of the Huns in the fourth century AD who pushed most of the Gothic tribes westward into the Balkans. It was here that Wulfilas, Bishop of the West Goths, created a Gothic alphabet (primarily derived from the Greek) and translated portions of the Bible into the Gothic language. Gothic was still spoken up into remarkably recent times, surviving in the Crimea as late as the sixteenth century.

Other than Gothic texts we also have the evidence of the runic inscriptions which appear to have been loosely derived from one of the north Italian or Etruscan alphabets of the first century AD. Runic inscriptions were employed widely over northern Europe from about AD 150 to 900, and still earlier is the solitary evidence of the Negau helmet, discovered in Yugoslavia and bearing the inscription *harixasti teiva* which is usually translated 'to Army-Guest (or Host), the god', putatively a dedicatory inscription to a Germanic god. The helmet is inscribed in a north Italian script and has been variously dated from about the seventh to the second century BC.

Other than direct textual evidence of the Germanic languages, we have the writings of classical historians, the most important of whom is Tacitus who described the location and culture of the early Germans in his *Germania*. Tacitus located most of the Germanic tribes about AD 100 in a region bordered on the west by the Rhine, to the south by the Main and on the east by the Oder. Earlier sources, such as Caesar in the first century BC, are somewhat less reliable but again place the Germans east of the Rhine. The earliest historical source, Pytheas, is generally understood to have located the Germanic tribe of the Teutones in present-day Denmark and the Gutones possibly in northern Germany.

Both the historical and inscriptional evidence indicate that the earliest Germanic-speaking peoples were largely distributed in the area of northern Germany and southern Scandinavia. To confine the Germans more precisely within this area we must have recourse again to the study of river names and early tribal names, especially among peoples lying immediately east of the Rhine. A few linguists suggest that the territory between the Oise and Aller may have been occupied by a linguistic group which was neither Celtic nor Germanic but which has been termed the *Nordwestblock*.[17] Although the existence of such a grouping in the first centuries BC is not universally agreed, the hypothesis at least poses a salutary reminder that some historically anonymous groups may have survived to the dawn of historical records and we

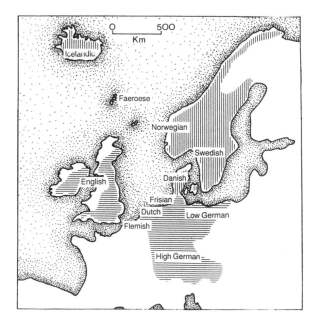

56 The distribution of the Germanic languages. The northern group is indicated by vertical hatching, the western group with horizontal. The eastern Germanic group, attested by Gothic, is extinct.

The Germanic Languages

Gothic (fourth century)

Jah hairdjos wesun in thamma samin landa thairhwakandans jah witandans wahtwom nahts ufaro hairdai seinai. Ith aggilus fraujins anaqam ins jah wulthus fraujins biskain ins, jah ohtedun agisa mikilamma.

Old English (tenth/eleventh century)

& hyrdas waeron on tham ylcan rice waciende. & niht-waeccan healdende ofer heora heorda. Tha stod drihtnes engel with hiq & godes beorhtnes him ymbe-scean. & hi him mycelum ege adredon.

Middle English

And schepherdis weren in the same cuntre, wakinge and hepinge the watchis of the nyzt on her flok. And loo! The aungel of the Lord stood by sydis hem, and the clerenesse of God schynedet aboute hem; and thei dredden with greet drede.

Low German (fifteenth century)

Unde de herden weren in der suluen iegenode wakende. Unde helden de wake auer ere schape. Unde seet de engel des heren stunt by en unde de clarheit godes ummevench se unde se vruchteden sick myt groten vruchten.

High German (sixteenth century)

Und es woren Hirten in derselbigen Gegend auf dem Felde bei den Hurden, die huteten des Nachts ihrer Herde. Und siehe, des Herrn Engel trat zu ihnen, und die Klarheit des Herrn leuchtete um sie; und sie furchteten sich.

Swedish

I samma nejd voro da nagra herdar ute pa marken och hollo vakt om natten over sin hjord. Da stod en Herrens angel framfor dem, och Herrens harlighet kringstralade dem; och de blevo mycket forskrackta.

And shepherds were in that same land abiding and keeping watch by night over their flocks. But the angel of the lord approached them and the glory of the lord shone about them, and they feared greatly.

57   A brief excerpt from the Gothic Bible compared with other Germanic groups. The hairda *'flock' is to be compared with English* herd *as well as Sanskrit* sardha-, *Lithuanian* kerdzius *and Middle Welsh* cordd *'troop'. As the word* nahts *'night' is part of very basic vocabulary, we find it very well attested across the Indo-European languages, e.g., Hittite* nekut, *Sanskrit* nak, *Greek* nyks, *Albanian* nate, *Latin* nox, *Old Irish* in-nocht, *Lithuanian* naktis, *Old Church Slavonic* nosti. *The word for 'fear'* agis *goes with Greek* akhos *and Old Irish* agor *'fear'.*

would be ill-advised to imagine that all of Europe or Asia was occupied by only those branches of the Indo-European languages recorded in history.

The area demarcated by the historical and linguistic evidence back to the first century BC has provided archaeologists with an independent sense of security in their identification of the earliest Germanic region. Continuity of settlement and culture can be clearly observed from the initial historical emergence of the Germanic tribes in the first centuries AD back to the Iron Age Jastorf culture. This culture, appearing about the fifth century BC, was the dominant Iron Age

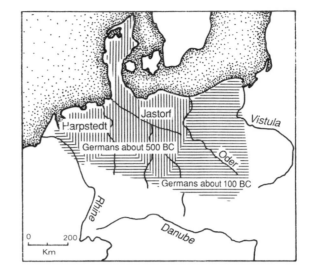

58   The distribution of the early Germans of the Jastorf and Harpstedt cultures and their historical distribution by about 100 BC.

culture of Northern Europe and the continuity of its settlements, cemeteries, and distribution accords well with the historical locations of the earliest-known Germanic tribes. Consequently, the Jastorf culture and probably the neighbouring Harpstedt culture have provided Germanicists with a generally agreed-upon Germanic homeland. This also finds reinforcement from the linguists who suggest that those sound changes that transformed a late Indo-European dialect into Proto-Germanic probably occurred about 500 BC.

There is a strong temptation to push the Proto-Germanic presence in this same region back further in time. Certainly, no major body of archaeologists would argue that the Jastorf culture was anything other than a direct descendant from the Later Bronze Age of the same area. This can be demonstrated by the continuity of settlement and cemetery practices which are as much in evidence here as between the Jastorf culture and the historical period, but we cannot really penetrate beyond this and still hope to retain the name Proto-Germanic in a linguistically meaningful sense.

We can see, then, that the Jastorf culture was Proto-Germanic by common agreement. What preceded it may also have been Proto-Germanic or perhaps late western Indo-European, or some other state of the evolution of the Indo-European languages for which we have no precise name. We will have good reason to return to this problem at the end of this chapter.

Italy

While many may carp with Metternich's dismissal of Italy as not a nation, but only 'a geographical expression', this is a particularly apt description for the Indo-Europeanist. By the end of the eighth century BC, Greek colonists in southern Italy had introduced the alphabet which subsequently spread throughout the Iron Age cultures of the Italian peninsula. The resulting inscriptions have opportunely preserved the evidence for a variety of different languages that were, for the most part, soon to become extinct. A linguistic map of Italy set to a notional date of 500 BC gives some indication of the linguistic complexity of Italy prior to the expansion of Latin by the Romans. It is for this reason that we must now abandon our usual framework of presenting an Indo-European group under its ethno-linguistic heading, for we will have to confront all of the linguistic evidence from Italy at one time.

In discussing the linguistic history of Italy it is best to begin with the evidence for non-Indo-European languages. By far the most important example is Etruscan which provides us with over 10,000 inscriptions and some short texts in a language which the overwhelming majority of linguists have concluded is not Indo-European and not demonstrably related to any other language except for some inscriptional evidence on the island of Lemnos in the east Mediterranean. This raises the entire problem of Etruscan origins which has filled volumes every bit as large as this one and is as heatedly debated as any of the problems concerning Indo-European origins. There is no easy solution, since the evidence is extremely self-contradictory. Nevertheless, the present tendency in Etruscan research is to adopt the most economical thesis: the Etruscans were a non-Indo-European people native to Italy who adopted many items and styles of east Mediterranean provenience by way of trade. The similarity between Etruscan and the Lemnian inscriptions must be acknowledged and is admittedly difficult to explain. One thesis sees both Etruscan and Lemnian as remnants of a continuum of non-Indo-European 'Mediterranean' languages which spanned the eastern and central Mediterranean before the intrusion of Indo-European speakers. But the similarity between Etruscan and Lemnian is, I believe, too great to be explained by anything other than a more

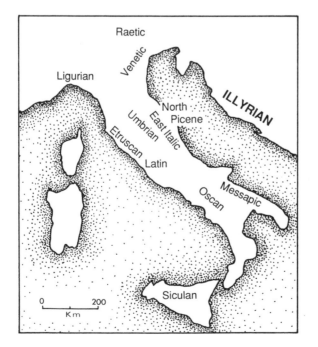

59 *The distribution of the major languages of Iron Age Italy.*

	Etruscan	Latin	Proto-Indo-European
1	thu	unus	*oinos
2	zal	duo	*duwo
3	ci	tres	*treyes
4	sa	quattuor	*k^{w}etwores
5	mach	quinque	*penk^{w}e
6	huth	sex	*s(w)eks
10	sar	decem	*dekmt
brother	ruva	frater	*bhrater
daughter	sech	filia	*dhugəter
son	clan	filius	*sunus

60   *The non-Indo-European nature of Etruscan is clearly seen in this comparison between it, Latin and Proto-Indo-European.*

direct and immediate historical connection, possibly involving a visit to Lemnos by Etruscan traders.

Perhaps one of the reasons that it is slightly easier to accept Etruscan as a native language of Italy is that there is other evidence for non-Indo-European languages in the region. A large body of linguistic opinion supports the argument that both place names, particularly in the western Alpine region and in Sardinia, and many of the words in Latin and the Romance languages unanalyzable from the standpoint of Indo-European, derive from a pre-Indo-European substrate. This evidence is, of course, very similar to that which we have seen employed to substantiate a pre-Greek population and it must be admitted that only the Etruscan language offers us conclusive textual evidence. Some have suggested that Ligurian, a language attested to the north of the Etruscans in a few glosses and local names, was also non-Indo-European (although heavily influenced by the Celts), but the linguistic evidence here is far too sparse to draw any firm conclusions. Similarly, in the eastern Alps where Raetic is also slightly attested, there have been claims that this language possesses distinctly non-Indo-European elements, for example, Raetic *tinake*, Etruscan *zinake*, but here again the inscriptional evidence is really very meagre. Nevertheless, when we combine all this evidence with Etruscan, the non-Indo-European place names and elements in Latin, and the proximity of at least northern Italy to conclusively non-Indo-European languages in southern France and Iberia, we have little doubt that the Indo-European languages were intrusive into Italy and that they were superimposed on a variety of non-Indo-European populations.

The most famous of the Indo-European languages in Italy is naturally Latin whose spread coincided with the expansion of the power of the Roman state. It is a tribute to the persistence of the Roman conquest that, out of the vernacular language spoken in its territories at the height of the Roman empire, there emerged the Romance languages of French, Spanish, Portuguese, Italian, Romanian and others, with approximately 550 million native speakers today, rendering Italic the second largest group of Indo-European speakers. But at the time we have drawn up our linguistic map, Latin would appear to have been confined to the territory about Rome with its nearest linguistic neighbour seen in the dialect of Faliscan immediately to its north. Far more controversial are attempts to relate Latin closely to Siculan, a language spoken in eastern Sicily and attested by only three inscriptions and some glosses.

Down the spine of Italy ran the major group of Osco-Umbrian. Oscan itself was the language of the Samnites and it probably did not become extinct until the first centuries AD if graffiti on the walls of Pompeii can be any guide. There are about 200 inscriptions plus the usual glosses and personal names. Umbrian is better attested with the Iguvium tablets, religious texts inscribed on bronze which date back to about 200 BC. The differences between Latin and Osco-Umbrian are as obvious as their similarities and linguists are unsettled as to whether a common Proto-Italic dialect was carried into Italy from whence the two major groups developed, or whether they represent independent developments, perhaps outside of Italy, which have gained similarities through long-standing contacts.

The major language of southeastern Italy, apart from that of the Greek colonists, was Messapic, which is known from about 260 inscriptions dating to approximately the sixth to the first centuries BC. A combination of ancient historical testimony tracing Messapic tribes to Illyria coupled with archaeological evidence for cross-Adriatic connections in ceramics and metalwork have prompted linguists to link Messapic with Illyrian. The hard linguistic evidence is minimal since there are no Illyrian inscriptions and the link must be based on personal and place names.[18] Consensus does support such a link but not without hesitation; a minority is more cautious and does not regard Messapic-Illyrian links as even discussable.

To the north of Messapic is Picene or East Italic which may comprise two different languages under the same name. Some of the Picene inscriptions

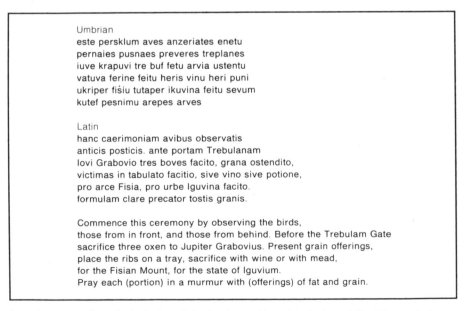

Umbrian
este persklum aves anzeriates enetu
pernaies pusnaes preveres treplanes
iuve krapuvi tre buf fetu arvia ustentu
vatuva ferine feitu heris vinu heri puni
ukriper fiśiu tutaper ikuvina feitu sevum
kutef pesnimu arepes arves

Latin
hanc caerimoniam avibus observatis
anticis posticis. ante portam Trebulanam
Iovi Grabovio tres boves facito, grana ostendito,
victimas in tabulato facitio, sive vino sive potione,
pro arce Fisia, pro urbe Iguvina facito.
formulam clare precator tostis granis.

Commence this ceremony by observing the birds,
those from in front, and those from behind. Before the Trebulam Gate
sacrifice three oxen to Jupiter Grabovius. Present grain offerings,
place the ribs on a tray, sacrifice with wine or with mead,
for the Fisian Mount, for the state of Iguvium.
Pray each (portion) in a murmur with (offerings) of fat and grain.

61   An excerpt from the beginning of the Iguvium tablets with Latin and English translation.

Messapic
klohizisthotoriamartapidovasteibasta
veinanaranindarantoavasti

'Here, Jupiter! Thotoria Marta gave to the city of Basta her land in [the
locality] of Darantoa . . .' ('Consensus' translation)

'Here, Jupiter! Under the *teutor-ship of Amartapidius, for the
inhabitants of Basta this law. They passed it (the law) in the Council of
Elders in Basta . . .' (Otto Haas translation)

'One should heed these things! I, Teutoria Marta, purchase in the city
of Basta the wine fields in Darantua . . .' (M.E. Huld translation)

62   *This inscription from Vaste is one of the longest texts in the Messapic language and
illustrates the problems in translating such marginally attested languages. The original
inscription runs for eight lines and there are no breaks between words. These must be determined
by isolating out repeated words or word-endings from which very conflicting translations may be
produced.*

extend back to about the seventh century BC and are among our earliest written
evidence in Italy. Unfortunately, the inscriptions, though easily deciphered,
are not easily translated. The southern inscriptions are at least transparently
Indo-European for example, *matereif patereif* = Latin *matribus patribus* 'to the
mothers and fathers', while the north Picene inscriptions pose far more
problems. These have been judged intuitively by some linguists to look like
Indo-European (even though we cannot translate a single word confidently!)
while others see them as evidence of the non-Indo-European natives. Those
who accept an Indo-European identification frequently derive them, like
Messapic, from the east Adriatic.

Finally, in the Veneto to the northeast we have Venetic, the language of the
Iron Age Este culture which is at least unqualifiably Indo-European. The over
200 inscriptions (though none over ten words long) were written from the sixth
to the first centuries BC. In addition, there is toponymic evidence which here
relates the territory of the Veneti to the tribe of the Liburni of Adriatic
Yugoslavia. Venetic is sufficiently well known to argue about its linguistic
affinities with other Indo-European languages. Similarities with Italic and
Germanic have all been suggested, especially with the former, but some
linguists regard Venetic as an independent Indo-European subgroup which
shares some similarities with other West European languages but not enough to
link it closely with any particular one.

When reviewing the origins of the Indo-European peoples of Italy we may
accept that they were intrusive and superimposed on a non-Indo-European
substrate. Since we find the evidence for non-Indo-European languages
increases as we move westwards either through Italy or along the Mediterranean coast, the most probable direction for Indo-European movements is either
from north of the Alps or across the Adriatic from the east. This becomes
particularly plausible when we consider that by the ninth century BC there had

North Picene
mimnis erut gaarestades
rotnem uvlin parten us
polem isairon tet
sut trat nesi krus
tenag trut ipiem rotnes
lutuis thalu isperion vul
tes rotem teu aiten tasur
soter merpon kalatne
nis vilatos paten arn
uis balestenag ands et
sut i akut treten teletau
nem polem tisu sotris eus.

63 The famous Novilara inscription is the longest example of the north Picene language. Scholars are divided on whether the language is Indo-European or not but are generally agreed that there is not a single word in this inscription that can confidently be translated.

developed three major archaeological provinces along Adriatic Italy which coincide well with three of our major linguistic groups. In the Veneto we find the Este culture first emerging at 900 BC, while both a Picene archaeological region and the Late Bronze Age cultures of Apulia and Basilicata provide our second and third archaeological units. All three of these provinces show longstanding and intense relationships with the east Adriatic, especially in metalwork, such that regular movements of people across the Adriatic Sea or along the northeast coast of Italy have frequently been postulated. These Balkan currents are relatively constant from at least the thirteenth century BC onwards, and they prevent us from chasing the illusive and oversimplistic model of a single invasion to explain the Picenes and the Messapi. Rather, there may have been long-term movements of Indo-European speakers into Adriatic Italy who, by dominating the larger and richer coastal sites, were in an optimum position to spread their languages into the smaller and poorer interior. These movements from the east would appear to define the most recent layer of Indo-European immigrants except, of course, for the fifteenth-century Albanian refugees who also crossed the Adriatic to settle in southern Italy and Sicily where today they still retain their own language.

Another putative intrusion is associated with the rapid spread of the Proto-Villanovan culture (or Pianello–Timmari horizon) which emerged over most of Italy about 1100–900 BC. Although it has long been considered a prime vector of the Indo-European languages, it must be admitted that it seems to provide us with precisely the type of evidence for which we are *not* looking in order to explain the linguistic diversity of Italy, since it displays a remarkable cultural uniformity over almost the entire peninsula. It is in this period that we see the widespread appearance of cremation cemeteries employing biconical urns, and a wide variety of Central European metalwork that includes fibulae, razors, pins, swords, and sheet bronze work such as buckets, helmets and armour. The introduction of cremation with urns, and the metalwork, have been attributed in the past to Urnfield invaders from the north of the Alps who penetrated northern Italy to produce a major upheaval in culture. Present archaeological models dismiss schemes of massive Urnfield invasions as grossly simplistic relics of all-too-traditional archaeological thinking. Nevertheless, attributing the similarities between Italy and Central Europe to vaguely defined models of persistent cultural contacts or orientations still leaves room for some element of folk-movement, even if nowhere on the scale of those who dreamed of Late Bronze Age warriors bursting through the Alpine passes. The results of such movements, however, become linguistically obscure when we recall that the same cultural phenomenon which underlies areas of Indo-European speakers such as the Osco-Umbrians, also provides the immediate foundation of the Villanovan culture of Etruria which we recognize as the earliest archaeological manifestation of the non-Indo-European Etruscans.

Retreating in time to the next potential intrusion we arrive at the appearance of Middle Bronze Age industries in northern Italy, especially the Po Valley. Here the emergence of the Terramare culture, the initiation of cremation burials into what was previously an inhumation area, the abandonment of earlier settlements, and both ceramic and metallurgical parallels with Central Europe, particularly Hungary, are all cited as evidence for immigrants.

Finally, a still earlier series of intrusions has been proposed to explain the emergence of the three major Eneolithic/Early Bronze Age cultures of Italy the Remedello, Rinaldone and Gaudo. It has long been argued that these three cultures were the result of an invasion(s) of a warrior aristocracy which introduced metallurgy, a new burial rite, and new ceramics, as well as a marked change in the earlier social system. The archetypal evidence derives from the Rinaldone culture of Tuscany which offered evidence of a clear status male burial in the Tomb of the Widow at Porte San Pietro. In a stone-cut tomb was found a man accompanied by a stone battle-axe, copper daggers, an arrowhead and pot, and a woman with evident skull injuries suggesting that she was dispatched on the death of her husband according to the rite of suttee as practised in ancient India. Other Rinaldone graves offer typically Indo-European evidence such as horse remains and an abundance of copper objects including daggers, axes, awls and a halberd. To the north, in the Po Valley, was the Remedello culture with its large cemetery where metal daggers, halberds, axes and awls accompanied burials. The metal is reputed to have come from the Alpine foothills of Central Europe; some silver items have also been linked to Central Europe. In all of these cultures the physical remains have been interpreted as a basically dolichocephalic (long-headed) population among whom an intrusive brachycephalic (broad-headed) people settled.

Venetic:	mego	zontasto	sainatei	reitiiai	porai	egeotora
Latin:	*me*	*donavit*	*sanatrici*	*reitiae*	*bonae*	*egetora*

	aimoi	ke	louzerophos.
	(pro) Aemo	*et (que)*	*liberis.*

'Egetora gave me to the Good Reitia the Healer on behalf of Aemus and the children.'

64　A Venetic inscription from a bronze nail. Here it is translated into Latin and English.

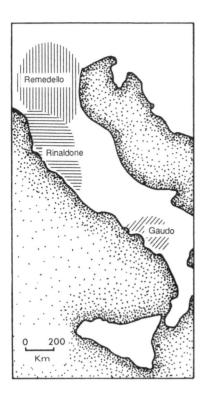

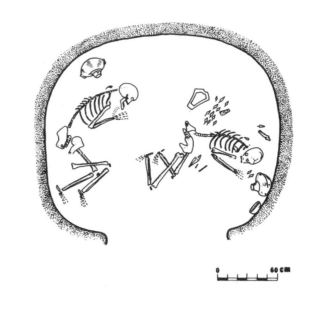

65,66   The major Early Bronze Age cultures of Italy. On the right is a burial from the Rinaldone culture of Tuscany – the Tomb of the Widow.

These arguments for intrusion have, as all others, been attacked and the continuity with earlier Neolithic traditions and the lack of clear external sources for invasion have been emphasized. A middle ground holds to some small intrusion but mainly to continuity among the inhabitants, although this school does attribute social change to the introduction and exploitation of metals.

These different waves of intrusion are still major discussion points of Italian archaeology and no theory can be considered as holding the upper hand for any period. Obviously there are problems even if one accepts some of the intrusions. For example, to suggest that the Rinaldone culture of about 2700 BC represented Indo-Europeans derived either from Central Europe or along the Mediterranean coasts runs into the obvious problem that it explains Indo-Europeans in a territory that emerges later as Etruscan. No one has managed to construct a fully integrated model of successive intrusions, from both the north and the east, which provides a perfect fit with the successive series of different Indo-European languages in Italy. While the Adriatic coast combines archaeological evidence with a certain degree of linguistic plausibility, our search for the earlier Oscans, Umbrians and Latins remains far more elusive. That Italy was Indo-Europeanized from some time after 3000 BC and prior to 800 BC there is little doubt. That one can also postulate a number of intrusions from outside Italy and still hold to an essential continuity of cultural development in many areas of Italy is also defensible. In a region where both the amount of archaeological evidence and our models for interpreting it still leave very much to be desired, this is perhaps all that we can expect at present.

The Celts

Although Celtic speakers are now confined to the Atlantic periphery of Europe, their Iron Age ancestors once dominated Western and Central Europe, occupied vast stretches of Eastern Europe, invaded both Italy and Greece, colonized central Anatolia, and, in the guise of mercenaries, even fought in the armies of Egypt. Their history during the last five centuries BC is that of a rapidly expanding host of different tribes and tribal confederations and it is small wonder that the Greeks counted them as one of the great barbarian *ethnoi* of the ancient World, although today they represent the smallest surviving group of Indo-European speakers. In examining their origins, we will first briefly review the evidence for the different Celtic languages, seek out and exclude those areas where we know the Celts to be demonstrably intrusive, and then attempt to trace them back to their earliest appearance in the archaeological record.

The Celtic languages are traditionally divided into two major geographical groups – Continental and Insular. The Continental languages are those recorded in the first centuries BC. Our evidence includes inscriptions in the Greek, Latin or Iberian scripts; coin inscriptions; place names and, naturally, the personal names preserved in the works of classical historians such as Caesar. Most of our evidence for the Continental Celtic languages is assigned to three major linguistic groups. There is Gaulish, spoken in the province of the same name, and evidenced by nearly 100 inscriptions, the majority of which are confined to southern France. There is also Lepontic, a Celtic language known from about 70 inscriptions which derives from the Alpine region to the north of Milan. The third is Hispano-Celtic (or Celtiberian) whose inscriptions are localized to a triangle drawn between Zaragoza, Burgos and Guadalajara, but by way of coins and place-names is attested over the northern two-thirds of the

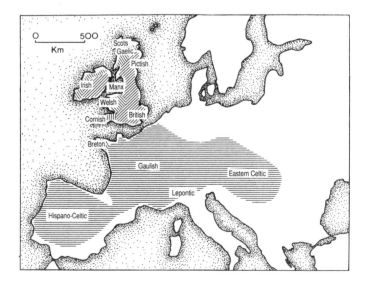

67   The distribution of the Celtic languages. The continental languages are indicated with horizontal hatching, while the two groups of insular Celtic languages – Goidelic and Brittonic – are indicated with diagonal hatching.

Iberian peninsula. None of these inscriptions predates the third century BC. A fourth linguistic group, the Celtic languages of Eastern Europe, is meagrely noted in place and personal names. The Continental Celtic languages became extinct largely through the expansion of the Roman empire or the southerly movements of Germanic tribes.

The Insular Celtic languages are found in Great Britain, Ireland and, by way of transplantation, Brittany. Although we possess a little very early evidence such as the sixth-century BC labelling of Britain as Albion and Ireland as Ierne (modern Irish Eire), most of our linguistic data does not begin until the incorporation of Britain into the Roman empire. Our earliest major source for Ireland is Ptolemy's gazetteer of the known world which dates to about the second century AD and provides over fifty names of peoples and places of Ireland. By the middle of the first millennium AD the Irish had developed their own script (*ogham*) for inscribing grave memorials. It was also during this time that the Gaelic language of Ireland was carried to both Scotland and the Isle of Man. The Brittonic languages of southern Britain survived the Roman conquest to evolve into Welsh, Cornish and Breton, the last of which was at least partly the product of British refugees who fled to the continent. Today there are perhaps three and a half million speakers of the various Insular Celtic languages.

Our starting point for discussing the expansion of the Celts is their equation with the La Tène period of Western Europe which flourished during the last five centuries BC. The coincidence of the evidence of historical sources which begin by the sixth century BC, the subsequent distribution of Celtic written

---

Old Irish

Froech macc Idaith di Chonnachtaib, mac-side do Be Find a ssidib, derbsiur-side do Boind. Is e laech as aildem roboi di feraib Erenn ocus Alban, acht nibo suthain. Dobert a mathair di bai dec do assint sid, it e finda auderga. Boi trebad occo co cenn ocht mbliadnae cen tabairt mna cucai. Coica macc rig rop e lin a theglaig comais cutrummai friss uili eter cruth ocus ecosc.

Froech son of Idath of the Connachta (was) son to Be Find of the fairy-mounds, (and) herself sister to Boand. He was the warrior who was the most handsome of the men of Ireland and Scotland, but he was not long-lived. His mother gave to him 12 cows from the fairy mound, white with red ears. He maintained his house for eight years without taking a wife to himself. Fifty sons of kings were the number of his household, all similar to him in age, in form and in appearance.

---

68   An excerpt from the Old Irish tale Tain Bo Froich *'Cattle Raid of Froech'. Froech's mother 'Be Find' is literally 'woman blonde' where* be *is derived from Proto-Indo-European* *gᵂena- *'woman' (cognate with Sanskrit* gana, *Greek* gyne, *Old Prussian* genna, *and English* queen *where it underwent a special semantic development). The* derb-siur *is the 'true-sister', the latter element of which is cognate with the Indo-European words for sister, e.g., Sanskrit* svasar-, *Greek* eor, *Latin* soror, *English* sister. Boand *derives from* bo *'cow' and* find *'white' where* bo *falls within the series of cognate Indo-European words for the cow: Sanskrit* gaus, *Greek* bous, *Umbrian* bum, *Latvian* guovs, *Tocharian* ko *and English* cow.

*1 (top) The Hittite king Tudhaliyas IV (1250–1220 BC) depicted
in the embrace of the god Sarumma on the wall of a rock chamber at the cult site
of Yazilikaya. The divinity was a Hurrian god adopted by the Hittites.*

*2 (above) Twelve gods marching in procession from the Hittite cult
site of Yazilikaya. The physical features of the divinities – hooked noses,
square faces, high cheek bones – have been considered typical of the Hittite
population.*

3 Eighth-century jug from a child grave at Gordion, the capital of the Phrygians.

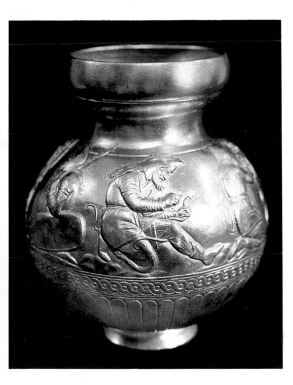

4 (above) Silver plaque from Luristan. The central figure is commonly interpreted as the Iranian primeval god Zurvan who produced the two competing forces of later Zoroastrian religion – Ahuramazda and Ahriman. The depiction of young, adult and aged groups of people further emphasizes Zurvan's character as the god of time. The plaque dates to about the eighth or seventh century BC.

5 (left) A Scythian strings a bow on a golden vase from the tomb at Kul Oba. The scene is one of four and may depict Scythes, the eponymous ancestor of the Scythians, in his successful stringing of Herakles' bow. Note that he carries his own bow in typical Scythian fashion in his gorytus, or bow case, fastened to his belt. Fourth century BC.

6 (right) The expansion of the Iranians to the west is most dramatically emphasized in this relief of a Sarmatian cavalryman carrying a battle standard (windsock). From a funeral stele in Chester, one of the Sarmatian veteran camps in Britain.

7 Seal impression from Mohenjo-daro. These seals, written in the Indus script, provide the only information for the language of the Indus Valley civilization. Still undeciphered, possibly undecipherable, the language of the scripts most likely belongs to the Elamo-Dravidian family.

8,9 Two Vedic gods of the early Indo-Aryans. Above is Agni, the god of fire and the hearth, whose name is cognate with Latin ignis *'fire', found in English 'ignite'. On the left is Indra, the archetypal god of war, who is commonly depicted holding his club, the* vajra.

10 (top) A detail of the 'Warrior Vase' from Mycenae which depicts a troop of bearded Greek warriors wearing horned helmets. The peculiar devices hanging from their spears have been variously interpreted as standards, slings or even bags for carrying provisions. Twelfth century BC.

11 (above) Sixteenth-century BC stele from Grave Circle A at Mycenae. The scene has been variously interpreted as a battle scene between an armed charioteer and a foot soldier, or a chariot race customary in funeral games such as those described in the Iliad. In the latter interpretation, the standing figure is an umpire monitoring the turn of the chariot.

12 Silver-gilt Thracian plaque of the mid-fourth century BC from Letnitsa. The figure is probably female (Thracian women wore their hair shorter than males who wore their hair in a top-knot) and she may be feeding a three-headed serpent, a motif known widely in Indo-European tradition.

13 (above) Illyrian cavalry fighting depicted on a seventh-century BC belt from Vace, Slovenia. Not only are the weapons and clothing of the two warriors different but even the manes of the horses vary.

14 (right) Illyrian warrior armed with axe, double spears and shield. The figure is from a bronze situla from Vace, Yugoslavia and dates to the seventh or sixth century BC.

15 (above) A silver plaque from Mora-
via depicts a Slav nobleman on horseback and with
his falcon.

16 (right) Face-urn from about the fifth
century BC from northern Poland. The tradition of
decorating urns with human faces began earlier in
Central Europe and was then adopted by the
prehistoric Balts.

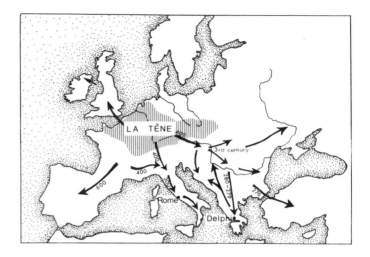

69   The La Tène culture and the course of Celtic expansions in the first millennium BC.

testimony, place names and the Celtic character of the La Tène culture is not challenged. Consequently, the expansion of La Tène material culture into areas peripheral to its earlier distribution is assigned to the historically attested migrations of the Celts. In Hungary, Romania and Yugoslavia, for example, there is abundant evidence of intrusive Celtic finds, both metallic and ceramic, coupled with Celtic cemeteries and occasionally fortified settlements. These began to appear in the fourth century BC when Greek authors record the expansion of the Celts towards Southeast Europe. Similarly, Celtic migrations and temporary conquests in Italy are seen in the distribution of La Tène artefacts in the peninsula. Hence the expansion of the Celts to Eastern Europe and the central Mediterranean can all be broadly associated with the appearance of La Tène material in these regions.

Unlike Eastern Europe, the evidence for Celtic expansions along the Atlantic pose more problems. We have seen, for example, that Celtic languages were established in the Iberian peninsula. The earliest historical attestation for the Celts in Iberia is the fifth century BC, for what few earlier sources exist lack references to conclusively Celtic populations. They do, however, assist us in the central problem of our survey since they help to exclude Iberia as an early location of Indo-Europeans. This is evident not only from the inscriptional evidence of at least two major non-Indo-European entities in the Iberian peninsula – Iberian, attested along the eastern coast of Spain, and Tartessian which is known from inscriptions covering the southern quarter of Iberia – and also from the only surviving non-Indo-European language of Western Europe, Basque. The Basque language appears to have been spoken over a much larger area than its present confinement to the Pyrenees would now indicate, and place-name studies of northern Spain and southern France exclude this region as an early home of the Indo-Europeans. With non-Indo-Europeans well attested in the north, east and south of Iberia, the logical consequence is to consider this region with those other areas that require an *intrusion* to explain the presence of Indo-European speakers. The absence of substantial La Tène influences in Iberia indicates that the intrusion responsible for the Celts must have occurred earlier in the period from about 1000 to 500 BC when there are more abundant associations between Iberia and the Urnfield and Hallstatt cultures of France, which are regarded as ancestral to the La Tène. There is some linguistic support for this hypothesis since the Celtic language spoken in Spain appears to have avoided the famous (though perhaps phonologically trivial) shift from Proto-Celtic q to p that occurs in all of the other Continental Celtic languages.

The expansion of the Celts to the British Isles poses its own special problems. There are no remnant pre-Celtic languages in the British Isles although Pictish, the language recorded in inscriptions over southeastern Scotland, may have retained a non-Indo-European element in what little of its vocabulary is recorded. Otherwise, the earliest evidence for Indo-Europeans in Britain or Ireland are the Celts. As the concern of our study is Indo-European origins rather than Celtic arrivals, we can avoid the archaeological minutiae involved in tracing Celtic migrations into Britain and Ireland and speak in broader terms. General archaeological and linguistic opinion assigns the intrusions which carried the Celtic languages into Britain and Ireland to sometime during the first millennium BC, although some scholars still hold to an earlier date. Certainly the similarity between the earliest evidence for Brittonic and Ogham Irish are too close to permit them a long separation in time, and they share the same Late Bronze Age and Iron Age vocabularies of their continental relations.

General opinion, therefore, traces the earliest historical Celts back to the continent and the La Tène culture, or to its immediate predecessor, the Hallstatt culture, at least in Western Europe.[19] In so doing, we can trace the earliest Celts to a broad band stretching from eastern France to Bohemia from 800 BC onwards. Since it is with little difficulty that archaeologists can trace the Hallstatt back to the Urnfield culture (1200–800 BC) or yet earlier periods, some prehistorians have glibly asserted that a 'Proto-Celtic' culture can be discerned all the way back to the Early Bronze Age. This can only be done, however, if one maintains a blissful ignorance that a proto-language, at least to a linguist, must meet certain minimal linguistic requirements. In the case of Proto-Celtic we are

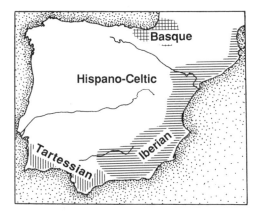

70 *Non-Indo-European languages and Hispano-Celtic in the Iberian peninsula.*

Q and P Celtic			
Proto-Indo-European	Old Irish	Welsh	Translation
kʷetwores	cethir	pedwar	4
(kʷenkʷe)	coic	pump	5
kʷer-	cruth	pryd	form
kʷrmi-	cruim	pryf	worm
kʷrei-	crenaim	prynu	buy

71   The Celtic languages are often divided into Q and P Celtic since Proto-Indo-European *kʷ yielded a 'k' sound (written c in Irish), but a 'p' sound in Gaulish and Brittonic.

talking of a state in the linguistic continuum, involving both the phonetic and grammatical changes which occurred after the dissolution of Proto-Indo-European, but which is immediately ancestral to the known Celtic languages. Proto-Celtic is, in a sense, a process whose beginning cannot be precisely dated, but linguists would be increasingly uncomfortable with the use of the term as one recedes back in time from the end of the second millennium BC. Hence, although the archaeologist may perceive continuity in the archaeological record, the linguist may prefer to employ less specific terms to describe the language of these distant ancestors of the Celts. Since this is the natural direction of our own inquiry, we will now leave the trail of the individual Indo-European groups and see if there are any broad patterns that may help to explain the origins of the Europeans in general.

Earlier Configurations

In our review of the origins of the Indo-European languages of Europe, it has become apparent that while some of the various languages are intrusive into non-Indo-European territories, for example, Greek, Italic and Hispano-Celtic, there are no grounds for seeking the immediate origins of any Indo-European group outside Europe. We have traced the individual Indo-European languages back to an area that includes eastern France and Holland on the west, southern Scandinavia and the Baltic Sea on the north, the upper Volga and Dnieper on the east, and the territory north of both the Alps and peninsular Greece on the south. Throughout the third and much of the second millennium BC it is likely that this territory consisted of Indo-European dialects that stood somewhere between the language we reconstruct as Proto-Indo-European and the 'branches' of Proto-Celtic, Proto-Germanic and so on. It is now our object to examine briefly the interrelationships between these different language groups and discover if they have any widely accepted expression in the archaeological record.

In general, the dialectal relationships among the various Indo-European languages are congruent with their earliest geographical locations. Similarities that link two or more languages, the isoglosses of linguistic science, are frequent, and provide the type of evidence that suggests that various groups were once geographically proximate to one another. When the Dative-Ablative ending *-bhyos (Sanskrit *vrkebhyas* 'to the wolves') appears as *-mos in Germanic (Gothic *wulfam*), Baltic (Lithuanian *vilkams*) and Slavic (Old Church Slavonic *vlikomu*), this argues for some form of close association between the ancestral speakers of these different languages which accounts for why they all adopted the same dialectal form. On the basis of this and much more abundant evidence of phonetics, grammar and vocabulary, we can speak of a continuum of Slavic-Baltic-Germanic that stretched over Northern Europe from east to west. We have already seen how Slavic on the east shares obvious correspondences or contacts with Iranian, while Germanic displays close contacts via loan words with Celtic. It has long been argued that Celtic and Italic also share many similarities of phonetics and grammar and even an Italo-Celtic branch of Indo-European has been suggested along the lines of Indo-Iranian. This is now much disputed, although Italic is regularly included with the other West European languages.

If an archaeologist is set the problem of examining the archaeological record for a cultural horizon that is both suitably early and of reasonable uniformity to postulate as the common prehistoric ancestor of the later Celtic, Germanic, Baltic, Slavic, and possibly some of the Indo-European languages of Italy, then the history of research indicates that the candidate will normally be the Corded Ware culture. At about 3200–2300 BC this Corded Ware horizon is sufficiently early to predate the emergence of any of the specific proto-languages. In addition, it is universally accepted as the common component if not the very basis of the later Bronze Age cultures that are specifically identified with the different proto-languages. Furthermore, its geographical distribution from Holland and Switzerland on the west across Northern and Central Europe to the upper Volga and middle Dnieper encompasses all of those areas which we have seen assigned as the 'homelands' of these European proto-languages.

Although the Corded Ware horizon may provide a plausible foundation for a number of the Indo-European groups in Europe, it does not account for all of them. We have also seen how Greek, Illyrian, Thracian, probably Messapic and East Italic, and possibly some of the other languages of Italy appear to derive from Southeast Europe. In addition, it is from this region that one normally obtains the intrusive Phrygians and Armenians who appear in Western Asia. The linguistic evidence suggests that Greek, Armenian, Iranian and Indic share certain similarities which indicate a chain of languages stretching from the Balkans across the Pontic and on into Central Asia. There is some evidence that Thracian shares some similarities with the eastern *satem* languages as well as Phrygian. Illyrian and the languages attested from Adriatic Italy tend to relate more easily with the western languages. Whatever the precise relationships, this evidence does not remove these languages from a staging area or earlier home in Southeast Europe, an area which lies essentially out of the distribution of the Corded Ware horizon.

Since we have already proposed migrations from the Balkans into Greece as early as the third millennium BC, logic compels us to assume that by this time Southeast Europe was already a source of Indo-European languages. This is

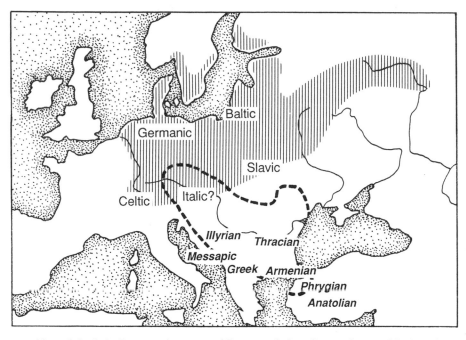

72 Most of the Indo-European languages of Europe and Anatolia may be traced back to the earlier territories of the Corded Ware horizon (indicated by vertical hatching) and the Balkan-Danubian complex (dotted line).

certainly not at variance with majority opinion among Southeast European archaeologists who seek the earliest appearance of Indo-European speakers in the discontinuity that follows the Late Neolithic/Eneolithic cultures of the region. The date for this must be very generally set to about 3500 BC and includes a wide variety of local cultures, for example, Maliq III in Albania; Karanovo VII or Ezero in Bulgaria; and Baden-Kostolac in the west Balkans. The Balkan-Danubian complex has been proposed as a convenient label for all of these cultures, and it does provide a basis after which continuity is the dominant theme of the archaeological record.

We may anticipate then that both the Corded Ware horizon and the Balkan-Danubian complex are essential to any explanation of the origin of the Indo-Europeans of Europe. Both the specific character of these different cultures and the problem of their ultimate origins – be they indigenous or intrusive – will be the topics of Chapter Eight when we attempt to trace the expansion of the Indo-Europeans. Before we can do this we shall have to abandon our historical evidence and seek from other sources what the earliest Indo-Europeans held in common.

CHAPTER FOUR

Proto-Indo-European Culture

> When we have only the reconstructed
> protolanguage, however, we still have a glorious
> artifact, one which is far more precious than
> anything an archaeologist can ever hope to
> unearth.
>
> MARY HAAS, 1969

Traditionally, there have been two methods employed by Indo-Europeanists to reconstruct Proto-Indo-European culture. One involves the straightforward comparison of the cultural traits or practices of the different Indo-European peoples in the hope that we can isolate common elements and project them back to the Proto-Indo-European period. This technique is voluminously illustrated throughout the pages of most general handbooks of Indo-European culture where the authors amass numerous references to the behaviour and institutions of the different Indo-European peoples. Often this makes for the best of reading but the entire logic of such an approach, at least when applied to the more obviously functional categories of culture, is certainly suspect.

We may take a familiar example by examining briefly how Indo-Europeanists have long observed similarities between the organization and behaviour of the war-bands (*Männerbunde*) depicted in the histories and literature of various Indo-European peoples. Here we find, from India to Germany and Ireland, a series of recurrent motifs in the organization of these warrior sodalities – egalitarian structure, frenzied berserker-like behaviour in war and sometimes in peace, the use of wild animals such as wolves as totems, and a tendency to operate outside the normal jurisdiction of society which often leads to conflicts between the warriors and the formal political and religious élites of the community.

Does such evidence permit us to extrapolate such warrior sodalities back to Proto-Indo-European society? Many have certainly found the image of young Indo-European berserkers sweeping across both Europe and Asia as attractive vehicles for carrying out the expansion of the Indo-European languages. Naturally, no one argues that such warrior sodalities are exclusively Indo-European and we can cite many other examples drawn from Asia, Africa and the New World, especially among the Plains Indians. Nevertheless, if the warrior sodalities constituted a formal segment of Proto-Indo-European society, this might well be translated into certain archaeological expectations such as the systematic deposition of weapons with the burials of young males. Too often, this has prompted archaeologists to equate the discovery of warrior burials throughout most of Eurasia with the traces of Indo-European expansions.

The very fact that war-bands are by no means a uniquely Indo-European phenomenon should caution us against reading into the archaeological record an Indo-European behind every burial accompanied by a stone or metal battle-axe. Warfare is the product of environmental, economic and social circumstances that can be found anywhere, and there is no reason for assuming an inherently warlike character for the Indo-Europeans.

More importantly, our evidence for Indo-European war-bands is derived from very different time periods with none before the Late Bronze Age. We may be struck by the similarities between the heroes of medieval Germanic and Irish tales and the Indic war-god Indra who leads his band of hell-raising Maruts through the hymns of the *Rig Veda*, but their behaviour is more apt to be *generic* responses to their particular cultural circumstances than the direct *genetic* inheritance from common ancestors and institutions which existed thousands of years earlier. To suggest otherwise is to assume implicitly that the structural organization of warfare among the Indo-Europeans remained essentially static for several thousands of years. Any archaeologist engaged in the study of warfare in Europe could not fail to remark on the numerous changes in war technology, defensive architecture and the organization of warfare from the Late Neolithic to the Dark Ages, and any attempt to read medieval Irish military institutions into the Eneolithic of Western Europe would be transparently fallacious. In short, we cannot be entirely confident in our reconstructions when they are based *solely* on the ethnographic residue of later Indo-European peoples. Consequently, in this chapter we will keep to the second method of cultural reconstruction, linguistic palaeontology.

Long before August Schleicher had initiated the reconstruction of Proto-Indo-European linguistic forms, linguists had already begun to reconstruct the culture of its speakers. The same correspondences which demonstrated the affinity of the different Indo-European languages also pointed to the shared cultural content of the Proto-Indo-European vocabulary. The series of words for sheep seen in Luwian *ḫawi-*, Sanskrit *avis*, Greek *o(w)is*, Latin *ovis*, Lithuanian *avis*, Old Irish *oi* or English *ewe* provided ample proof that the Proto-Indo-European community knew the **owis* 'sheep'. It was from just such comparisons that Adalbert Kuhn, in 1845, attempted to produce a capsule description of Proto-Indo-European society. He described the culture of the original Indo-European speakers as settled (words for village, fort, house); engaged in both agriculture (grain) and stockbreeding (cattle, sheep, goat, pig, horse, dog); and politically evolved to the level of the state (king).

We have advanced far beyond Kuhn's first attempts, and a century and a half of lexico-cultural reconstruction has produced a vast amount of research including whole encyclopaedias of Indo-European culture. But any survey of these sources would soon make it clear that agreement on some issues is difficult to find. The reasons for this are sound, if not a bit daunting.

It is extremely uncommon, for example, for the majority of Indo-European languages to share the remnants of the same Proto-Indo-European word. Loss of the 'original' vocabulary seems to have been high and is especially likely to have affected languages only known in written form within the past 1,000–2,000 years. If this is the case, in how many different languages must the same word occur to be counted as a Proto-Indo-European word? There is really no wholly acceptable configuration of correspondences that may be utilized, although one general rule of thumb demands at least a shared correspondence between a European and a non-adjacent Asian language in order to attribute the word to high Indo-European antiquity. Others might assign different criteria such as correspondences from any three languages provided that at least one was not immediately adjacent to the others. For reasons that will become more obvious below, it is prudent to demand both a European and an Asian cognate.

A second problem frequently encountered is the variation in the meaning of a cognate word in various languages where it is far easier to reconstruct the original sound of the word than what it actually meant. When the Greek word for oak is the same as the Germanic word for beech and the Russian word for elder, on what grounds does one ascribe an original Proto-Indo-European meaning to the word?

Loan words pose another obvious problem, although by no means so great as some have imagined. In the history of Indo-European studies, there can always be found a few who challenge the entire validity of our lexico-cultural reconstructions since they maintain that it is impossible to know whether a particular word has been inherited from Proto-Indo-European into the various daughter languages or whether it has merely been borrowed from one language to another through time. All too frequently such warnings are capped with some example wherein the naïve linguist blunders into ascribing coffee, cigars and coca-cola to the Proto-Indo-Europeans because of the transparent similarity of these words in the modern European languages.

In a sense, any new word is a loan word which spreads from a single speaker or small group of individuals to all other speakers of a language. If these all converse in the same idiom, then the word will be accepted and pass for native. If, on the other hand, the word crosses a language border, it will be articulated according to the rules of the language borrowing the word. When this is different from the donor language, then one is often able to discern that it is a loan rather than inherited word. In English, for example, we have two words for cattle – *cow* and *bovine* – that we might wish to relate to similar words in other Indo-European languages. We could easily set our word *bovine* against the series that includes Greek *bous*, Latin *bos*, and Old Irish *bo* but we would never mistake it for the inherited English outcome of Proto-Indo-European $g^w ous$ since Proto-Indo-European g^w could never produce a *b* in English (nor would the ending of the word be explained). Only *cow* can be the inherited form, while bovine (and beef) are clearly loan words ultimately derived from Latin *bos/bovem*. Moreover, even *bos* is not the expected Latin outcome of the Proto-Indo-European word (which should have yielded something like **vos* in Latin), and so linguists regularly regard *bos* as a loan either from Umbrian where we do find the initial *b* (*bum*, cf. Latin *bovem*), or from some similar non-Latin dialect of Italy. Even when we are dealing with closely related languages such as Old Norse and Old English, we can discern the numerous Norse loan words in English, for example, egg, ugly, keel, sky, skill and many others. It it this ability to recognize when loan words are present that generally inspires in linguists the confidence to determine whether words are inherited from Proto-Indo-European or are later borrowings between already differentiated Indo-European languages. Indeed, linguists have devoted a substantial amount of research into identifying later loan words as a means of elucidating the contacts between the different Indo-European languages in prehistory. To take a familiar example, we can identify Celtic loan words for iron and lead in Germanic which fit neatly with the archaeological evidence that indicates contacts between Iron Age Celts and their northern neighbours. Similarly, the Germans also borrowed certain social terms, for example, ruler and servant, from their Celtic neighbours. This is not to say, of course, that there are not genuine difficulties in the analysis of some words, but historical linguists are not naïve in this and they bring to their data an arsenal of techniques which greatly reduces the chance of reconstructing nonsense within prehistory.[20]

Unfortunately, our confidence in the reconstruction of cultural items often tends to be inversely proportional to their archaeological utility. For example, while no one would doubt that the linguistic evidence indicates that the earliest Indo-Europeans knew the dog, it would be vastly more useful if we were certain whether they knew the eel, the turtle, the salmon, or other more geographically circumscribed species. The reason for our inability to recover with certainty some of these words lies embedded in the basic Indo-European hypothesis. An expansion of Indo-European speakers over a vast area took many of them out of their earlier environment so that they experienced radical changes in their cultural ecology before they emerged into history. By this time they had often abandoned those parts of their vocabulary that they no longer needed and the remaining trace of a particular Proto-Indo-European word may be left in only a handful of languages. These may be preserving an old inherited word, but they may also be later creations confined to a particular area of the Indo-European-speaking world. This is particularly true when we consider the contrast between the European and the Indo-Iranian languages.

If we employ the traditional procedure of not admitting a word as proto-Indo-European unless it has at least one European and one Asian reflex, then we must encounter the Indo-European fault line. The textual remains of Tocharian and the Anatolian languages offer only limited opportunities to evaluate the cultural content of the Indo-European languages of Asia. Indic and Iranian, on the other hand, provide us with a vast body of evidence but also with histories uniquely Asian and apparently essentially pastoral. For this reason we often find that words reflected in many European languages do not have a reflex in Indo-Iranian. Paul Friedrich, for example, presents us with no less than eighteen categories of Indo-European trees, but few of these find any reflex in either the Indic or Iranian languages. This has been a problem that has troubled linguists for well over a century and which has invariably been resolved in one of three ways. Some propose that the Europeans retained the Proto-Indo-European vocabulary and the Indo-Iranians moved off from a European homeland, losing many terms as they immigrated into their new Asian environments; alternatively, it was the Indo-Iranians who retained the inherited vocabulary while those peoples who moved west into Europe created new words in their new surroundings; finally, some would propose a homeland large enough for both branches to encompass a great variety of economies and environments. For the present it will be better to hold all of these mutually conflicting theories in the backs of our minds and preclude no solution to the homeland problem. Rather, let us take a brief survey of the more important elements of the reconstructed Proto-Indo-European culture.

Environment

The physical environment of the Indo-Europeans offers us few clues as to where they were situated. They knew both plains and mountains, rivers and lakes. The weather vacillated enough to give them words for hot and cold, including snow and ice. Only three seasons – winter, spring and summer – are reconstructible, with a word for autumn lying beyond our powers to recover. This evidence has repeatedly been pressed to demonstrate more about the Proto-Indo-European environment and economy than the weight of the comparisons can carry. It is unequivocally true that winter is the best-attested season and that summer is reasonably well reconstructed. The word for spring appears to be a somewhat later linguistic formation and consequently some have argued for an environment that sees a rapid transition between summer and winter, that is, a more southerly environment. The absence of an autumn and therefore of a harvest season, has also been embraced by those who imagine the ancient Indo-European peoples to have been pastoralists rather than agriculturalists who would surely have maintained a word for this season. Since British and American English do not commonly agree on the name for autumn (or fall), it would be more than risky to put too much credit on such arguments.

The word for sea is perhaps one of the more problematic. That a word existed (*mori) is most certain. However, it seems originally to have meant swamp, marsh land or lake, rather than a larger body of open water. In addition, it is found only in European languages and not in Indo-Iranian other than Ossetic – an Iranian language contiguous to Europe although originating further to the east. Some have argued then that the Indo-European community did not originally live near the sea – which sea, of course, was the primary issue since such an hypothesis would deny both the Baltic and Black Seas, possibly the Caspian or indeed any large body of water. On reflection, it should seem obvious that this argument is a logical embarrassment since one would be hard pressed to set a people down anywhere in Eurasia without finding some large body of water conveniently situated to cry out for a name.

The botanical evidence for the Proto-Indo-European environment is what interests us most here. Armed with quaternary pollen diagrams, we should be able to employ this evidence to delimit the area of the Proto-Indo-European community and learn something of the arboreal culture of the earliest Indo-Europeans. Naturally, any method so elegant and simple in concept is generally impossible to execute.

A survey of the standard Indo-European handbooks reveals that anywhere from three to eighteen trees have been reconstructed for the Proto-Indo-European landscape. The main problem here lies in the paucity of cognate names in any of the Asiatic languages and the abundance of correspondence that can be found in the European languages. If we adhere to the rule that there must be at least one cognate in Europe and one in Asia, then our conception of the Proto-Indo-European forest must, of necessity, be limited. The birch is perhaps the best attested, and one may suggest that its peculiar and useful bark is the reason for its retention in six language groups. The willow would also meet the minimum requirements and its lexical association with words indicative of intertwining suggests that one of its uses was in the production of osiers for plaiting such things as baskets. The elm could be Proto-Indo-European and here we have a tree whose use would probably include foddering livestock. Ash, another possible Proto-Indo-European term, is often associated with words meaning 'spear shaft' which indicate one of its main uses. If one accepts a certain amount of special pleading concerning the root *doru-, which normally means tree but sometimes specifically oak, then this tree should also be set to the Proto-Indo-European landscape. To omit it is difficult given its overall utility as fodder, a source for wooden tools, its use in architecture and its association with the religion of many Indo-European peoples. Perhaps somewhat less solid are attempts to assign the yew and the pine to Proto-Indo-European. The former is also found mixed with terms for archery in a number of languages and is sometimes associated with ritual or legalistic functions.

What can we say from such a collection of trees? Actually, very little, since they are all reasonably at home over most areas of the northern hemisphere and can be found widely in temperate Europe, the Caucasus, Siberia and Asia Minor. Only in areas such as Central Asia and the east Caspian would they appear to be less at home, or in areas further to the south.

Not included in the list of Proto-Indo-European trees is the most celebrated arboreal item of the Indo-European homeland problem, the beech. We can reconstruct a *bhaǵos on the basis of words in five different groups. But the Germanic (Old Norse *bok*) and Latin (*fagus*) forms mean 'beech' while the Slavic (Russian *buzina*) indicates 'elder', and Albanian (*bunge*) and Doric Greek (*phagos*) mean 'oak'. The importance of the word lies in the fact that the beech was traditionally confined west of a line (the famous 'beech line') from Königsberg (the Baltic) to Odessa on the Black Sea. Such a distribution effectively excluded a Proto-Indo-European home set on the Russian or Asiatic steppe. Naturally, without an Asiatic cognate this argument was refuted by those who asserted that it was a late European term, not a Proto-Indo-European word. Then, an apparent cognate was discovered in Kurdish (*buz*), a clearly Asiatic language of the Iranian branch, which supported a Proto-Indo-

European acquaintance with the beech. This was later overturned when the Kurdish form was shown not to be cognate with the word for beech, but rather with the elm (*myg-). Even if we admit to a Proto-Indo-European 'beech', late holocene pollen diagrams show that the beech extended as far east as the Don river and that another species of beech spanned the Caucasus, thus robbing the term of much of its geographical utility.[21]

Against all of this is a series of fair to excellent European cognates for the juniper, poplar, apple, maple, alder, hazel, nut, linden, hornbeam and cherry. This provides us with the classic conundrum: was the homeland in a heavily forested zone and did the Asiatic Indo-Europeans abandon their arboreal terms as they moved through steppe and desert, or was the homeland set in a very thinly wooded area and it is the Europeans who have innovated? Alternatively, did the homeland straddle both forest and steppe or desert zones? If we could answer those questions, the present book would take a distinctly different approach from the one it does. In any event, it is clear from the wild animals known to the Proto-Indo-European communities, that the environment must have included some tree cover.

More than a hint of forests comes through our survey of the wild mammals known to the Proto-Indo-European speakers. Reasonably solid reconstructions provide us with the otter and beaver, the wolf, bear, lynx, elk, red deer, hare, hedgehog, mouse and possibly roe deer. Without at least riverine forests we could not explain the retention of names such as the beaver and the otter, while the bear, red deer and elk also indicate that the setting was certainly not entirely confined to the open steppe or desert.

The names of the Indo-European birds pose a particular problem for the linguist since they are often imitative of the actual calls of the birds. One of the most obvious examples can be seen in the series: Sanskrit *kokila-*, Greek *kokkyx*, Latin *cuculus*, Lithuanian *kukuoti*, Russian *kukusa*, Middle Irish *cuach*, and English *cuckoo*, in which the root *kuku* is so clearly onomatopoeic that one cannot entirely trust the results of such comparisons. The birds most commonly reconstructed to Proto-Indo-European include the eagle and possibly some other large bird of prey. In addition, the goose, crane and duck are also all attested in the strict sense, and we may note how all of these require a habitat in or near water. Less certain are the more clearly onomatopoeic names of the hen, owl, hoopoe and crow.

If we turn now to fish, the quantity of names shrinks abruptly and forms great controversy. A Proto-Indo-European *loksos* has frequently played a part in delimiting the Indo-European homeland, since it has often been taken to mean exclusively the salmon (*Salmo salar*) which would pitch the Indo-Europeans into the drainages of the Baltic Sea. But there is fairly sound evidence that the word is more likely to have referred to the salmon trout and hence is of no great geographical utility. The second term, the eel, is also of questionable status (linguistically) and has similarly been employed to exclude the Pontic-Caspian region. Even if admitted, one may note that the eel actually does frequent the major rivers of the Pontic up to the Sea of Azov. Furthermore, a correspondence between Sanskrit *saphara* and Lithuanian *sapalas* provides the minimum requirement for a Proto-Indo-European fish, possibly belonging to the carp family. Two Proto-Indo-European words for fish itself also exist, and Eric Hamp has suggested that one of them, *$p(e)ik$-sk 'the speckled one', derives from the denotation of the trout.

Among reptiles and amphibians, the snake is the best reconstructed but this is of almost no value since there is no possibility of specifying what type of snake. The turtle has occupied a slightly controversial place. It is not *sensu stricto* Proto-Indo-European but has been employed to exclude certain areas of Europe such as Scandinavia. Even if admitted to Proto-Indo-European it still would not delimit an area any smaller than most of Eurasia. We can reconstruct words for both bee and honey. The native distribution of the honey-bee covers most of Europe and North Asia but excludes the desert and steppe regions to the east of the Caspian and Aral Seas. A Proto-Indo-European *$wobhsa$ 'wasp' is reconstructed from seven different language groups.

If we try to draw the environmental evidence together and eschew as much prejudice towards particular theories as we can, we arrive at a landscape which included some trees and certainly enough to provide forest environments for a number of wild mammals. A river-bank or lake-side orientation is discerned from some of the animals and birds, although in terms of prehistoric settlement this is hardly surprising. That a number of the trees such as birch and willow are so closely linked with temperate climates does suggest a region of at least seasonally cold temperatures. Beyond this we cannot fairly go other than to conclude that to set the Proto-Indo-Europeans exclusively in the open steppe (and not forest steppe or river valleys), or in a desert region, would seem to be incongruous with the Proto-Indo-European vocabulary.

Economy

That the subsistence economy of Proto-Indo-European society was based on stockbreeding with some agriculture is impossible to deny. Indeed, some of the most widely and best-attested words in the Indo-European languages are those which concern domestic animals, and, of these, words relating to cattle are probably among the most prolific.

Cattle raising is well embedded in the Proto-Indo-European vocabulary, with no less than three basic terms – cow, ox and steer – all attested within the strict sense. In addition, secondary products such as butter, and possibly some form of cheese, can also be attributed to the Proto-Indo-European vocabulary although these terms may relate to the products of sheep or goats as well. The same may also be said for Proto-Indo-European words for meat, marrow and herd. The use of oxen for traction is suggested by the reconstructed terms for yoke and plough, and, as we shall later see, wheeled vehicles would most likely have been drawn by oxen at the time of the earliest Indo-Europeans.[22] The importance of cattle is also reflected in a frozen expression 'to drive cattle', generally used in the sense of cattle raiding and found in Celtic, Italic and Indo-

Iranian. Finally, the cow as a special beast of sacrifice is indicated by the Sanskrit-Greek correspondence of the word for the special sacrifice of 'one hundred cows'.

Sheep are also spectacularly well attested in the Indo-European languages with cognates in no less than nine major language groups. Their function in the economy certainly included wool, as both this word and a word for weaving are attested. More problematic is their traditional association with the word for wealth where we find a Proto-Indo-European *pek̑- (to comb) frequently associated with *pek̑u- (livestock, possessions). It has long been regarded as reasonable that there was an irreversible semantic development that led from a word 'to comb' and a noun 'sheep' (the woolly animal) to livestock in general and finally to wealth, hence German *Vieh* 'cattle' and English *fee*. More recently, however, this was challenged by the late Emile Benveniste who argued that the semantic development should indeed be reversed and begin with a concept of 'movable possessions' which, under the influence of later cultural developments, was gradually specified to sheep. Whatever one's position on this debate, it would be wise not to read into the linguistic evidence any case for the economic primacy of sheep in Indo-European society and to note only their clearly evidenced presence and their utility as wool-bearing animals.

The goat has posed perennial problems for linguists since its lexical correspondences tend to be between only a few languages and are not nearly so well attested as sheep. Nevertheless, there are sufficient correspondences to grant it Proto-Indo-European status and, indeed, it would be difficult to imagine a stockbreeding regime in Eurasia that did not employ both sheep and goat, although the goat might well have been secondary in importance. It is associated with words for hides which provides at least one index of its function, and dairy products may also be expected.

The pig has been a major issue of economic reconstruction since, unlike the other livestock, it permits more specific economic and environmental conclusions. For those who imagine the Proto-Indo-European economy to have been that of pastoral nomads, then the domestic pig should have occupied the same position of anathema among the Indo-Europeans as it does among Semitic speakers. On the other hand, for those who imagine that the Indo-European community had a settled agricultural economy, the pig was one indication of stability since it is an animal that is normally excluded from any regime of pastoral nomadism. The linguistic evidence for 'pig' is unequivocal as a Proto-Indo-European *su- is found widely (English *swine*, Latin *sus*, Indic *su-*). The term seemed to refer to the pig generically, and the Indo-Iranian terms were specifically applied to the wild pig. It is possible to imagine, therefore, that the underlying meaning of the word was a wild pig. This opposes the other reconstructible word, *pork̑o-*, which is clearly associated with domestic pigs but limited in its distribution to the European languages. The convenient explanation for this state of affairs is that the Proto-Indo-European community was acquainted with the wild pig but only upon the migration of its European branches into the settled agricultural regimes of Europe did some of them acquire a word for the domestic pig. Alternatively, of course, one might argue for the disappearance of the *porko- among nomadic Indo-Iranians as they migrated from their European homes. Fortunately, neither of these arguments is necessary since Benveniste has demonstrated that the automatic ascription of *su- to a wild pig is not justified because it is applied exclusively to the domestic animal in the European languages. Furthermore, linguists discovered reflexes of *porko- in Indo-Iranian. Today, therefore, it would be difficult to deny the domestic pig a place in the Proto-Indo-European economy and the opposition of *su and *porko is interpreted not as that between a wild Proto-Indo-European and a domestic European species but as between the name of the adult and young form of the domestic species.

That the horse was known to the Proto-Indo-European community is undeniable as can be seen from the impressive series of correspondences: Hieroglyphic Luwian a-su-wa; Mitanni a-as-su-us-sa-an-ni 'horse trainer'; Sanskrit asva; Avestan aspa-; Tocharian A yuk; Tocharian B yakwe; Mycenaean i-qo; Greek hippos; Latin equus; Venetic eku-; Old English eoh; Gaulish epo-; Old Irish ech, while Lithuanian retains the feminine asva 'mare'. As all of these words regularly indicate a domestic horse, linguists are generally agreed that the Proto-Indo-European *ekwos 'horse' was also domesticated. It is not only widely attested in the Indo-European languages but it is about the only animal name to figure prominently in the personal names of the earliest Indo-Europeans, for example, the Indic Asva-cakra, Old Persian Vist-aspa, Greek Hipp-arkhos and Phil-ippos, Gaulish Epo-pennus and Old English Eo-maer. Moreover, the word is also extended to deities such as the divine twins of Indic religion, the Asvins, and the Gaulish goddess Epona. We will later examine its role in Indo-European mythology and ritual, but for now we merely emphasize the degree to which the domestic horse is embedded in the culture of the earliest Indo-Europeans. Problematic is the fact that in many areas of Eurasia where the domestic horse first appears there were also wild horses present, and there is no relict of a lexical opposition between the wild and domestic horse.

Finally, the word for 'dog' is comfortably and uncontroversially ascribed to the Proto-Indo-European vocabulary and, because of the linguistically archaic structure of the word, it is attributed to the earliest layer of the vocabulary as one might expect from the first domesticated animal.[23]

Although lexical correspondences across all Indo-European languages for livestock are easily found, the vocabulary related to agriculture is somewhat more limited. One commonly accepted word for an unspecified 'grain' is attributable to Proto-Indo-European in the strict sense along with words for 'to sow' and for some form of grinding instrument such as a quern stone. The word for field *agros is well attested, but whereas in the European languages it designates a cultivated area, in Indo-Iranian it refers only to an open plain. Words for both plough and sickle, however, can be solidly reconstructed to Proto-Indo-European. A much larger common agricultural vocabulary is to be found confined to the languages of Europe. Here we find many words associated with agriculture – ploughshare, seed, grain, mill, furrow, barley and millet. And, of course, the usual opposition between an agricultural west and a pastoral, nomadic east has frequently been given as the explanation for this dichotomy, with the attendant arguments for lexical loss or innovation depending on where one wishes to locate the Indo-European homeland. For our purposes it will be best to limit our conclusions to the observation that, on the basis of the available lexical residue, at least some agriculture, including the plough, was known to the Proto-Indo-European community; we can go no further than that until we have seen evidence for the rest of the cultural vocabulary.

Settlement

Most of the terms concerning settlement and architecture are so generic that they do not offer anything but the vaguest image of a Proto-Indo-European settlement. Words for house, post, door and door-post are all reasonably well founded. The correspondence between Sanskrit *vraja* 'hurdle' and Old Irish *fraig* 'wattled wall' has indicated to some that we may imagine walls constructed from wattling while associated words for wall, clay and dough suggest the use of daub. A common word for hearth is also attested.

When we go beyond the basic sphere of habitation to larger constructs we move into a more interesting but also more debatable region. Cognates derived from Proto-Indo-European **w(e)ik̑-* are found across a number of languages with meanings as circumscribed as house (Greek *(w)oikos*) to village (Latin *vicus*, Gothic *weihs*) and clan (Indic *vis-*). On the basis of this one might assemble the meanings together and derive them from a word which designated a small settlement whose members were related – anything from a body of houses belonging to an extended family up to a clan.[24]

Finally, we have a common word for a fortified enclosure seen in such diverse languages as Sanskrit *pur*, Greek *polis* and Lithuanian *pilis*. Although the meaning of some of these words evolved into that of 'city', their original reference to merely a fortified high place is reasonably secure (Greek *akropolis* 'high fort'), and we may imagine that some form of fortified settlement or refuge existed in the Proto-Indo-European landscape.

Technology

A variety of words for different types of pots and bowls are reconstructible to Proto-Indo-European and are seen in such comparisons as Sanskrit *caru*, Old Irish *coire* and Old Norse *hverr*, although it must be admitted that the lexical reconstructions fall far short of the type of description which might prove useful to the archaeologist. Only the correspondence between the Tocharian expression *tseke . . . peke* and Latin *fingo . . . pingo*, 'I form . . . I paint', has been pressed to the conclusion that the Indo-Europeans employed painted pottery, a conclusion by no means guaranteed by such meagre evidence.

The vocabulary of metallurgy is poorly and controversially represented. The primary utilitarian metal would appear to be that ancestral to the series Sanskrit *ayas* 'metal, iron'; Latin *aes* 'bronze'; Old Norse *eir* 'bronze, copper'; and English *ore*. Generally, the fundamental meaning of the word has been taken to indicate 'copper', and the meanings 'bronze' and 'iron' have been seen as later semantic developments. While the time-scales involved with Proto-Indo-European would certainly seem to preclude 'iron', they do not necessarily exclude 'bronze' as the original referent. But the absence of any common words for tin in the Indo-European languages might support the exclusion of bronze from Proto-Indo-European culture unless, of course, the Proto-Indo-European **ayes* was imported bronze and the technique of its manufactures was unknown to the earliest Indo-Europeans. A second word for copper, apparently related to the Proto-Indo-European root **reudh* 'red', is also known, but here its similarity to Sumerian *urud* 'copper' has led to much speculation about cultural relations between the Indo-Europeans and the Sumerians or possibly an intermediate party. Finally, cognate words for whetstone in Sanskrit, Greek and Germanic also suggest the use of metals by the Proto-Indo-European community.

There are two possibilities for precious metals, both of which are hampered by their derivation from roots so productive and so obvious that one is not certain that they were not independent formations rather than relics of an ancestral word. Gold, for example, is closely linked with words meaning bright or yellow, while silver is clearly derived from the word for white. Total certainty about these metals is difficult to find, although a strong case can be made for the Proto-Indo-European community having been acquainted with silver.

We have already seen that secondary technologies associated with agriculture and stock-breeding were known to the Proto-Indo-Europeans. There is certainly sufficient evidence to indicate sewing, spinning and weaving of wool. In addition to wool, the Proto-Indo-Europeans knew hemp, and a word for flax or linen is shared among most European languages. The linguistic evidence tells us little about the appearance of Proto-Indo-European clothes (**wes-*) other than that the word for belt (**yos-*) can be attributed to the earliest Indo-Europeans. The grinding of grain, and the yoking of animals for traction, are evident in the correspondence of Sanskrit *yugam*, Greek *zygon*, Latin *jugum*, English *yoke* and other cognates. The Indic and Greek correspondence clearly indicates a yoked pair of animals, and we may have to do with either the plough or, more interestingly from a cultural-historical perspective, wheeled vehicles.

One of the more noteworthy areas of the Proto-Indo-European cultural lexicon is that concerning wagon terminology. It includes several words for wheel, as well as one for axle, and another for nave. Beyond these generic terms we are helpless in trying to recover a more specific image of the construction or appearance of the Proto-Indo-European cart or wagon but, as we shall see later, its mere existence proves to be an extremely important cultural marker.[25]

In addition to land transport, there also exists the clear series of cognates: Sanskrit *naus*, Greek *naus*, Latin *navis*, Old Irish *nau*, and so on, which indicate the existence of a Proto-Indo-European *nau- 'boat'. Means of propulsion is limited to a set of cognates indicating oars.

With regard to Proto-Indo-European weaponry, the most unequivocal reconstructions concern the bow, bowstring and arrow, all of which support the existence of archery within the Proto-Indo-European community. A thrusting weapon such as a dagger is usually postulated on the basis of the cognates Sanskrit *asis* 'sword' and Latin *ensis* 'sword'. Here again, we are confronted with meanings which appear to be too recent to project back into the Proto-Indo-European community without assuming that the name of some thrusting weapon later developed into the word for sword in Sanskrit and Latin. Alternatively, it has been suggested that the root *nsi- meant only 'black' and that we have before us merely parallel developments in Sanskrit and Latin for an iron tool or weapon.

Finally, one might have expected that the Proto-Indo-Europeans would have left us with better evidence for their word for axe. As it is we have three different terms of varying degrees of controversy. Tomas Gamkrelidze and Vyachislav Ivanov cite the comparison of Hittite *ates-*, Old English *adesa* and possibly Sanskrit *-adhiti*, all indicating an axe. There is also the notorious correspondence between Greek *pelekeus* and Sanskrit *parasu-* which are traditionally compared with Akkadian *pillaq-*. The Akkadian word actually means 'spindle' and 'spike'. This word has very probably been borrowed into Greek and Indo-Iranian from a foreign source and everything about the structure of the word suggests that it is not a native Proto-Indo-European word. The last possible term is the perplexing series of cognates associated with Proto-Indo-European *akmon. It is perplexing because the same word yields both the meaning of stone (and hammer) and sky. Hans Reichelt attempted to explain this double meaning by postulating an Indo-European belief in the sky as a stone vault. More recently, J. Peter Maher has proceeded from the underlying root meaning of *ak 'sharp' to suggest that the word originally indicated a sharp thing, that is, an axe, which would naturally have been fashioned from stone (Maher had in mind the classic 'battle-axes' of the Corded Ware culture). The same word also provided the basis for terms referring to sky and hammers or missiles, frequently associated with Indo-European thunder gods. This complex of seemingly unrelated meanings is resolved along the same lines known to anyone familiar with the history of early antiquarian studies. As late as the eighteenth century there were still scholars who persisted in the common folk-belief that stone axes were the residue of thunderbolts (hence thunderbolts, elf-shot in English or Donnerkeil in German). This, Maher maintained, was merely the retention of earlier Indo-European beliefs that metaphorically associated axes with phenomena such as thunder and lightning.

Social Organization

There is a sort of horrible irony in the fact that, while modern archaeologists are greatly interested in reconstructing the social systems of prehistoric peoples, historical linguists offer the archaeologists such detailed reconstructions that they are still beyond archaeological retrieval even when we know what to look for. Nothing can make years of attempts to recover social systems on the basis of detailed studies of mortuary evidence appear so futile as to be informed by a linguist that the Proto-Indo-European community appears to have employed an Omaha-type kinship system, since no one knows what this should look like 'on the ground'. All linguistic evidence suggests that Proto-Indo-European society was patrilineal in descent and male dominated according to that much-overworked term patriarchal. We lack a common term for husband or wife although we can recover a Proto-Indo-European *widhewa 'widow'. We cannot reconstruct a common word for marriage for Proto-Indo-European; but as we have seen, many Indo-European languages do employ the same Proto-Indo-European verb *wedh- 'to lead (home)' when expressing the act of becoming married, from the groom's point of view. This suggests that the residence rules of the Proto-Indo-Europeans involved the woman going to live in the house of her husband or with his family.

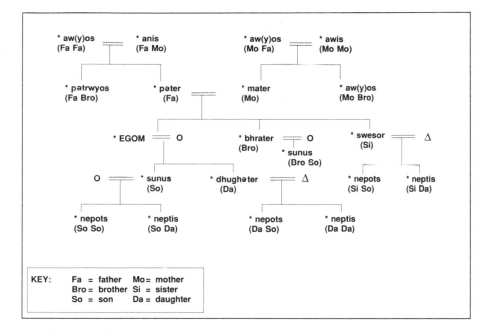

*73 Proto-Indo-European kinship terms reconstructed according to the Omaha system. One of the characteristics of the Omaha system is the skewing of generations where the same term is used for both grandfather and mother's brother, e.g., *aw(y)os: Hittite huhhas 'FaFa, MoFa', Armenian hav 'FaFa, MoFa', Old Church Slavonic uj 'MoBro', Old Prussian awis 'MoBro', Latin auus 'FaFa, MoFa', Old Icelandic afi 'FaFa, MoFa', Old Irish aue 'grSo'; reciprocally, the same term is proposed for grandchild and nephew, e.g., *nepots: Sanskrit napat 'grSo, descendant', Avestan napa 'grSo, descendant', Greek nepous 'descendant', Albanian nip 'grSo, nephew', Old Church Slavonic netii 'SiSo', Lithuanian nepuotis 'grSo, SiSo', Old English nefa 'grSo, SiSo', Latin nepos 'grSo, SiSo, SiDaSo', Old Irish nie 'SiSo', and Cornish nie 'grSo, nephew'. The reconstruction of the underlying Proto-Indo-European meanings are by no means universally agreed and many linguists argue that some meanings such as 'nephew' for *nepots were actually very late developments in the individual Indo-European languages and not inherited from the proto-language.*

Among the kinship relations, the roles of the mother's brother and the corresponding sister's son is of especial interest. The basic linguistic forms appear to be *aw(y)os for both the mother's father and mother's brother and *nepots for both grandson and sister's son, a pattern that some argue is congruent with the skewing of generations found in the Omaha system.[26] Throughout the Indo-European world we observe a well-known pattern of behaviour predictable from the kinship structure of the Indo-European languages. In general, the father occupies the role of stern disciplinarian as do father's brothers who, in a patrilineal system, are all competing for positions of authority over their younger kinsmen (and potential competitors). On the other hand, in a patrilineal system the maternal uncle is outside the lineage and his behaviour is generally that of both an affectionate and friendly counsellor. It is in this light that the statement of Tacitus on the early Germans, 'A sister's sons are considered to be related to her brothers as nearly as to their own father', and other historical references, are to be understood. It follows naturally, then, that as a man would have an especially close relationship with his own maternal uncle, similarly he would occupy the same role towards his sister's sons, the Proto-Indo-European *nepots. Beyond this particular pattern of behaviour, it has also been suggested that fosterage outside one's own family appears to be strongly associated with this same pattern: for example, Beowulf is raised by his maternal grandfather; the Irish champion Cú Chulainn is fostered by his maternal uncle Conchobor; Roland and Charlemagne, and so on. As we will see in the next chapter, this particular relationship of *nepots to uncle received special elaboration in Indo-European mythology.

Beyond the family, several institutions appear. One is the clan, and its leader (*weik-potis) is seen in the striking comparison between Avestan vispaitis 'clan-chief, household chief', and Lithuanian viespats 'lord', formerly 'clan-chief', together with its very nontransparent Albanian cognate zot 'lord'. But beyond the level of the clan it is more difficult to proceed confidently. We do know that in ancient Iran the tribe was designated the zantu, a word with impeccable Indo-European origins and coming from the same root which yields words like Latin gens 'race, tribe', Old Norse kind 'follower', and English kin but here we speak of identity of root and not of word and it is impossible to know whether we are dealing with an inherited word for tribe or not.

Two terms seem to be associated with some form of military organization. The most familiar derives from Proto-Indo-European *teuta- which is reflected in the Persian word for mob (toda) but is translated more generally as 'people' in Oscan touto, Old Irish tuath, Latvian tauta, Old High German diota (whence Deutsch), arguably Hittite tuzzi-, and in personal names recorded among the Greeks, Illyrians and Gauls. Furthermore, there is the correspondence of Hittite lahha- 'campaign', Mycenaean ra-wa-ke-ta (lawagetas) 'commander', Greek la(w)os 'people under arms' and Phrygian lawagtaei 'commander'. To what extent either of these terms can be extrapolated back into Proto-Indo-European society to indicate war-bands or more abstract conceptualizations of the people under arms is debatable. Nevertheless, few would deny that this evidence indicates the existence of some form of military institution among the earliest Indo-Europeans. The vocabulary of strife is also seen in a Proto-Indo-European word for blood revenge or blood payment which is attested in Avestan and Greek.

The apex of Proto-Indo-European society, according to the standard handbooks of Indo-European culture, was ruled by a king whose title has usually been secured by the textbook series: Sanskrit *raj*, Latin *rex*, Gaulis *rix*, Old Irish *ri*, and possibly Thracian *Rhesos*. It has been assumed that this Proto-Indo-European **rēǵ-* was not necessarily the secular ruler whom one might normally envisage. Linguists have argued that the root of the noun is **reǵ* which provides such meanings as stretch, draw out in a straight line, and straighten. Our English word right is a reflex of this root, and the same opposition which we employ between what is straight or right and what is bent or crooked, that is, dishonest or wrong, is encountered throughout the Indo-European languages (see Chapter Five). Jan Gonda and Emile Benveniste sought in the basic etymology of the word a hint of the original function of the Proto-Indo-European **reǵ-*. Gonda suggested that the word meant one who stretches or reaches out, a metaphor for the formal activities of a king who is often depicted in Indo-European tradition as fulfilling his duties with outstretched arms. Benveniste argued that the fundamental meaning was 'one who determined what was right'. This suggested a leader who was more concerned with maintaining social and moral order than a secular sovereign exerting coercive power over his subjects or leading them in battle. Indeed, Benveniste proposed that there may have been more overtly priestly functions associated with the Proto-Indo-European king in that the root meaning of 'stretching out' or 'straightening' might be associated with duties such as laying out limits, be they demarcations of sacred territory within a settlement, the settlement itself or the borders of national territories.

This whole concept of Proto-Indo-European kings has recently been challenged. First, Andrew Sihler has argued that the underlying root is not 'to arrange in a straight line' but 'be efficacious, have mana'. Then Hartmut Scharfe reviewed the Vedic evidence, our only body of material providing an Asiatic cognate, to discover that the word *raj* in the earliest Vedic texts was not the masculine noun meaning king but a feminine noun indicating 'strength, power'. If this is accepted, then we no longer have evidence for Proto-Indo-European kings, and our testimony is limited to Celtic and Italic, two languages which share numerous similarities and which suggest a particular political development among some late Indo-European groups of Western Europe. Scharfe does observe that the correspondence between Sanskrit *rajan-* and Greek *aregon* suggests a Proto-Indo-European word for 'protector' or 'person with power or charisma', but not 'king'. The highest socio-political level that Scharfe attributes to the Proto-Indo-Europeans is our **weiḱ-potis* 'the master of the clan' which we have already reviewed above.

We must also take a brief glance at that most loaded of Indo-European words – Aryan. As an ethnic designation, the word is most properly limited to the

Indo-Iranians, and most justly to the latter where it still gives its name to the country Iran (from the Avestan genitive plural a*iryanam* through later Iranian *eran* to *iran*). The great Persian king Darius described himself as Aryan. The term was also used widely in India where it referred to one who was a member of the community (though details of who was included in the community have been the topic of wide and unsettled debate). Whether this ethnic designation was limited to the Indo-Iranians or not is difficult to say. A possible cognate occurs in Hittite, for example, where it indicates 'kinsman, friend', and there also appears here the negative expression *natta ara* 'not proper to the community', that is, 'not done'. Although some claim that this root can be found in the names of many other Indo-European peoples, for example, Irish *Eriu* and *aire*, this would require more argument than is worth the effort and we are safer to remain with the general consensus that it does not rather than to pursue this matter further.[27]

Conclusion

Our review of Proto-Indo-European culture omits volumes that have been written about the reconstructed vocabulary, since much falls either under the category of predictable phenomena or else under items not readily retrievable by the prehistorian from any source other than language. Day, night, earth, sky, clouds, sun, moon and star can all be found in the reconstructed Proto-Indo-European vocabulary. We may be confident that the Proto-Indo-Europeans were physically similar to us and that many of their anatomical parts are linguistically retrievable through the comparison of the Indo-European languages. Indeed, it is bizarre recompense to the scholar struggling to determine whether the Proto-Indo-Europeans were acquainted with some extremely diagnostic item of material culture only to find that they were far more obliging in passing on to us no less than two words for 'breaking wind'. English dictionaries may occasionally shrink from including such vulgar terms as 'fart' but the word gains status when set within the series: Sanskrit *pardate*, Greek *perdo*, Lithuanian *perdzu*, Russian *perdet'*, Albanian *pjerdh* 'to fart loudly' (distinguished from Proto-Indo-European **pezd-* 'to break wind softly').

Turning to more crucial matters, we can see that the presence of words for pottery, domestic animals and agriculture in the Proto-Indo-European lexicon argues that the community was at least Neolithic and that it would be senseless to assign the Proto-Indo-Europeans to the earlier hunter-gatherer societies of the Mesolithic. Moreover, we encounter in the Proto-Indo-European vocabulary not only words that one associates with the original 'Neolithic Revolution' but also the lexical residue of what Andrew Sherratt has termed a later 'Secondary Products Revolution'. These include the secondary uses and products of domestic animals which can be seen in dairy products, wool and textiles, wheeled vehicles, yokes, ploughs and the domestic horse. Sherratt suggests that these secondary products only emerged in Europe several thousand years after the initial appearance of the Neolithic economy.

When we consider the most recent terms of the inherited Indo-European vocabulary, most are not evidenced in Eurasia prior to the fourth millennium BC. The earliest wheeled vehicles are clearly a fourth-millennium phenomenon whether they be initially found in Mesopotamia, the Caucasus, the Pontic-Caspian steppe or along the Danube. The horse appears to have been first domesticated about the beginning of the fourth millennium and such metals as silver are rarely found anywhere in Eurasia prior to the fourth millennium BC. Since caution teaches us that the evidence gained from future excavations will most probably increase the antiquity of any invention, we might then assign a notional date of about 4500 BC as the earliest probable time for the culture reconstructed from the inherited vocabulary of the Indo-European languages. We have already seen from our review of the evidence for the earliest Indo-Europeans in the historical record that a terminal date for the Proto-Indo-Europeans would be set not much later than 2500 BC, possibly somewhat earlier. In the broadest terms then, the Proto-Indo-Europeans were a Late Neolithic or Eneolithic society which began to diverge about 4500 to 2500 BC.[28] This is the time-frame we will employ when we embark on our quest to discover the homeland of the Indo-Europeans. But first we must review yet one more source of cultural information that might offer an insight into the nature of Proto-Indo-European society. We need to examine briefly the massive evidence for the religion and mythology of the Indo-Europeans.

CHAPTER FIVE

Indo-European Religion

The oldest religious rites of Indo-European
peoples do not presuppose temples or idols. Nor
is there a reconstructible term for 'temple'. But
there is a 'worship', conceived as a hospitable
reception with a meal, consisting of slaughtered
animals, and accompanying recitation of poetry,
the 'celestials' coming, as it were, on a visit to
the 'earthly ones'.

PAUL THIEME, 1964

In what did the Proto-Indo-Europeans believe, or, to use their own words, to
what did they 'put their hearts'? This archaic expression is still preserved in a
roundabout way in English where the Latin verb *credo* 'I believe' has been
borrowed to fashion our English *creed*. This word finds cognates in Old Irish
cretim, the Hittite *karatan dai*, Indic *srad-dha* and Avestan *zrazda-*. Admittedly
with some linguistic difficulty, the Proto-Indo-European expression appears to
have been built from the words for heart (**kerd-*) and put (**dhe*). In order to
examine the ideology of the Proto-Indo-Europeans we will require access not
only to the direct evidence of the reconstructed vocabulary but also to the less-
tangible evidence of the myths of the various Indo-European peoples. As Indo-
European mythology has attracted an enormous volume of scholarly interest,
we will prune the subject down by concentrating our attention primarily where
the evidence for Indo-European religion may tell us something of the ritual
behaviour and structure of Proto-Indo-European society.

Although philologists have long been interested in the religion of the ancient
Indo-Europeans, the results produced by the type of linguistic reconstruction
we employed in the last chapter are neither numerous nor always particularly
solid. One of the more obvious correspondences can be seen in the similarity of
Sanskrit *devas*, Latin *deus*, Lithuanian *dievas*, Old Irish *dia* and the Old Norse
plural *tivar* 'gods'. In addition, there is that most striking of all comparisons:

	sky	father
Sanskrit	dyaus	pita
Greek	zeu	pater
Latin	Ju	piter
Umbrian	Iuve	patre
Illyrian	Dei	patyros
Hittite	ᴰSius	—
Proto-Indo-European	*dyeus	pəter

Although we can produce a fairly facile translation of Proto-Indo-European *dyeus pater* as 'Father Sky', we cannot be confident that we understand the role of this god in the religion of the Proto-Indo-European community. Some would doubt that 'father' here connoted a progenitor of gods or man but rather, as has long been argued, that it signalled only the type of authority which one associates with the Latin *paterfamilias*. Secondly, we find this same god at the apex of some Indo-European religions such as Greek and Roman, but of less obvious importance in others such as Indic. Some have regarded the ascendancy of 'Father Sky' in the Mediterranean to have been a relatively recent phenomenon involving the conflation of an earlier Proto-Indo-European god with local Mediterranean weather/storm deities.

Most other lexical correspondences tend to be associated with predictable natural phenomena. For example, a sun-god (or goddess) is normally postulated on the correspondence of Sanskrit *Surya*, Gaulish *Sulis*, Lithuanian *Saule*, Germanic *Sol* and the Slavic *Tsar Solnitse*. Furthermore, we may reconstruct common names for moon and dawn, both of which appear as divine figures in various Indo-European religions. A somewhat more difficult correspondence may conceal a thunder- or rain-god behind the debatable comparison of the Indic rain-god *Parjanyas*, Lithuanian *Perkunas*, Slavic *Perun*' and the Norse *Fjörgyn*, the mother of Thor whose credentials as a thunder-god hardly need defending.

With such correspondences it is small wonder that many Indo-Europeanists were content to view the Proto-Indo-European pantheon as little more than the theomorphization of the major elements of nature. To press beyond this level of comparison required a certain amount of linguistic legerdemain which yielded rarely accepted equations. Some, for example, could point to the possible linguistic similarity between Kerberos, the guardian dog of the Greek Hades, and the epithet *sabala* 'spotted, varicoloured' (*kerbero?*), the standard epithet of one of the dogs of Yama, the Indic god of the dead. And even after more force than the comparative method in linguistics will normally allow, all one gains by postulating such a correspondence is the somewhat incongruous image of a Proto-Indo-European canine guard of the realm of the dead who answered to the name of 'Spot!'

More promising perhaps are those mythological reconstructions whose linguistic credentials are reasonable although they do not necessarily provide us with a clear image of their place in Proto-Indo-European ideology. Certainly one of the more intriguing examples is the comparison of the Indic (and Avestan) *Apam Napat* 'grandson/nephew of water' with Latin *Neptunus* and the Irish *Nechtain*. The latter two preserve only the element *nepots* 'grandson or nephew' but were still closely associated with water, the Latin god as the Roman equivalent of Poseidon, the god of waters, and the Irish figure Nechtain who maintained a sacred well. The *nepots* also figures prominently in eschatological literature. The epic traditions of a number of Indo-European peoples preserve an account of the 'final battle', for example, Kurukshetra in the great Indian epic, the *Mahabharata*; the 'Second Battle of Mag Tured' among the early Irish; Ragnarok among the Norse; and several others. A common structure has been found to underlie these different accounts which casts the *nepots* in the role of the protagonist against his evil opponent.

We also have the correspondence between the Indic Manu, the ancestor of the human race, and the Germanic founder-figure Mannus. The Indic god Aryaman, a deification of the concept of Aryan-hood, may share a Celtic cognate with the Gaulish Ario-manus and Old Irish Airem. Finally, we may note the similarity between the Indic god Bhaga 'sharer or dispenser of goods' (which, via its Iranian cognate was lent into the Slavic languages as the word for god), and the Phrygian Zeus Bagaios.

But all of these comparisons have never been regarded as entirely satisfying and it seems that straight lexical reconstructions of Proto-Indo-European divinities have proved far less rewarding here than they have for the reconstruction of other aspects of culture. If any further progress is to be made, some argue, then it requires the replacement of a method based on comparative philology with a 'new comparative mythology'.

Dumézil and tripartition

The foundation of much of what is currently written about Indo-European mythology has its origins in the sociological approach to the study of religion championed by Emile Durkheim. He and his followers proceeded from the assumption that myths expressed certain social and cultural realities. The attractiveness of such an approach is immediately apparent to anyone who has pondered the range of social structures reflected in the mythologies of various peoples. The Sumerians, for example, appear to have venerated a pantheon of gods organized according to an archaic version of their own social order. Among the Indo-European peoples we find the old Germanic social system and values encapsulated in the Old Norse pantheon housed at Valhalla, while the ancient Greek Olympus more closely reflected the more complex and specialized institutions of early Greek society. Moreover, the myths of a people were not only to some extent ciphers of their (often archaic) social structures, but they also reinforced social behaviour and served as divine charters for political realities. The Scythian origin myth, for example, records how their neighbours, the Agathyrsi and Geloni, had to resign themselves to subservience to Scythian power since their eponymous ancestors (Agathyrus and Gelonus) had failed in a mythic contest of strength to string Herakles' bow. Scythes, the progenitor of the Scythians, had naturally accomplished the task and secured a divine charter guaranteeing the superior social position of the Scythians. With such an approach, the study of Indo-European religion invites our closest attention since the antiquated social realities which might be preserved in the myths of different Indo-European peoples may shed some light on the nature of Proto-Indo-European society itself. It is obvious, however, that if we are to pursue this line of inquiry, we must abandon our hesitation stated at the beginning of the last chapter at employing such evidence. Reconstruction of Proto-Indo-

European ideology by comparing the structures of the myths of different peoples without further linguistic support differs little from other cross-cultural comparisons similarly obtained. Yet to dismiss such evidence here would exclude any discussion of the work of the majority of scholars now engaged in the study of Indo-European myth. So much for my procedural rigour.

An obvious starting point to such an investigation is how the various Indo-European peoples perceived the social divisions of their own communities. Among the earliest attested is the familiar division of society in Vedic India into the *brahmanas* 'priests', *ksatriyas* 'warriors' and *vaisyas* 'herder-cultivators', with the *sudras*, the lowest group, outside the Aryan community and composed of the suppressed indigenous population. Such a scheme has not only been remarkably persistent in India until the present but is quite analogous to the social divisions imputed to other Indo-European societies as can be seen in the following table:

		India	Iran	Greece (Ionian bioi)	Rome	Gaul
I	priests	brahmanas	athravan-	priests and magistrates	flamines	druides
II	warriors	ksatriyas	rathaestar-	warriors	milites	equites
III	herder-cultivators	vaisyas	vastrlyo fsuyant-	labourers and artisans	quirites	plebes

All of this evidence suggests a conceptual framework among early Indo-European-speaking peoples that tripartizes society into three classes: priests, warriors and herder-cultivators. Is a residue of such a system also recoverable from Indo-European mythology?

An emphatically affirmative answer to this question is given by the eminent French comparativist Georges Dumézil and his colleagues and followers. They have produce a vast corpus of evidence that has apparently formed a foundation for interpretation solid enough to withstand not only its bitterest critics but even the frequent excesses of its over-zealous supporters.

Dumézil argues that the evidence for tripartition of Indo-European society can be seen in one of the earliest sources of Indo-European religion – the treaty between Matiwaza, King of Mitanni, and the Hittite king, dating to about 1380 BC and discovered in the archives of Bogazköy (Hattusa). The Mitanni king, as we have seen before, evoked the names of the transparently Indic gods Mitra, Varuna, Indra and the Nasatyas. The first two names are characteristically found co-joined in the Vedas, that is, Mitra-Varuna, and they represent, according to Dumézil, the two main aspects of Indic sovereignty. Mitra personifies the concept of contact and governs the legalistic aspect of sovereignty while Varuna's domain pertains more appropriately to the magical or religious. The god Indra is the warrior-god par excellence while the Nasatyas are twins, associated closely with horses, and find their clearest roles in the maintenance of health in both livestock and people. In short, the three fundamental estates of Indo-European society are presented in canonical order in the Mitanni treaty.

This same tripartite division is seen over and over again throughout the mythologies of the Indo-European peoples. Herodotus records, for example, how the kingship of the Scythians was awarded to one of three brothers who could pick up three heavenly (but burning) objects that fell to the earth – a cup, an axe, and a plough with yoke. The first is regarded as a symbol of the ritual and sovereign function, the axe is the instrument of war and the plough with yoke are clearly symbols of the cultivator. The pre-Capitoline divine trio in ancient Rome consisted of the sovereign Jupiter, the war-god Mars and, finally, Quirinus, the patron of the people. Or, to take a more well-known example, preparatory to the disastrous judgment of Paris in Greek mythology, the three goddesses in competition each attempted to bribe Paris with a primary aspect of their own character. Hera offered sovereignty, Athena promised military prowess while Aphrodite promised the love of the most beautiful woman in the world, an arguably obvious aspect of fertility.

Tripartition is by no means limited to divine figures but permeates other aspects of society. Medicine, for example, is also divided when we find that, according to Pindar, the Greek healer Asklepios heals sores with spells, wounds with incisions and exhaustion with herbs and potions. A similar system is encountered in the Iranian *Avesta* where three types of medicine are listed: spell-medicine, knife-medicine and herb-medicine. Diseases and cures pertaining to the sovereign class are healed with spells appropriate to the techniques of priests. Wounds inflicted in battle, or fractures, are the province of surgery. Wasting diseases that threaten general well-being are treated with herbs and potions.

These comparisons are almost limitless and new articles invariably add to the number of canonical recitations of Indo-European tripartition. The underlying system, according to Dumézil, is one where society is encapsulated in three basic elements or, to use the Dumézilian expression, 'functions':

1 The first function embraces sovereignty and is marked by a priestly stratum of society which maintains both magico-religious and legal order. The gods assigned the sovereign function are often presented as a pair, each of which reflects a specific aspect: religious such as the Indic Varuna or Norse Odinn, and legal such as Mitra or Tyr.

2 A second military function assigned to the warrior stratum and concerned with the execution of both aggressive and defensive force, for example, the war-gods Indra, Mars and Thor.

3 A third estate conceptualizing fertility or sustenance and embracing the herder-cultivators. Here the mythic personages normally take the form of divine twins, intimately associated with horses, and accompanied by a female figure, for example, the Indic Asvins (horsemen) and Sarasvati, the Greek Castor and Pollux with Helen, the Norse Frey, Freyr and Njörth.

Although the tripartite conceptual system proposed for the ancient Indo-Europeans offers some opportunity for archaeological confirmation, it is a bit surprising to see how little use of archaeology has been made by those interested in comparative mythology. One of the few exceptions has been an attempt by

Dumézil himself to analyze one of the Luristan bronzes according to Indo-European mythology. The bronze capitol, dated to about the seventh or eighth century BC, is illustrated with seven registers, the upper and bottom two of which can be dismissed as primarily ornamental. It is the three central friezes that offer, according to Dumézil, iconographic evidence of the Indo-European system of tripartition. The upper register portrays two figures symbolically co-joined by both holding the same palm in the centre. The left hand figure stands next to an altar, a clear association with religious functions, while the right hand figure stands next to a bovine. Dumézil reminds us that the bull was the titular animal of Mitra, and he identifies the two figures as the sovereign gods Varuna and Mitra. The middle register depicts a figure standing between two lions with a bird overhead. Dumézil suggests that the figure is quite probably of Indra, the Indic warrior-god. Of the 36 mentions of a bird in the *Rig Veda*, 23 of them are associated with Indra while another 6 occur with the Maruts, Indra's warrior band. Twelve of the 13 mentions of a lion in the *Rig Veda* are connected with Indra or the Maruts. The lower register depicts two figures, interpreted as the Indic divine twins, the Asvins, assisting an older figure, an iconographic representation of an incident in the *Rig Veda* where the twins rejuvenate an old man.

Whether one is impressed by this interpretation or not, it must be admitted that there is ample room for archaeological 'testing' of the tripartite model.

One of the more obvious symbols of social tripartition is colour, emphasized by the fact that both ancient India and Iran expressed the concept of caste with the word for colour (*varna*). A survey of the social significance of different colours is fairly clear cut, at least for the first two functions. Indo-Iranian, Hittite, Celtic and Latin ritual all assign white to priests and red to the warrior. The third function would appear to have been marked by a darker colour such as black or blue. Unfortunately, the preservation of coloured textiles among a prehistoric people is possible but seldom encountered and one must seek more enduring markers of Indo-European social classes.

Perhaps a potentially more rewarding area for examination can be found among the ritual animal sacrifices that we encounter among the early Indo-Europeans. The evidence of these rituals, especially those preserved in ancient India and Rome, demonstrates how a hierarchy of different victims were sacrificed to, or associated with, the various divinities who filled out the major social 'functions' of Indo-European mythology. In the Indic *sautramani*, for example, the priestly Sarasvati received a ram, the warlike Indra obtained a bull, and the Asvins, the twins who represented the third estate, were offered a he-goat. In the *Avesta*, the great goddes Arədvi Sura Anahita, who embraced all three functions, received the sacrifice of horses, cattle and sheep. The Roman purification sacrifice of the *suovetaurilia* preserved within its very name the identity of its three ritual victims – *su* 'pig', *ovis* 'sheep' and *taurus* 'bull'.

Although the sacrificial sequence in these and other rituals was clearly hierarchical, the precise identity or sequence of the victims sacrificed was not rigidly observed within the same culture, much less between different Indo-

74–77 *Luristan bronze covering for a quiver dating to about the eighth or seventh century* BC *(L. 8.25 cm). Georges Dumézil has interpreted the figures as representatives of the three Indo-European 'functions'. Three Registers are shown in detail. From top to bottom, Register 3: The 'sovereign' figures; Register 4: The 'warrior' figure; and Register 5: The 'twins'.*

European peoples. In examining the Indic evidence, for example, Jaan Puhvel notes that where the horse is identified as one of the victims it is dedicated to the warrior-god, while a sheep or hornless ram is offered to the priestly deity and cattle or goat to those representing the third estate. But where the horse is absent from the ritual, cattle replaces it and the third function receives a goat or pig. The Roman evidence shows even greater variability, and in the Greek triple sacrifice known as the *trittua*, we find that the animals are often a ram, bull and a boar.

The difficulties involved in extrapolating from this type of evidence to the Proto-Indo-Europeans are fairly obvious. While the horse may normally be associated with a warrior-deity and the sow is certainly an archetypal third-function fertility symbol, we can see how exceedingly difficult it is to assign specific socio-ritual identities to the other victims. As Jaan Puhvel observes, the important factor may not necessarily rest in any inherent symbolism associated with a particular species but rather to whom they are to be sacrificed, different gods requiring different constellations of three ritual victims. We need not totally despair of such evidence in seeking to understand better the earliest Indo-Europeans since we are clearly discussing a series of domestic animals all known to the Proto-Indo-Europeans. We may hope to find some evidence for tripartite or triple sacrifice even if we cannot be secure of the precise beliefs that prompted the ritual behaviour.

Horse sacrifice

Some would maintain that the *premier* animal of Indo-European sacrifice and ritual was probably the horse. We have already seen how its embedment in Proto-Indo-European society lies not just in its lexical reconstruction but also in the proliferation of personal names which contain 'horse' as an element among the various Indo-European peoples. Furthermore, we witness the importance of the horse in Indo-European rituals and mythology. One of the most obvious examples is the recurrent depiction of twins such as the Indic Asvins 'horsemen', the Greek horsemen Castor and Pollux, the legendary Anglo-Saxon settlers of Britain, Horsa and Hengist (literally Horse and Stallion) or the Irish twins of Macha, born after she had completed a horse race. All of these attest the existence of Indo-European divine twins associated with or represented by horses.

The major ritual enactment of a horse-centred myth is supported by evidence from ancient India and Rome and, more distantly, medieval Ireland. The Indic ritual is the *asvamedha*, probably the most spectacular of the ancient Indic ceremonies. It began in the spring under the direction of four priests, acting under the patronage of the king who was dedicating the sacrifice to the divine representatives of his warrior class. A prized stallion was selected as the victim and after rituals initiating the ceremony, the stallion was set free to wander for an entire year, 400 warriors trailing behind to ensure that the course of the stallion was neither interfered with nor that it had contact with mares.

Ancilliary rituals took place throughout the year until the horse was returned for the final three day finale. This involved, among other things, the horse pulling the king's chariot, a large sacrifice of a variety of animals, and the smothering of the horse, after which the king's favourite wife 'co-habited' with the dead stallion under covers. The horse was then dismembered into three portions, each dedicated to deities who played out the canonical order of Dumézil's three 'functions'.

The *asvamedha* bears comparison with the major Roman horse sacrifice which was known as the *October Equus*. Following a horse race on the ides of October, the right-sided horse of the team was dispatched by a spear and then dismembered, again in such a fashion as to indicate its 'functional' division into the three estates. As with the Indic ritual, the major recipient of the sacrifice was the warrior-god (Mars). In medieval Ireland, and through the admittedly somewhat jaundiced eyes of the Norman Geraldus, we read how in the inauguration of one of the tribal kings of Ulster, a mare was sacrificed and then dismembered. In a classic example of Ulster pragmatism, the pieces of horse flesh were then boiled in order to make a great broth in which the king subsequently bathed while devouring the morsels of meat.

A detailed analysis of this and other material has led Jaan Puhvel to propose a Proto-Indo-European myth and ritual which involved the mating of a figure from the royal class with a horse from which ultimately sprung the famous equine divine twins. He offers some additional linguistic support for such a ritual in the very name of the Indic ceremony, the *asvamedha*. This derives from the Proto-Indo-European **ekwo-meydho* 'horse-drunk', attesting a ritual which included both a horse and drunkenness. This is quite comparable to the personal name Epomeduos which is found in ancient Gaul and appears to derive from **ekwo-medu-* 'horse-mead'. The modern English *mead* is transparently part of the same series that gives us Sanskrit *madhu-*, Greek *methy*, Old Church Slavonic *medu*, Lithuanian *medus*, Old Irish *mid*, and Tocharian B *mit*, all of which provide us with our word for the Proto-Indo-European alcoholic and ritual drink **medhu* 'mead'. Hence, both the Indic and Celtic worlds still preserve the ancient Proto-Indo-European name of a horse-centred ceremony involving intoxication.

The horse ritual warrants one more comment since it illustrates all too well how a comparison of myths may lead us along paths that appear to be contradicted by archaeological evidence. Both the *asvamedha* and *October Equus* clearly concern the sacrifice of a draught horse and in a striking instance of parallelism, both require that the horse in question excels on the right side of the chariot (cf. a Hittite ritual where the vehicle is drawn by a mule on the left side and a horse on the right). Clearly, this suggests that the horse is selected from a paired chariot team. But archaeological evidence indicates that the horse was not likely to have been employed in paired draught until the invention of the spoked wheel and chariot, which is normally dated after about 2500 BC and, consequently, some time after we would have assumed the disintegration of the Proto-Indo-European community. Indeed, the entire concept of horse-twins totally points to paired draught, while the archaeological evidence suggests that this should not be so at the time-depth we normally assign to Proto-Indo-European. Although cultural borrowing or parallel development may be suggested, this is a problem yet to be resolved.

One final element of ritual associated with the horse sacrifice is the distribution of its anatomy after its death. In the *asvamedha*, for example, we have seen how the horse was butchered and offered to three different deities who can be assigned tripartite functions in Dumézilian fashion. As animal remains frequently accompany burials, we may hope that Indo-European rituals may shed some light on the patterns of offerings discovered in the archaeological record of the earliest Indo-Europeans.

The cattle cycle

We have already seen how lexical correspondences permit us to reconstruct proto-Indo-European expressions for 'to raid for cattle' and 'sacrifice of a hundred cattle'. At first glance we might regard these as the chance residue of the vocabulary concerning the secular (raiding) and sacred (sacrifice) disposition of cattle in Proto-Indo-European society. But in an extensive examination of the role of cattle in both society and belief among the Indo-Iranians, and a number of peoples of East Africa, Bruce Lincoln suggests the paramount role of cattle in early Indo-European economy and religion.

From mythological evidence primarily drawn from the Indians and Iranians, but also from the Greeks, Romans, Germans, Celts and Hittites, Lincoln reconstructs an Indo-European myth of the first cattle raid. This concerned a hero figure *Trito* 'third' (Vedic *Trita Aptya*, Avestan *Thraetaona Athwya*, Greek *Herakles*, Norse *Hymir*, Hittite *Hupasiya*) who loses his cattle to a three-headed monster, normally a serpent, which at least in Indo-Iranian tradition is closely associated with local non-Indo-European populations. In a return encounter *Trito*, with the assistance of the Indo-European warrior-god, defeats the three-headed monster and recovers his cattle. Lincoln suggests that this cattle-raiding myth served as a charter which both helped to define the role

78   Bruce Lincoln suggests that the early Germanic Gallehus horn (c. AD 400) depicts a three-headed figure from the Indo-European cattle-raiding myth.

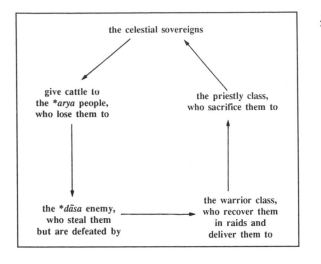

79   The structure of the 'cattle-keepers' myth'.

of the warrior in Indo-European society (the proper activity of the warrior was cattle raiding), and sanctioned Aryan cattle raiding against foreigners who, according to the myth, had previously robbed the Aryans.

Lincoln brings this warrior-class-centred myth into contrast with the myth of the first cattle sacrifice which served to underpin the position of the priest. This myth, about which we will have more to say below, involved the sacrifice of both a man and an ox (or bull) from whose parts the world was created. On a practical level this myth chartered the position of the priest who sacrificed victims to a sky-god who then bestowed both men and cattle on the kings or warriors of the Aryans in exchange. These were then expected to turn over cattle to the priest for sacrifice so that the cycle which secured the free flow of cattle through both human society and the cosmos was perpetuated.

Lincoln argues that the striking similarities which he finds between the cattle-keeper's religion of the Indo-Iranians and East Africans is due to similar ecologies where possession of cattle defined the economic basis of society. Both cattle raiding to secure more of the principal commodity and cattle sacrifice to recompense and perhaps manipulate the deities were natural developments of such cattle-based societies. These two different activities encouraged the formalization of two separate classes – warriors and priests – whose own behaviour was patterned after the myths of the first cattle raid and first sacrifice. Although Lincoln's study is primarily directed at the behaviour of the Indo-Iranians, his frequent recourse to general Indo-European mythology, especially in the reconstruction of these mythic charters, suggests that the roots of the cattle-keeping religion and world view, with its attendant social ramifications, might also be projected back to Proto-Indo-European society.

Human sacrifice and punishment

Human sacrifice is not a common occurrence among the rituals of the earliest Indo-European peoples, although there is hardly a group where some evidence for it cannot be found. In Germanic and Celtic tradition the evidence amounts to a reasonably well-supported pattern of 'The Threefold Death', wherein we can see human sacrifice or punishment applied in a clear trifunctional fashion. The manner of execution was carried out in a manner appropriate to the three Dumézilian functions. The ancient Gauls, for example, made offerings to three gods – Esus, Taranis and Teutates – by recourse to hanging, burning and drowning, respectively. This pattern is replicated in the pagan Germanic punishments of hanging, stabbing and drowning, each technique correlated to the crime for which the victim was convicted. The underlying scheme suggests that human sacrifice to a deity occupying a priestly or juridical role (or the death penalty for one who violated these particular interests) was death by hanging. A violation of the warrior code, or an offering to the god(s) of war, most appropriately awarded death either by burning or by the sword. Fertility deities were satisfied by drowned victims. Although the best evidence is primarily confined to the westernmost Indo-Europeans, there is some additional support to indicate that threefold sacrifices may have been more widespread.

War of the Functions

Certain striking parallels concerning the Roman account of the Sabine War, the Norse myth concerning the war between the Aesir and the Vanir, and the Indic epic *Mahabharata* have provided support for a Proto-Indo-European 'War of the Functions' from which some have drawn important conclusions about the formation of the Proto-Indo-European community. Basically, the parallels concern the presence of first- (magico-juridical) and second- (warrior) function representatives on the victorious side of a war that ultimately subdues and incorporates third function characters, for example, the Sabine women or the Norse Vanir. Indeed, the *Iliad* itself has also been examined in a similar light. The ultimate structure of the myth, then, is that the three estates of Proto-Indo-European society were fused only after a war between the first two against the third. From this mythic model, it has been suggested that the possible historical reality underlying the myth may be the conquest of settled agriculturalists by a non-sedentary community. This comes too close to one popular archaeological solution to the Indo-European homeland problem to pass without comment.

The idea that there existed an historical reality behind the 'War of the Functions' is both highly speculative and unnecessary. We have already seen, for example, how the origin myth of the Scythians was constructed to serve as a social charter of behaviour and status within the Pontic region, that is, an Agathyrsi or a Geloni was subservient to a Scythian because his ancestors were incapable of stringing Herakles' bow, while Scythes, the ancestor of the Scythians, was successful. Similarly, if we admit a Proto-Indo-European 'War of the Functions', this need not reflect anything more than a reminder to the productive members of society that they remain subservient to both priests and warriors, a situation divinely chartered by a mythical war which their ancestors lost but whose historical validity is no more secure than Herakles' bow.

Dualism and Indo-European ideology

We have already seen how Dumézil and his colleagues propose a pattern of dualism that cuts across the tripartite structure of Indo-European ideology. The first or sovereign function, for example, is expressed through paired gods (Varuna-Mitra, Jupiter-Dius Fidius, Odinn-Tyr) who are each respectively charged with the magico-religious and juridical-contractual aspects of rulership. The divine twins provide even more obvious evidence for dualism.

The significance of twins in Indo-European mythology can be readily seen in the creation or foundation myths of the Indo-Europeans. The Proto-Indo-European *yem- 'twin' underlies the name of a god common to the Indo-Iranians (Indic *Yama*, Avestan *Yima*) who becomes the progenitor of mankind. In a recent study, Jaan Puhvel argues that the underlying form for the name of Remus, the brother of Romulus in the story of the founding of Rome, was actually *iemus*, the early Italic form of Proto-Indo-European *yemos 'twin'. In Norse mythology, mankind is formed from the remains of a giant whose name, Ymir, has also been derived by some from the Proto-Indo-European word for twin. Furthermore, Tacitus relates how the early Germans were the descendants of Mannus and Tuisto, the latter of which again means twin. Among the Celts we have the tale relating the foundation of Emhain Macha, the ancient capital of Ulster, which was explained by recourse to a myth in which Macha gave birth to *emuin* 'twins', again derived from Proto-Indo-European *yem-. Analysis of all these tales indicates that the Proto-Indo-Europeans believed that the progenitors of mankind were *Man (Indic *Manu*, German *Mannus*) and *Twin, the latter of which was sacrificed and carved up by his brother to produce mankind. To this Bruce Lincoln adds the coincidental sacrifice of a bovine integral to this myth in India, Iran, and among the Norse and Irish.

We can go beyond the dualism expressed by twins to outright binary opposition as one of the underlying structures of Indo-European ideology. The most familiar example can be seen in how the Indo-Europeans treated the basic directions. As we have seen, the opposition between the Proto-Indo-European words for right and left also presents a systematic opposition between the concepts of propitious, healthy, strong, dexterous (Latin *dexter*, Sanskrit *daksina*, Avestan *dasina-*, Lithuanian *desine*, Old Church Slavonic *desn*, Greek *dexios*, Old Irish *dess*, Albanian *djathtë*, and so on, from Proto-Indo-European *deks-), and the left which is unfavourable, unsound, weak, or, to use the Latin again, *sinister*. This opposition is also sexual since the right side or right hand is regularly associated with males and the left with females. Furthermore, the opposition also carries into the cardinal directions: the propitious south lay to the right (the Sanskrit and Irish words for right also mean south), while to the left lay the malevolent north, thus demonstrating that Proto-Indo-Europeans faced east to *orient* themselves. This right—left polarity is naturally not confined to the Indo-Europeans but can be found throughout the world. Nevertheless, securing this polarity to Proto-Indo-European society does provide the archaeologist examining the position and orientation of burials with another clue for tracking the course of the Indo-Europeans.

The analysis of Indo-European ideological structure in terms of binary opposition is hardly removed from the structuralist approach of Claude Lévi-Strauss who proposes a universal tendency to mediate between opposites. Bruce Lincoln has viewed the organization of Indo-Iranian ideology in a similar light, offering it as an alternative tool for understanding Indo-Iranian social theory. Here, for example, the *arya* are contrasted with the aboriginal (and, from the Aryan perspective, inferior) *dasa*. In turn, the *arya* are subdivided into upper classes versus commoners, a system which Lincoln also finds in Caesar's account of early Celtic society. The upper classes are subdivided between sovereigns and warriors, while the sovereigns are composed of a binary opposition between priests and kings. In a somewhat similar vein, Einar Haugen has examined Norse ideology in terms of minimal oppositions.

Some have sought an explanation for the ideological dualism in the social structure of Proto-Indo-European society. Tomas Gamkrelidze and Vyachislav Ivanov, following the work of other linguists, propose that the Proto-Indo-European system of marriage involved the exchange of women between two opposing moieties. This fundamental division of Proto-Indo-European society into two 'halves' could not help but engender an ideological response in Indo-European religion. Harkening back to earlier approaches to the mythological evidence, they propose an opposition between the two primary Indo-European deities: *dyeus pɔter*, the god of the clear sky, charged with the maintenance of religious order, versus *perkuno* – the god of storm, thunder and patron of war. More interestingly, they emphasize dual political leadership among the early Indo-Europeans. Citing Homer's account of the Achaian forces in the *Iliad*, they note how frequently the tribes listed are led by two rulers, while the dual kingship of ancient Sparta continued this tradition. Other evidence such as Horsa and Hengist leading the Anglo-Saxon settlement of Britain has already been mentioned. But is this meant to suggest dual kingship among the Proto-Indo-Europeans? We can no longer avoid the central problem of employing the evidence of comparative mythology to construct a picture of Proto-Indo-European society.

Mythology and Reality

Some of the critics of the 'new comparative mythology' harbour suspicions regarding how its proponents seem to tease out of any Indo-European document some evidence for tripartition. Others suggest that the three divisions of society proposed by Dumézil for the Indo-Europeans are so 'natural' and generic to any society that they cannot be usefully employed as a diacritic for marking Indo-European culture. Some scholars engaged in the analysis of myth do not criticize Dumézil and his school; they simply ignore it as an irrelevancy to their own approach to the mythology of individual Indo-European peoples. But if one embraces the concept of tripartition, then it seems to offer unparalleled information for the archaeologist who wishes to correlate the concept of Indo-European with the archaeological record.

The prehistorian is provided with a capsule description of Proto-Indo-European society divided into three major classes – priests, warriors and herder-cultivators. We may expect to see these classes marked by colour, totem, animal or any other form of culture-loaded symbolism. We may expect to discover the remains of animal sacrifices, especially that of the horse, or its ritual dismemberment. Triads of animals may occur in burials or other sacrificial contexts. Burials of males and females may exhibit variations in position and orientation similar to that indicated by the linguistic evidence. The most optimistic may even imagine that the Indo-European 'War of the Functions' underlies an historical reality, and search the archaeological record for the incorporation of an agricultural society into that of non-agriculturalists. How likely are we to be disappointed?

There can be little doubt that the links between the reconstructed ideology and their expressions in material culture or behaviour of a prehistoric people may be far less than we hoped for in the last paragraph. Dumézil himself has insisted that his Indo-European civilization is one 'of the spirit', and that it need not be tied down to the real Proto-Indo-European world. Ideal worlds of myths, one may argue, are just that, and although they may be an expression of social realities, these need never take the corporeal forms required by the archaeologist. Squeezing priest burials out of the archaeological record of most Indo-European peoples, for example, has been a nearly impossible task. Any archaeologist examining the burial remains of the Celts in a La Tène cemetery may well wonder whatever happened to the facile generalizations concerning their social structure derived from myth and early ethnographers such as Caesar. The isolation of clear-cut classes or 'functions' is very difficult in Iron Age contexts when one might be more hopeful of discerning occupational classes than in the Eneolithic or Early Bronze Age. Perhaps most ironic is the fact that, even if archaeologists find it impossible to demonstrate the social structures predicted by mythologists, it will have absolutely no effect whatsoever on their continued publication of yet further examples of social tripartition and other aspects of Indo-European religion and ideology.

If we must accept these difficulties then we must be honest about the utility of the new comparative mythology in elucidating Proto-Indo-European culture. Many of its practitioners would admit that the society which lies behind their reconstructions is an idealized one that need not be reflected in the cultural record, nor can it ever be effectively tested. Such an untestable hypothesis is, of course, no hypothesis at all, and its utility as an explanatory device is far better left to comparative mythologists who can play by different rules. They are not speaking the same language as the prehistorian. But how can we use arguments about the mythic reinforcement of social realities without assuming a relationship between social structure and myth? Here the resolution of this contradiction, perhaps more intuitive than logical, will be to hold the mythological evidence out for examination against the archaeological record, yet not make demands for proof higher than its own practitioners would willingly admit.

CHAPTER SIX

The Indo-European Homeland Problem

This Aryan family of speech was of Asiatic origin.
A. H. SAYCE, 1880

This Aryan family of speech was of European origin.
A. H. SAYCE, 1890

So far as my examination of the facts has gone it has
led me to the conviction that it was in Asia Minor
that the Indo-European languages developed.
A. H. SAYCE, 1927

We begin our search for the homeland of the Indo-Europeans with the deceptively optimistic claim that it has already been located. For who would look further north than Lokomanya Tilak and Georg Biedenkapp who traced the earliest Aryans to the North Pole? Or who would venture a homeland further south than North Africa, further west than the Atlantic or further east than the shores of the Pacific, all of which have been seriously proposed as 'cradles' of the Indo-Europeans? This quest for the origins of the Indo-Europeans has all the fascination of an electric light in the open air on a summer night: it tends to attract every species of scholar or would-be savant who can take pen to hand. It also shows a remarkable ability to mesmerize even scholars of outstanding ability to wander far beyond the realm of reasonable speculation to provide yet another example of academic lunacy. It is sobering to recall that one of the greatest prehistorians of this century, V. Gordon Childe, dismissed his own researches into Indo-European origins as among the most *childish* things he wrote. It is no easy task to get one's bearings in a problem where most of the proposed solutions show a remarkable ability to be dismembered and securely entombed in one generation only to rise again to haunt later scholars. One does not ask 'where is the Indo-European homeland?' but rather 'where do they put it *now*?' Reflect for a moment that one of the most extensively argued solutions to the Indo-European problem at present has been advanced by the distinguished Soviet linguists Tomas Gamkrelidze and Vyachislav Ivanov who situate it either in or near Armenia, precisely in the same region that James Parsons set it nearly 230 years ago. The evidence and reasons for such a solution have naturally changed radically, yet the range of actual locations has not. So,

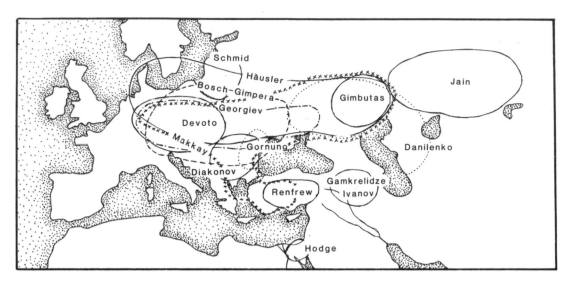

80   The modern 'consensus': A map of some of the solutions to the Indo-European homeland problem proposed since 1960.

lest one imagine that 230 years of research has carried us closer towards the truth, or perhaps that more negotiable concept of consensus, one need only glance at a map of some of the solutions to the Indo-European problem which have been proposed since 1960. We hardly need any encouragement to pause briefly before embarking on our own quest to consider precisely what we are looking for.

Defining the homeland

Once we acknowledge that the historically attested Indo-European languages must derive from an earlier common or Proto-Indo-European language, logic also requires us to accept the existence of prehistoric communities which spoke that language. We may, of course, question the validity of the precise forms of our linguistic reconstructions and whether they represent exactly, or even approximately, the actual speech of the Proto-Indo-Europeans. We may also dismiss a wholly uniform dialectless proto-language as extremely improbable, and admit that there must have been considerable linguistic differences throughout the Proto-Indo-European speech community. But the actual existence of these Proto-Indo-European speakers, who must have left traces in the archaeological record of Eurasia, cannot be denied.

When we attempt to reconstruct these Proto-Indo-Europeans we tend to telescope the cultural, linguistic and mythological similarities of the various historical Indo-European groups back into the prehistoric past. This tempts us to imagine the expansion of the Indo-Europeans from their original homeland much in the same fashion as a cosmologist surveys the origins of the universe from an initial 'Big Bang': running the cameras in reverse we follow the trails of energy and matter back to a singularity. But, for the Indo-Europeans, there can be nothing resembling a singularity. Only by assuming the preposterous notion that the Proto-Indo-European language originated simultaneously with human speech itself can we imagine it to have been anything other than a segment of the overall continuum of human speech in Eurasia. The Proto-Indo-European homeland is essentially the spatial expression of a vaguely defined temporal division of that linguistic continuum. Such a definition necessarily involves both the discipline of the historical linguist and the archaeologist, and each ignores the arguments of the other at his or her peril since the evidence for Proto-Indo-European speakers is a product of linguistics while the location of a prehistoric people is more properly the domain of the archaeologist. We have seen in Chapter Four that the evidence of the Indo-European vocabulary indicates that the Proto-Indo-Europeans should have existed broadly within the period 4500–2500 BC. There is both linguistic and archaeological evidence that can aid us in locating these Proto-Indo-Europeans within Eurasia at this time. There are also very serious problems of theory and method which will affect the validity of our solution. In the remainder of this chapter we will examine some of the approaches that have the greatest claim to our attention as well as some of the more general problems associated with the search for the Indo-European homeland.

The neighbours of the Proto-Indo-Europeans

A peculiar tendency among a number of nineteenth-century linguists was the strange desire to insulate the Indo-European homeland by great natural barriers, the Hindu Kush or the Himalayas proving particularly popular. Here primitive 'Aryans' were believed to have 'perfected' their language before bursting out over the rest of Eurasia. But if human experience be any guide, we must assume that during the fifth to the third millennia BC the Proto-Indo-Europeans were surrounded by other linguistic groups. In this section we will try to obtain a notional image of the prehistoric linguistic situation in Eurasia and to seek to locate the Proto-Indo-Europeans through their relations with their linguistic neighbours.

First of all, we must try to imagine the Proto-Indo-Europeans occupying a territory among a large number of other linguistic groups. In Chapter Two we made a little rough estimation to postulate a territory of about 250,000–500,000 square kilometres for a major Bronze Age language, based on the historical disposition of the Near Eastern languages. If we were to take the main linguistic groupings of Europe today (Celtic, Germanic, Slavic, Finnic, Hungarian, Basque, and so on.), or to undertake calculations based on the major language groups attested for Iron Age Europe, the size of our individual linguistic territories would fall, on average, somewhere between 500,000–750,000 square kilometres. Furthermore, Sydney Lamb in his estimation of the number of linguistic entities in North America on the eve of European colonization reckoned about twenty-three language families which were represented by about 350 languages. If we apply these figures to the entire territory of North America, we would estimate that each of these language families would have occupied an area of about 1,000,000 square kilometres, while the individual languages would each have occupied about 65,000 square kilometres. Lamb estimated that, around 4000 BC, the number of languages in North America was probably of the order of 150–210, roughly half the number encountered historically. This would suggest an average size for each language somewhere in the range of 115,000 to 160,000 square kilometres. Similar rough estimates could be made from many more of the world's languages. It is, of course, not the precise figures that are important but the order of magnitude. Generally, before the emergence of major state languages we encounter most linguistic entities in the world occupying areas that range from the extremely small up to about 1,000,000 square kilometres. Consequently, we may postulate the size of the Proto-Indo-European homeland falling within the range of about 250,000–1,000,000 square kilometres, a figure which is in fair accord with most solutions to the homeland problem as suggested by both linguists and archaeologists. A similar area is also suggested for the homelands of many other language families, and where there are substantial deviations from such an average they tend to be downward rather than towards a yet larger area.

We should remind ourselves why there seems to be an upper threshold to the size of a linguistic area, a 'maximum permissible area' as it has once been termed. Here we must recall that languages are always in the process of change and therefore, as the area of a given language grows in size, it will become increasingly difficult for all of its speakers to intercommunicate and change together along the same lines. Rather, there will be increased tendencies towards regionalization where linguistic change will follow different local paths of development. It is also highly probable that the economic system of the speakers of a given language will play a significant role in the size of area in which relative uniformity will be maintained. Mobile subsistence economies such as hunter-gatherers, or more certainly pastoral nomads, frequently retain linguistic uniformity over a wider area than is typically found among agriculturalists among whom long-term village settlement will probably promote regional developments. As the time-depth for Proto-Indo-European is set roughly to the Neolithic-Early Bronze Age, we may expect that there were a substantial number of different languages across Europe and neighbouring parts of Asia at this time.

Our picture of a linguistically fragmented Eurasia 4500–2500 BC is also a natural consequence of accepting an average linguistic area of about 250,000–1,000,000 square kilometres. As with the North American evidence cited above, there remains today only a small number of language families attested in Europe whose ancestral proto-languages can be projected back into prehistory. We may conclude, therefore, that a considerable number of languages (potential language families) have totally disappeared sometime between 4500 BC and the emergence of historical records in Europe. Applying our estimate of the average size of linguistic territory, there should have been something of the order of twenty to forty different languages occupying Europe at the same time as Proto-Indo-European. Now, it might strike one as improbable that so many languages or language families have disappeared without trace, but our earlier review of the historically attested disappearance of Hattic, Hurrian, Sumerian and Elamite in the Near East should have prepared us for just this sort of conclusion. Indeed, Iberian, Tartessian, Basque and Etruscan, remnant languages on the southwest periphery of Europe, suggest something of the magnitude of linguistic diversity that probably once prevailed over the rest of Europe. All of this emphasizes the incredible success that the Indo-Europeans achieved in expanding over territories many times greater than that from which they originated. This too is not without some analogic support. We know from the historical record that the Turkic language, confined in the sixth century AD to a region no larger than we would normally posit for Proto-Indo-European, virtually exploded over an area in excess of 2,500,000 square kilometres by the ninth century AD. Here, of course, the highly mobile character of Turkish society provided them with an advantage in their expansions and their ability to establish an exceptional linguistic uniformity over a gigantic region.

Now we must push beyond the theoretical probability that the Proto-Indo-Europeans had many linguistic neighbours to see whether it is possible to locate their homeland on the basis of their relationships with these neighbours. The remnant non-Indo-European languages of Western Europe, such as Basque, Iberian and Etruscan, offer us no evidence that would closely relate them to the Indo-European family, although one may always discern the occasional late loan word between Etruscan and Latin or Iberian and Celtic. Essentially, these languages offer us no compelling reason to seek an Indo-European homeland in Southwest Europe, nor has this area ever been a serious candidate. Of far greater importance in our search is the Finno-Ugric or Uralic languages.

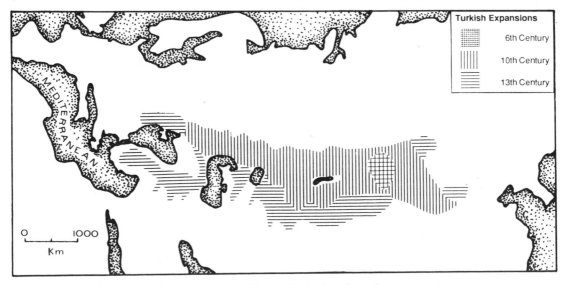

81 The historical expansion of the highly mobile Turks indicates how fast a language group might spread.

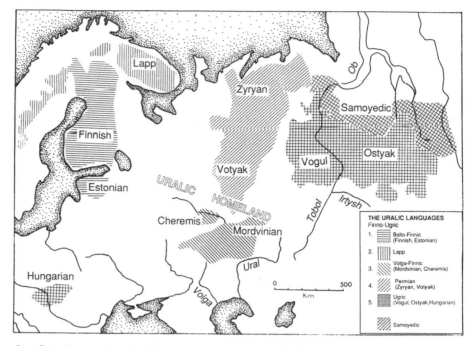

82   Distribution of the Uralic languages and their probable homeland.

The Finno-Ugric languages include Finnish, Estonian, Hungarian, and the Lappic, Permic and Volgaic languages. All of these are found to the west of the Urals, that is, in Europe itself, except for Vogul and Ostyak which occupy a wide area of the Ob drainage immediately east of the Urals. All of these Finno-Ugric languages may be taken as one major branch of a Uralic family whose other branch is the Samoyedic languages of northern Siberia. What is of greatest importance to the Indo-Europeanist is that these languages exhibit a convincing number of loan words borrowed from the Indo-European family when they were still largely undifferentiated in their own homeland. Knowing the location of the Finno-Ugric homeland permits us a rough approximation of the early Indo-Europeans.

Some may naturally query using the Finno-Ugric languages as an anchor for the Proto-Indo-Europeans as seeking one unknown via another, but here we should remember that the Finno-Ugric homeland, despite the considerable amount of debate concerning its location, does not present the same magnitude of problems as the Indo-European homeland. The Finno-Ugric languages generally fill out a territory stretching from the northeast Baltic across Russia to east of the Urals (Hungarian was a medieval intruder into Eastern Europe from the Volga region and is most closely related to Vogul and Ostyak). This confines the search for the Finno-Ugric homeland to an area much smaller than the Indo-European one. In general, most proposed Finno-Ugric homelands tend to be confined to a strip about 1,000 kilometres long and 200–300 kilometres wide, stretching from the middle Volga east to the middle Ob, that is, an area of about 300,000 square kilometres. There are some who would seek the homeland further west as far as the Baltic, or to the southeast as far as the Aral Sea, but most solutions centre on the smaller area. Consensus, therefore, situates the earliest Finno-Ugrians in the forest zone of Eastern Europe-western Siberia among a variety of hunting-gathering-fishing cultures, many of whom may be embraced archaeologically under the Comb and Pit-marked Pottery tradition. It is now for us to see if it is possible to relate the Indo-Europeans to this region.

The substantial number of loan words of clear Indo-European origin that are found across the Finno-Ugric languages suggest that they were borrowed when the latter was still a proto-language. The precise time at which these loans occurred is a delicate problem. It is generally acknowledged that many of the words were borrowed from the Indo-Iranian languages and not Proto-Indo-European, since the borrowed words have already undergone the characteristic changes expected of the Indo-Iranian languages. For example, we find that Finnish *porsas* and Votyak *pars* 'pig' are clearly derived from an Indo-Iranian *parsa* – and not the Proto-Indo-European *porkos* (cf. Latin *porcus*). This, and other examples such as Finnish *sata* 'hundred' which is comparable to Indic *satam* and Avestan *satəm* (and not Proto Indo European *kmtom*, cf. Latin *centum*) all suggest that these loans were made sometime during the third or second millennia BC. While most would see these loans as unequivocally Proto-Indo-Iranian and hence notionally about 2000 ± 500 BC, a few have argued that they are distinctly Iranian loans although dating to approximately the same period. Consequently, we have reasonably solid evidence to maintain that about 2000 BC Indo-Iranians were providing a series of lexical items, pertaining particularly to agriculture (such as pig, goat, grain, grass) and technology (hammer, awl, gold), to Finno-Ugric peoples situated roughly between the middle Volga and the Ob. This would place the Indo-Iranians to their immediate south (lower Volga-Ural) and helps confirm the location of the earliest Indo-Iranian tribes as suggested in Chapter Two.

The evidence suggestive of a relationship between Indo-European and Finno-Ugric at a still earlier date is of greater interest. Here we are speaking of a series of possible loan words which would appear to have derived from Proto-Indo-European itself. In addition, there are also some striking similarities between the personal endings of the verb and some of the case endings of the noun between Proto-Indo-European and Proto-Uralic. Such similarities have suggested to some that the relationship between the two language families might not be two languages in contact but rather that they both derive from a still earlier common source which may be termed Proto-Indo-Uralic. Whatever way one reads the evidence, there is a substantial body of linguistic opinion which sees Proto-Indo-European and Proto-Uralic or Finno-Ugric as being closely related and consequently once adjacent to one another. With the Uralic languages occupying the northern forest zone, it is most probable that the Proto-Indo-European territory at least included a substantial portion of the forest-steppe or steppe zone of the Volga-Ural region.

After Finno-Ugric, the possibility of Semitic-Indo-European relations has the greatest demand on our attention. Since well into the last century, and indeed still earlier, there have been frequent attempts to demonstrate parallels in vocabulary between the Indo-European languages and the Semitic languages of the Near East. The number of lexical comparisons, depending on one's source and to some extent imagination, is sizeable, and may approach 100–200 among its more ardent proponents. Some of the comparisons invariably find a place in Indo-European handbooks such as Proto-Indo-European *(s)tauro and Proto-Semitic *tawru '(wild) ox', or Proto-Indo-European *septm and Proto-Semitic *sab' 'seven' (alone of the numerals). In the more extensive lists of comparisons, agricultural words constitute approximately a quarter of all the words allegedly shared by Indo-European and Semitic.

Unlike comparisons between Indo-European and Finno-Ugric, the Semitic relations do not really have a general acceptance despite the fact that there are a number of most energetic supporters of genetic links between the two families. Certainly, any linguist running through some of the longer lists of comparisons encounters far too many cases of special pleading. Indeed, in a recent survey of the supposed Semitic—Proto-Indo-European loan words, especially those referring to agriculture and animals, Igor Diakonov has winnowed out almost all of the proposed comparisons except for goat, wild cattle and horn, all three of which he argued were probably derived from a common third source. Now there are, to be sure, some comparisons that will simply not go away such as Greek pelekeus, Indic parasu- 'axe' which is normally set beside Akkadian pilaqq 'spindle, spike', itself a possible loan from Sumerian balag. This would appear to be a typical 'wander word' moving along trade routes between various peoples from the Aegean to the Indus. Similar suggestions have been employed to account for possible similarity between Akkadian sarpu 'silver' and vaguely similar words in Germanic, Baltic and Slavic. But these, and occasionally other attempts to establish correlations between other Near Eastern languages, are quantitatively minute, qualitatively poor, and certainly do not reflect the unimpeachable pattern of evidence which we find with the agricultural and technological loan words that were borrowed from Indo-Iranian into Finno-Ugric. These indicate what intimate contacts between two language families should look like and this is not at all what we find in the Near East. There are, of course, some possible loans between individual Indo-European languages, as we have already seen between the Indo-Aryans and the Hurrians (Mitanni), or possibly Hittite and Hurrian. On the other hand, there is no convincing evidence that would set Proto-Indo-European in direct contact with the languages of the Near East although it is always possible that a few words may have passed between these two different families through intermediary languages.

A third family to be seriously proposed as possessing considerable similarity with Indo-European is Kartvelian. This is the major language group of the south Caucasus which is spoken by four million people, among whom the overwhelming majority speak the Georgian language. Although some lexical evidence has been cited (Tomas Gamkrelidze lists about twenty words), the primary case for Indo-European—Kartvelian relations is typological and concerns comparisons in the phonetic and grammatical systems of the two families. With such a case it is far easier to argue a very distant genetic link between the two families rather than some historical association played out during the period of Proto-Indo-European existence. Moreover, some scholars explain Kartvelian—Indo-European similarities by contact between the two, when the Anatolians came into long-standing contact with their Kartvelian neighbours to their east.

Even more remote are the attempts to associate the early Indo-Europeans with the Altaic languages, especially Turkic, whose home is situated generally in the region of the Altai. Other than the occasional correspondence between Turkic and Tocharian, for example, Turkish *öküz* 'ox' from Tocharian B *okso*, there is really no solid evidence to draw the Proto-Indo-Europeans so far to the east.

To sum up this section, during the fifth to third millennia BC Proto-Indo-European was but one of a considerable number of languages spoken across Eurasia. It seems likely that the majority of the languages existing then have left no trace and now lie beyond our ability to recover. Of those languages to have survived into the historical record, those that comprise the Finno-Ugric family exhibit the strongest relationship with Indo-European and suggest that at some time they were both neighbours. That the Proto-Indo-Europeans shared a border with the Finno-Ugric speakers somewhere in the vicinity of the forest-steppe zone of south Russia appears to provide the most economical explanation of the evidence. But we would be overplaying our hand to imagine that it provided the *only* explanation since a contact relation or earlier genetic relation between Proto-Indo-European and Finno-Ugric could also have been played out directly west of the Finno-Ugric languages, as has been suggested by Oleg Trubachev. This would be an area that might include the northwest of the Soviet Union extending towards the Baltic and into Central Europe. But the attraction of a more southerly location for Indo-Europeans has the additional advantage of explaining any putative contacts with both the Caucasian and Near Eastern languages.

Internal linguistic evidence

It has long ago been argued that we may look within the structure, the distribution and the interrelationships of the Indo-European languages, to gain some insight as to where they were situated before their major dispersal or, at least, before they were earliest attested. The nature of this evidence and the approaches to it vary widely and we will proceed from some of the simpler forms of reasoning to a few of the more esoteric means of locating the Indo-European homeland.

One of the most obvious approaches to our problem is to ask which candidate for a possible Indo-European homeland is most plausible from the geographical point of view. This basically requires us to set all other factors other than distance to zero and assume that the point of origin most conveniently located to the extremes of the total area of the Indo-Europeans provides the simplest solution. Naturally, this merely leads us to accept the centre of the language family's distribution as its most likely point of origin. When we apply such a rule to the distribution of the Uralic languages we would place a centre somewhere in the Urals, and for the Turkic languages we would seek its homeland somewhere in the vicinity of the Altai, locations which are at least congruent with the primary range of modern opinion. By the first century BC, a period late enough to encompass most known Indo-European languages, we find that they are distributed from approximately 10 degrees west longitude (the Celts of northwest Iberia and Ireland) to 90 degrees east longitude (Eastern Iranians, Tocharians). The north—south dispersion is much smaller lying between about 60 to 20 degrees latitude, that is, between the Germans and the Indo-Aryans, and it is clear that the basic axis of Indo-European expansions should be east—west. Consequently, the centre point for the linear expansion would be approximately 40 degrees east longitude, the area of the Don river in south Russia. A homeland, therefore, that stretched somewhere between the Black and Aral Seas would be most convenient in terms of explaining the early geographical distribution of the Indo-European languages if only the factor of distance is considered. But a convenient explanation which ignores all the other variables is hardly a compelling one without further support.

Any historical linguist would have good cause to argue that the dispersal of a language family is far more reliably measured in terms of languages than in kilometres, since it is the individual languages which form the constituent elements of the family. From this perspective there is something very lopsided about our selecting 40 degrees east longitude as the centre of dispersion since only the Armenian, Indo-Iranian and Tocharian languages are found east of it while all other Indo-European languages lie to its west.

The western bias of the Indo-European languages was observed as long ago as the mid-nineteenth century when most scholars were automatically assuming that the homeland lay in Asia, the 'mother of nations'. It was at this time that the first serious proponent of a European homeland, the British ethnologist and philologist Robert Gordon Latham, argued that an Asian homeland violated the basic principles of natural science. When confronted with two branches of Indo-European – a European branch that occupied a vast area and which was extremely diverse versus the relatively homogeneous dialects of the Indo-Iranian group in Asia – one must naturally conclude that the latter were derived from the area of the former in the same way as one would derive an isolated species from the territory of its genus. Consequently, it was far more logical to imagine that the Indo-Iranian languages had moved away from the mass of other Indo-European languages rather than the converse, and to argue otherwise was to engage in the same type of absurdity as assuming that the Finno-Ugric languages originated in Hungary.

Although Latham never occupied a central place in the development of historical linguistics, his line of argument is still widely utilized today. The principle implicit in his argument is that linguistic differentiation is a product

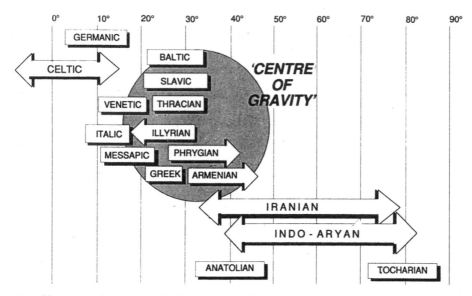

83   *The centre of gravity of the Indo-European languages.*

of time, hence we may expect that where there is greater diversity the language family must have existed there for a greater time. Conversely, the appearance of relatively similar close-knit dialects suggests a recent occupation of a given territory. The idea of the 'centre of gravity' of a language family for determining the homeland area has been widely applied among the languages of the world, especially in North America but also in Africa. If we were to apply it here to the Indo-Europeans, we would find the area of greatest diversity to lie very roughly in Central-Eastern Europe where Italic, Venetic, Illyrian, Germanic, Baltic, Slavic, Thracian, Greek and possibly both Armenian and Phrygian took their more immediate origins. Such a solution pitches the homeland to about 20–30 degrees longitude, considerably west of our earlier solution based solely on distance. It also raises two further issues or factors which themselves have served as routes to the Indo-European homeland. The first concerns the internal configuration of the Indo-European languages. While it may be quite attractive to dismiss the Indo-Iranian languages as a later offshoot of the European languages, the existence of the very 'un-Indo-Iranian' Tocharian languages forces us to consider other alternatives. Secondly, the centre of gravity principle, which implicitly depends on time as the major factor of linguistic diversification, ignores other, possibly more important, factors which might induce the linguistic fragmentation we encounter in Central-Eastern Europe. These are topics which we cannot afford to ignore.

Earlier, when we examined the tree versus wave models of the Indo-European language, we noted the obvious tendency for various Indo-European languages to share common features with some, rather than others, of its sister languages. The most obvious division was the distinction between the *centum* and *satem* languages. In the nineteenth century, many linguists placed exceptional importance on the fact that Celtic, Germanic, Italic and Greek all maintained a Proto-Indo-European *k while eastern languages such as Baltic, Slavic, Armenian, and Indo-Iranian all revealed an s-sound. The west–east division suggested that the Proto-Indo-Europeans had divided like cell mitosis, and some even sought a major physical barrier to explain the sound shift, the Vistula river proving popular at one time. Naturally, the symmetry of this model was shattered when both the Anatolian and the Tocharian languages were also revealed to be centum languages. Some attempted to retain the traditional division by invoking migrations of heroic length from the west to explain the later positions of the Tocharians. The internal relationships of the Indo-European languages, therefore, does bear on their relative geographical positions and, consequently, on the Indo-European homeland itself.

The internal configuration of the Indo-European language is essentially established by examining the phonetic, grammatical and lexical (vocabulary) similarities that are shared between each language. The fact that the centum languages retain the Proto-Indo-European *k, while the satem languages change it to an s, is an example of a phonetic isogloss (similarity). An example of a grammatical isogloss is the augment, the prefacing of a Proto-Indo-European *e- to verbs to form a past tense, which is found in Greek, Armenian, Phrygian, and the Indo-Iranian languages (Greek *ephere*, Armenian *eber*, Sanskit *abharat* 'he bore' from the root *bher- 'bear'), but nowhere else. Finally, there are isoglosses which involve vocabulary. For example, Italic, Celtic and Germanic all share the same word *netr 'snake' (Latin *natrix*, Old Irish *nathir*, Old English *naeddre* [Modern English *adder*] which is not found in any other Indo-European language). These isoglosses, which are numerous and varied, derive from either of two situations: they are examples of old Proto-Indo-European words or forms which have been retained only in some but have disappeared in other Indo-European languages; or they are innovations developed across adjacent dialects in a later stage of Indo-European after dialectal unity had collapsed. The word for snake cited above is a good example of the second situation since it cannot be ascribed to Proto-Indo-European but rather appears to be an innovation of the west Indo-European languages of Celtic, Italic and Germanic. Within historical linguistics there are considerable areas of disagreement over the status of many of the isoglosses yet there are also regions of broad, though by no means universal, agreement. Basically, they concern the nature of linguistic relationships experienced by the speakers of the various dialects between the period which we denote Proto-Indo-European and the emergence of each individual language. No solution to the Indo-European homeland problem can afford to ignore these configurations.

The Anatolian languages appear to have preserved a number of archaic features, for example, laryngeals and heteroclitics,[29] and they lack a number of other characteristics such as grammatical gender, which is commonly found in the other Indo-European languages. Although the absence of some forms may certainly be attributed to attrition, since Anatolian was introduced into a territory densely settled by non-Indo-European speakers, there is still sufficient evidence to convince most linguists that the ancestors of the Anatolian languages separated from their other Indo-European relations at a relatively early time. It is precisely for this reason that the hypothesis of an early migration into Anatolia by Indo-European speakers is popular with many linguists.

A central group of Indo-European languages comprised of Greek, Armenian, Iranian and Indic, would all appear to share some of the latest innovations in the development of the Indo-European languages, for example, the augment. This is historically explained by assuming that the ancestors of all of these languages were once geographically more closely associated than we find them in historical times. On the basis of our excursus into the individual origins of each of these groups we may suggest a chain of central Indo-European dialects stretching from the Balkans across the Black Sea to the east Caspian.

There are other closely associated languages or configurations which conform well with the historical position of the various languages. For example, historical linguists recognize many shared similarities among the west Indo-European languages of Celtic, Italic and Germanic. Another recognizable chain of isoglosses links Germanic specifically with Baltic and Slavic while the latter two share a number of features with Iranian and Indic. All of these relations are geographically plausible and suggest that the relative position of most of the Indo-European languages has probably not altered greatly. By this is meant that we do not find compelling reasons to associate Celtic more closely with Iranian, for example, and hence have to devise complicated geographical hypotheses to explain their origins. In general, this indicates that the expansion of the Indo-European languages was broadly centrifugal from a more central homeland rather than linear from one of the extremes.

Finally, we may glance at the temporal relationship between the various languages. We have already seen that the geographically more central languages, from Greek east to Indic, all appear to share late innovations. On the other hand, there are also several features that have traditionally been regarded as archaisms and which are preserved only in Celtic, Italic, Phrygian, Anatolian and Tocharian. The fact that the archaisms are situated on the periphery of the Indo-European world, while the innovations are found towards the centre, conforms with one of the well-known models of what is commonly known as linguistic geography: peripheral languages conserve while central languages innovate. To what extent this is a universally applicable norm is quite debatable, but this model does seem apt for the distribution of languages in the Indo-European family. In concrete terms it implies a central area composed of the ancestors of the Greek-Armenian-Iranian-Indic group, and a peripheral area of Indo-European dialects which both retained certain archaic features of Proto-Indo-European and avoided the later innovations of the central group. Temporally, this indicates that the ancestors of the peripheral languages had already dispersed before the central region had innovated. Geographically, a homeland which conforms to this model will have obvious attractions to the historical linguist. Again, then, the region between Central-Eastern Europe across the east Caspian provides a plausible homeland. Certainly, situating the Indo-European homeland to either the western or eastern extreme of the Indo-

European dispersion would conflict with almost all of the evidence for the internal configuration of the Indo-European languages.

Interference and substrates

Our emphasis on how languages change naturally through time should not eclipse other factors responsible for the fragmentation of the Indo-European language family. While the expansion of the Indo-European languages requires human migration, it also must have involved the assimilation of a vast number of non-Indo-European peoples. Although the aboriginal populations would come to adopt the Indo-European tongue, the ultimate result might very well have been affected by their native language, its phonetic system, grammar and vocabulary. This is a phenomenon experienced by anyone who undertakes a second language, and we can hardly fail to hear the differences between English as it is articulated by a Frenchman, a Chinese or an Indian. The impact of the substrate language on the newly adopted one is known as *interference* and, since the mid-nineteenth century, linguists have often argued that the degree of interference provides a clue to the location of the Indo-European homeland. It is reasoned that where the Indo-Europeans travelled least from their homeland we should expect the least foreign interference and, consequently, the most conservative languages. Conversely, where we find the most radical deviations from Proto-Indo-European, we may assume strong interference from substrate populations whose territory should consequently be excluded from the homeland area.

Theoretically, we should want to compare the proportion of each language's vocabulary, grammar and phonetic system with reconstructed Proto-Indo-European and then determine which languages seemed the most conservative and which had diverged the greatest. Unfortunately, we must ensure with such a procedure that we are comparing like with like. But how do we compare Hittite, for example, against Lithuanian, when the former was already extinct 2,500 years before the latter was first attested? The later a language is first attested, the greater opportunity for it to have undergone changes stemming from its contacts with other languages *after* it has taken up its historical position. Greek, for example, which has a very long textual tradition, reveals approximately four times the number of inherited Indo-European words in its vocabulary as does Albanian which is first attested very late and, in the meanwhile, had borrowed heavily from its neighbours. Finally, there is no recognized means of measuring degrees of conservatism and weighing each change in phonetics, grammar or vocabulary against another. We must ultimately trust to impressions that cannot help but be subjective.

Subjective or not, there are probably few linguists who would not admit that there is fairly clear evidence for substrate languages affecting some of the Indo-European languages. Even as early as the Vedic period, Dravidian loan words began to appear in Indic, while we have already reviewed some of the evidence for non-Indo-European vocabulary in Anatolian and Greek. On a much broader scale, the Celtic languages of both Britain and Ireland underwent an extremely brusque restructuring which has often been attributed to the influence of native non-Indo-European-speaking populations. These observations, of course, only serve to exclude peripheral areas which we would have rejected as potential homelands on other grounds. There is for Northern Europe an extensive, bitter and thoroughly inconclusive controversy on whether the systematic change of all Proto-Indo-European consonants in Germanic should be attributed to non-Indo-European natives who spoke 'broken' Indo-European. Further east we find far less discussion of substratal influences and a much greater acknowledgment of conservatism. This is especially seen in the case of Lithuanian which exhibits an astounding retention of the Proto-Indo-European forms as can be seen in the declension of the Indo-European word for 'wolf' below:

	Proto-Indo-European	Sanskrit	Lithuanian
Nominative	*wlkʷos	vrkas	vilkas
Vocative	*wlkʷe	vrka	vilke
Accusative	*wlkʷom	vrkam	vilka
Genitive	*wlkʷosyo	vrkasya	vilko
Ablative	*wlkʷod	vrkad	vilko
Dative	*wlkʷoi	vrkaya	vilkui
Locative	*wlkʷoi	vrke	vilke
Instrumental	*wlkʷo	vrka	vilku

What is most striking is that Lithuanian shows roughly the same general retention of the Proto-Indo-European forms (naturally mitigated by minor sound shifts) as does Sanskrit, despite the fact that the latter language is attested nearly 3,000 years earlier than Lithuanian. This apparent archaism has mesmerized many linguists for over a century now and has led some to the conclusion that the Indo-European homeland must have lain in or near the Baltic. The case for a Baltic homeland has been augmented by a series of studies made by Wolfgang P. Schmid who has argued that the Baltic region even retains the Proto-Indo-European names for rivers. This hydronymic evidence we will pass over, since attempts to analyze river names in terms of Proto-Indo-European itself tend to be wildly subjective and seldom convince the majority of historical linguists.[30] Nevertheless, we are still left with the apparent conservatism of Lithuanian. Moreover, Vittore Pisani has observed that those languages west of the Baltic all show an abandonment of the Indo-European free accent[31] while Lithuanian and a number of the Slavic languages retain traces of it. And here we can observe that, although Slavic is not quite so conservative as Lithuanian, it still displays an extremely high retention of Indo-European noun forms.

The evidence of Lithuanian, and to some extent Slavic, has predisposed many to seek the homeland in this region of Eastern Europe, or at least proximate to the Baltic and Slavic territories. It would be misleading to imagine that both of these branches of Indo-European did not show marked innovations as well as conservatism, and this is especially apparent in the verbs.

Nevertheless, this cannot detract from the overall, subjective if you will, impression that the Indo-European languages of Eastern Europe have shown a stronger tendency to retain earlier Indo-European forms than have some of their neighbours. But this alone does not provide a secure solution to our problem. We have no more right to assume that interference is the prime cause of language change than the other factors upon which solutions have been constructed. Moreover, even if we were to attribute the conservative nature of Lithuanian to a lack of interference from non-Indo-European substrates, this need not indicate the absence of non-Indo-Europeans in the Baltic region but merely the effectiveness of intruding Indo-Europeans at assimilating a native population. Recall here the trivial impact of the Celtic languages of Britain on the development of English. Here some future linguist, ignorant of the evidence of both history and placenames, might conclude that England had always been occupied by Germanic-speaking peoples.

While our excursus into the internal linguistic evidence cannot provide us with a conclusively demonstrated homeland, it does emphasize a recurrent pattern of support for a homeland which should lie between Central Europe and the east Caspian.

Linguistic palaeontology

One of the most widely recognized techniques for delimiting the Indo-European homeland is linguistic palaeontology, the same method employed in the reconstruction of the cultural vocabulary of the Proto-Indo-Europeans. When we apply it to the homeland problem, we compare the reconstructed Indo-European vocabulary against the archaeological and environmental record in order to determine what region in Eurasia best corresponds with the linguistic evidence. While there are the invariable problems of method associated with this approach, linguistic palaeontology does rest on a logical basis which can assist us in delimiting the Indo-European homeland.[32]

A starting point for all discussion must be the time-depth of our comparisons. All of the evidence so far reviewed indicates that the Proto-Indo-European language, as we reconstruct it, possessed a cultural vocabulary consistent with a date of roughly the fourth millennium BC. We may extend it somewhat in either direction, but not very much. Since we know that the Anatolian languages had already appeared by about 2000 BC and that the Indo-Iranians should have emerged by that time as well, any date more recent than 2500 BC for Proto-Indo-European becomes increasingly implausible. There is, perhaps, a bit more latitude in extending the concept of Proto-Indo-European earlier than the fourth millennium BC, but anything much prior to 5000 BC would locate the Proto-Indo-Europeans temporally long before the earliest evidence for a number of the apparently later items – wagon, domestic horse, wool, yoke, plough – that are well established in the Proto-Indo-European vocabulary, plus others such as silver which are arguably Proto-Indo-European. Since one still comes across scholars asserting that the origins of the

Indo-Europeans may well be traced to the Palaeolithic, we should pause to discuss our lower time limit for the concept of Proto-Indo-European.

On brief reflection one could hardly dispute that the distant Palaeolithic ancestors of the Proto-Indo-Europeans possessed many words ancestral to those which later emerged in the Indo-European languages. We could hardly be surprised that Palaeolithic people, occupying the area of the homeland, had names for the trees, wild animals, implements, kinship categories, and natural features expected of any human society. On the other hand, we would be astounded if they possessed precisely the same words articulated in the same phonetic system and utilized with the same grammatical endings as their descendants many thousands of years later. This would violate all human experience. Rather, we might conjecture that a hunter speaking a distant ancestor of what later emerged as Proto-Indo-European may have called a cow **ngu in 10,000 BC, which later evolved into **$ngʷu$ by 7000 BC, then **$gʷuo$ by 5000 BC to emerge in Proto-Indo-European as *$gʷous$. Now, no form antecedent to the reconstructed Proto-Indo-European form can be termed Proto-Indo-European. This is not linguistic nit-picking but essential logic which, if ignored, leads swiftly to absurdity unless one is also content to thrust Proto-Englishmen into the Palaeolithic because the English language also retains reflexes of Proto-Indo-European vocabulary, for example, 'cow' from Proto-Indo-European *$gʷous$. Linguistically, the only way to proceed any further back in time than Proto-Indo-European is to assume the genetic relationship between Indo-European and another language family and attempt to reconstruct their common ancestor from their individual proto-languages. This has indeed been attempted on both a small scale, such as Proto-Indo-Uralic or Proto-Indo-Semitic, to vast constructs such as Nostratic which argues for a common ancestor for the Indo-European, Uralic, Altaic, Kartvelian, Hamito-Semitic and Dravidian languages. These controversial theories do not concern us here and we may merely emphasize that there were no more Proto-Indo-Europeans in the Palaeolithic than there were Proto-English or proto-Frenchmen. Our Proto-Indo-European is the slice of one particular strand of the linguistic continuum, falling about 4500–2500 BC.

Once we have established the appropriate time-frame for our search, what items of the Proto-Indo-European vocabulary are most diagnostic for locating the homeland? In Chapter Four we reviewed the Proto-Indo-European environment but it did not offer many useful markers. The existence of a word for mountain *$gʷer(ə)$ (Sanskrit *giris*, Greek *deiros*, Old Church Slavonic *gora*) have led some to assume that the Indo-Europeans must have originated in a mountainous landscape, candidates ranging from the Himalayas in the nineteenth century, to Armenia as recently suggested by several Soviet linguists. On the same line of reasoning, these latter exclude the plains of Northern Europe and the entire Pontic-Caspian region. Surely, one need not live on a mountain to have a name for it, and neither the North European plain nor the Pontic-Caspian steppe is so far distant from marked topographical relief that their occupants could have dispensed with a word for mountain.

The arboreal vocabulary of Proto-Indo-European has played a much more significant role in the homeland problem. In general, most of the tree names that can be solidly attested for Proto-Indo-European are so ubiquitous that they cannot be used to delimit the homeland much further than we already have. Only the beech has provided more circumscribed limits for the homeland, on the traditional argument that it did not grow east of the Königsberg-Odessa line and so excluded both a steppe and an Asiatic origin for the Indo-Europeans, but we have already seen that this word cannot bear the weight of such inferences. Even if we were to assume Proto-Indo-European status for it, despite the lack of a single Asiatic reflex of the word and grave doubts about its original meaning, then the beech excludes Atlantic Europe, and that part of Europe east of a line from Moscow to Rostov on Don, but not the Caucasus where a variety of beech is well represented. On the other hand, the Volga and east Caspian do lie decidedly outside the distribution of the beech.

Of the Indo-European wild fauna, almost all the reconstructed species have such broad distributions that they do not normally lend themselves to delimiting the homeland. The one major exception, at least from the perspective of the history of the homeland problem, is the Proto-Indo-European word *lokŝos which has frequently been taken to mean 'salmon' (*Salmo salar*). The salmon has a very restricted distribution in Europe and its imputation to Proto-Indo-European suggested that the homeland must have included the rivers which drain into the Baltic, hence Northern Europe. More recent and exhaustive examination of this word has, however, prompted Richard Diebold to reverse this conclusion. According to Diebold, the evidence indicates that the original referent was not 'salmon' but probably the anadromous 'salmon trout' (*Salmo trutta*) which is ubiquitous. In addition, a number of linguists have also argued for the reconstruction of the smaller speckled 'brook trout', thus providing two salmonids for Proto-Indo-European. Diebold presses the argument further by observing that none of the other salmonids – huchen, char, greylings – is attested for Proto-Indo-European and that their names were created as each individual Indo-European language came into contact with these new species. Now, there is only one area

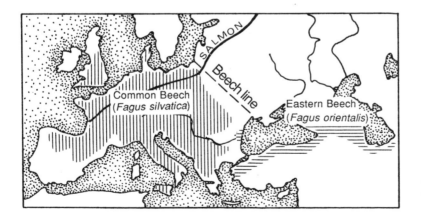

84 The 'beech line' and the distribution of the salmon, Salmo salar.

in which the two salmonids attested for Proto-Indo-European are found to the exclusion of all others – the Pontic-Caspian. Consequently, the fish that was once employed to dismiss the steppe region can be used to support it. To decide the homeland problem on such an argument involves us in the subtle issue of the admissability of negative evidence.

To argue the location of the homeland from what items are *not* attested to Proto-Indo-European involves us in *a silentio* evidence. This has been frequently employed (and criticized) in the history of the problem. If the Indo-Europeans do not share a common word for amber, for example, how can one imagine that the homeland included the Baltic region where amber was of such importance? How can the homeland be situated in the Mediterranean or the Near East if we cannot reconstruct to Proto-Indo-European words for oil, olives, grapes, the ass, or many other environmental terms typical for this region? While the absence of a single word can be set aside as a matter of chance, can the absence of an entire series of words relating to a specific environment be so quickly dismissed? Or are all arguments based on negative evidence, to be dismissed as inconclusive no matter what their quantity or pattern? Linguists know all too well that, if we apply any form of strict scrutiny in determining the Proto-Indo-European status of a word, there are numerous examples of words which the Proto-Indo-Europeans must have had but which we cannot reconstruct, for example, we can reconstruct 'eye' and 'eyebrow' but not 'eyelid'. Furthermore, we have already seen how one may reject tying a word and the homeland too close together when all one needs to assume is that the bulk of the Indo-Europeans moved outside the distribution of the particular item at an early time. As no one has been able to resolve this epistomological issue, the reader must decide how much worth should be placed on these arguments.

A corollary to examining patterned absences in the proto-lexicon is the analysis of the shifts in meanings of reconstructible Proto-Indo-European words. A good example is provided in Proto-Indo-European *bherǵo- 'birch'. This is one of the few tree names that can be strongly reconstructed to Proto-Indo-European. It denotes the birch in Indic (*bhurja-*), Iranian (Ossetic *bärz*), Germanic (*birch*), Baltic (Latvian *berzs*) and Slavic (Russian *berëza*). However, its meaning has been shifted in Italic where Latin *fraxinus* refers to the ash, and the word is absent from Greek. Generally, linguists have argued that its shift or absence in Mediterranean languages is motivated by the fact that the birch is either absent or rare here, and hence when the Indo-Europeans first entered this region they either dropped the word from their vocabulary or shifted the meaning of the word to another species. In Paul Friedrich's extensive list of Proto-Indo-European (or early Indo-European) tree names, about half of the Greek reflexes of these words exhibit shifts in meaning, a pattern which is quite congruent with other evidence for the later Indo-Europeanization of Greece.

If we move from the wild to the domestic fauna, then we find several items of interest. The most obvious and frequently discussed is the horse which is very well reconstructed to Proto-Indo-European and is normally taken to refer to the domestic horse. This is not where the matter ends, however, since we know that wild horses during the Proto-Indo-European period were also to be found over a broad area of Eurasia, including areas where we also know of domestic horses. Yet there is only one word for horse in Proto-Indo-European, and it does not distinguish between wild and domestic. The consequence of this is that while Proto-Indo-European *ekwos probably refers to the domestic horse it might well also have included the wild horse.

During the relevant period, Eurasia can be divided into three broad categories with regard to the exploitation of the horse. The first category includes all of those areas where there appears to be a virtual absence of horse remains. This would mean most of the Near East, including Anatolia, with a very few exceptions which are normally attributed to the importations of horses from the steppe to the north. It also comprises the Balkans. The earliest horses in Greece do not appear prior to about 2000 BC which is consistent with a late Indo-Europeanizing of Greece. There is a little early evidence for horses on some east Balkan sites but this is generally interpreted as the westernmost extension of either wild horses or possibly contacts with domestic horse-breeders from the Pontic-Caspian. There is no evidence whatsoever for horses in the Neolithic period of the Carpathian Basin although very small numbers of horses do begin to appear, again from the east, during the fourth millennium BC. The other regions excluded from the primary range of the horse lie outside of serious homeland consideration, for example, the Apennine peninsula, southern Iberia, and Ireland, although they further emphasize the later movements of Indo-Europeans into these regions. If the horse, either wild or domestic, is employed as a major marker of the Proto-Indo-Europeans, then we would exclude most of Southeastern Europe from the homeland.

The second category includes areas where horses appear to have survived the Late Pleistocene and continued to be exploited through the Neolithic, albeit as wild animals and as extremely marginal resources. Here we speak of the occasional presence of horse bones on sites of Central and Northern Europe. While the number of bones may not be great, they do occur at a sufficient time and distance from the major East European centre of horse breeding so that they cannot be immediately dismissed as merely the product of contacts with the Ukraine. Consequently, unless one demands that the Proto-Indo-European *ekwos referred only to the domestic horse, we cannot use this animal to exclude either the Neolithic cultures of the Danube or the TRB (Trichterbecher, that is, Funnel Beaker) culture of Northern Europe as possible Indo-European homelands.

The third category is the actual centre of the natural range of wild herds of horses, specifically the tarpan, and the earliest-known centre of horse domestication. The main core of this region is to be found from the Dnieper river east to the Volga, and possibly on into Asia. It is extremely difficult to determine its eastern limits, but the presence of domestic horses in the Afanasievo culture of southern Siberia by the third millennium may suggest earlier predecessors. During the fourth millennium BC, the domestic horse appears to have expanded westwards and accounts for the increasing percentages of horse remains in the northwest Pontic and the earliest appearance of the horse in the Balkans and Carpathian basin. Thus, if one wishes to confine *ekʷos to the domestic horse, then linguistic palaeontology suggests that the border of the homeland should not lie much further west than the Black Sea.

In evaluating the evidence from these three categories, we recognize that the Indo-European homeland may be most conveniently set to the Eurasian steppe, but we are under no compulsion to come solely to this conclusion. If the Proto-Indo-European *ekʷos included also the wild horse, then there are no grounds for confidently excluding Central and Northern Europe as potential homeland territory. Still, it must be admitted that they offer slight support for the horse-centred society which we commonly project to the Proto-Indo-European period, and on balance the evidence of the horse better supports the steppe and forest-steppe. Finally, it is difficult not to see the absence of the horse in the Balkans as serious grounds for again challenging its claim to be included in the homeland.

The earliest evidence for wheeled vehicles outside of territories either demonstrably non-Indo-European, for example, Sumer, or implausibly Proto-Indo-European – such as the Kuro-Araxes culture of south Transcaucasia where Hurro-Urartian languages appear – is to be found among a number of fourth-millennium BC cultures in Europe. These include the TRB culture of Northern Europe which reveals an acquaintance with wheeled vehicles by the mid-fourth millennium BC; the Late Copper Age Baden culture in the Carpathian Basin and other late Copper Age cultures of northern Italy which date from the latter half of the fourth millennium BC; and the Pontic-Caspian region where numerous remains of wheeled vehicles begin to emerge towards the end of the fourth millennium BC. Tomas Gamkrelidze and Vyachislav Ivanov, interestingly enough, have noted that one of our words associated with wheeled vehicles, Proto-Indo-European *kʷekʷlo- bears striking similarity to the words for vehicles in Sumerian gigir, Semitic *galgal-, and Kartvelian *grgar. With the putative origin of wheeled vehicles set variously to the Pontic-Caspian, Transcaucasia or to Sumer, we may be witnessing the original word for a wheeled vehicle in four different language families. Furthermore, as the Proto-Indo-European form is built on an Indo-European verbal root *kʷel- 'to turn, to twist', it is unlikely that the Indo-Europeans borrowed their word from one of the other languages. This need not, of course, indicate that the Indo-Europeans invented wheeled vehicles, but it might suggest that they were in some form of contact relation with these Near Eastern languages in the fourth millennium BC.

In general, the other solidly reconstructed technological items tend either to reinforce a border ranging from Northern Europe across the Pontic-Caspian, or to expand it considerably. The plough, for example, solidly attested to Proto-Indo-European, is known by way of ploughmarks in a number of fourth-millennium BC sites in Northern Europe extending from Britain to Poland.

Copper is widely attested throughout Europe during the fourth millennium BC and cannot be employed as a useful geographic marker. Silver, somewhat more contentiously ascribed to the Proto-Indo-European vocabulary, does have a largely East European distribution throughout the later fourth millennium BC and, if accepted, would effectively exclude Northern Europe from the homeland area. But anyone conversant with the history of the homeland problem realizes that an argument dependent on a single item, particularly a linguistically contestable one, cannot hope to achieve universal agreement. Rather, we must take our lead from the general pattern of correlations between linguistic palaeontology and the archaeological record.

A summary view of linguistic palaeontology engaged in evaluating the plausibility of an Indo-European homeland somewhere in Europe confines our attention primarily to the territory embracing the TRB culture of Northern Europe, the later Neolithic descendants of the Linear Ware culture of the Danubian drainage, the Eneolithic cultures of the Pontic-Caspian region and, perhaps, southern Siberia. The further one moves to the north, west or south of this broad band, the less plausible the territory becomes as a potential homeland congruent with the cultural vocabulary of the Indo-Europeans. Some areas, such as the Carpathian Basin, are merely transitional between what is acceptable and what is implausible. We have pushed the linguistic evidence about as far as we may; now it is the turn of the archaeologist.

Archaeology

There have been over a century of archaeological solutions proposed for the Indo-European problem. The implicit assumption behind almost all of these is the belief that a linguistic entity can be located and its expansion traced in the prehistoric record. There has, unfortunately, been a suprising lack of concern for actually tying a prehistoric linguistic entity to the types of cultural debris encountered by the archaeologist. Anyone with the least familiarity with current archaeological literature recognizes that Gustav Kossinna's dictum of 1911, that sharply defined archaeological cultures invariably correspond with clearly marked ethnic groups, holds little attraction for today's archaeologist. Certainly we need not add to the litany of warnings that pots do not equal people. Nevertheless, while one may deny the necessity of assuming an invariable one-to-one correlation between an archaeological and a linguistic entity, it is equally perverse to assume that there can be no correlation between the two. There is sufficient evidence, for example, to indicate correlations between cultural trait lists and various linguistic groups in North America, which is hardly surprising since we might well expect that cultural traits are more easily shared by a people with the same language than between peoples excluded by linguistic barriers from easy intercourse and interaction.[33] Hence, archaeologists are seldom embarrassed at attributing the Celtic language to the bearers of La Tène remains, Germanic to the Jastorf culture, or various Bantu languages to certain African ceramic styles. The emphasis here must naturally be on inexact equations since one can always cite some exceptions – such as peoples sharing the same language but possessing radically different cultures, as in village versus Bedouin Arab; or different linguistic groups participating in cultures barely distinguishable from another, as among the linguistically diverse Pueblo Indian villages in the American Southwest. These exceptions are normally sufficient to dissuade most archaeologists from attempting to link a culture with a linguistic group unless the culture is proto-historic, like the Celts, and the gap between the archaeological and written records is not great. The linguistic identity of archaeological cultures more distant from the historical record may be thought to lie beyond reasonable inference. This is not, however, an option open to the archaeologist engaged in the Indo-European homeland problem, and we will have to follow the archaeological evidence as best we can.

We may anticipate that any evaluation of an archaeological solution to the homeland problem will involve us in three major issues. The first is the nature of the archaeological entity selected for the homeland. We have already seen that there are some constraints on the area that we might select, although we must recall that at about 4000 BC the number and variety of potential homeland cultures in Eurasia is so great that the territory of the maximum permissable homeland area could normally accommodate at least several different cultures. This cannot help but lead to a certain vagueness no matter what our solution.

Our inability to be precise is further enforced when we concern ourselves with tracing the actual migrations of the Indo-Europeans. Setting aside for the moment the enormous difficulty of tracing a folk migration in the archaeological record, we must remember that we are also attempting to delimit the territory of a linguistic entity which we cannot date with the precision which we apply to an archaeological culture. We might, for example, equate the area of a culture dating from 4500 to 3500 BC with the homeland, when Proto-Indo-European may have not terminated until a millennium later, by which time it occupied a vastly larger area. Conversely, a culture dating from 3500 to 2500 BC might actually represent a stage in the linguistic continuum after the formation of individual Indo-European language groups. We are dealing with general trajectories rather than absolute borders when we attempt to apply the evidence of archaeology to the homeland problem.

The more concrete problem here is naturally whether we can trace the movement of a prehistoric people in the archaeological record. For those who engage in such risks, there is basically a rough hierarchy of evidence that ranks burials as among the more significant evidence for migration and intrusion, closely followed by changes in architecture, ceramics and economy while other items of technology, especially metallurgy, are more often explained by means other than the expansion of ethnic groups. Much current modelling in archaeology tends to emphasize almost every possible means of explaining the spread of a new cultural manifestation other than actual migration. Exchange systems, prestige chains, peer-polity interactions, similar cultural evolution or internal structural reordering independent of external stimuli are frequently advanced against former models of culture changes that instinctively sought to introduce a new people with every new pot or burial. Such a predisposition against finding migrations in the archaeological record is primarily the luxury of prehistorians since any archaeologist operating within historical periods confronts so much evidence for both the historically attested and archaeologically evidenced movement of peoples that it would be ridiculous to dismiss them. Only a misguided (and I hope hypothetical) prehistorian would seek to explain Anglo-Saxon cemeteries in southern England as the result of a continental cult-package or the increased militarization of native British populations following the structural collapse of Romano-British society. Indeed, for the historical archaeologist the problem of correlation is often reversed – there is definite historical evidence for folk movement but precious little archaeological support. This raises one topic which simply cannot be ignored.

Frequently, even when some evidence for migration is grudgingly acknowledged, it is claimed that the evidence is far too slight to account for the assumed linguistic changes. Those who pursue the matter further must engage in argument by decibel – it is the vehemence of the advocacy for or against invasion rather than an appeal to commonly accepted criteria of how much evidence is needed to validate or invalidate the case for a folk movement. If the intrusive origin of the English people is firmly reflected in the archaeological record, the Scots occupy the reverse position. Historical evidence relates how peoples in Ulster migrated to western Scotland in the fifth to sixth centuries A D. The linguistic evidence before this time clearly indicates that various Brittonic languages were spoken in Scotland prior to this colonization and after it we find the transplanted Gaelic language expanding through Scotland. Yet no archaeologist reviewing the sparse evidence for both Ulster and western Scotland would independently declare that there was sufficient evidence to substantiate a linguistic expansion from Ulster to Scotland. The same could be said of the introduction of Breton to Brittany from southern Britain, and many other historically attested but so far archaeologically unverified movements of people.

The issue here, I would argue, is not so much the archaeological record but the misconceptions or at least preconceptions that many archaeologists bring to it, especially those who require unequivocal archaeological evidence for intrusions. Colin Renfrew has recently illustrated this attitude when he writes how archaeologists have now come to the 'realization that there have been far fewer wholesale migrations of people than once had been thought'. He is accurate in describing the general 'mood', at least of archaeologists in Western Europe, but he also exhibits the type of confusion archaeologists tend to share about linguistic problems. First, this new 'realization' has not, in my opinion, much to do with the actual number of migrations be they fewer or more; it concerns how archaeologists discuss the phenomenon of culture change in the archaeological record when there are no other historical or linguistic constraints on the material. Hence to suggest that the presence of a particular type of vessel, the beaker to take a familiar example, and several other 'foreign' elements, were introduced into Britain by an immigrant population is now regarded as *passé* in many archaeological circles. Archaeologists would now seek other explanatory means for accounting for their presence. If, on the other hand, we had possessed later Neolithic texts in one language and found a new language expressed in 'Beaker texts', then I am confident that the evidence previously dismissed as insufficient to support migration would be eloquently assisting us in determining the time of arrival and pattern of movements of these new people. This illustration is, I think, less hypothetical than it might seem.

Witness for example how Renfrew himself treats the origins of the Insular Celts in his own study of Indo-European origins. The archaeological evidence for Iron Age intrusions is weighed insufficient to be interpreted as a migration, hence, we cannot explain the Insular Celtic languages by Late Bronze Age or Iron Age migrations into the British Isles. This throws us back onto the more archaeologically visible introduction of the farming economy into Britain and Ireland in the late fifth millennium BC. But when we come to later Celtic movements such as those into Scotland from Ireland during the first millennium AD a different model is introduced – élite dominance, suggesting a small number of people at the apex of a hierarchy who bring about a linguistic transformation. Why? Both Scotland and Ireland are of similar size; both come to adopt the essentially same Gaelic language. The archaeological evidence for intrusions into Ireland during the Late Bronze Age or Iron Age is certainly no poorer than that for movements from Ireland to Scotland in the first millennium AD. But linguistic and historical evidence constrains Renfrew to accept the later migration (without a shred of convincing archaeological evidence) and yet he rejects any Bronze or Iron Age migration (élites or otherwise?) into Ireland. I do not dispute that the dominance of an Irish élite in western Scotland probably led to the widescale adoption of Gaelic there, but I do dispute that any archaeologist can hope to pronounce on what linguistic displacements did *not* happen in the prehistoric record.

I believe we must discern between two epistomological phenomena: evidence for putative migrations generated entirely by a closed interpretation of the archaeological record; and the issue of migration generated by a reading of the linguistic or historical evidence. In an ideal world there should be no distinction between the two and any archaeologist should be able to establish the validity of a particular invasion hypothesis independent of whether there is historical or linguistic evidence for it. My experience with the literature concerning both prehistoric and historic migrations convinces me that this is not yet the world we live in, and that archaeologists play by different rules depending on the nature of the problems confronting them.

This whole problem of distinguishing linguistic intruders in the archaeological record is aggravated by the fact that our ability to provide the necessary precise dating for the evidence of population movements lessens as we proceed into prehistory. A Dark Age migration that is at least apparent is normally based on data such as a series of well-defined cemeteries extending over one to several centuries and apparently intrusive into the region we find them. Although problems most certainly exist, archaeologists can at least point to intrusive Anglo-Saxon, Longbard, Gepid, Avar, or Sarmatian cemeteries. In much earlier periods, however, we neither have such abundant data nor can we order it within the fine tuning of a century, hence any intrusion that has resulted in the almost predictable adoption by the newcomers of elements of the native culture will seldom, if ever, be particularly obvious. Returning to the spread of the Athapascans in North America, we find some of them practising a sub-Arctic culture in their Alaska-Canadian homeland; others who migrated south into the Pacific Northwest were assimilated into the classic wealth and prestige-obsessed cultures of their neighbours; and those who pressed further south, adapting to both the new environment and acculturating towards the native occupants of the American Southwest. The language persisted but the cultural evidence of its speakers was shed each time it came into a new area. It is a fortunate prehistorian who recovers an intrusive population before it begins to assimilate towards the native culture.

The lessons of all this are several. The archaeologist can identify what appear to be discontinuities in the archaeological record. He may interpret them as evidence of intrusions, or, as Renfrew remarks, reclassify what were once taken to be intrusions into something else. So long as there is no compulsion from linguistic or historical evidence, this is a game that archaeologists are best left to play alone. There is, I believe, a corollary to this: archaeologists would be better off not wasting their time assigning unnecessary linguistic identities to their putative intrusions. Arguments that the 'Beaker folk' may have introduced an Indo-European language into the British Isles (though not one that evolved into anything for which we have evidence), or that the appearance of the royal tombs at Alaca Hüyük in central Anatolia were the result of Indo-Europeans (but not the ancestors of the Hittites), seem to me to be idle. Dealing with the real problems of language intrusion is difficult enough without speculating about the spread of unattested languages. The archaeologist may also assert that there is no obvious evidence for an intrusion or a discontinuity at a particular time, though he or she cannot pretend to control all the possible data and exclude the possibility of a linguistic intrusion. The most positive pronounce-ment that can be made is that both archaeological and linguistic or historical evidence seem to be congruent with one another in suggesting linguistic intrusion; the most negative is that the evidence from the various disciplines do not seem to form a congruent picture.

Finally, there is another issue that is almost invariably ignored yet which is of equal consequence as the previous one. Even if we feel that the evidence does admit of a folk movement, how do we assess that it effected a linguistic replacement? As we have seen, intrusive populations may well find themselves assimilated by their hosts rather than the reverse, especially when migrations will often involve a smaller population intruding into the territory of a larger. It is perhaps here that the analysis of the changing structures within society is most productive and we will seek to explore this further in Chapter Eight.

17 The face of an ancient German. The famous Tollund man, recovered from a Danish bog, illustrates the appearance of the Iron Age German. The rope around his neck suggests that he met his death through punishment or sacrifice.

*18 (above) Cast bronze helmet plates from Torslunda in Sweden
depict hard-pressed Scandinavians and monsters. The plates date to the sixth
or seventh century AD.*

*19 (right) Detail of two scenes of Iron Age life in northern Italy
from the Certosa situla from Bologna. The upper register depicts preparations
for a feast while the lower illustrates either a contest or duet involving two
musicians.*

20 *Scene from the Gundestrup cauldron. The plate illustrates troops of infantry and cavalry wearing Celtic regalia and blowing the typical Celtic horn, the carnyx. The scene on the left is generally interpreted as a ceremonial*

drowning scene, the classic method of dispatching a victim to a 'third function' fertility deity in Western Europe. The cauldron is probably of east European manufacture, though later transported to Denmark.

21 (above) Burial from Khvalynsk cemetery, Volga region. Accompanying ornaments include shell beads and copper rings imported from the Balkans.

22 (below) Typical communal burial pit of the Dnieper-Donets culture from the site of Nikolskoye.

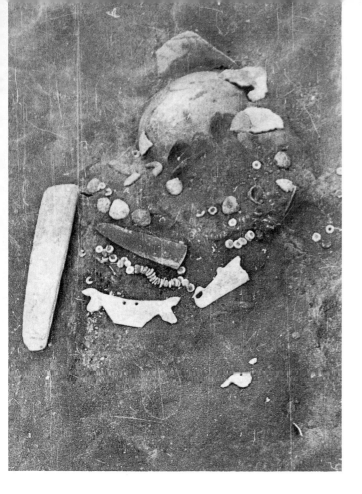

23 (top left) Burial from the Sezzhee cemetery in the middle Volga region. The individual was accompanied by a stone axe, knife, bead necklace and zoomorphic bone plates.

24 (top right) Reconstruction of the robust Cro-magnon features of a Dnieper-Donets male from Nikolskoye.

25 (above) Reconstruction of a Dnieper-Donets female.

26 (left) Reconstruction of a male from the Sredny Stog site of Alexandria. For those who hold to a Pontic-Caspian homeland, this represents, in general, the physical type of the earliest Indo-Europeans.

27 (left) The Kernosovka stele, discovered in 1973, provides one of the finest examples of Eneolithic art of the Pontic region. It reveals a moustached figure with club, dagger and three axes above the belt, while below it are depicted a large rectangle and two animals, identified as horses.

28 (below) Clay model of a four-wheeled wagon from the Baden cemetery of Budakalasz. This provides some of the earliest evidence for wheeled vehicles in Danubian Europe in the late fourth and early third millennia BC.

Throughout this chapter all of the evidence reviewed so far predisposes us to assume that the Proto-Indo-Europeans were situated, broadly speaking, in a territory extending from Central or Northern Europe on the west across the Pontic-Caspian and possibly into southern Siberia. We see little reason to support an Indo-European homeland that included either Western Europe, Mediterranean Europe, the Balkans, or the Near East. Western Europe, and certainly the southern Mediterranean, have never really been considered serious candidates for the homeland. The same cannot be said, however, for Southeast Europe (the Balkans and Greece), since some linguists and archaeologists have proposed that the Proto-Indo-Europeans might be placed in this territory. We need to take a closer look at the case for and against Southeast Europe.

In a world where the archaeological record refuses to shout out evidence for massive Indo-European migrations, one might well sympathize with Colin Renfrew when he retreats to the expansion of the Early Neolithic in Europe as the only 'basic and widespread cultural and economic change' that might account for the spread of the Indo-European languages. Here, Renfrew is following the conventional wisdom that maintains that Neolithic colonists from Western Asia, probably Anatolia, crossed into Greece during the seventh millennium BC where they established Europe's earliest Neolithic communities. During the course of generations, the descendants of these colonists maintained a 'wave of advance' gradually carrying the new subsistence economy both northwards through the Balkans and westwards from Greece through the central and western Mediterranean. Further advances continued northwards along the Danube drainage to the Atlantic and Baltic, while others pushed eastwards around the northwest shores of the Black Sea where they adopted pastoral economies and spread further east across the steppe. The superior productive capacity of these early agriculturalists ensured their success at assimilating the local Mesolithic communities and the spread of their own (Indo-European according to Professor Renfrew) language(s) from Anatolia to the peripheries of Europe. The differentiation and internal relationships of the Indo-European languages were then established according to the 'wave model' of linguistic change.

In establishing the mechanism of linguistic expansion, a 'wave of advance' of farming communities progressively colonizing new territories over a period of generations, Colin Renfrew accepts a traditional model for the spread of the Neolithic economy. This has been recently challenged by some revisionists who, like Graeme Barker, argue that 'the various systems of initial farming which we can discern were developed by the indigenous population rather than by newcomers'. This position is rather extreme, and seems to flourish among only a handful of British universities. On the other hand, most archaeologists specializing in the origins of the European Neolithic would not accept that the expansion of the farming economy could be entirely attributed to a wave of advancing farmers whose own origins lay ultimately in Anatolia. Rather, we distinguish in the archaeological record areas where a strong case can be made for actual colonization from Asia, for example, Southeast Europe (Greece and the Balkans), probably the Linear Ware territory of Danubian Europe, and other areas where the evidence of continuity from the preceding Mesolithic suggests the local adoption of the new economy by indigenous populations. This is especially seen along the peripheries of continental Europe, in the western Mediterranean, in Northern Europe and in the forest, forest-steppe and steppe zones of Eastern Europe.

If we accept the traditional argument that farming communities did cross from Asia to colonize Southeastern Europe, then it would indeed be difficult to resist the notion that they served as vectors for spreading new languages into Europe. The issue is whether the new languages were Indo-European, as Colin Renfrew has proposed. Given all the evidence reviewed so far, I find this one of the least likely hypotheses. Since Renfrew's book is admittedly speculative, I do not intend to dwell on those points which seem to be particularly implausible, for example, early Neolithic Proto-Indo-Iranians in the Zagros and Indus, 'Proto-Irish' in Ireland about 4500 BC, and so on, since they are peripheral to the main thrust of his argument. Rather, I will examine the core of Renfrew's solution to the Indo-European homeland problem as this also has a bearing on the alternative solutions.

Renfrew draws the Indo-Europeans from the earliest Neolithic communities of Anatolia, including eastern Anatolia, broadly the region from Çatal Hüyük to Çayönü. As we have seen before, with the emergence of the earliest written sources, this region not only exhibits Indo-European populations (Hittite, Luwian and Palaic), but also at least two apparently unrelated non-Indo-European groups: Hattic and Hurrian. Thus, part of the area designated as the Indo-European homeland emerges as non-Indo-European with our first historical records. The only way I can account for this within the framework of Renfrew's model is to assume that later non-Indo-European languages spread into the area of the former homeland, or to assume that two or more language families grew up in the same area and at the same time. There is little to be said in favour of either idea. I am puzzled by a solution that propels Indo-Europeans out of their Anatolian homeland such that they traverse over 3,000 kilometres to arrive in Ireland in the course of two millennia, yet require 5,000 years to advance the 100 or 200 kilometres (if that much) east to Armenia? When the Armenians occupied the former Urartian kingdom about Lake Van, was this a reoccupation of the Indo-Europeans' former territory, or the furthest eastern expansion of the Indo-Europeans from their Anatolian home? Since neither Phrygian nor Armenian can be said to have evolved from Anatolian, and their presence in their respective locations surely requires some form of migration, it seems that in order to sustain Renfrew's model of Indo-European origins we have to propose some form of reflux movement and later migrations which are, of course, quite contrary to his attempt to propose a simple archaeologically visible migration of Indo-Europeans.

An Indo-European homeland which was confined to only south-central and western Anatolia (and hence avoided having to explain Hurrians and Hatti in the Indo-European homeland) could be regarded as a geographical adjustment which might avoid some of the former criticism, although one might note that it requires us to derive the Indo-Europeans from only a handful of sites. But problems still exist since we simply cannot ignore the substantial proportion of the placenames of Anatolia that are unanalyzable as either Indo-European or within the framework of the Anatolian dialects, for example, Parnassos (in both Anatolia and Greece) with a root *parna* 'house' attested in Hurrian *purni* and Egyptian *pr*. In short, there is a case to be made for non-Indo-European substrates across all Anatolia and on into Greece, and I would have thought it far more plausible to associate these with the spread of the Neolithic economy from this region rather than what are almost universally taken to be intrusive Indo-Europeans.

The time-depth for an expansion of the Indo-Europeans in the early Neolithic about 6500 BC is wholly incongruent with our reconstruction of the Indo-European vocabulary. Renfrew attempts to address this problem either by denying the utility of linguistic palaeontology or by attempting to defend his proposed homeland against its findings. For example, the presence of copper in early Neolithic Anatolia indicates that his 'homeland' cannot be excluded on the grounds that the Proto-Indo-Europeans had a word for copper. Nevertheless, as we have seen before, terminology for wheeled vehicles is so abundant and deeply embedded in the Indo-European languages that we must accept their ascription to Proto-Indo-European if the comparative method means anything. Similarly, the horse, which is not attested in any form in Anatolia until the fourth millennium BC, and in Greece until the third, and is again thoroughly embedded in the reconstructed vocabulary as well as in Indo-European ritual, makes a seventh-millennium BC homeland in Anatolia or Greece quite unacceptable. If Andrew Sherratt is correct in placing the development of his 'Secondary Products Revolution' in the Late Neolithic, then words for yoke, plough, wool, and so on, all solidly attested to Proto-Indo-European, would also render an association between the earliest Neolithic and the Indo-Europeans extremely unlikely; the same might be said of Proto-Indo-European silver. While most wild animal terms are rather ubiquitous in Europe, Anatolia and Greece do seem to lie beyond the range of the beaver, another word which can be ascribed to Proto-Indo-European. Even the social and kinship terms which indicate at least that the Proto-Indo-Europeans were patrilineal and 'patriarchal' (and possessed some form of warrior sodality) do not seem to fit the agricultural societies we find in the early Neolithic cultures of Greece and the Balkans.

An Indo-European homeland in Anatolia makes it impossible to explain the structural and lexical similarities between Proto-Indo-European and Uralic, the linguistic family that would appear to be most closely related to Indo-European. Rather, we are required by Renfrew to seek the emergence of Indo-European in a milieu of non-Indo-European languages, such as Hattic and Hurrian, which are structurally worlds apart from Indo-European and provide no grounds to suggest anything other than late contacts. Given that the time-depth suggested by Renfrew for Proto-Indo-European is also broadly contemporary with the emergence of the early Neolithic societies in Southwest Asia, I think we would have the right to expect far greater similarities between Proto-Indo-European and the other languages of this region if this were the home of the Indo-Europeans.

The evidence for a non-Indo-European substrate in Greece, shown in placenames, personal names, tribal names, and cultural terms – some post-dating the Neolithic – seems a reasonable supposition despite all of the problems in sorting out the various layers. Moreover, we have other evidence such as shifts in tree names which make a circumstantial case for assuming an expansion of Indo-Europeans into the Mediterranean and not out of it.

Concerning the origin of the Indo-Europeans of Asia, Renfrew must press his wave of advance around the northwest shores of the Black Sea to explain the origin of Indo-Iranian pastoralists of the Pontic-Caspian steppe and beyond. We will see in the next chapter that such a model is specifically rejected by most if not all Soviet archaeologists engaged in the study of this region. Unlike other peripheral areas where we might propose later expansions from Central Europe during the Bronze or Iron Age to protect Renfrew's hypothesis, there is no body of evidence to suggest anything other than the gradual acculturation of steppe populations well beyond the frontier of the 'wave of advance' colonists. Failure to account for the origins of the Indo-Iranians (and Tocharians) invalidates any putative solution to the homeland problem.

An Anatolian homeland is at variance with the time-depth for the fragmentation of the Indo-European dialects, based on linguistic criteria. According to Renfrew's theory, the language ancestral to Greek was already in Greece by about 6500 BC. Indo-Iranian, following the less implausible of Renfrew's two (implausible) hypotheses,[34] was spoken by descendants of the earliest farming communities who pushed around the Black Sea by the fourth millennium BC and then adopted a pastoral economy and expanded across the steppe. This would indicate that, when we first encounter these languages, they have been separated for over 5,000 years despite the fact that they share what are generally regarded as numerous late isoglosses. The temporal separation between them, according to Renfrew's theory, seems wholly incongruent with what we understand of the Indo-European dialects, and we can only achieve this (lesser?) implausibility by selecting an archaeological interpretation of the origins of the steppe pastoralists that seems contradicted by the archaeological evidence. There are other examples of how Renfrew's theory disregards any notion of the internal relationships of the Indo-European languages. He derives Italic from a seventh- or sixth-millennium Neolithic expansion from Greece across to Italy, yet we know that Italic and Greek are divided by far more isogloss bundles than join them. In short, the whole question of the time-depth involved with his expansions is at variance with almost all current thinking on the problem.

One could compile more objections, such as, if the Indo-Europeans were in Crete since 6000 BC, why can't we read Linear A? Why does it appear to have been devised for a language whose syllabic structure is radically different from the structure of Indo-European words? I would argue that the cumulative weight of these arguments indicates that any attempt to tie the initial Neolithic colonization of Europe to the spread of the earliest Indo-Europeans is really not congruent with either the linguistic or archaeological evidence and, indeed, does not even provide the economy of explanation which should have been one of its major attractions. Anatolia is the wrong place at the wrong time and migrations from it give the wrong results. A brave run, perhaps, but Renfrew's solution is not a convincing one.

Maintaining Renfrew's speculative vein, I would agree that there may have been some population movement from Anatolia to Greece and on into the Balkans beginning in the seventh millennium BC. I would agree that it could have introduced a new language, though it is always possible that pre-Neolithic populations on both sides of the Bosporus spoke the same or related languages. If they did introduce a new language, I would have expected a language similar perhaps to a distant ancestor of those that are historically attested in Anatolia such as Hattic, and that this would provide us with our earliest retrievable evidence of substrate languages in Anatolia and the Aegean. This language may well have been spread through Southeast Europe where, in the course of several millennia, it underwent regional differentiation in the farming villages of the various cultures of this region. It may possibly have been extended somewhat further into Danubian Europe. However, the survival of native languages after their gradual adoption of agriculture particularly throughout the Mediterranean, and the rest of the European periphery, would have ensured that Neolithic Europe was divided into numerous unrelated languages, probably language families. Only Etruscan, Tartessian, Iberian, Basque and Indo-European survived into the written record.

If we can reject outright an association of the Proto-Indo-Europeans with the Early Neolithic of western Anatolia and the Aegean, we need only briefly comment on the Balkans as a suitable homeland. This area has been proposed by a number of linguists, most recently perhaps, Igor Diakonov. It should be noted that Diakonov, like other linguists who have postulated a Balkan homeland, such as Boris Gornung, exclude Greece from the homeland and require a later expansion from the Balkans into Greece to explain the appearance of the Greek language. Here I must join Renfrew in the conventional wisdom which makes it nearly impossible to separate the Early Neolithic communities of the Balkans from those of Greece since they both appear to have taken their origin from the same background of Neolithic colonization, and their differences are trivial compared with their similarities in both material culture and behaviour. In short, a Balkan homeland is merely an Anatolian-Aegean origin once removed and fails for all the same reasons.

Only brief mention need be made regarding the archaeological plausibility of the Indo-European homeland recently proposed by Gamkrelidze and Ivanov which is set to the region of eastern Turkey, the southern Caucasus and northwestern Iran, roughly in the location of Armenia. First, there is really no archaeological evidence whatsoever for an expansion from this region, much less an historical pattern of migrations, that might account for the later positioning of the Indo-European languages. Furthermore, with the possible exception of Johannes Schmidt's attempt to place the Proto-Indo-Europeans near the Babylonians because of what he believed were similarities in their numerical systems, there has probably never been a solution to the homeland problem that has so obviously confined the Proto-Indo-Europeans in an area virtually surrounded, if not itself occupied, by historically attested non-Indo-European peoples. Gamkrelidze and Ivanov have much to say that is innovative and interesting but their solution to the homeland problem is wholly without archaeological support.

We can better examine the possibility of an archaeological solution if we separate the Indo-Europeans territorially into the divisions suggested earlier at the end of Chapter Three. First, we have the territory of Northern and Central Europe which, during the period that we assign to the Proto-Indo-Europeans, was occupied primarily by the Neolithic TRB culture and later by the Globular Amphora and Corded Ware cultures. The last of these occupies a vast territory by the third millennium which is thoroughly congruent with the more immediate origins of the later Celts, Germans, Balts and Slavs, and possibly the Italic-speaking peoples. The second major region comprises much of Southeastern Europe from which we would most conveniently derive the Illyrians, Thracians, Dacians, Greeks, and possibly the Anatolians, Phrygians and Armenians. It is also a likely staging area for some of the Indo-European peoples of Italy. Finally, we have the third major region encompassing the Pontic-Caspian steppe where we naturally look for the earliest Indo-Iranians and the most likely home of the Tocharians. We could draw a circle around this entire area set to 2500 BC and there would be few who would argue that we had not fairly encompassed all of the known Indo-European peoples or their more immediate lands of origin. Can we call this the solution to the homeland problem and leave it as settled? If we could, the next two chapters would certainly be far less controversial though also probably less interesting. But to accept such an enormous territory as the homeland requires us to spread the Proto-Indo-Europeans over an area of 2,000,000 square kilometres, or more. It would also require us to accept the inclusion within the homeland of extremely diverse cultures which some archaeologists insist share no historical or genetic connection. We really cannot avoid at least making an attempt to discover a smaller area that might better explain the formation of Indo-European languages across this larger region by about 2500 BC. Besides, there is one model which does claim to provide both the archaeologists and linguists with exactly that for which they seem to be looking.

Although the hypothesis of an Indo-European homeland situated exclusively in the Pontic-Caspian steppe has been advanced a number of times this century, the present formulation of this theory owes much to the publications of Marija Gimbutas who has argued for over twenty-five years that the Proto-Indo-Europeans should be identified with her Kurgan tradition. This term embraces a series of cultures occupying the steppe and forest-steppe of the southern Ukraine and south Russia. By the fourth millennium BC this region evidences all of the attributes of a putative Indo-European society reconstructed from linguistic evidence – including the most geographically indicative such as the domestic horse and wheeled vehicles. Settlements are few and most of the various cultures of the region are known primarily through their mortuary practice. This normally involves burial in an earthen or stone chamber, the frequent presence of ochre, and in many instances the erection of a low tumulus (Russian *kurgan*). Grave goods may include weapons and animal remains, especially of sheep/goat, but also of cattle and horse. The capsule image of the Kurgan tradition is a warlike pastoral society, highly mobile (hence the paucity of habitation evidence), which employed both wagons drawn by oxen and rode horses. These people seemed to have originated in the eastern steppe, perhaps in the Volga-Ural region, and to have pushed westwards until they burst in on the later Neolithic or Eneolithic cultures of Eastern and Central Europe and brought about a thorough transformation of European society. They also expanded southwards through the Caucasus to occupy Mesopotamia; some pushed beyond towards India while others remained on the steppe and pressed eastwards where they passed into Central Asia, the staging area of the Iranian and perhaps the Tocharian migrations.

The expansion into Europe, the most closely argued part of the hypothesis, is attributed to three waves of folk movements spanning the centuries from about 4000 to 2500 BC. The evidence for this expansion rests on a variety of novel traits and transformations seen in the development of European prehistory. Very briefly these can be summarized.

The evidence for a change in mortuary practice plays a primary role in both the Kurgan theory and almost any attempt by an archaeologist to substantiate a claim for population movement. Into the territory of Southeastern Europe,

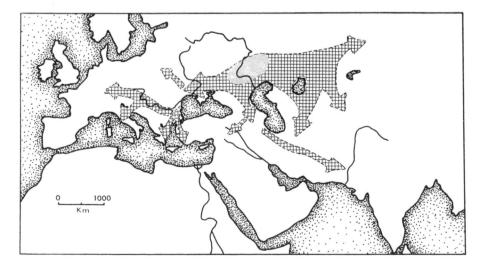

85   The Kurgan homeland and its expansions according to Marija Gimbutas.

characterized by Gimbutas as sexually egalitarian and peaceful, there appear alien burials morphologically identical to those on the steppe. These are generally confined to males and are accompanied by weapons – arrows, spears and knives; and by symbols of power – horse headed sceptres. The rite of suttee, the sacrificial execution of a woman on the death of her husband, is indicated in some burials suggesting the patriarchal character of the warrior-pastoralists who superimposed themselves on the local agricultural populations.

The economy of the pastoralists is seen as being imported into the Danube region by Kurgan intruders. Gimbutas suggests that the lack of good grazing land in the steppe probably impelled the Kurgan migrations into Southeast Europe. The earlier stable agricultural economy is seen to collapse in the face of the intruders, and the post-Neolithic economies of the region rapidly emphasize stockbreeding over agriculture.

An important component of these movements is the spread of the domestic horse from the steppe into the Danube region. Horse bones, cheek pieces (here largely limited to the northwest Pontic agriculturalists), and the horse-head sceptres are all cited as evidence of Kurgan intrusions.

Earlier stable tell settlement in the east Balkans disintegrates under the pressure of Kurgan populations and most sites are abandoned. There is a general population dislocation with the final phases of a number of Balkan Neolithic cultures being played out in marginal lands such as islands or mountain cave sites. In addition, characteristic cultural markers of those societies, generally ceramic, appear to be pushed increasingly westwards under the pressure of eastern invaders. Actual settlement remains decrease with new more mobile communities, or else there emerge defended chieftain's strongholds built either in stone, such as Ezero in Bulgaria, or in wood, such as Vucedol in northern Yugoslavia.

A rapid disintegration in fine ceramics, and the almost complete disappearance of painted wares, is attributed to the Kurgan people who themselves were content to fashion fairly crude shell-tempered cooking vessels. The copper industry of the Eneolithic Balkans collapses and is gradually replaced by arsenical-bronzes whose form and provenience are attributed to the Caucasus metallurgical centres via the steppe. The vector for this technological change is identified by long-distance Kurgan exchange. The Kurgan people also introduced the wheeled vehicle to the Balkans and Central Europe.

A society identified as essentially matrifocal, that is, centred on females, and which is emphasized by virtually thousands of female clay figurines, abruptly disappears under the Kurgan warriors whose religious attention was more attracted to warlike sky-gods and sun worship. The new religion is especially seen in the erection of stone stelae in the Alpine region on which are depicted horses, wagons, sun bursts, and especially weapons – axes, spears, arrows and daggers – characteristic of the warlike society that honoured such principles.

Finally, there is some evidence that there was an infusion of a new physical type into the Danube region which can easily be traced back to the steppe region. Here we are talking of a Proto–Europoid C type which is identical to skeletons examined in the steppe region and which are now found mixed with autochthonous Mediterranean types associated with the earlier Neolithic of Southeast Europe.

These Kurgan intrusions, therefore, are credited with causing the collapse of the Southeast European Eneolithic cultures and their subsequent amalgamation into mixed Kurganized societies. Kurgan elements inherent in some of these societies then spread north and westwards where they underlie the transformations taking place in Northern Europe and result in the formation of the Corded Ware horizon. Similar evidence for migration – kurgans, horses and warriors – are also seen in the south Caucasus and Anatolia providing an intrusive culture for the Indo-Europeans of Anatolia. The expansion of such elements eastwards, as in the Early Bronze Age cultures of south Siberia, establish a Kurgan entity in the zone from which we derive Iranian peoples.

The Kurgan solution to the Indo-European problem would thus appear to solve our problem economically by providing a homeland congruent with the Proto-Indo-European culture as reconstructed by linguistics and occupying a geographical situation compatible with the most plausible expansion of Indo-European speakers. The archaeological evidence for the expansions is not limited to a few traits which might be easily dismissed as the result of exchange, but is rather all the major features of a culture in the course of expansion into alien territory. The warlike society of these mobile invaders provides the Kurgan people with an appropriate means of expansion and an explanation for their success at colonizing vast areas.

The Kurgan solution is attractive and has been accepted by many archaeologists and linguists, in part or total. It is the solution one encounters in the *Encyclopaedia Britannica* and the *Grand Dictionnaire Encyclopédique Larousse*. It describes Indo-European expansions in a framework congruent with expectation, and perhaps most importantly, it derives the Proto-Indo-Europeans from the Pontic-Caspian region, a territory which its bitterest opponents would normally admit was at least Indo-Iranian and undisturbed by population intrusions since the beginning of the Neolithic. Opposition to the Kurgan solution does not lie with those who would argue that the Pontic-Caspian steppe was not the territory of the earliest Indo-European speakers, but that the Proto-Indo-European homeland must have been larger; there is no alternative homeland from which archaeologists would derive all of the cultures of our late Indo-European territory. One might at first imagine that the economy of argument involved with the Kurgan solution should oblige us to accept it outright. But critics do exist and their objections can be summarized quite simply – almost all of the arguments for invasion and cultural transformations are far better explained without reference to Kurgan expansions, and most of the evidence so far presented is either totally contradicted by other evidence or is the result of gross misinterpretation of the cultural history of Eastern, Central and Northern Europe. In the next two chapters we will examine the evidence in more detail to determine whether it is in fact possible to isolate a more confined Indo-European homeland.

CHAPTER SEVEN

The Archaeology of the Proto-Indo-Europeans

> Archaeology can offer nothing new to the study
> of Proto-Indo-European civilization. For any
> candidate culture advanced by archaeologists as
> the Proto-Indo-European culture, only two types
> of evidence can be offered: evidence that
> conforms to the evidence offered by linguists,
> which will be tautological (although helpful as
> support and external validation), or evidence that
> differs from the linguistic evidence, which will
> then call into question whether the candidate
> ought not to be rejected in favor of another that
> better fits the linguistic evidence.
>
> BRUCE LINCOLN 1981

The evidence examined so far suggests that Proto-Indo-European speakers occupied the region between the Dnieper river on the west and the Ural on the east sometime during the fifth to third millennia BC. Such an assertion would probably be embraced by most scholars, linguists or archaeologists engaged in the study of the earliest Indo-Europeans. This consensus, however, swiftly collapses if we also assert that these two rivers formed the precise boundaries of the Proto-Indo-Europeans and that the homeland was effectively confined between 30 and 50 degrees longitude. Many claim that the border of the Proto-Indo-Europeans should extend west to include the territories of the TRB (Funnel Beaker) culture of Northern Europe and the Linear Ware culture and its descendants in Danubian Europe. The consequence of accepting such an expansion generally relegates the Pontic-Caspian region to the immediate ancestors of the Indo-Iranians. Other scholars would not halt the eastern borders of the Proto-Indo-Europeans at the Ural but extend them into southern Siberia. Nevertheless, whatever one's preference, there is still general agreement that an examination of the Dnieper-Ural region from the fifth to the third millennium BC should have little difficulty intersecting Proto-Indo-European communities. We will first review the archaeological evidence from this territory, therefore, and then, in the next chapter, extend our examination both east and west to establish the limits of the Proto-Indo-Europeans.

Dawn of the Proto-Indo-Europeans

By about 9000 BC the northern retreat of the glaciers across Ice Age Europe invited the radical alteration of the environment of the Pontic-Caspian in directions still recognizable today. Released from their refuge areas, a succession of trees colonized the lands north of the Black Sea. In general, the southernmost region formed a broad band of essentially steppe vegetation where trees were primarily confined to river valleys. To the north lay the forest-steppe which invited the establishment of communities of birch, pine and willow at first, then hazel, and finally elm and oak by the sixth millennium BC. These trees are, of course, all reconstructed to the Proto-Indo-European vocabulary although they are hardly confined to the Ukraine and south Russia. Nor do the animals which have been recovered from archaeological sites date to this period. These include dog, wild pig, wild cattle, red deer, wild horse, bear, fox, wolf, lynx, beaver and hare, plus an equal number of species not reconstructible from the Indo-European languages such as reindeer and saiga antelope. We may speculate that at least some of the names of these trees and animals were distantly ancestral to the forms we later ascribe to Proto-Indo-European. To argue otherwise would suggest that the Mesolithic ancestors of the Proto-Indo-Europeans totally abandoned their inherited vocabulary in later periods which is hardly probable. We may imagine, then, that during the Mesolithic some of the communities occupying the banks of the great river valleys of the southern part of the European USSR probably spoke languages that would later evolve into Proto-Indo-European.

The Mesolithic period begins about 9000 BC and ends about 6000 BC by which time the native populations of the Pontic-Caspian began to adopt the manufacture of ceramics and the keeping of domestic animals. When examining the Mesolithic from our own particular perspective, we are tempted to seek some form of broad cultural uniformity that might presage the later formation of the Proto-Indo-Europeans. The primary archaeological evidence is stone tools and the determination of cultural boundaries is mainly based on analyzing the forms of these tools, their method of manufacture and their distribution as a percentage in various assemblages. For much of the Pontic-Caspian the stone industries are characterized by the production of geometric microliths or tiny flint blades. Since almost all subsequent development in this region appears to have been established on this Mesolithic base, some have perceived in this wide distribution of geometric microliths the foundation of the later Proto-Indo-European ethnic region, but most archaeologists today would be extremely sceptical of ascribing ethno-linguistic identities to vast lithic techno-complexes. In addition, a closer examination of this region indicates much greater cultural complexity.

The best studied area of our region is the Ukraine where over 300 sites have been ascribed to at least twenty different Mesolithic cultures or groups. Half of these groups are assigned to the Early Mesolithic (ninth to seventh millennia) and the other ten are attributed to the Late Mesolithic (seventh to sixth millennia BC). These cultures can be grouped into two major cultural territories. The cultural groups of the southern steppe zone are technically similar to the broad Azilo-Tardenoisian tradition of Western Europe in their generally exclusive reliance on microliths. They share industrial similarities which link them to the Danube and the Near East as well as to their own Late Palaeolithic ancestors. The physical type of this southern region, attested by the remains in the cemetery of Voloshskoe and other sites, is described as gracile and Old Mediterranean. This contrasts sharply with the more robust Cro-Magnon physical type which is usually associated with the northern forest-steppe and which appears to intrude southwards into the steppe zone by the Late Mesolithic. The northern zone had a macro-microlithic industry which some would relate to the Swiderian-Kunda groups of Poland and the Baltic.

The archaeological evidence across the Pontic-Caspian suggests that settlement was limited almost exclusively to the river valleys and the shores of what have since become dried lakes. With a hunting-gathering-fishing economy, populations were likely to have been both sparse and well scattered except where natural conditions especially favoured fishing and permitted larger communities. This would seem to have been the case on the lower Dnieper where we find nearly ninety burials in the Mesolithic cemeteries of Vasilevka and Voloshskoe. Here the dead were generally buried flexed on their sides, and ochre was occasionally employed in the burials. A number of individuals had suffered violent deaths, apparently from arrows. These may have been victims of perennial disputes over fishing rights to the most favoured locations. The cemeteries were almost exclusively composed of adults whose average age at death was about thirty-five years.

The society indicated by the archaeological evidence for the Mesolithic clearly predates the type of culture that we reconstruct from the Indo-European languages, and we can again emphasize how nonsensical it is to chase Proto-Indo-Europeans back to the Mesolithic not to speak of the Palaeolithic. Indeed, as the physical environment of the Mesolithic was markedly different from that of the earlier Ice Age, it is probable that some components of the vocabulary concerning the environment may have only been formulated during the Mesolithic. We should also note that the mixture in both physical types of the population and cultural groups that runs throughout the Mesolithic should shatter simplistic delusions about any physical or ethnic purity that might be attributed to the Indo-Europeans.

Emergence of Proto-Indo-European Society

As we saw in Chapter Four, the Proto-Indo-European vocabulary clearly reflects an economy that emerged in Eurasia only with the Neolithic period. Very broadly, this form of economy which sees the exploitation of domestic animals and the first traces of village settlement appears in the Pontic-Caspian by approximately the sixth millennium BC. Most archaeologists would seek an external source for the earliest appearance of domestic livestock, agriculture, pottery and the other paraphernalia of the earliest farming communities.

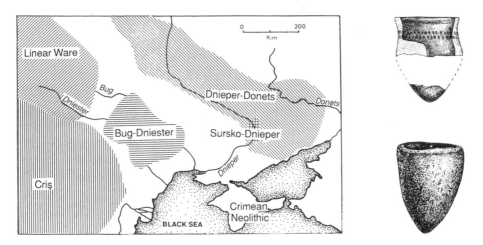

86–88 Early Neolithic cultures in the west Pontic region. On the right are a clay pot and a stone vessel from the Sursko-Dnieper culture.

The evidence for an expansion of the Neolithic economy from the southwest is largely centred on the origins of the Bug-Dniester culture which is known from about fifty sites situated primarily on the southern Bug and another ten on the river Dniester. By the late seventh millennium BC there begins to appear the first traces of domestic animals, such as pig and cattle, in what are otherwise typical hunting-fishing settlements. By at least the sixth millennium BC there is also evidence for pottery. The settlements tended to be small with nine huts on Baskov Island representing the most substantial site. The economy here was primarily based on hunting red and roe deer, wild pig, and fishing. The lithic technology is still firmly rooted in the preceding Mesolithic which has generally argued for a substantial degree of continuity in this region. The presence of domestic livestock on Bug-Dniester sites has normally been explained as the result of stimulus from neighbouring farming communities to the west. Similarly, the pottery has been regarded as a feature also borrowed from neighbouring agricultural populations.

Apparently some slight immigration from the west and subsequent acculturation of the native population stimulated the creation of the Bug-Dniester culture. The expansion of farming populations throughout the Balkans had progressed to the fringes of the Pontic region where both the Criş culture in the southwest and the Linear Ware culture on the northern Dniester appear by the late sixth millennium. The fabric and decoration found on Bug-Dniester sites ties them closely to the Balkans and we may agree with Pavel Dolukhanov and others who characterize the Bug-Dniester culture as the result of hunter-gatherers who have adopted some of the forms of the Neolithic economy and technology from neighbours, or from small groups of farmers, who may have expanded out of regions of higher agricultural potential into the forested region of the Dniester and beyond.

The subsequent cultural development in this western Pontic region sees much more intensive interactions and possible migrations from the Balkans that ultimately result in the emergence of the Tripolye culture. We will have more to say about this below.

East of the Bug-Dniester culture this same general form of primary hunting-gathering-fishing economy which sees the introduction of some pottery and domesticated animals also emerges on the middle Dnieper. Here the poorly known group of Sursko-Dnieper sites are to be found. Situated on the islands of the Dnieper and occupying small areas which evidence semi-subterranean huts, the Sursko-Dnieper population also practised an economy largely dependent on hunting and fishing with some possible traces of domestic animals such as cattle. Pointed based pottery, manufactured in both clay and stone, is also a characteristic of this culture. The lithic industry lies in the preceding Mesolithic and argues again for distant contacts and the adoption of some Neolithic traits by otherwise predominantly hunting-gathering populations. There are no absolute dates for this culture but it is generally correlated with other sites which date to the sixth millennium BC. Contemporary with these developments were the appearance of pottery and possibly domestic animals among hunting-gathering populations in the Crimea.

It would appear that the area from the Dniester to the lower Dnieper and Crimea was largely one which saw the gradual adoption of Neolithic traits by native Mesolithic populations. The Mesolithic foundations of these early Neolithic cultures are largely associated with the more southerly Mesolithic cultures. The expansion of the Neolithic economy from the west to the Bug-Dniester culture can be argued on the basis of the temporal priority and proximity of neighbouring agricultural communities in the Balkans and Moldavia. However, extrapolating this process from the southern Bug to the Dnieper and the Crimea where there is a gap of several hundred kilometres does pose some problems. Why this is so critical to the problem of the Indo-European origins will be evident later when we have examined the origins of the Neolithic cultures of the Volga and Caspian area.

By the early fifth millennium BC there emerged in the Ukraine one of the most extensive of the Neolithic cultures of the Pontic-Caspian region, the Dnieper-Donets culture. The culture is known from over 200 sites. It initially appeared on the middle Dnieper to the northern Donets and then expanded in almost all directions apparently absorbing other local Neolithic groups. The settlements of this culture are not well known and tend merely to repeat the pattern encountered elsewhere with its sparse evidence for semi-subterranean huts. The ceramics were initially pointed based, but flat-based wares emerge in the culture's later phases. Lithic technology continues the macro-microlithic forms of the preceding Mesolithic period although the later phases see the appearance of larger flint and polished stone axes and the disappearance of microliths. The economic evidence from the earliest stages is almost exclusively from hunting and fishing. The prey included wild cattle, elk, red and roe deer, wild pig, onager, fox, wildcat, hare and bear. In subsequent stages there appears to have been an increase in population and an advance southwards into the steppe. The later stages see the growing importance of domestic animals –

cattle, sheep/goat, pig, horse and dog – and the initial appearance of agriculture.

Far better known than the settlements are the approximately thirty cemeteries which have yielded about 800 burials. They generally exhibit a recurrent pattern of burial in elongated pits with groups numbering from two to a dozen buried together in rows, or in large collective burial pits. Individual burial is also known. The burial position is extended on the back with variable orientation, and the dead were frequently sprinkled with ochre, a custom that we will see continues into subsequent periods. Although ceramics are not often included as burial gifts, there is an assortment of other items, especially ornaments such as beads fashioned from shell, stone, deer or fish teeth or, very rarely, copper. Flint tools also occur. The most famous of the cemeteries is Mariupol which is located near the Sea of Azov and which yielded 122 burials. In addition to the grave gifts mentioned above, there were also exotic items such as axe-heads carved from porphyry, and copper rings, all of which attest exchange relationships with the Caucasus. The slight increase in grave gifts in the later periods has suggested to some archaeologists that we are witnessing a gradual growth in the complexity of social organization as agriculture and stockbreeding became more important in the Dnieper-Donets culture.

The great number of burials also provides considerable evidence for the physical type of the Dnieper-Donets population. They are predominantly characterized as late Cro-Magnons with more massive and robust features than the gracile Mediterranean peoples of the Balkan Neolithic. With males averaging about 172 centimetres in height they are a fairly tall people within the context of Neolithic populations.

The physical type, the extended supine burial position, the continuity with the preceding macro-microlithic industry, and similarities in ceramic decoration with the sub-Neolithic cultures of the northern Forest Zone have all suggested a northerly origin within the Ukraine, and the foremost authority on the culture, the Ukrainian archaeologist, Dmitry Telegin, assigns them to a broad cultural region that spanned the Vistula in Poland southeast to the Dnieper. We will later see how this might bear on establishing the limits of the Proto-Indo-Europeans. Conversely, we should also note that Alexander Formozov argues for an essentially 'southern' origin for the Dnieper-Donets culture that does not relate it to more northerly sub-Neolithic cultures.

On the lower Don there also emerges a local Neolithic culture which takes its name from the well-stratified site of Rakushechny Yar. Several radiocarbon dates from this site attest the appearance of ceramics by about 5000 to 4500 BC among an essentially hunting-fishing population which gradually adopted stockbreeding.

East of the Don, the earliest Neolithic cultures are only now emerging into an interpretive framework among Soviet archaeologists who have been greatly increasing our knowledge of the eastern steppe and forest-steppe over the last few decades. Before this, little more was known than numerous scatters of pottery and flint distributed over dune sites in the middle and lower Volga region. These were undatable except in the vaguest sense and in the absence of full scale excavations of secure cultural layers they could generally be dismissed as camp sites of sub-Neolithic hunter-gatherers who had gained some use of ceramics from their western or southeastern neighbours. While this interpretation of many of the small camp sites may still stand, there are now an increasing amount of data that suggest that the course of the Neolithic on the easternmost fringe of Europe may have been far more complex and interesting than previously imagined. Moreover, it raises some spectacularly difficult issues concerning Indo-European origins.

Stretching from the southern Urals across the Volga and on westwards to the Manych depression is the Seroglazovo culture of the Pre-Caspian region. It is attested from nearly 100 sites, mainly surface finds, which include egg-shaped pots and lithic industries still firmly derived from the Mesolithic. The sites are almost invariably situated along river or lakeside shores which would have been far more abundant then, when the Caspian Sea was much larger than at present. This provided a regimen of deltas and marshes along the southern fringe of the Seroglazovo culture. Radiocarbon dates for the maximum transgression of the Caspian suggest that the Seraglazovo culture dated to the seventh or sixth millennium BC.[35]

To the north, principally in the forest-steppe of the middle Volga and extending eastwards to the southern Urals (the Agidel culture), there also lie a substantial number of recently excavated Neolithic sites. Here we speak not only of the recurrent remains of egg-shaped vessels or lithic traditions reminiscent of the Mesolithic but also of evidence for domestic livestock.

The economy of these eastern sites was based on both hunting-fishing and stockbreeding. The hunted remains included the usual prey encountered across most of Europe and in the Proto-Indo-European vocabulary. According to Gerard Matyushin and Aida Petrenko, the domestic animals included the

89   Early Neolithic cultures of the Caspian and southern Urals.

horse, frequently the predominant species, cattle and ovicaprids. Domestic pig is conspicuously absent. Radiocarbon dates are not numerous and are quite controversial in that they suggest that the Neolithic economy had emerged here by at least the sixth millennium BC, if not earlier.

In discussing the origins of this most easterly of European Neolithic cultures, Soviet archaeologists have often directed their attention to the southeast, specifically the southeast Caspian, and beyond, where one encounters the earliest evidence for domestic animals in the Old World. This is prompted by several factors. We have already seen that the earliest farming communities of the west Pontic do not predate the sixth millennium, and it is extremely difficult to tie the earliest appearance of domestic livestock on the eastern forest-steppe with a stimulus so distant and apparently too late. Secondly, the appearance of domestic sheep in the economy of these eastern sites suggests direct contacts with the areas of original sheep domestication in the Near East, since Soviet archaeologists do not regard the sheep as native to the Volga-south Ural region. Furthermore, the sequence of egg-shaped ceramics bears a generic similarity with the earliest pottery of the southeast Caspian which should date back to the seventh millennium BC. Hence, an explanation which sees an expansion of the Neolithic economy from Central Asia provides a form of solution to the problem of the earliest Neolithic cultures of the Volga-Ural region. It also offers an historical association between the easternmost Neolithic populations of the Pontic-Caspian and their Asiatic neighbours. Yet one can hardly disguise the problems inherent in such a model since the distance between the earliest Neolithic cave sites of the south Caspian (for example, Djebel, Dam-Dam-Chashma and Belt) is not only very great but also they are separated by vast deserts. Clear intermediaries between them and the north Caspian-southern Urals are not yet forthcoming although one can hardly pretend that this region has been extensively surveyed. The only generalization one can make about a south Caspian origin for the Neolithic of the Volga-Ural region is that it is hotly disputed.[36]

Another possible route for the Neolithic economy, especially ovicaprids, might lie across the Caucasus. We now have radiocarbon-dated Neolithic-Eneolithic settlements such as Toyretepe, Gargalartepesi, Shulaverisgora, Imirisgora, Kharamis Didigora and Arukhlo I that all calibrate to the sixth millennium BC, while the site of Shomutepe has indicated a seventh-millennium date. These early sites reveal faunal assemblages with ovicaprids totalling 50 per cent or more of the remains, followed by cattle and then pig. If sheep were indeed absent from the Pontic-Caspian Mesolithic, the Caucasus would provide a somewhat more proximate source for their introduction than the Balkan Neolithic cultures, especially as sheep are known from Mesolithic sites in Georgia. Unfortunately, evidence for early Neolithic settlement immediately to the north of the Caucasus has not yet been discovered.

While the details of the initiation of the farming economy in the Pontic-Caspian remain a major problem, we can still make some general observations. The archaeological record is rather clear in reflecting quite substantial hunting-

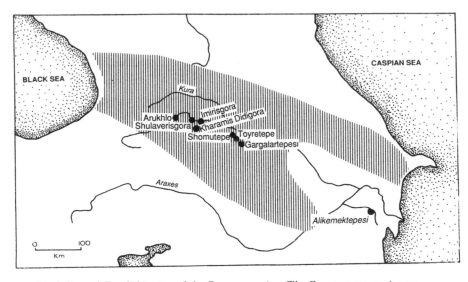

90 Neolithic and Eneolithic sites of the Caucasus region. The Caucasus mountains are indicated by shading.

gathering-fishing populations in this region, with relatively stable adjustments to their environment. This is particularly to be seen in the large cemeteries of the lower Dnieper but also elsewhere in this same region. The gradual adoption of ceramics, then possibly of some domestic livestock together with evidence for cultivation, are all very much congruent with the picture of an essentially gradual shift in economy, the indigenous populations accepting various alien items into their culture as they saw the need. There is no evidence for intrusive farming colonists as we find in the Balkans other than that clearly marked by the borders of such farming cultures as the Criş, Linear Ware and Tripolye. This is the eastern limit of any proposed 'wave of advance' and beyond it we have only indigenous communities for which there is no evidence of extermination or absorption by intrusive farmers. This is particularly obvious of the more easterly early Neolithic sites which lie up to 1,000 kilometres distant from the Balkan-derived cultures, and indicates that a correlation between Indo-Europeans and the Pontic-Caspian region appears to be one that involves exclusively native European populations rather than populations which took their origin in Western Asia at the beginning of the Neolithic.

The possibility that the Neolithic economy and technology was introduced into the Pontic-Caspian region from more than one direction has certain linguistic implications. If one accepts a direct historical link from the Near East either across Central Asia or the Caucasus to the Pontic-Caspian, this might well provide a convenient venue for the diffusion of words associated with the new productive economy. But providing a solution for one desperate to account for a few of the apparent similarities between Proto-Indo-European and some Near Eastern words involving livestock and agriculture raises another problem.

Our evidence so far appears to indicate that the Pontic-Caspian received Neolithic influences from the Balkans, and possibly both the Caucasus and east Caspian, and it is extraordinarily difficult to envisage a process by which the same terminology either diffused or was invented on both sides of the Pontic-Caspian. If we accept a dual or triple source for the Neolithic economy of the Pontic-Caspian then we may have to look to other processes for the apparent uniformity of agricultural terminology among the Indo-Europeans. A long process of convergence among the various Pontic-Caspian communities might possibly have resulted in a generally shared vocabulary among linguistically related groups. Alternatively, one area of the Pontic-Caspian may have achieved some form of ascendancy over the entire region thereby assimilating what may have been linguistically diverse neighbours. If this occurred, it should have taken place by the Eneolithic which marks the final period in which we may properly assert the existence of a Proto-Indo-European-speaking community.

The Eneolithic period of the western Pontic

The Eneolithic is generally marked by the addition of copper artefacts to the otherwise Neolithic technology. This distinction is fundamentally superficial since copper objects such as beads or awls also occur in cultures which have been universally described as Neolithic, and even during the Eneolithic period many cultures shown to possess copper objects did not utilize them as a significant part of their industrial technology. Nevertheless, the appearance of metals in many societies has often correlated with the emergence of widespread exchange relations, a more ranked social system and, at least in a European context, also a rise in warfare, defensive architecture, increased dependence on the pastoral component of the economy, horse domestication and wheeled vehicles. Both the lexico-cultural evidence of the Indo-European languages and

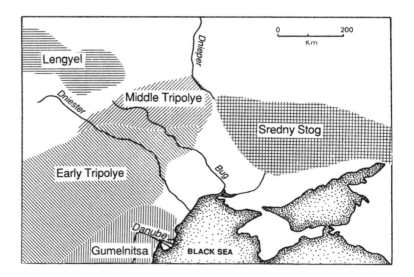

91   Eneolithic cultures of the west Pontic region.

our best estimates for the terminal period of Proto-Indo-European existence direct our attention to the Eneolithic.

During this period the western frontier of the Pontic-Caspian was delimited by several different cultures. In the far southwest, towards the Danube, was the Gumelnitsa culture which occupied eastern Romania and Bulgaria and whose continuity with the preceding cultural evolution of the Balkan Neolithic lies essentially unassailable. It is for precisely this reason that we have excluded it as non-Indo-European since it would require us to ascribe to the entire Balkans an original Indo-European identity which we have found incompatible on other grounds.

The major western neighbour of the Pontic-Caspian Eneolithic peoples was the Tripolye culture, the western variant of the Cucuteni-Tripolye continuum that spanned Romania to the Ukraine and whose existence ranged over 1,500 years. In the Ukraine alone there are approximately 1,000 sites of this culture known. These range from small settlements comprising only about a dozen houses to vast settlements whose structures number in the hundreds. The increasingly defensive nature of these settlements throughout the course of the Eneolithic, and the intensified contacts with their eastern neighbours, will demand comment in the next chapter. At present, our interest is primarily drawn to the origins of the Cucuteni-Tripolye culture.

Although some have claimed a local derivation rooted in the earlier Bug-Dniester culture, both the accumulation of evidence over the past decades and general opinion now emphasize the essentially Balkan roots of this culture. It first appears in Romania where the Pre-Cucuteni I phase dates to about 5000 BC. The earliest sites find their closest parallels in the architecture, ceramics, figurines, lithics and economy of the Boian culture of Romania. It is from this region that the Cucuteni-Tripolye culture seems to have expanded eastwards into the Prut-southern Bug region where Tripolye sites begin to emerge about

92 *Reconstruction of a Tripolye settlement.*

4500 BC; it then spread both northeastwards towards the Dnieper and southwards towards the northwest shores of the Black Sea. The initial extension into the Ukraine would naturally have carried these people into the earlier territory of the Bug-Dniester culture, but the marked distinctions between the two have generally indicated that the agriculturally more advanced Tripolyeans virtually assimilated the preceding inhabitants. Therefore, the Cucuteni-Tripolye culture, like the Gumelnitsa culture to its south, appears to derive from the great Balkan block of Neolithic cultures, which we have good reason to set outside the range of Proto-Indo-European candidates.

North of the Tripolye culture, on the northwest border of the Ukraine and Moldavia, the Eneolithic is represented by the Lengyel and TRB cultures. As both of these occupied very substantial regions in which the putatively Indo-European Corded Ware horizon subsequently appears, we have no *a priori* grounds to exclude them from the Proto-Indo-European world. We will examine their relationship with the Pontic-Caspian region in the next chapter. It is now time to examine those Eneolithic cultures whose origins would appear to lie with the indigenous populations of the Pontic Caspian and who have the surest claim to being designated Indo-Europeans.

The Early Eneolithic of the Pontic steppe and forest-steppe

The Eneolithic cultures of the Pontic-Caspian emerge by 4500 BC and subsequently evolve into Early Bronze Age cultures by about 2500 BC, if not earlier. Since these dates coincide almost precisely with the suspected floruit of the Proto-Indo-Europeans before the emergence of distinct Indo-European groups, we are justified in examining this period more closely than the preceding one. Our attention will focus on those areas of material culture or behaviour that seem to pertain most to our reconstructions of Indo-European society.

In broad terms, all of the cultures which we are about to encounter take their origin from their Neolithic antecedents in the Pontic-Caspian although precise derivations are very much open to debate. The earlier Eneolithic cultures embrace a series of individual cultures, all of which are distinguished in archaeological nomenclature, but which also display recurrent traits that point either to long-standing mutual contacts or underlying genetic relations. These include the Sredny Stog, Novodanilovka, Lower Mikhaylovka-Kemi Oba cultures in the west and the Samara, Khvalynsk and southern Ural Eneolithic cultures in the east. In addition, residual Neolithic cultures such as the Dnieper-Donets culture lingered in some regions to be contemporary with some of the Early Eneolithic cultures before finally being absorbed by them. By the end of the Eneolithic period, about 3500–2500 BC, most of the Pontic-Caspian region was occupied by the Yamnaya (Pit-grave) horizon. The successors of the Yamnaya culture are set to a period in which one generally assumes the emergence of already differentiated Indo-European-speaking peoples. It is during the course of the Eneolithic period that those who support

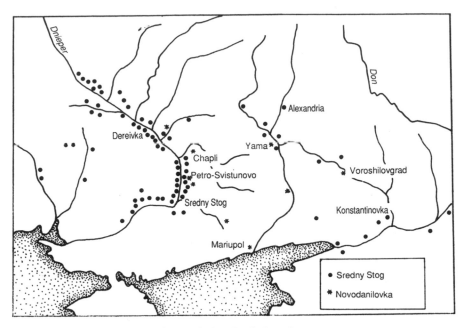

93   Distribution of the Sredny Stog and Novodanilovka cultures.

the Pontic-Caspian as the *exclusive* homeland of the Indo-Europeans argue for their initial expansion.

The Sredny Stog culture is easily the best known of the Early Eneolithic cultures of the Pontic-Caspian. It is attested by approximately 100 sites located primarily along the middle Dnieper and extending eastwards to include the Donets and the lowermost reaches of the Don. Both radiocarbon dates and synchronisms with the better-dated Tripolye culture indicate that this culture flourished about 4500–3500 BC.

The evidence for settlements in the Sredny Stog culture is not extensive and the site of Dereivka on the middle Dnieper is by far the most impressive. An area of over 2,000 square metres was apparently bordered by some form of fence which enclosed several houses, work places and areas of ritual activity. The houses were slightly sunk into the ground, rectangular in shape, with the largest measuring 13 by 6 metres. Hearths were found within them. Scattered about the site were various activity areas including a place for repairing fish gear and processing one's catch, a potter's workshop, and a place where bones were worked into tools. Semi-subterranean huts are also known from Alexandria, and surface dwellings, similar to those from Dereivka, have been uncovered at Konstantinovka on the lower Don. At Dereivka, in addition to more secular activities, there was also some evidence for ritual. This included a deposit consisting of the head of a stallion accompanied by the left footbones of a horse, the remains of two dogs, and a figurine in the shape of a wild boar. Beneath one of the walls of a house was discovered a pit with the burial of a dog.

The economy of the Sredny Stog culture was based on stockbreeding, agriculture, hunting and fishing. The domestic livestock, in terms of the

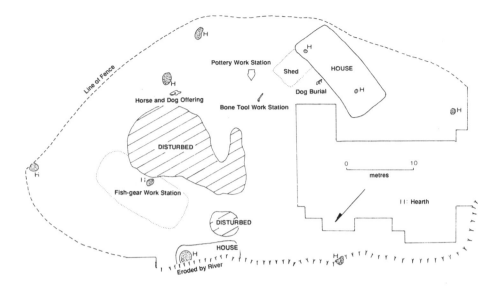

94   Plan of the Sredny Stog site of Dereivka. The area indicated with solid lines was heavily disturbed without proper excavation.

attested number of individuals from five Sredny Stog sites, included horse, sheep/goat, cattle, pig and dog. The horse served both as a meat source, evidenced by the slaughter patterns which specifically reflect the butchering of young males, and for transport. Antler cheekpieces for fixing the bit in the horse's mouth are known from Dereivka and other Sredny Stog sites. This evidence, coupled with the logical requirements of controlling herds of horses from horseback, supports the thesis that the horse was probably ridden at this time. Generally, archaeologists are sceptical that the horse could also have been employed for traction. Both the small size of the animals (average withers height of 136 centimetres) and the absence of a suitable harness would have rendered these earliest domestic horses poorly suited to pull the heavy timber carts or wagons that are first attested in the Eneolithic.

Although the horse would have revolutionized transportation and the mobility of the Sredny Stog people, it is questionable whether it alone provided the complete prerequisites for true steppe nomadism involving the cyclic exploitation of steppe pastures on a year-round basis. While sheep were well suited to the steppe, the presence of domestic pigs on Sredny Stog sites points to a settled regime, although one that was amassing the technological and economic requirements which might permit specialized nomadic pastoralism. It is always very difficult to evaluate the comparative values of stockbreeding versus agriculture in prehistoric sites, yet the evidence for half a dozen querns and about a dozen grinders from Dereivka at least indicates the processing of plant foods, although these may not necessarily have been domestic. In general, Soviet archaeologists assume that stockbreeding provided the primary core of the Sredny Stog economy.

The wild animals hunted by the Sredny Stog population included a wide range of prey attested throughout Europe. The primary game animals were red and roe deer, elk, wild boar and, again reminding us more forcefully of the riverine environment of these sites, beaver and otter. Badger, wolf, fox and hare are also represented in the faunal samples. Birds such as mallard, pintail duck, goose, teal and coot were recovered as well.

Finally, there can be little doubt that fishing also played a role in the Sredny Stog economy. The discovery of net sinkers, fishhooks, and fish remains at Dereivka confirms the exploitation of wels, perch, roach, red-eye, carp and pike. Unio and Palludino shells were also collected extensively.

The technology of the Sredny Stog culture provides several areas for comment. Ceramics were still bag-shaped with rounded or pointed bases which clearly reflect their local forest-steppe ancestry. The fabric of the vessels was frequently tempered with crushed shell which provides a useful technological, and some would claim ethnic, marker for the Pontic-Caspian region. By the later period of the Sredny Stog culture, the so-called Dereivka period following 4000 BC, cord ornament appears on the pottery setting a pattern which subsequently emerges over much of the rest of Europe at a later date. The implications of this design technique will assume greater importance when we attempt to trace the expansion of the Indo-Europeans.

The lithic remains of the Sredny Stog culture contain much of what we might expect of most Eneolithic societies across Europe. Knives, scrapers, arrowheads, spearheads are all known. Among the antler tools, the most interesting are the hammers and mattocks which occur in great abundance at Dereivka. The excavator, Dmitry Telegin, argues that the hammers were close range weapons and served an analogous function to the stone battle-axes which appear later in the Eneolithic. Cheekpieces for horses were also fashioned from antler.

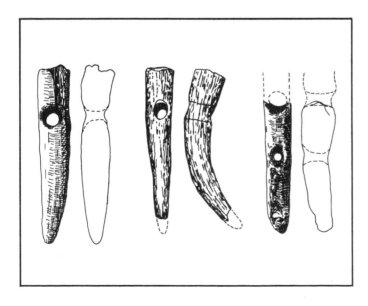

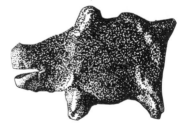

95, 96 Antler cheek pieces and wild boar figurine from Dereivka.

Copper objects are rare in the Sredny Stog culture and generally consist of little more than beads, although Telegin suggests that copper tools did exist at Dereivka as evidenced by traces of copper oxides on worked bone and the requisite techniques employed in working antler into tools. Evgeny Chernykh has demonstrated by spectral analysis that the copper was derived from the Balkan-Danubian region and probably passed eastwards via the Tripolye culture to the Sredny Stog.

A number of Sredny Stog cemeteries have been uncovered and reveal relatively uniform burial rites. The graves are simple pits without any evident surface marker such as a mound. The deceased were buried on their backs but with their legs flexed (in distinction to the customary extended positions of the Dnieper-Donets culture), and they were frequently strewn with ochre. Grave gifts were few and included pots and tools. At Dereivka one of the graves was accompanied by a pot imported from the Tripolye culture.

The disposition of the burials within the cemetery is also distinguished from the previous Dnieper-Donets culture where numerous burials were interred in a series in group pits. In the Sredny Stog culture the burials tend to be grouped into small numbers, two to five, which are separated from other small groups within the same cemetery. Soviet archaeologists see in this a shift in social organization where the various small groups indicate family or other kinship units who retained their distinct identities even within their cemeteries.

The Sredny Stog cemeteries also provide information about both the physical appearance and life-spans of the population. In general, the Sredny Stog people are described as proto-Europoids of medium to tall stature, more gracile than the Dnieper-Donets people but still quite robust when compared with their contemporaries in the Tripolye culture. From the small Sredny Stog cemetery on Igren island, Ina Potekhina has examined the demographic structure of the population. Males who had achieved adulthood died on average

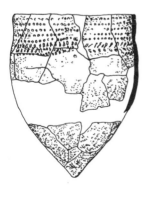
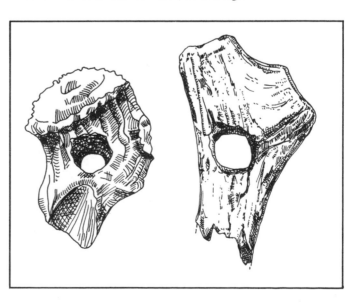

*97, 98   Pointed-based pot and antler
'hammer-axes' from Dereivka.*

about the age of thirty-six years while the few females in the cemetery, contrary to the usual pattern observed in prehistoric cemeteries, outlived the men and died at about forty-four years of age. If the very high rate of infant mortality is taken into consideration, the average age at death for the entire population was about twenty-seven years.

There are quite marked similarities between the burials of the Sredny Stog culture and those of the Novodanilovka group which also occupied the lower Dnieper and the steppe region of the Ukraine contemporary with the early Sredny Stog culture. The Novodanilovka burials are grouped into small cemeteries, generally not exceeding half a dozen burials, among which Chapli, Yama, Voroshilovgrad and Petro Svistunovo are the best known. The burials are in the supine position with legs flexed, orientation is to the east or northeast, and the deceased was sprinkled with ochre – all of which are characteristics also seen in the Sredny Stog culture. Where they differ is in the elaboration seen both in the construction of the tombs and in the grave goods. Generally, the grave pits are lined with stone slabs and the burials are richly accompanied with a wide assortment of goods. Included among these are stone tools of which long flint knives, arrowheads and spearheads are quite typical. The flint is of high quality and was obtained from the Donets region. Polished stone axes, fashioned from slate or serpentine, maces made from stone, antler or even copper also occur. About a dozen copper bracelets are known; their function is indisputable, as they have been found about the lower arm bones of a burial at Chapli. Other ornaments include rings, beads and pendants of copper, and pendants fashioned from boar's tusk, animal teeth and shell. Globular vessels with slightly pointed bases also occur with the burials.

The interpretation of the Novodanilovka group is made extremely difficult because of the total absence of any settlement sites. Other than a few hoards of copper or flint objects, such as the Goncharovka hoard with 150 knife-like blades, the Novodanilovka burials are without a clear cultural context. They were initially assigned to the Sredny Stog culture but are now recognized by

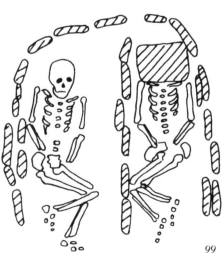

100   Typical long flint knife of the Novodanilovka group (L. 13.7 cm).

99   Novodanilovka burial at Yama (1.8 × 1.85 m).

101   Copper bracelet from Chapli (D. 6 cm).

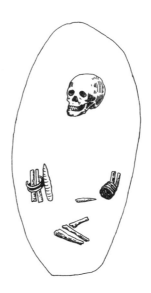

102   A Novodanilovka grave at Chapli yielded a status burial wearing bracelets of copper that had been imported from the Balkans.

Ukrainian archaeologists as an independent group, putatively composed of specialist flintworkers engaged in the long-distance exchange of flint and possibly copper. That future discoveries within the Sredny Stog settlements may extend the range of its objects and practices to include the more exotic items found in Novodanilovka burials is always possible, and it has been suggested that these graves merely represent wealthier members of the Sredny Stog culture. What is most important is the pattern of broad general similarity between the different cultures and groups occupying the Dnieper-Ural area.

The third major Ukrainian cultural entity of the earlier Eneolithic is the Lower Mikhaylovka-Kemi Oba culture which spans the region between the lower Dnieper and the Crimea. The lower Dnieper variant, the Lower Mikhaylovka culture, synchronizes roughly with the later part of the Sredny Stog culture, while the Kemi Oba culture of the Crimea extends into the later Eneolithic.

Some settlements have been ascribed to the Lower Mikhaylovka culture, the most famous being the eponymous site of Mikhaylovka where the Lower Mikhaylovka remains underlie the later Yamnaya settlement and fortifications. Here semi-subterranean houses were found, one of which measured about 15.5 by 5 metres. The faunal remains from Lower Mikhaylovka were not abundant but include sheep/goat, cattle, horse, pig and dog, in that order, with some traces of hunting. The ceramics are different from the Sredny Stog culture and are flat-based with raised necks. Of special note is a low pedestalled bowl which may be interpreted as a censer, analogous to similar ritual paraphernalia encountered regularly in this region throughout later prehistory.

Burials and associated rituals have attracted special attention. The burials are placed in low mounds (*kurgans*) and the presence of stone rings, cromlechs, is frequently noted. Hearths have been discovered built on top of the kurgans, on their periphery or within the burial pit itself. Grave goods are rare but may include pottery, copper awls or shell ornaments.

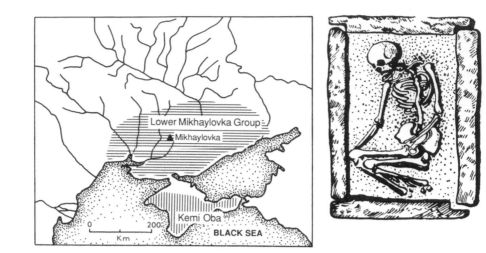

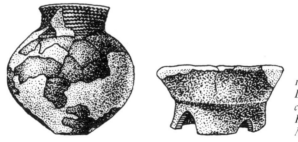

103–106   The distribution of the Lower Mikhaylovka-Kemi Oba cultures. Above is a burial from Kemi-Oba. Left are a Lower Mikhaylovka pot and censer.

One of the more striking recent discoveries of the Lower Mikhaylovka group is the existence of altars or offering places. Beneath a kurgan at Kalanchak was found a circular area on which lay the fractured remains of an anthropomorphic stone stela with traces of ochre; potsherds; and animal bones. Similar deposits have been found elsewhere.

To the south, in the Crimea, are the remains of the Kemi Oba culture which is primarily represented by small cemeteries. Besides those features which are similar to the Lower Mikhaylovka group, for example, kurgans, cromlechs, eastern orientation, and so forth, there are several other features of considerable interest. A number of the tombs which have been built as stone cists have included painted ornament on the walls. Of greater representational interest are the carved stone stelae on which are depicted the heads and arms of figures, and which are covered with both geometric and more realistic ornament. A fine example of this is the stone stela that derives from Kernosovka. The stela stood 1.2 metres high and depicts the head, including a face with a moustache and beard; arms; and phallus. On the front surface of the stela are carved images of what have been interpreted as tools such as mattocks, a battle-axe, and animals including two horses. There are about seventy such figures known from the Pontic region. Considerable evidence exists that they were employed in Later Eneolithic burials, especially in the construction of Yamnaya graves where they were used to cover the deceased. This was clearly not their original purpose since they were constructed to stand upright, and Dmitry Telegin suggests that they were originally manufactured by the Lower Mikhaylovka-Kemi Oba culture and later appropriated by Yamnaya tribes who reused them in their own burials.

These major cultural groups – Sredny Stog, Novodanilovka and the Lower Mikhaylovka-Kemi Oba cultures – all constitute the primary Eneolithic cultures of the lower and middle Dnieper to the lower Don region in the period 4500–3500 BC. Their origins are by no means clearly understood though no one would deny a strong degree of continuity from the preceding Surski and Dnieper-Donets cultures in their development. But other impulses, seen in ceramics, metal working, and the elaboration of burial ritual by using stone, point to more distant contacts with the Tripolye culture to the west, and especially the Eneolithic cultures of the north Caucasus to the southeast.

We have already noted the potential importance of the Caucasus in stimulating the Neolithic economy in the Pontic-Caspian region. The association of the northern Caucasus with the Pontic-Caspian is much more clearly seen in the Eneolithic period. One of the earliest north Caucasian sites of importance is the cemetery at Nalchik. Here were found 147 burials placed under very low mounds which together formed an extensive low kurgan covering an area of about 300 square metres. Although twelve of the burials were found in the supine position with legs flexed (as we frequently encounter in the steppe), the majority were deposited on their sides, males on their right and females on their left. Ochre frequently accompanied the burials. Grave goods included pendants fashioned from animal teeth, flint tools, and a series of marble bracelets. The earliest burials at Nalchik are dated to the Eneolithic. Other than a few other burials and a single settlement site, there is little local context for the Nalchik cemetery which appears to straddle the world of both the steppe and the Caucasus.

Nalchick precedes the Maykop culture which takes its name from the famous royal barrow at Maykop southeast of the Sea of Azov. The massive quantity of gold and silver ornaments and vessels has long been the subject of archaeological debate: what were their precise chronological and cultural relations with the Bronze Age cultures of the Near East, Anatolia, and their neighbours in the Caucasus? The sites of the Maykop culture appear to cluster in the Kuban region from whence they extend eastwards across the northern Caucasus. Burials are typically found beneath kurgans which generally employ stone constructions such as cromlechs and stone cists. The deceased are found buried either in the supine position with legs flexed, or on their sides. Copper objects are a frequent burial accompaniment.

The origins, interpretation and absolute dates of Nalchik and the Maykop culture are perennial topics of debate. Their origin, for example, is variously attributed to a yet unidentified local Neolithic population, or to a northward expansion of the Eneolithic cultures of the Caucasus. More important from our point of view is the elaboration of their burials, with stone constructions which

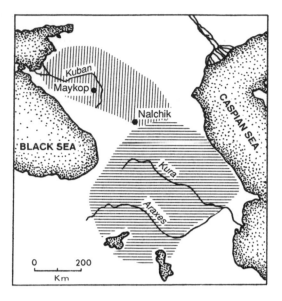

107 Location of the Maykop (vertical hatching) and Kuro-Araxes (horizontal hatching) cultures.

many archaeologists see as a source for the stone-built tombs encountered in the Lower Mikhaylovka and Kemi Oba cultures. Similarly, they offer ceramic parallels for some of the cultures on the steppe. Finally, in their strategic position between the steppe and the major metallurgical centres of the Caucasus, the northern Caucasus becomes an important factor in the cultural development of the Pontic-Caspian in the Later Eneolithic and Bronze Ages.

Early Eneolithic in the East

The Eneolithic successors of the earlier Seroglazovo culture are the Samara culture of the middle Volga forest-steppe, and the Pre-Caspian culture to its south. Both cultures are still very poorly known and their formulation as cultural entities is relatively recent. The Samara culture, which takes its name from the river Samara, was only discovered in 1973. Its major site is the cemetery of Sezzhee where many of the practices and some of the grave goods encountered in the Dnieper-Donets culture are paralleled. The burials are in flat graves, extended on their backs, and often powdered with ochre, especially the graves of children. The majority of graves were accompanied by goods that included polished stone axes, shell beads, pendants of animal teeth, bone tools, ceramics, and small plates fashioned from boar tusk or shell which would be sewn on garments, a practice most notably attested in the Dnieper-Donets cemetery at Mariupol. In addition, figures carved from tusk or bone also occur in the graves. They were fashioned into the shapes of horses, cattle and ducks. The possibility that the horse was employed ritually in the burial rite is suggested by the discovery of horse skulls and other bones in the overburden of the cemetery.

The distinctive shell-tempered Samara ceramics are known on other sites throughout this region and, according to Igor Vasiliev, ceramically influenced the forest cultures to the north. This provides a point of mutual contact between a segment of what we presume to have been Proto-Indo-European speakers and the region most often favoured as the probable homeland of the Uralic languages.

The Pre-Caspian culture to the south is very poorly known with little more than twenty sites identified. These are generally on heavily eroded dune surfaces where material from different periods has been mixed together. The sites are, as a rule, situated along the shores of dry lakes and are composed of flat-based ceramics, quartzite tools and occasionally animal bones. Both the Samara and Pre-Caspian cultures are synchronized with the Dnieper-Donets culture to the west.

The successor to both the Samara and Pre-Caspian cultures is known as the Khvalynsk culture which takes its name from the major cemetery of Khvalynsk, situated on the right bank of the Volga. This cemetery covered an area of about 1,100 square metres and revealed the remains of 158 burials. The cemetery reflects striking similarities with both the Dnieper-Donets and Sredny Stog cemeteries. While there are forty-five individual burials, the majority were placed in group pits ranging from a pair to as many as seven together. The burials were normally in the supine position with legs flexed, often covered with ochre, and orientated from north to east. The graves were simple pits, though a number had been covered with stones.

The grave goods from the Khvalynsk cemetery are exceedingly rich and include about fifty pots, again employing crushed shell temper; beads fashioned from Unio shell, bone and stone; dentalium shell pendants; stone arrowheads and axes; bone harpoons, fishhooks and knives; and animal bones. Here, too, were uncovered figures carved from boar tusk and shell, and about forty copper objects. These included spiral bracelets and rings and, like the Sredny Stog copper, spectral analysis indicates that the copper was originally derived from the Balkan-Danubian region far to the west. In the overburden of the graves there were found the bones of domestic horse, cattle and sheep/goat.

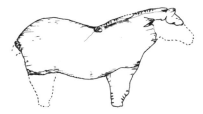

108 Horse figure from Sezzhee (L. c. 12 cm).

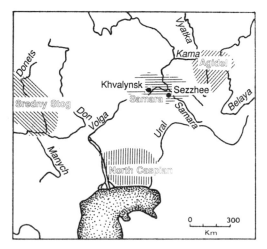

109 Distribution of Eneolithic cultures of the Caspian-middle Volga region.

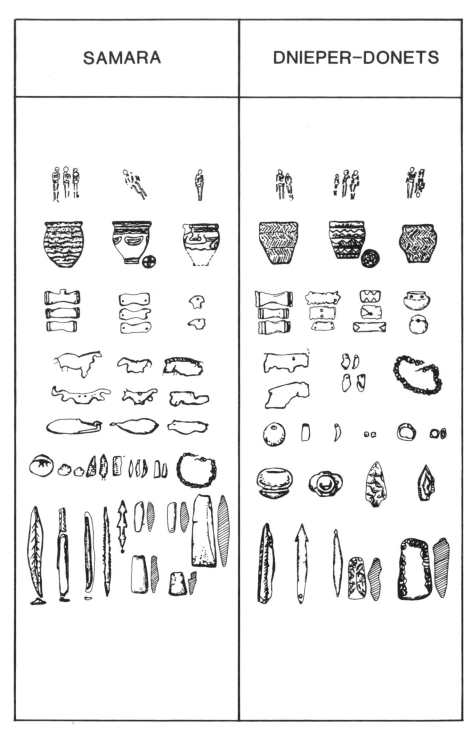

SAMARA	DNIEPER-DONETS

110   Comparison of material from the Samara and Dnieper-Donets cultures.

111   (Opposite) material from the Khvalynsk and Sredny Stog-Novodanilovka cultures.

KHVALYNSK	SREDNY-STOG

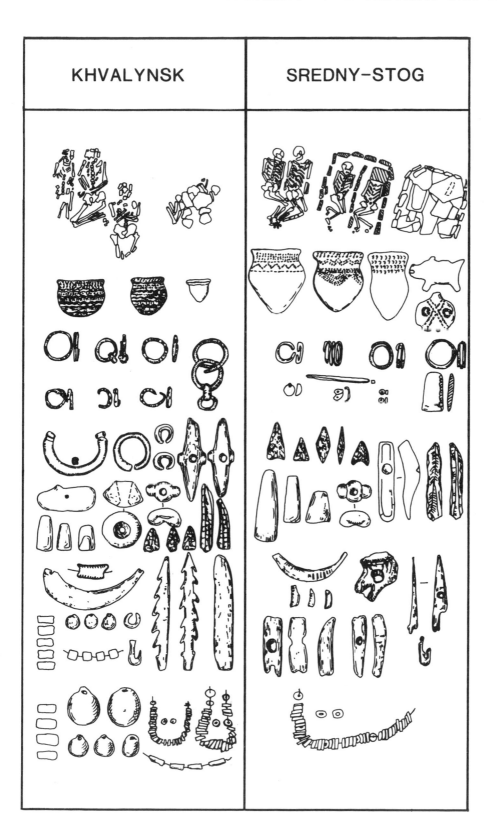

Igor Vasiliev points out that, excluding the differences in ceramics, there are striking similarities in burial ritual and technology between the Khvalynsk and the Sredny Stog cultures. To these we may add, naturally, the presence of domestic horse, which is apparently known as early in the middle Volga-south Urals as on the middle Dnieper. The similarities suggest to Vasiliev that there was a broad Sredny Stog-Khvalynsk horizon embracing the entire Pontic-Caspian during the Eneolithic. This, he suggests, replaced an earlier broadly uniform horizon, associated with the Dnieper-Donets culture, that not only occupied the west but also evidenced strong influences on the middle Volga Seroglazovo and Samara cultures.

In attempting to explain why we should have such widely similar material and ritual behaviour across the entire Pontic-Caspian, Vasiliev touches on the issue of cultural priority. In the Ukraine, the later phases of the Dnieper-Donets culture appear to coexist with the Sredny Stog culture until they are finally absorbed. In such a situation, according to Vasiliev, it is doubtful that one can argue for an entirely local evolution from the Dnieper-Donets to the Sredny Stog. Rather, he directs our attention eastwards to the middle Volga where the transition between the intervening cultures of the Neolithic and Eneolithic clearly indicate local development. The possibility that the Sredny Stog-Khvalynsk horizon was achieved by impulses moving from east to west can be proposed even if Ukrainian archaeologists emphasize what they perceive to be continuity between the Neolithic and Eneolithic. Indeed, this hypothesis, that the Ukrainian Eneolithic cultures were in part derived from movements from the Volga, has been argued by a number of Soviet archaeologists, though previously there was little chronological control of the data, nor was there the evidence for cultural development on the middle Volga.

We are still far from understanding precisely why there should have developed such a broad band of similar cultures across the Pontic-Caspian during the Early Eneolithic. Obviously, a general *Drang nach Westen* would help explain the uniformity of the stockbreeding vocabulary of the Proto-Indo-Europeans, but this should not be accomplished at the expense of other pertinent archaeological data. It is clear that metallurgy was diffusing in the opposite direction, and we must envisage a very broad area which formed a sphere of constant mutual relations, especially with regard to exchange. The increased mobility produced by the domestication of the horse was also probably an important factor. The extent to which actual folk movements were involved is not yet clear, but they can hardly be dismissed. The ultimate result of these interactions and possible movements is to be seen in the Late Eneolithic. Here the greatest similarities arise with the Yamnaya culture, one of the major cultural-historical entities of prehistoric Europe.

The Yamnaya cultural-historical area

The final Eneolithic culture of the Pontic-Caspian region, and the last cultural entity which may putatively be assigned a Proto-Indo-European date, is the

Yamnaya (Pit-grave) culture. The major floruit of this culture, substantiated by more than seventy radiocarbon dates, is about 3600–2200 BC. Its territory embraced the entire Pontic-Caspian from the Bug and Dniester rivers on the west across to the Ural and Emba rivers on the east. Such a territory, stretching 3,000 kilometres across, is so vast that many archaeologists accept the terminology of Nikolai Merpert and refer to a Yamnaya cultural-historical area rather than to a single culture.

The immediate origins of the Yamnaya culture are complicated and still very much disputed, although there is general agreement that both the Sredny Stog and Khvalynsk cultures were the primary foundations for the Yamnaya groups of their respective regions. While these certainly underlie some of the local Yamnaya variants, it should be noted, however, that Merpert envisages nine different regional variants in this vast continuum.

The Yamnaya culture is overwhelmingly evidenced by the remains of its burials rather than from settlements. Evidence for occupation sites is almost unknown in some of its regional variants, and where they do occur in sizeable numbers, they frequently tend to be insubstantial camp sites suggesting a mobile form of economy. This is especially true in the steppe region of the Volga where Yamnaya remains are recovered from the same type of dune camps as in the preceding Neolithic period.

There are, however, some major exceptions to this pattern, especially along the lower Dnieper where the site of Mikhaylovka offers the most substantial remains of a Yamnaya settlement. Here, overlying the earlier Lower Mikhaylovka phase, were stratified two substantial phases of the Yamnaya culture. The earlier occupied an area of about 1,500 square metres. Both semi-subterranean and surface structures, the latter with stone foundations, were recovered, along with a great quantity of ceramics, tools and faunal remains. The later Yamnaya phase saw the expansion of the settlement to cover an area of

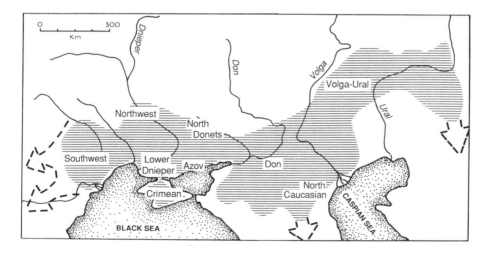

112   The regional groups of the Yamnaya cultural-historical region.

1.5 hectares, and the erection of fortifications consisting of both a ditch and stone walls which still stand to a height of 2.5 metres. Several varieties of solidly constructed houses were discovered, including both small oval-shaped dwellings similar to the previous phase, and large rectangular houses with one to three rooms. These structures were built on stone foundations up to a metre high and then completed in wood and daub. Although Mikhaylovka is the largest of the fortified Yamnaya sites it is not unique, and several other stone fortified sites are known.

Mikhaylovka offers by far the largest single sample of economic remains from the Yamnaya culture. Here were recovered over 50,000 identifiable bones of domestic and wild animals. The domestic fauna consisted primarily of cattle and then sheep/goat, with substantial remains of horses and some pig. The most typical wild fauna included the onager, red deer, aurochs, wild boar, saiga (the steppe antelope), and a variety of other species such as otter, fox, wolf, hare and beaver. Querns and flint sickle blades indicated that agriculture was practised. The faunal remains from the site of Repin on the Don were primarily those of domestic horse.

While the existence of agriculture in the Yamnaya culture is not disputed, the general opinion is that the culture was overwhelmingly centred on stockbreeding which may have become so specialized in some of its regional variants that it permitted pastoral nomadism. Valentin Shilov has called attention to the natural conditions of the open steppe where salty soils and sands would have precluded any serious development of agriculture yet would have provided excellent conditions for pastoral economies. It is in precisely these areas that Yamnaya camp sites have been encountered in the Volga-Ural region. Furthermore, Yamnaya burials are known from the deep steppe far

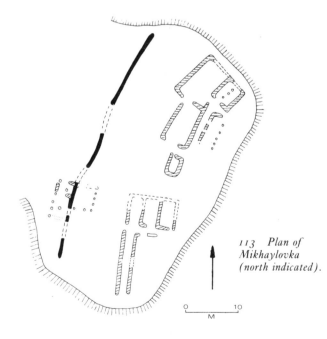

113 Plan of Mikhaylovka (north indicated).

114 Yamnaya burial with remains of wagon (3.5 × 2.6 m).

from the major rivers that might have provided the regime necessary for stable farming settlements. Although the primary source of faunal remains for much of the Yamnaya region is to be found in grave offerings, these do indicate a marked predominance of ovicaprids, precisely the animals that would best exploit the steppe environment. Even in areas such as the lower Dnieper, Ukrainian archaeologists argue that such sites as Mikhaylovka may have served as centres on which camp sites of semi-nomadic pastoralists depended.

The general picture of the Yamnaya economy is varied and dependent on the natural conditions in which its populations found themselves. In the major river valleys, where agricultural soils and forested environment provided the necessary basis for mixed farming settlements, the Yamnaya culture appears to have followed such an economy. Nevertheless, the increased development of stockbreeding, especially the utilization of both the sheep and domestic horse, assisted in the expansion of human settlement out from the river valleys into the deep steppe. Another obvious factor in the development of mobile economies was the invention of wheeled vehicles.

Wagons are first attested in the Pontic-Caspian during the Yamnaya period. Quite numerous remains of wheels, and even some entire wagons, have been recovered from Yamnaya burials. They show the use of both the two-wheeled cart and the four-wheeled wagon. There is consensus that the means of traction was oxen, as the vehicles with their heavy solid wooden wheels would have been far too heavy for horses to pull at this time. The wagon is traditionally seen as one of the prerequisites for successful exploitation of the open steppe, since it provided the necessary mode of transport for both family and property which was necessary in a mobile economy. Horse riding, which we have already seen in the Sredny Stog culture, is also evidenced in the Yamnaya culture. A pair of wooden cheekpieces was recovered from a Yamnaya kurgan at Vinogradovka, near Odessa.

The range of Yamnaya technology is not extensive. In addition to the variety of flint tools employed in the subsistence economy there is also a range of weapons – for example, flint arrowheads, daggers, stone battle-axes and maces. Bone and antler tools such as mattocks, harpoons and awls have also been recovered. Ceramics vary according to region but in some instances continue the pattern of shell and sand-tempered wares with decoration executed by cords and comb stamping. There is more copper than in earlier periods, with the production of awls, knives, chisels and adzes. While previous metallurgical developments appeared to be the result of long-distance contacts with the Balkan-Danubian region, we now find the beginnings of localized Yamnaya metallurgical centres. In the lower Dnieper copper appears to have been acquired from the Caucasus region and developed under its stylistic influence, although with its own independent production, as evidence for copper working at Mikhaylovka suggests. In the Volga-Ural region local copper resources began to be exploited.

The primary evidence for the Yamnaya culture, as mentioned above, is burials. In general the burial ritual involved the digging of a shaft (the *yama* 'pit'

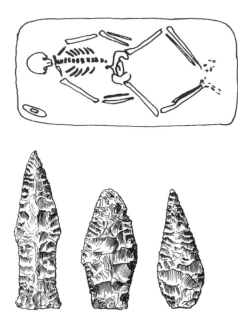

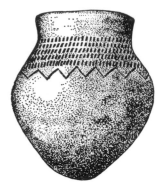

115–118   A burial from Vinogradovka, oriented with head to the west. A Yamnaya pot, daggers and spearhead.

grave) and depositing the body of the deceased, at least in the earlier periods, on the back with legs flexed and head oriented east or northeast. Some extended supine burials are also known. The deceased might lie directly on the floor of the pit, but there are also frequent traces of wooden planks or reeds and rushes being employed as a floor. The use of ochre is quite frequent and hence the culture is often termed the *Ockergrabkultur* (ochre-grave-culture) in German archaeological literature. The burial might be surrounded by a cromlech, or covered with stones, or timber planks might form a roof over the pit and a hearth might be placed next to the burial. The most notable feature, however, was the erection of a kurgan over the grave. Into this kurgan might be deposited subsequent Yamnaya burials or indeed burials from later periods extending all the way to the Middle Ages. In terms of grave goods, these might range from none, especially with the majority of typologically early graves, to an impressive quantity of items. Goods might include pots, copper knives and awls, boar-tusk pendants, and an assortment of bone and stone tools such as flint sickle blades, scrapers, stone axes and harpoons. Occasionally bird bones, generally interpreted as primitive flutes, have been found. Wheeled vehicles or individual wheels might accompany a burial.

Animal bones are an intriguing accompaniment to many burials and the principal species represented were ovicaprids, cattle, horse, dog and some wild animals. These remains may often be interpreted simply as joints of meat presented as food offerings; however, other rituals were also at play. Frequently the skull and forelegs of a sheep, or much more rarely of a horse, are encountered in a grave and indicate the presence of a 'head and hooves' cult. In some cases the forepart of the animal might have been erected directly over the burial. Knucklebones of sheep were also found frequently. Knucklebones are, of course, a familiar gaming device, and the association between the knucklebone, or astragalus, and words for dice is known in various Indo-European languages. Their presence in Yamnaya burials may be explained as offerings of gaming pieces but one should also note that they show a very strong correlation with the burials of young children. At Berezhnovka on the Volga, for example, one child was accompanied by sixteen astragali which may have served as toys or ornaments.

The origin of the Yamnaya culture is still a topic of debate. Essentially, the major issues concern which area of the Pontic-Caspian exhibits the greatest continuity of culture between the earlier and later Eneolithic, and whether chronologically earlier burials might be attributed to a particular region. Some archaeologists, such as Igor Vasiliev and Marija Gimbutas, argue that the earliest Yamnaya burials occur in the Volga region, and that the evidence for continuity between the Neolithic across the Eneolithic is so unassailable that one must attribute a priority to this region with regard to Yamnaya origins. Others, such as Dmitry Telegin, would find that the Yamnaya burials of the Ukraine are so distinctly related to the preceding Sredny Stog culture that it is unnecessary to seek an external origin. Although there are a great number of radiocarbon dates, none pertains to what are universally admitted to being the most archaic Yamnaya burials. At present, we can only surmise that there was a very rapid expansion of distinct ceramic types and burial ritual over a vast area. Nikolai Merpert has suggested that the almost instantaneous spread of elements so closely associated with expressing ethnic identity – ceramic style and burial ritual – may indicate the existence of substantial tribal unions engaged in intense contacts with one another. This would certainly be in accordance with our image of the Pontic-Caspian region as an enormous sphere of continual interaction and mutual influences, in which cultural traits and human groups traversed with great rapidity. If the inhabitants of the regions also shared a broadly similar language at this time, this would no doubt have assisted in the rapid diffusion of common cultural traits, and the creation of a broadly similar cultural horizon.

Proto-Indo-European culture

Any attempt to compare the linguistic evidence for Proto-Indo-European culture with the archaeological evidence of our supposed homeland region invites a certain dread among those with more than a passing familiarity with the literature on the subject. Precisely the same evidence employed to paint the Indo-Europeans into a Baltic landscape has been used to set them securely in the ancient Bactria of northern Afghanistan. There is indeed a curious tendency among some enthusiasts to assume that when the Proto-Indo-European vocabulary refers to clouds, rain and ice, these elements were somehow specifically abusing the inhabitants of their own particular homeland and nowhere else. Consequently, it must be admitted at the outset that the great majority of items concerning Proto-Indo-European environment or culture can hardly be ascribed exclusively to the Pontic-Caspian region rather than to elsewhere. On the other hand, if we do assume that the Pontic-Caspian region was inhabited by Proto-Indo-European speakers, then we can hardly avoid evaluating the extent to which the linguistic and archaeological evidence correspond.

As expected, the Pontic-Caspian offers plentiful referents for the admittedly generic terms for the landscape which we can reconstruct linguistically. There are ample plains and rivers and other natural features. The problematic Proto-Indo-European *mori- be it an inland sea, salt lake or marsh, could still be accommodated within the Pontic-Caspian. Here there were several major bodies of water plus numerous deltas, marshes and now dried lakes that once served as primary settlement locations during the Neolithic-Eneolithic.

The Proto-Indo-European vocabulary clearly attests words for mountains and high places. This fact has been pressed by the Soviet linguists Tomas Gamkrelidze and Vyachislav Ivanov to support their hypothesis that the homeland was in a mountainous region (Armenia). They dismiss as potential homelands the 'flatlands encompassing the whole of eastern Europe, including the Pontic'. As we have already observed, this surely raises the linguistic evidence to literally too great a height, since one hardly need live on a mountain to have a name for it. It is true that most of the mountain ranges such as the Carpathians, Crimean, Caucasus and Urals are largely peripheral to the Pontic-Caspian cultures, but we should never forget that geographical terms are merely perceptual categories. There is quite obvious relief within the Pontic-Caspian, and we should surely be astonished if its inhabitants actually lacked a word for mountain or hill.

The climatic evidence is vague. The current conditions of the Pontic-Caspian vary in aridity as one moves eastwards and it is valid to characterize even the western part as possessing a moderate and somewhat arid climate with hot summers and short, mild winters. Currently the Pontic-Caspian sees about forty to eighty days of snow lying per year, and the conditions during the Eneolithic are assumed to have been drier but colder than at present.

From the arboreal point of view, the Pontic-Caspian offers a number of diverse environments. The forest-steppe and the river valleys could provide all the necessary arboreal referents, while the steppe would have contributed little, and the semi-desert of the Caspian almost nothing. All the strongly attested tree names do find their counterparts in the Pontic-Caspian during the Neolithic-Eneolithic. It must be admitted that the beech, the most debatable arboreal item, did have a much more limited distribution. The common beech was barely found east of the Dnieper, while the eastern beech was confined to the Caucasus and Crimea. In such a situation one could hardly be surprised if the word is attested only in the European languages and does not find a reflex in the more easterly Indo-Iranian languages.

The wild fauna reconstructed linguistically can be correlated with remains recovered from archaeological sites, although they are not unique to our area.

Both the Indo-European vocabulary and the archaeological evidence emphasize a variety of riverine fauna such as beaver and otter, and one should not imagine the Pontic-Caspian purely as an arid steppe region. There are, of course, some animals known from the steppe sites, such as onager and saiga antelope, that are in no way reconstructible to Proto-Indo-European, though this is hardly surprising given their extremely limited distribution.

The economy which we envisage from linguistic evidence for the Proto-Indo-Europeans is well-enough mirrored in the archaeological evidence. Agriculture is attested, but nowhere does it seem to have been the primary subsistence component of the economy. Indeed, in the Volga-Ural steppe, and possibly also in areas of the western steppe, there are reasons to exclude agriculture as a serious factor in the economy. Rather, the emphasis of the archaeological remains appears to be primarily on stockbreeding. Evidence has been found for all the basic livestock. There are no grounds to prefer sheep or cattle as the primary species since they vary with the particular ecological situation of each settlement. The domestic pig, a controversial animal among linguists, does appear to be of secondary importance throughout the Pontic-Caspian. It is attested minimally in the west and seems, so far, to have been absent in the east prior to the second millennium when it does appear on Bronze Age sites. This is coincidental with fairly intense relations running from the south to the north. As we have mentioned before, the Uralic languages acquired their name for the domestic pig from Indo-Iranians, and it is attractive to imagine this loan occurred here in the Volga-Ural region during the second millennium BC when Indo-Iranians may well have been in contact with their Uralic neighbours.

The most significant linguistic-archaeological correlation among the domestic animals is the horse, which is known at least from the fourth millennium BC, or earlier from the Dnieper east to the southern Urals. It is not simply present, but all the evidence indicates intense exploitation and a role in ritual. All of this helps underwrite the apparently equo-centric practices that are shared by many Indo-European peoples. Where the horse occurs either to the south or immediately west of the Pontic-Caspian, this is generally explained by contacts with the natural home of the horse. This strengthens the Pontic-Caspian's claim to homeland status though it does not entirely secure it against other areas. Domestic horse remains are reported from both Central Europe in the Altheim culture and the North European TRB culture, but it should be emphasized that there is no evidence that these cultures exploited the horse in their economies or ritual on the scale we find in the Pontic-Caspian.

The reconstructed vocabulary for settlement architecture is imprecise, and it is impossible to know whether the Proto-Indo-European *weiḱ-, which spans such meanings as house, village or clan, might appropriately be assigned to a small settlement such as Dereivka. The postulated evidence for some form of fortified enclosure on the basis of Sanskrit, Greek, Armenian and Lithuanian can at least find a plausible referent in sites such as Mikhaylovka which are known from about 3000 BC.

The basic assortment of Neolithic-Eneolithic technology evidenced from language is also mirrored on Pontic-Caspian sites. Obviously, little can be made of the fact that both the Proto-Indo-European lexicon and these sites exhibit, for example, pottery, grinding stones and arrowheads. The Proto-Indo-European thrusting (?) weapon, indicated by the Sanskrit-Latin cognates for 'sword', may find its ultimate origin in either the long flint blades from the Sredny Stog and Novodanilovka cultures, the flint daggers known in the somewhat more recent Yamnaya burials, or in the earliest bronze daggers, which we will encounter in the next chapter. Copper is well attested and could offer the probable referent of the Indo-European basic metal term (*ayes-) and, as we will see below, silver is also known in the Pontic-Caspian from about the fourth millennium BC. If one accepts the linguistic existence of a Proto-Indo-European word (*(a)rgentom) for this metal, the Pontic-Caspian offers an especially attractive fit for a metal conspicuously absent from most of Europe at this time.

The technology of the 'Secondary Products Revolution', which involves the plough, milking and other dairy products, wool, and wheeled vehicles, is all clearly indicated in the Proto-Indo-European vocabulary. The actual archaeological evidence has seldom been assembled for discussion of this topic – faunal reports rarely explore the precise patterns of exploitation of livestock. The apparent increase in numbers of sheep, at least among communities exploiting the open steppe, may be associated with the words for wool and combing in the Indo-European languages. Indeed, Sandor Bökönyi has recently suggested that a new type of sheep, which was larger and offered more wool, had been introduced into the steppe region from Asia. Instruments putatively employed in assisting in milking cattle have been found on Yamnaya and later sites, and a primitive plough is recorded from Mikhaylovka. Only with wheeled vehicles and animal traction are we on really well-discussed ground, and there is abundant evidence for carts and wagons from at least 3000 BC onwards. This again is an attractive link with the linguistic evidence at a suitably early date although it is still not a unique correlation. Models of wagons are known from the Baden culture in Hungary at about this same time, and a four-wheeled wagon is depicted on a pot from a TRB site in Poland.

Although there has been a vast amount of literature on the burial remains and ritual of the Pontic-Caspian Eneolithic cultures, we are still far from being able to pronounce authoritatively on the social structure of their communities, nor are we able to make apt comparisons with our linguistic evidence. Burials may range widely in wealth but it is difficult to postulate evidence for a Proto-Indo-European 'protector', 'man with charisma' or 'master of the clan' on this evidence. One of the problems here is the nature of our mortuary evidence. Kurgans frequently contain multiple burials, and we are seldom certain that our sample of burials derives from the same general period. There is no question that some graves are markedly wealthier than others, but if we cannot compare them confidently with contemporary burials, we have no solid basis for evaluating the structure of Pontic-Caspian society in detail. We can only note, as observed by Alexander Häusler and others, that very often the primary burial in a kurgan belongs to a male. Indeed, Maryana Khlobystina, in examining the distribution of burials by sex on the Volga, noted that the overwhelming majority belonged to males and children. Consequently, she suggested that females were buried elsewhere, probably in not-yet-discovered flat graves, and that the emphasis on male burials indicated the strong patriarchal nature of steppe society.

Given the nature of our evidence, one can imagine how elusive Georges Dumézil's three classes might be in the archaeological record. Elena Kuzmina suggests that those burials accompanied by horse remains might claim to represent the nobility postulated by the Dumézilian school. It we look at an isolated case, such as Khutor Khryashchevskogo I, we certainly find an attractive candidate for a royal figure. In this late steppe burial, the deceased was accompanied by a horse skull, several pots, a metal spearhead, several arrows, a mace and a stone hammer. But this burial is hardly typical of all horse-associated burials, many of which are accompanied by only additional animal remains, or nothing else.

Evidence for age-sets is slight. In his compendious survey of steppe burials, Alexander Häusler notes how some kurgans appear to be given over primarily to children's burials. In addition, he notes a certain tendency for older males to correlate with a southwesterly orientation. We should also emphasize that relatively wealthy burials of children are quite common, and there are obviously important issues concerning the ascription of wealth and status among the Pontic-Caspian populations; these warrant closer study. As we have already mentioned, the burial rites which follow the Dnieper-Donets culture do exhibit a shift from collective burials in large pits to smaller group pits, or individual burials arranged in small groups within a larger cemetery. Some Soviet archaeologists have interpreted this shift as a structural reordering of society that sees the emergence of family or clan burial plots.

We may hope to find evidence of Indo-European ritual behaviour on the anthropomorphic stone stelae and in the remains of animal sacrifices. It is not difficult, for example, to read into those stelae which depict male figures bearing battle-axes the representation of a sky-god, thunder-god or, more abstractly, the warrior function. Naturally, given the ease with which we can squeeze three of our postulated Proto-Indo-European divinities out of the same block of stone, our actual ability to make a credible association between the iconographic evidence and Indo-European myth is clearly suspect. It is remarkable that, given the iconographic detail on some of the stelae, this source of information has been largely bypassed by those most involved in reconstructing Proto-Indo-European religion. We might emphasize that the stelae do not exclusively depict male figures wielding axes, but a number portray a female figure apparently wearing a necklace of beads. Other motifs include what appear to be two large footprints, and stylized trees.

There is abundant evidence for the deposition of animal remains in graves, and also for special sacrificial areas. In a rough survey of animal remains in tombs across the Pontic-Caspian, we generally find sheep as the most frequent offering, followed by cattle, and then horse. We may wish to read these figures as inversely proportional to the status of the offering, keeping in mind the victims sacrificed to the Iranian goddess Arədvi (100 horses, 1,000 cattle, 10,000 sheep). On the other hand, Nikolai Merpert suggests that the paucity of cattle and horse remains compared with those of sheep may have had more to do with economic factors, since the steppe tribes were perhaps less inclined to waste valuable traction animals on ritual occasions.

Some form of horse sacrifice is, at least according to both the ritual and mythic evidence, one of the expected patterns of ritual behaviour which we might predict for the Proto-Indo-Europeans. We have already seen the sacrifice of the stallion and dogs at the Sredny Stog site of Dereivka, and archaeologists have been quick to link this ritual deposit with the type of horse sacrifices we later encounter in India. If we expand our attention to the ritual sacrifice of three different species, one of which is the horse, then there are some examples which would not be out of place in an Indo-European 'trifunctional' ritual. At Grushevka a 'ritual' pit was uncovered which contained the bones of horse, cattle and sheep, while the same three species were also found in a burial at Gerasimovka I. These are exceptions, however, rather than patterns, since normally the remains of horse – often the skull or forelegs – is either found alone or accompanied by only one other species such as sheep or cattle.

We have already mentioned the problem of establishing some form of explanation for the divine twins so often encountered in Indo-European mythology. Mortuary evidence offers us the Yamnaya burial at Novoalekseevka 6/14, where the skeleton of a one-year-old child was found lying between two horse skulls. This is an exceptional burial, and there really is very little evidence

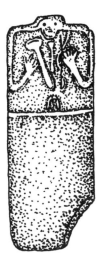
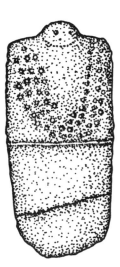

119 'Warrior' figure armed with axe, mace and bow on a stela from Natalevka (H. 1.6 m).

120 Female stela from Utkonosovka.

121 Two figures (twins?) on a stela from Kazanki (H. 1.17 m).

122   Two-headed horse from Sezzhee (L. 7 cm).

to postulate the twinning or doubling of horses, in draft or ritual, among the Pontic-Caspian tribes of the Eneolithic. The only other explicitly ritual context is from the cemetery at Sezzhee. Here, above the group of richest burials, the excavators discovered a ritual area which included the skulls and legs of two horses, as well as two pots, a harpoon and shell beads, all sprinkled with red ochre. At Sezzhee we have also the broken remains of a figure purportedly depicting a two-headed horse although two-headed cattle figures are also known from the site. Two horses are depicted on the lower register of the Kernosovka stela.

Finally, one further element of equine ritual may be seen in the horse remains from Dereivka. In her analysis of the faunal evidence from the site, Valentina Bibikova observed that of the eighteen whole metacarpals recovered, seventeen of them were from the left leg. From this we may postulate some form of ritual prohibition against breaking the left foreleg of the horse which may lead us back to the right-left dichotomy so often observed among the Indo-Europeans.

Provided that our expectations do not demand precise detail, most of the archaeological evidence from the Pontic-Caspian does make a reasonably solid fit with our reconstruction of Proto-Indo-European culture. In some areas, such as those pertaining to the domestic horse and wheeled vehicles, the fit is particularly striking, and we cannot find such close correspondences among many other Eneolithic cultures of Europe. None of this, however, is sufficient to impell us to claim the Pontic-Caspian as the exclusive homeland of the Proto-Indo-Europeans. This can only be acknowledged if the proponents of a Pontic-Caspian homeland can demonstrate expansions from this region which account for the dispersion of the Indo-European languages.

CHAPTER EIGHT

Indo-European Expansions

The Aryans left their homes . . . on the 1st of
March. This settles the question of the climate
of their original home. Had their homes been
situated in a moderate zone, the Aryans would
never, of their own free will, have made their
exodus so early; they would have delayed it, if
not until May, at any rate until the middle of
April.

RUDOLPH VON IHERING, 1897

The preceding chapter has provisionally assigned the earliest Indo-European speakers to the Pontic-Caspian region. As this territory encompasses well over 300,000 square kilometres, it indicates an area whose size is certainly comparable to the territory of a major linguistic entity. We are therefore reluctant to assign additional territory to this 'homeland' unless compelled to do so by other evidence. But we can only avoid enlarging our prospective homeland area if we can actually trace an expansion from this region, carrying us into all of those territories where we subsequently encounter the historical Indo-Europeans. If this can be accomplished we are afforded with a solution to the homeland problem expressed at the right order of magnitude and not so large as to be linguistically implausible or geographically meaningless. Many scholars, both archaeologists and linguists, do support the notion that the Pontic-Caspian region defines the Indo-European homeland. Now we must evaluate whether we really can limit the Proto-Indo-Europeans to such a confined homeland and trace their expansions from it.

If we demand absolutely conclusive archaeological evidence for folk movements from the Pontic-Caspian, and the subsequent absorption of peripheral regions by intruders from the steppe, then our task is hopeless. It is too much to expect that we now have all of the archaeological evidence at hand, or indeed that archaeologists even agree on the nature of the evidence required to demonstrate population movements, much less the linguistic absorption of native populations by intruders. Rather, we can do little more than trace plausible trajectories of Pontic-Caspian peoples into a number of critical territories. We need to demonstrate that peoples from the steppe expanded into Southeastern Europe to effect the formation of the immediate ancestors of the Indo-European peoples of the Balkans and Greece, and of those languages of Anatolia whose origins have been directly linked to the Balkans, such as Phrygian, Armenian, and possibly the Anatolian languages themselves. We are also required to establish a genetic link that seriously involves the Pontic-Caspian in the formation of the Corded Ware horizon of Northern and Central Europe, since it provides the presumed staging area for the later emergence of the Celts, Germans, Balts, Slavs and possibly other Indo-European groups. And, finally, we must discover traces of Pontic-Caspian expansions into Asia to explain the creation of the Tocharians and Indo-Iranians. As we began our survey, in Chapter Two, with the Indo-Europeans of Asia, we will examine this region first.

Expansion into Asia

Although many details may be disputed, there is most certainly a serious case for an expansion of peoples from the Pontic-Caspian into the steppe and forest-steppe east of the Urals. These movements appear to have begun as early as the fourth millennium BC, and they may have continued over several millennia by which time the major patterns of migration in this region were dramatically reversed by Turkic-speaking peoples such as the Huns.

The easternmost culture to claim a relationship with the Pontic-Caspian is the Afanasievo whose remains are primarily confined to the Minusinsk Basin and the Altai. Burials provide the most frequent evidence – over 400 graves from approximately fifty cemeteries – but about ten settlements are also known. The distribution of these sites indicates that the Afanasievo people exploited both riverine territories as well as the deep steppe. The settlements, at least those on the Yenisey, are insubstantial, and are commonly interpreted as the seasonal camps of pastoralists who raised cattle, sheep/goat and, significantly, domestic horse. Although wheeled vehicles are not directly attested, archaeologists suspect that the Afanasievans possessed them. The cultural successor to the Afanasievo culture, the Okunevo culture, does exhibit evidence for wheeled vehicles, despite the fact that its economy appears originally to have been based on hunting and gathering. Consequently, we attribute the introduction of wheeled vehicles among the Okunevo people to their immediate and technologically more advanced predecessors.

The Afanasievo dead were interred in rectangular pits which were covered by kurgans and surrounded by cromlechs and rectangular stone enclosures. The deceased were buried flexed on their side or, more notably, on their backs with their legs flexed, the traditional burial posture known from the Pontic-Caspian. Ochre was included in burials. The grave goods included pointed based pots, similar in general form to those of the Pontic-Caspian, and decorated with stamped impressions. Indeed, Maryana Khlobystina has synchronized the Afanasievo ceramics from the Altai with parallel developments of Yamnaya ware on the Volga. Censers decorated with ochre were part of the Afanasievo ritual paraphernalia. Formally, they closely resemble similar cult artefacts known from the Pontic-Caspian. In addition to the predictable stone and bone tools found in the graves, there were also objects of copper, gold and silver. Faunal remains of sheep, and more rarely of cattle and horse, were

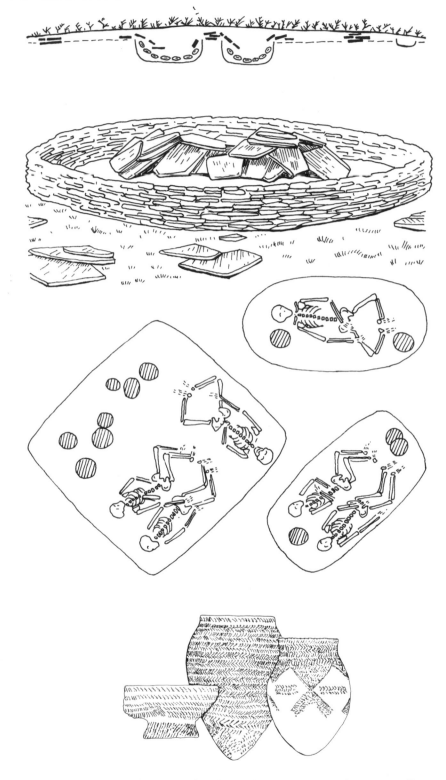

123, 124 Afanasievo kurgan and burials, together with pottery and a censer (tallest vessel c. 25 cm).

found in the fill of the burials and were interpreted as the residue of funeral feasts. Khlobystina notes that, like the earlier Yamnaya burials on the Volga, the earliest Afanasievo tombs in the Altai were confined exclusively to males and children.

In contrast to the physical type of their neighbours, the Afanasievo people have repeatedly been classified as Europoids by Soviet anthropologists, who find their closest parallels with the Yamnaya populations of the Pontic-Caspian. Traditionally, Soviet archaeologists have dated the Afanasievo culture to the mid-third millennium BC; however, radiocarbon dates indicate that this culture probably began before 3000 BC and then continued throughout much of the third millennium.

From the above, it is not difficult to understand why archaeologists have often associated the Afanasievo culture with the Pontic-Caspian. Similarities in burial ritual, material culture, economy and even in physical type all point towards the Pontic-Caspian. Moreover, if Elga Badetskaya is correct when she finds no solid evidence for stockbreeding on the Yenisey prior to the Afanasievo culture, then we have a hint of an explanation as to how this culture managed to spread so far to the east. Possessed with an already-developed mobile economy based on stockbreeding, populations from the Pontic-Caspian could swiftly have expanded to exploit the vast steppe and forest-steppe east of the Urals. Such an expansion would, no doubt, have brought the ancestors of the Afanasievo culture into contact with the various local sub-Neolithic communities whom they eventually assimilated. This model seems plausible enough but it has always faced one major obstacle – the distance between the Ural, the traditional eastern limit of the Pontic-Caspian cultures, and the Yenisey, is in the order of 2,000 kilometres!

The enormous gap between the Pontic-Caspian and the cultural territory of the Afanasievans is too obvious a difficulty to be ignored. This gap, however, may have more to do with the paucity of archaeological exploration in the intervening territory than to a genuine absence of intermediate sites. As our archaeological evidence to both the east and north of the Afanasievo culture reveals only hunting-gathering peoples, an Afanasievo origin somewhere to the west is all that we can seriously entertain. Recent discoveries now suggest the existence of intermediate sites that might help fill the gap between the Ural and the Yenisey. Tamilla Potemkhina, for example, has uncovered cemeteries at

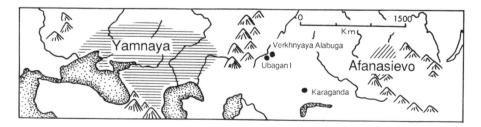

125 The region between the Yamnaya and Afanasievo cultures.

Verkhnyaya Alabuga and Ubagan I in the Tobol drainage east of the Ural. The graves included burials in the supine position with legs flexed, the use of ochre, bone plates similar to those recovered from the Khvalynsk cemetery of the Volga, pointed-based pots similar to both Yamnaya and Afanasievo vessels, and copper artefacts provenanced by spectrum analysis to the Yamnaya region. These burials were in flat graves typologically similar to the very earliest Yamnaya burials of the Volga-Ural group. While Potemkhina observes that these burials indicate that the Yamnaya culture extended further east than had previously been suspected, Elga Badetskaya maintains that, had the ceramics from these sites been found on the Yenisey or the Altai, they would probably have been ascribed to the Afanasievo culture. Further east of the Tobol, on the Karaganda, a burial has been uncovered which was again in the classic Yamnaya posture and accompanied by a vessel similar to Afanasievo ware. In short, the evidence is slowly accumulating to support the existence of a vast extension of material culture, economy, ritual behaviour and physical type from the Pontic-Caspian eastwards to the Yenisey by about 3000 BC.

To suggest an extensive band of communities historically related to the Pontic-Caspian across the West Asiatic steppe is of obvious linguistic interest. As we have seen above, some linguists would require for Tocharian origins a model which would place their ancestors on the 'archaic' periphery of the Proto-Indo-European dialects. This would explain why they did not participate in the series of linguistic innovations experienced by their nearest historical neighbours, the Indo-Iranians. In purely temporal terms, an expansion of Indo-European speakers as far east as the Yenisey as early as the fourth or early third millennium BC might adequately account for the early separation of the ancestors of the Tocharians from their other Indo-European relations. It does not, of course, place them specifically in their later historical position in the Tarim Basin, which lies nearly 1,000 kilometres to the south. This distance, however, is not insurmountable when one considers that we have several thousand years to account for the movement of these apparently mobile Indo-Europeans either south of the Altai or through Mongolia into Chinese Turkestan. Indeed, long ago Sergei Kiselev suggested that the border of the Afansievo culture may well have extended further south than is presently known. Kiselev referred to the discovery of sherds of pottery, with decoration similar to Afanasievo ware, recovered by Sir Aurel Stein in the western part of Chinese Turkestan, the area immediately adjacent to the earliest-attested Tocharian-speaking people.

Recent excavations have also suggested that the trajectory of Pontic-Caspian movements was not only to the east but also towards the south where steppe elements have been found in the fourth- or third-millennium BC cemetery of Tumek-Kichidzhik. The site is located south of the Aral Sea and is assigned to the Kelteminar culture, the major Neolithic (but with a hunting-gathering-fishing economy) culture of the east and southeast Caspian. As well as clearly local traits such as lithics and ceramics, the grave goods included ornaments of bone and boar tusk which were nearly identical to goods found in the Samara and later cultures on the middle Volga. In addition, the burial rite – extended supine position, northern orientation, ochre – and the proto-Europoid physical type also relate to the steppe. Alexandr Vinogradov links these steppe influences with the southern movement of sheep-rearing pastoralists who expanded to take advantage of the desert and semi-desert conditions of this region. This is a pattern that was maintained through the early Bronze Age where we find traces of steppe burials on the northern borders of the proto-urban settlements of Central Asia.

The later Steppe Bronze Age of western Siberia provides us with our second major watershed that may be associated with the expansion of Indo-Europeans in Asia. Traditionally, the second millennium BC of the west Siberian steppe is primarily represented by the Andronovo culture. This, in fact, is a cultural label that embraces a series of local cultural groups which occupied the forest-steppe and steppe from the Urals to the Yenisey and from the northern border of the forest-steppe south to the Pamirs of Tadzhikistan. Admitting the existence of predictable regional variation, this enormous region does find similar ceramics and metal types, a predominantly stockbreeding economy, and a range of broadly similar mortuary practices and ritual traditions. Today the concept of a unified Andronovo culture has been seriously challenged by a number of Soviet archaeologists who prefer to regard the regional variants as independent cultures existing within the context of a vast sphere of interactions that generated the similarities mentioned above. Radiocarbon evidence suggests that the Andronovo culture may have begun to emerge in the early second millennium BC.

Few, if any, archaeologists would deny a general Indo-Iranian identity for most of the bearers of the Andronovo culture, nor would they deny its fundamental genetic association with its western neighbours in the Pontic-Caspian. These connections are not only of the more general kind – primarily

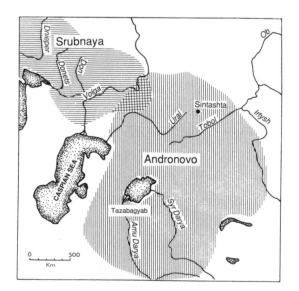

126 Generalized distribution of the Andronovo and Srubnaya cultures.

stockbreeding economy, domestic horse, wheeled vehicles, *kurgan* burials – but they also involve the specifics of ceramic form and decoration, as well as the types of metal implements and ornaments. Indeed, the Pontic-Caspian successor to the Yamnaya culture, the Bronze Age Srubnaya (Timber-grave) culture, appears to have penetrated east of the Volga, and Srubnaya burials are known from the east Caspian.

The Indo-Iranian identity of the Andronovans is founded on both cultural and geographical evidence. The cultural remains from the Steppe Bronze Age sites coincide with our expectations for the immediate ancestors of those Indo-Iranians whom we later encounter in the historical record. The terrain of the region was one normally selected for a mobile economy founded on stockbreeding, and with few exceptions this is what we encounter. The herd consisted of cattle, sheep/goat and horse, and there appears little or no place for the domestic pig, a situation predicted by the poor lexical preservation of the inherited Indo-European word in the Indo-Iranian languages *east* of the Urals. The horse was clearly domesticated (it accounts for from 12 to 27 per cent of the domestic fauna), and was employed both in traction as well as being ridden: horse psalia, designed to hold the bit in the horse's mouth, are found on Andronovo sites, and paired horse burials suggest its use in drawing vehicles. A clay model of a horse with a perforation through the mane, putatively for attachment to a vehicle, is known from one of the southernmost Andronovo variants. More spectacular evidence for the chariot-borne aristocracy encoun-tered in the later historical record is the major cemetery at Sintashta in the south Ural steppe. Here the remains of chariots and sacrificed horses clearly presage the later royal burials of the steppe tribes such as the Scythians, or their more easterly Iranian cousins, who buried their dead in the spectacular chambers recovered from the Pazyryk cemetery of the Altai. Vladimir Gening, the excavator of Sintashta, has utilized Indic and Iranian religious literature as a key to interpreting the rituals evident in the cemetery. He calls attention to the ritual horse sacrifice (with as many as seven horses in a single burial chamber), dog sacrifice and the slaughter of domestic animals. Here also we might have a hint of the type of trifunctional animal sacrifices known from early Indo-European literature. In pit 1 was discovered a sacrificial area apparently unassociated with burials. Within it were the remains (especially skulls) of horses, bulls and sheep.

Unlike earlier essentially pastoralist peoples, the Andronovans have left us with considerable remains of their settlements which were generally situated along small rivers and ranged from two to twenty houses. These were constructed of wood – pine, cedar and especially birch which, as we noted earlier, is one of the very few Proto-Indo-European arboreal names well-preserved in Indo-Iranian. Elena Kuzmina has suggested that settlement evidence may be used to identify the Andronovans with the Indo-Iranians. She emphasizes the differences between the dwellings of both the Indus civilization and the proto-urban communities of Central Asia, and those of the steppe pastoralists. The former involved brick and stone surface structures with small rectangular rooms in the order of 9 to 12 square metres. These, she argues, correlate with small family units and are in striking contrast to the semi-subterranean timber-built houses of the Andronovans which occupied areas from 50 to 300 square metres, dimensions suggestive of large extended families. The evidence from both the *Vedas* and the *Avesta* indicate that the Indo-Iranian house can only be paralleled by those of the steppe and not by the indigenous (proto-)urban settlements.

Further support for identifying the Andronovans with the Indo-Iranians is that all our evidence for the trajectory of the earliest Indo-Iranians is from the north to the south, and consequently the steppe is the most logical staging area for their later migrations. Finally, the territory of the Andronovo culture coincides with the later Iron Age territories of the historically attested Eastern Iranians – the Saka, Massagetae, Sarmatians, and Alans.

Although the Steppe Bronze Age peoples make an admirable fit with the territory and expected culture of the steppe Iranians, it is not easy to make a simple appeal to the Andronovo culture to resolve all the issues of Indo-Iranian origins. Neither Western Iranians putatively associated with grey wares, nor the Mitanni nor Indo-Aryans, and the variety of their possible congeners in the Swat Valley or Indus region, are closely linked to the Andronovo culture of the steppe.

When the archaeological evidence becomes so opaque then our only refuge, if we choose to pursue this problem further, is probability, and not a little intuition. We can, I think, accept as one anchor the assumption that the Late Bronze Age cultures of the steppe were, for the most part, the linear ancestors of at least the Eastern Iranians of the historical period. Once this is admitted, then where is the most likely location for the Western Iranians and the Indo-Aryans during the Bronze Age? It is reasonably safe to exclude them from land east of the Yenisey or north of the forest-steppe. It is always possible that some Iranians were situated to the west of the Andronovans in the Srubnaya culture of the Pontic-Caspian, and we have already reviewed the suggestion that these may have passed southwards through the Caucasus to form the Western Iranians. But as for the ancestors of the earliest Indo-Aryans (and, I suspect, Western Iranians since the Caucasian theory leaves much to be desired), it is most probable to seek them along the southern border of the Asiatic steppe during the second millennium BC, if not earlier. If they are not clearly evident in the archaeological record this is probably due to the nature of processes involved in any movement south from the steppe. In general, archaeologists concerned with the problem of Indo-Aryan or Western Iranian origins believe that it entailed gradual and protracted movements from the steppe through Central Asia. Such a movement would require the mobile populations from the Eurasian steppe to pass through a perimeter of the more advanced agricultural societies of Soviet Central Asia and northern Afghanistan. This would not only include intimate contacts with proto-urban towns, but even with outposts of the Harappan culture, such as Shortugai. Such contacts would then transform the material culture of the steppe pastoralists, especially in the spheres of

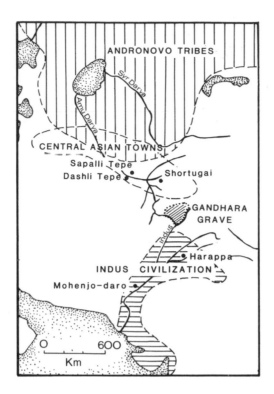

127 Many associate the Andronovo culture with the early Indo-Iranians. The southernmost Andronovo tribes would have had to pass through the cultural area of Central Asian urbanism and outposts of the Indus Valley culture (Shortugai) before arriving in the area of the Gandhara Grave culture (Swat Valley) or northwest Indus.

ceramics, architecture and metallurgy. For this reason, we should hardly expect to find our archetypal Andronovo pastoralists south of the steppe itself.

The process of cultural transformation outlined above is by no means hypothetical. South of the Aral Sea, and along the Amu Darya, there existed the Tazabagyab culture, frequently regarded as a local variant of the Andronovo culture. In addition to its livestock, including the horse, we also encounter irrigation systems along which small Tazabagyab villages, consisting of perhaps ten families, began to appear. We should also note that Tazabagyab burials signalled the sex of the deceased by burying males on their right side and females on their left, a trait that is hardly unexpected among the Indo-Europeans and which is encountered elsewhere in the Andronovo cultural region, such as at Tulkhar. Further east along the Amu Darya we encounter other Andronovo variants in Uzbekistan and Tadzhikistan which were either in direct contact or partly related to the more 'advanced' agricultural populations immediately to their south, including northern Afghanistan. Nataliya Chlenova has recently emphasized the importance of the major waterways of the area as historical routes which carried people between Central Asia and the Indus Valley. She notes that the southernmost Andronovo burials occur along the river Vaksh, which is less than 500 kilometres from the region of the putatively Indo-Aryan Gandhara Grave culture and may be reached by the river Kabul. Moreover, Elena Kuzmina perceives parallels between both the domestic architecture and burial rites of the Gandhara Grave culture, and the regional variants of the Andronovans to their north.

It is perhaps here that probability must yield to intuition, at least until the volume of excavated material from the region between the Indus and the steppe has been considerably augmented. The existence of Indo-Aryans and Iranians south of the steppe directs our attention to the complicated transition zone between the steppe and the band of more settled agriculturalists which extended from the Caspian east to the Amu Darya Basin, and beyond. Already by the fourth or early third millennium, steppe pastoralists had come into contact with Central Asian agriculturalists. Later we find the Dashli and Sapalli Tepe cultures emerging in the second millennium BC. These show a combination of factors – the indigenous traditions of the Central Asian proto-urban settlements such as Namazga and Altin Depe, and influences from the Andronovans. Their ceramics provide some of the better analogies for the type of pottery we find in the Gandhara Grave culture. Elsewhere in Central Asia Andronovo pottery is found on proto-urban sites, and Elena Kuzmina and others suggest that the steppe pastoralists may have been a major factor in the collapse of these sites in the late second millennium. With the steppe already occupied by Indo-Europeans from Afanasievo times, we may speculate that subsequent Indo-European populations evolved into the Indo-Iranians. We find some evidence on the major approaches into both India and Iran that indicates the movements of mobile pastoralists, possessed of the basic characteristics we might expect from the earliest Indo-Iranians. The details of how they ultimately arrived in their historic homes are still unclear, but the connection between the Pontic-Caspian and their immediate staging area in the steppe seems reasonable enough.

Expansion into the Caucasus

In our survey of Anatolian origins, we have seen that there are two schools of thought on the earliest appearance of the Anatolian languages. Some prefer a western entry via the Balkans while others have opted for an intrusion that carried Indo-European speakers from the Pontic south through the Caucasus and into eastern Anatolia. Although the eastern entry seems to involve some critical problems, not the least being its inability to trace a migration as far as the historical seats of the Indo-European-speaking Luwians, it has had an attraction for some linguists. These have emphasized that the Anatolian languages share certain features with the languages of the Caucasus (or, like the Caucasian languages, lack certain features found in all other Indo-European languages). Moreover, a number of linguists have claimed that the Caucasian languages, such as Kartvelian, must have been in close contact with an Indo-European language, presumably an archaic one such as we might expect from the ancestors of Hittite and Luwian.

An intrusion from the Pontic steppe into the Caucasus has been argued primarily by Marija Gimbutas. Her evidence is essentially founded on the appearance of kurgan burials in the steppe region of the confluence of the Kura and Araxes rivers. Among these kurgan burials are the three great mounds at

Uch-Tepe, the third of which has been excavated. This enormous mound measured 17 metres in height and 130 metres in diameter, and enclosed a stone-built chamber roofed with timber beams which have been dated to about 3500 BC. This, and other kurgans such as the one covering a wagon burial at Bedeni, have been interpreted as the tombs of the ruling elite who penetrated the local Kuro-Araxes culture from the Pontic-Caspian steppe. Other kurgans are known in western Georgia. In addition to what she sees as a kurgan burial rite, Marija Gimbutas also cites the settlement at Mingachaur as evidence of northern invaders. Here the rectangular semi-subterranean timber-built houses contrast with the typical Kuro-Araxes stone and clay-lined round houses. Finally, the appearance of Caucasian metallurgical types over the Pontic-Caspian is credited to intrusions by the Kurgan people into the Caucasus, who then transmitted the new techniques back to their kinsmen on the steppe. To this we might add the remains of horses, putatively domestic, from the site of Alikemektepesi in the steppe to the south of the Kura and Araxes. Soviet archaeologists cite this as the earliest evidence for domestic horse in the Caucasus, dated to the fourth millennium BC, if not earlier. Horse remains are regularly encountered on Kuro-Araxes sites.

If we compare this evidence with that of the Pontic-Caspian, then the similarities involve the use of the tumulus, burial chamber, and in some cases such as Uch-Tepe, the use of ochre. In several more detailed considerations of this material, Shan Winn relates it to the later royal burials at Alaca Hüyük, Trialeti and Maykop, which brings the steppe, the Caucasus, and northern Anatolia into some form of contact relationship. Winn emphasizes that the heirs to the Kurgan intrusions of the Kura-Araxes region are unlikely to have been an historical Indo-European group but, more plausibly, Hurrians. Nevertheless, he does entertain the possibility that Indo-Europeans passed through the Caucasus to occupy eastern Anatolia whence they progressively assimilated the Hatti of central Anatolia to form the later Hittites.

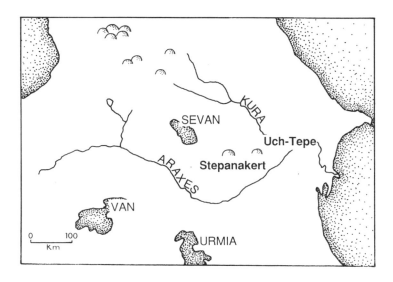

128 Kurgans in Transcaucasia.

The evidence for a Pontic-Caspian intrusion into the Caucasus is based largely on the work of Soviet archaeologists such as Karine Kushnareva, Tariel Chubinishvili and Rauf Munchaev who do not themselves explain these kurgan burials as the product of northern steppe intruders. Rather, they treat the barrows and the deposition of precious metals and wagons as a natural part of the process of social stratification witnessed throughout the Caucasus (the ceramics in the barrow graves are the same found in other forms of Kuro-Araxes burials). The Kuro-Araxes culture, with its relatively advanced metallurgy, distant exchange relations, and mixed farming subsistence basis could be expected to have evolved into a more ranked society which would have promoted the symbolic expressions of power and wealth. The social changes, therefore, can easily be dismissed as locally inspired, rather than intrusive, and there is no reason to deny to the ancestors of the Hurrians the same forms of display and social stratification which we might attribute to the Indo-Europeans. Similarly, exploitation of the steppe, and the creation of wealth-consuming pastoral societies in the Kuro-Araxes region, need not be specifically Indo-European, as numerous non-Indo-European populations throughout the Near East also evolved pastoral economies. We might also wonder about the antiquity of the Caucasian kurgans since the radiocarbon dates for Uch-Tepe are roughly contemporary with the earliest-dated kurgans on the Pontic-Caspian which are minute in comparison to this Caucasian tomb.

The evidence for Pontic intrusions through the Caucasus is neither abundant nor easy to evaluate. We may emphasize, however, that where the evidence for barrows is found, it is precisely in regions which later demonstrate the presence of non-Indo-European populations; hence the model of Pontic intrusions through the Caucasus at this time may be largely irrelevant to the question of Indo-European expansions.

Southeastern Europe and western Anatolia

By 6000 BC, farming communities were progressively expanding through northern Greece into the Balkans. From their first appearance, until about 4000 BC, they appeared to have enjoyed two millennia of uninterrupted development. This is seen in the expansion of population; the increasing density and size of settlements; the development of stone and early copper metallurgy; the refinement of subsistence strategies based on mixed farming; incipient craft specialization; elaborate ritual paraphernalia; and, probably, the evolution towards more complex social organization. Archaeologists witness this progressive development both in the correct ordering of the thousands of individual archaeological sites or, more conveniently, in a number of tells where the settlement debris of 2,000 years of continuous settlement has accumulated into massive mounds. The final phase of this development may be seen in the tells of south Bulgaria of the Karanovo VI period, the Gumelnitsa culture to its north, the late Vinča and contemporary cultures of the central and west Balkans and the Cucuteni-Tripolye culture on the western fringe of the Pontic region. It is during this final period of indigenous development, 4500–4000 BC, that archaeologists observe the earliest traces of direct contacts with the peoples of the Pontic-Caspian. In the subsequent millennia the evidence for contacts swells dramatically enough to convince archaeologists such as Vladimir Dumitrescu, Milutin Garašanin, Frano Prendi, Henrietta Todorova, and many others, that there was a sizeable influx of people from the Pontic region who laid the foundations for the Indo-European languages throughout Southeastern Europe. Some, such as Marija Gimbutas, would even credit them with the apparent collapse of two millennia of local development, and the total reorganization of the region under the aegis of Indo-European intruders. The evidence for this expansion of Pontic peoples is variable in quantity, complexity and credibility.

The earliest evidence for steppe peoples in Southeastern Europe is seen in the appearance of a series of interrelated objects and ritual behaviour that are without precedent in this area but which find close analogues in the Dnieper region during the Sredny Stog and Novodanilovka periods. The material evidence includes stone 'sceptres' fashioned in the shape of horse heads, typically encountered in the Pontic-Caspian but which are now also found in Southeastern Europe. Their total number exceeds thirty, and they may be divided into three types, largely on the degree to which they realize the actual features of the horse. The most realistic are mainly confined to the west of the Dnieper, with the exception of a sceptre from Terekli Mekteb in Dagestan. They are also found on Tripolye sites such as Fedeleşeni in Romania, and east Balkan sites such as Salcuţa and Casimcea in Romania, Rzhevo and Suvorovo in Bulgaria and Suvodol in southern Yugoslavia. It is widely accepted that these are objects ultimately of steppe inspiration, where the horse played an integral role in both economy and ritual and where a tradition of manufacturing stone-carved animal figures extends back well into the Neolithic. The context of the Suvorovo find is especially interesting since it accompanied a male burial in a

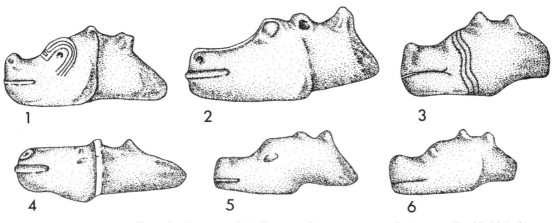

129   Horse-head sceptres of the Casimcea-Suvorovo type: 1 Casimcea, 2 Terekli-Mekteb, 3 Salcuta, 4 Suvorovo, 5 Fedeleseni, 6 Rzhevo. (The Suvorovo sceptre measures c. 17 cm long).

130   Some major Balkan sites showing early evidence for intrusions from the steppe. Sites with horse-head sceptres and burials with steppe features are indicated by dots; major settlements are indicated with triangles.

double grave. The male was provided with a sceptre, a pestle for grinding ochre, and long flint knives generically similar to those encountered in Novodanilovka burials. The accompanying burial, presumed to be female, wore a necklace of shell beads, again similar to those found in steppe burials and contrasting with the typical limestone beads of the native Eneolithic culture.

Even more than burial goods, the appearance of a specifically steppe burial ritual in Southeastern Europe is generally regarded as the most solid evidence for the presence of steppe intruders. The cemetery at Decea Muresului in central Romania offers nearly twenty graves displaying links with the steppe. These included long flint knives, Unio shell beads and stone maceheads similar to those recovered in the Novodanilovka group. The burial rite included the use of ochre and, more importantly, the positioning of the dead in the supine position with legs flexed, the classic Pontic-Caspian ritual which is unparalleled in the local cultures of Southeast Europe. The westernmost example of this particular form of burial was found in a single grave at Csongrád-Kettöshalom in eastern Hungary where a male was buried in the 'steppe position' and accompanied by a long obsidian blade, small copper beads together with limestone and shell beads, and a fragment of ochre. This complex of burials and stone sceptres is generally synchronized with steppe cultures dating to the centuries around 4000 BC. Even before this period, there is some ceramic evidence for contacts between the steppe tribes and the more settled agriculturalists immediately to their west.

Before 4000 BC, Tripolye sites begin to exhibit a ceramic that is widely known in archaeological literature as Cucuteni C ware. It is distinguished from the classic wares of the Balkans and northwest Pontic by the presence of crushed shell in the temper and by cord decoration, two features which typify the ceramics of the Pontic-Caspian steppe tribes. Such ware varies in quantity on

Cucuteni-Tripolye settlements but may easily account for 10 per cent of all ceramic remains on some sites. The presence of either steppe pottery or, more usually, pottery fashioned according to techniques regularly employed on the steppe, is generally interpreted as evidence for direct contacts between steppe pastoralists and their more settled Cucuteni-Tripolye neighbours. Such ceramic contacts are hardly unexpected, as we have already seen how Pontic-Caspian sites have been dated by the occasional presence of Tripolye wares in steppe burials.

Interpretations of this initial phase of Balkan-Pontic contacts vary, but even the minimal view admits that there is something more than distant trading relations involved. While some may be tempted to dismiss the evidence of stone sceptres as a widely distributed status item circulating among various local elites, an interpretation similar to that employed by some for the Bell Beakers – the sudden appearance of an alien burial rite in Southeast Europe which is also markedly similar to that of the steppe – does suggest an intrusive population. But, though intrusive, some East European archaeologists have not regarded it as evidence for a substantial invasion. Instead, Istvan Ecsedy and others argue that what we are witnessing is a limited Pontic presence in Southeastern Europe which was conservative enough to retain certain behavioural features carried from the steppe but which was also active enough to acquire luxury goods such as copper and obsidian in its new home.

The interrelationship between the settled agriculturalists of the northwest Pontic and the more mobile pastoralists of the steppe was not entirely symmetrical. Tripolye imports on steppe sites tend to be represented by well-made pottery often found within burials, clay figurines (again in burials) and copper objects. In a recent survey of such finds, Vladimir Zbenovich cites thirteen examples of Tripolye imports on steppe sites, frequently burials, between the Bug and Dnieper rivers. These imports, both by their nature and context, suggest prestige items acquired by the steppe pastoralists from their technologically more advanced neighbours. On the other hand, the various quantities of shell-tempered and cord-decorated wares that are found in increasing amounts on later Tripolye sites can hardly be interpreted as the result of an exchange between community leaders. Rather, like the occasional presence of antler cheekpieces on Tripolye sites, the steppe influences on their agricultural neighbours may be the result of direct contacts, possibly involving seasonal visits by Pontic-Caspian pastoralists to Tripolye settlements. This is also the pattern of behaviour attributed to Yamnaya herdsmen who may have gathered seasonally at major settlements such as Mikhaylovka. The relationship between the pastoralists and the settled farming communities may not have been purely symbiotic, since we find an increasing tendency towards larger, fortified settlements in the later Tripolye period. Maidanetskoe, for example, is an enormous Tripolye settlement with over 1,000 structures surrounded by several ditches. In human terms, then, the inhabitants of the large and usually fortified sites of the later Tripolye culture may have been forced to accustom themselves to the periodic visits, friendly or otherwise, of

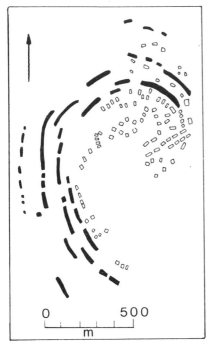

131   *Maidanetskoe is one of the largest late Tripolye villages. The surrounding fortifications are sometimes attributed to defensive measures against steppe pastoralists.*

132–134   *Objects from the Usatovo culture. (Top) painted ware of the Tripolye tradition; (right) dagger of arsenical bronze; (above) cord-decorated coarse ware.*

their steppe neighbours. Ethnographic evidence suggests a very fluid boundary between mobile and settled communities, and it is entirely probable that some pastoralists may have settled permanently whilst Tripolycans may have become integrated into the more mobile steppe communities. The resultant archaeological evidence certainly suggests the creation of hybrid communities.

By the middle of the fourth millennium BC we witness the transformation of Late Tripolye groups into new cultural entities. Probably the most noted is the Usatovo culture which occupied the territory from the lower Dniester to the mouth of the Danube. The available radiocarbon dates suggest that it flourished about 3500 to 3000 BC. In some aspects the culture retains traditional Tripolyean styles of painted wares and figurines and, at least for the Late Tripolye period, flat cemeteries. But, in addition, there also appears a ceramic technology that is fundamentally characterized by shell-tempered wares and cord ornament, a lithic industry shaped by steppe influences, and the use of large kurgans for burials. Metal objects are relatively abundant and include arsenical bronzes. Among objects found were a considerable series of daggers, along with axes, awls and rings, including rings made from silver which is a metal we would attribute to the Proto-Indo-Europeans. Economically, the subsistence basis differs from the typical Tripolyean cattle- and pig-based economy to one where ovicaprids are dominant and horse varies to between 10 and 15 per cent of the faunal remains.

The creation of such a hybrid culture is not easy to explain, and Soviet archaeologists themselves maintain no pretence of consensus. Some would see the presence of kurgan burials, which were sometimes more richly furnished than the more traditional flat cemeteries, as evidence that steppe overlords had superimposed themselves on the local Tripolye population. This is probably far too simplistic an explanation, especially since Tripolye communities do not even appear to have occupied this territory prior to the emergence of the Usatovo culture. Instead, we must also take into account 1,000 years of population growth to the north of the Usatovo culture on the middle Dniester and southern Bug, and subsequent expansion southwards where the traditional Tripolye economy was far less suited. Movement into this area, some argue, brought the Tripolyean element into contact with steppe pastoralists and possibly with communities from the Caucasus, all of whom participated in the creation of the Usatovo culture.

The apparent hybridization between steppe elements and formerly settled agricultural communities of Balkan origin is seen further to the west in the Cernavoda I culture of eastern Romania. Here, also, a coarse ware – similar to the Cucuteni C ware of Late Tripolye – appears, with its shell temper and cord decoration, together with the sporadic appearance of horse. This region, immediately south of the Cucuteni-Tripolye territory, was previously occupied by the Gumelnitsa (Karanovo VI) culture. During the fourth millennium, archaeologists perceive a structural reorganization of society across much of Southeastern Europe. Evidence for this comes from the abandonment of the tell sites which had flourished for several millennia; the displacement of previous cultures in almost every direction except eastwards; movement to marginal locations, such as islands and caves, or easily fortified hilltop sites such as Cernavoda I; and a general reduction in the major Eneolithic technologies of both fine ceramic manufacture and copper metallurgy. This abandonment and movement, often propelling neighbouring cultures into one another, operated against a background not only of somewhat elusive traces of hybridization with the steppe cultures such as the Usatovo and Cernavoda I, but also with continuous incursions of mobile pastoralists.

The cultural chaos of this period has produced something of a Balkan 'dark age'. The tell sites, for example, number in the order of 600 to 700. Their continuous development comes to a halt when they are abandoned about 4200 BC, and so far we only have evidence of several dozen being reoccupied during the subsequent Early Bronze Age, somewhere between 500 and 1,000 years later. Out of this period there later emerges a new cultural horizon that integrates cultures across Eastern Europe, including the northwest Pontic, and western Anatolia. Perhaps the most dramatic example of this new horizon is the settlement of Ezero in south Bulgaria. Here the accumulation of Neolithic and Eneolithic debris halts during the Karanovo VI period and then, after abandonment, we find the Early Bronze Age Ezero culture (Karanovo VII) beginning in the centuries around 3200 BC. On the ruins of the previous Eneolithic village was erected a settlement about 60 to 80 metres in diameter,

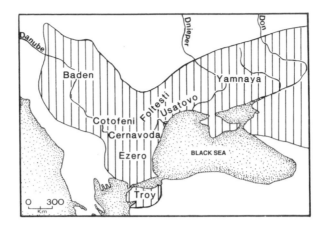

135 The circum-Pontic interaction sphere.

surrounded by stone walls. In subsequent periods the Ezero walls were extended, and throughout the Early Bronze Age Ezero took on the appearance of a citadel, providing a defensive focus to small unfortified settlements in the vicinity. The Ezero culture shares numerous similarities in fine ceramics, plastic art and metallurgy with other emergent Early Bronze Age cultures throughout Southeast Europe, particularly with the Baden culture of the Danubian region and the Coțofeni culture of Romania. This new Balkan-Danubian complex of related cultures was not confined to Southeast Europe but now extended across into northwest Anatolia and the Troy culture. It is important to emphasize that at Ezero, the excavators Nikolai Merpert and Georgy Georgiev discovered a sequence of ceramics clearly ancestral to, and then contemporary with, those found in the Troy culture. The evidence may still be regarded as tenuous, but a growing number of archaeologists now admit the temporal and cultural priority of Southeast Europe to the Early Bronze Age of northwest Anatolia. Once this is accepted, there is no great step to entertaining seriously the proposition that an influx of people from the Balkans carried both the material culture and possibly Indo-European languages into northwest Anatolia in the centuries around 3000 BC.

This consolidation in Southeast Europe was played out against a continuous background of further intrusions from the steppe. What was sporadically attested prior to 3000 BC swelled during the third millennium to provide unequivocal evidence for a movement of populations from the Pontic-Caspian steppe into the Balkans. If we take the lower southwest corner of the Soviet Union, the area between the Danube and the Dniester rivers, as our trip line, we find abundant evidence for the staging area of these highly mobile populations. In a recent study of the Eneolithic and Early Bronze Age kurgans of the region, Yevgeny Yarovoy lists over 1,000 excavated burials from some 118 sites in this region alone. Ukrainian archaeologists such as Ivan Chernyakov, Nikolai Shmagliy and Gennady Toshchev have examined the material classifying it into four periods: the pre-Usatovo burials which we have already referred to as evidence for the initial Pontic-Caspian contacts with Southeast Europe; the Usatovo kurgans; and the kurgan burials dating to the early and later Yamnaya

136 *The distribution of excavated kurgans (dots) in the lower Danube.*

137 *Kurgan burial at Ketegyhaza (head oriented to the west).*

periods. The bulk of the remains date to this later period which takes us though the third millennium BC.

The evidence for a westward movement of Pontic-Caspian peoples is not limited to the Danube; kurgan burials now appear in Romania, Bulgaria, Yugoslavia and as far west as the Tisza river in Hungary. These burials mirror the mortuary rite of the Pontic-Caspian with the supine flexed position, use of ochre, employment of wooden mortuary structures or mats of reed or grass, and even the physical anthropology of the deceased speaks for an intrusive population. Studies on kurgan burials in Romania, for example, have revealed that the more robust-appearing kurgan males averaged up to 10 centimetres taller than the native Eneolithic population. Grave goods such as silver earrings, copper beads, and the knucklebones of sheep (for children), all similar to items found in steppe burials, are known from these Balkan and Hungarian tombs. We can gain a hint of the magnitude of these migrations when we note that Istvan Ecsedy reports over 3,000 kurgans in Hungary alone, although only about forty-five have seen excavation.

A new cultural framework for Southeast Europe, erected against a backdrop of continuous population movements from the steppe, underwrites the historical connection between the Pontic-Caspian and Southeast Europe and Anatolia. It should be emphasized that, in many of the later Yamnaya burials, the ceramics recovered owe more to the cultures of the new configuration than to the steppe. These, and other features such as the stone-constructed citadels of Mikhaylovka, Ezero and Troy, have directed Nikolai Merpert's attention to a circum Pontic sphere of mutual interrelationships in architecture, ceramics and metallurgy in the Early Bronze Age.

The model for the prehistory of the fourth and third millennia derived from archaeology can accommodate the expectations of the historical linguists. One might imagine, for example, that the Anatolian languages were introduced into northwest Anatolia by the end of the fourth millennium BC, in association with the movement ascribed to the Balkan-Danubian complex. This would separate them earlier from their other Indo-European cousins. The innovating core which links Greeks, Armenians, Iranians and Indo-Aryans would have been the result of later linguistic developments during the third millennium, a period when highly mobile Yamnaya groups were moving into the Balkans but were still very much part of the chain of mutually related Pontic-Caspian—west Siberian steppe tribes. Alternatively, some might prefer to place the Greeks in western Anatolia by the third millennium BC, from whence they subsequently entered Greece. Either way, this puts Indo-European peoples in the Balkans, the putative staging area for each of the models of Greek migrations discussed in Chapter Three, as well as the appropriate area for the later development of either local (Thracian) or transported (Phrygian, Armenian) populations. This seems a plausible account for what might have happened but, again matters are never so simple.

Any interpretation of the archaeological puzzle of Southeast Europe during this transition period from 4000 to 3000 BC is likely to suffer from a lack of well-documented evidence. At the same time, one cannot ignore that a substantial number of leading East European archaeologists acknowledge an expansion from the Pontic-Caspian to be a major factor in effecting this transformation of society and, in general, that they identify these intruders as the earliest Indo-Europeans. It is difficult to deny that there is evidence for intrusions unless one's preoccupation with explaining all cultural change purely through local cultural processess precludes this concept. What remains for us here is to inquire whether this appeal to intrusion actually explains the presence of Indo-European languages in Southeast Europe and Anatolia.

In numerous works, Marija Gimbutas has argued that intrusions occurred in three waves. Southeast Europe is envisaged as initially having an essentially settled, agricultural, matrilineal, peaceful population, with an extremely rich artistic and religious vocabulary expressed through ceramics and figurines. This society was either destroyed or subjugated by essentially pastoral, warlike, patrilineal Kurgan tribes from the Pontic-Caspian steppe. Such a brusquely simplified presentation of this invasion hypothesis naturally rests most uncomfortably with many archaeologists, and one must surely question an explanation that focuses so intensely on elements such as the martial proclivities of the steppe intruders. Other factors were surely at play.

After two millennia of agricultural settlement one might expect there to have been a substantial growth in population in Southeastern Europe. Studies which have been made of settlement density appear to indicate that the distance between settlements, at least in some territories, was clearly diminishing as population increased. In Romania, for example, we find Early Neolithic Linear Ware sites spaced at intervals averaging 23 to 24 kilometres, while later Pre-Cucuteni sites are only 6 to 7 kilometres apart, and during the Cucuteni period itself they are only 3 to 4 kilometres apart. Defensive architecture such as palisades, ditches and earthen banks appear by the fifth millennium BC, for example, at Polyanitsa in Bulgaria, and precede any evidence for steppe intrusion, no matter how generously interpreted. Indeed, the expansion of the Tripolye culture into such arid areas as the northwest fringe of the Black Sea might be explained as the result of population pressure. Quite probably there were internal forces within society itself that were setting it on a new course.

External factors may also be taken into consideration. There is at least some evidence for increasing aridity during the Eneolithic which might have stimulated more interest in pastoralism. Many of the putatively late features of the Eneolithic economy, such as the plough, wheeled vehicles, domestic horse, yoke, dairy products, and woollen textiles, emerge in Southeastern Europe about the fourth millennium. As Andrew Sherratt has suggested, many of these features – such as plough agriculture and increased stockbreeding – would tend to enhance the male role in the productive economy. This, in turn, would effect a series of social changes which would influence inheritance systems and might promote patrilineality, clan associations, warfare, and a diminution in the status of the female in society, craft production and, possibly, religious ritual such as that so often expressed in Southeast European figurines. All of this might suggest that local processes may, in fact, have stimulated the creation of a society that matches our expectation of the Indo-Europeans. Nevertheless, when the steppe cultures both reflect the Proto-Indo-European vocabulary for these economic, technological and social changes, and offer substantial evidence for the introduction of the domestic horse, larger woolly sheep as well as, possibly, wheeled vehicles into the Balkans, we can hardly dismiss their presence as merely coincidental.

Here we should briefly consider Colin Renfrew's attempt to reverse the thrust of these arguments by suggesting that steppe pastoralism was ultimately derived from the Balkan cultures. Renfrew rejects a steppe homeland for the Indo-Europeans on three grounds: that it is founded on an uncritical reliance on linguistic palaeontology (which produces results incompatible with his own solution?); that it involves a 'migrationist' model (heretical to the 'immobilist' dogma?); and that it does not attend to the processes which led to pastoralism.

These processes indicate that steppe pastoralism must have developed from a mixed farming economy, and hence the Kurgan pastoralists must have been a secondary development from primary farming communities. According to Renfrew, these farming communities were the Tripolye culture. To the best of my knowledge, the suggestion that steppe pastoralism was preceded by more stable farming economies has not been disputed by anyone; that these communities should have been the Tripolye culture, however, is totally contradicted by all of the archaeological evidence so far reviewed. Neolithic farming populations spanned the entire region from the Dnieper to the Ural before the Tripolye culture had ever expanded towards the steppe, and it was east of the Dnieper that we see societies acquiring the necessary prerequisites to master the steppe. When some of the regional variants of the Tripolye culture did begin to advance into the steppe, about 3500 BC, they were the *last*, not the first to do so.

If we accept the arguments for some form of expansion from the steppe into Southeastern Europe as sufficient evidence for a Pontic-Caspian homeland, then we must envision the resulting society of the late fourth millennium BC as a hybrid production of native Balkan populations and intrusive Indo-Europeans. We can only hypothesize that the changes, both internally and externally induced, may have been sufficient to so disturb native development that less-numerous intrusive populations, with a more mobile economy, found themselves socially more competent to sustain their languages and achieve the gradual linguistic assimilation of the indigenous population. Towards the end of this chapter we will discuss the processes that may have assisted the expansion of the Indo-European languages.

The evidence suggests that a Pontic-Caspian origin for the Indo-Europeans of Southeast Europe and western Anatolia can at least be seriously entertained. Here we are hardly talking of proof but rather of a working hypothesis whose own integrity is supported by the substantial evidence for actual intrusions from the steppe seen in the spread of kurgan burials, the simultaneity of appearance of a series of economic traits that are all lexically attested in Proto-Indo-European, and the widely accepted interpretation of a structural reordering of Southeast European society coincidental with the appearance of these steppe intruders. Appeals to authority, naturally, only help underwrite the seriousness with which the hypothesis should be considered, not its validity.

Central and Northern Europe

Probably the most controversial, and certainly the most discussed, region of Indo-European expansion is the territory of Northern and Central Europe, from whence we commonly derive the linguistic ancestors of the Celts, Germans, Balts, Slavs and possibly others. During the Eneolithic there emerge within this region two cultures which exhibit striking cultural similarities over extremely broad areas. The slightly earlier and territorially more confined Globular Amphora culture appears in the centuries around 3500 BC, and is encountered from central Germany to northern Moldavia. Beginning slightly later is the Corded Ware horizon, with its over twenty regional variants. These stretch from the Netherlands on the west to the upper Volga and middle Dnieper on the east, and are found as far north as Scandinavia and as far south as Switzerland.

The Corded Ware culture has always occupied a position of special prominence within the remit of Indo-European origins. Although the evidence for Corded Ware settlements is still quite sparse, it has provided a large body of mortuary data as attractive to archaeologists on the trail of the Indo-Europeans as that recovered from the Pontic-Caspian. Corded Ware burials occur both in flat-grave cemeteries and under tumuli. The dead were buried singly or, more rarely, in pairs or larger groups, generally in the flexed position on their sides or backs. The orientation and burial posture were normally determined by sex: males were often buried on their right side, their heads to the west and faces to the south; females were buried on their left side and as their heads were oriented to the east they too faced south. In this light, the sexual dimorphism in Corded Ware burials exhibits what many would assume to be an overt expression of Indo-European ideology (we have already seen the same distinction at Nalchik, Tulkhar and in the Tazabagyab culture). Some would also regard as significant that the dead of both sexes faced south, the direction which the Indo-Europeans held to be auspicious as the related words for right, skilful and south indicate. It should be emphasized that the mechanics of expressing the opposition of the sexes need not have been executed in a uniform fashion among all of those embracing the same ideology. Hence, in some variants of the Corded Ware horizon males are found on their left side while females are buried on their right. This need not signal, as has been suggested, the retention of earlier 'matriarchal' ideologies, but is far more easily explained as a variation in the technique of expressing the same ideology, that is, males are buried right side up rather than right side down.

Sexual dimorphism is also exhibited in the nature of some of the grave goods. While cord-decorated amphorae may be found in both male and female graves, the cord-decorated beakers tend to correlate with males in a number of

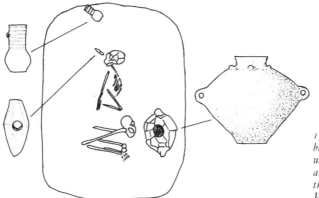

138   Typical Corded Ware burial of a male accompanied with an axe, beaker and amphora. The burial is from the Corded Ware cemetery of Vikletice in Czechoslovakia.

cemeteries. Both of these are ceramic type fossils of the culture that provide it with its most common name (*Schnurkeramik* 'corded ware'). In addition, another major trait of the burials is the frequent inclusion of a stone-perforated battle-axe with male burials which has provided some of its variants with the alternative name of Battle-axe culture (*Streitaxtkultur*). Other grave goods include pottery, arrowheads, bone needles, boar-tooth pendants for males, canine-tooth ornaments for females, and copper ornaments.

A number of factors account for the prominence of the Corded Ware culture in our discussion. The paucity of settlement sites traditionally predisposed archaeologists to view the Corded Ware culture as predominantly that of a mobile, pastoral people. This was reinforced by the presence of tumulus burials, a major characteristic of other pastoral peoples, most notably in the Pontic-Caspian. The extremely wide territory of Corded Ware occupation is suggestive of an expansion across much of Europe which was far more easily explained by tying it to mobile pastoralists rather than to settled agriculturalists. The presence of weapons in the burials, and the clear sexual dimorphism, reinforced the image of an essentially warlike, pastoral people. When this was coupled with evidence in the Corded Ware culture for domestic horse and wheeled vehicles, there was no problem in completing the image of a people which superimposed both their culture and language over a vast territory. Both the archaeological evidence, and expectation, encourage us to regard the Corded Ware culture as a classic expression of prehistoric Indo-Europeans, much as the Eneolithic cultures of the Pontic-Caspian have done.

The preponderance of what many have considered to be obvious Indo-European traits assisted the Corded Ware culture in being identified as not merely an Indo-European culture but as the homeland culture of the Proto-Indo-Europeans, especially among some German archaeologists of the early twentieth century. But, despite strenuous attempts, no one has ever been able to generate a serious case for relating the Corded Ware culture to the Indo-Europeans of the Balkans, Greece or Anatolia, much less to those of Asia. It is also generally admitted that the Eneolithic cultures of the Pontic-Caspian cannot be in any way directly derived from the Corded Ware culture or its predecessors. It is enough to remember that the Corded Ware culture is essentially a third millennium phenomenon and clearly post-dates the earliest appearance of Pontic-Caspian Eneolithic cultures. It is for these reasons that any attempt to assign an Indo-European identity to the Corded Ware peoples must be confined to a state of linguistic development that is ancestral to a number of specific Indo-European linguistic groups, but not to all of the Indo-European languages. It is also obvious, then, that establishing the correct relationship between the Corded Ware and Pontic-Caspian regions is essential to the entire problem of determining the earlier territorial boundaries of the Proto-Indo-Europeans.

We begin our review of Corded Ware–Pontic relationships with the evidence for chronology. There is an extensive series of radiocarbon dates for the Corded Ware horizon which are distributed quite unequally over their various regional variants. They indicate a span for the horizon from about 3200 to 2300 BC, with most dates falling in the third millennium BC. We have already seen that the seventy, or so, dates from the Yamnaya culture fall within the same very broad range, although they begin somewhat earlier (about 3600 BC), which is further emphasized by the fact that no typologically early Yamnaya burials have been dated. Although the Yamnaya culture may have begun earlier than the Corded Ware, there is no real case for an expansion of Yamnaya invaders across the North European plain, producing the Corded Ware horizon. Intrusive steppe burials as we previously encountered in Southeast Europe are generally absent from the Corded Ware region, and on what little anthropological data we possess, there is no reason whatsoever to associate the Corded Ware populations, themselves quite heterogeneous, with the physical type which we encounter on the Pontic-Caspian steppe. All of this indicates that any attempt to relate the two territories takes a different form from that which we employed in the Balkans.

Generic similarities offer the principal grounds for relating Corded Ware with the steppe. Tumuli, single burial, the supine flexed position in some instances, the use of especially constructed chambers, inclusion of cord-ornamented pottery, tooth pendants, weapons and animal remains, are all part of the burial rite of both regions. In a recent comparison of the burial practices of the two cultures, Lothar Kilian isolated twenty-three diagnostic features. He argued that the Corded Ware burials possessed a series of traits not found in the Pontic-Caspian – amphorae, cord-decorated beakers, battle-axes – which are the essential markers of the Corded Ware culture. In contrast, the steppe burials utilized egg-shaped pottery, hammer-head pins, ochre and a variety of

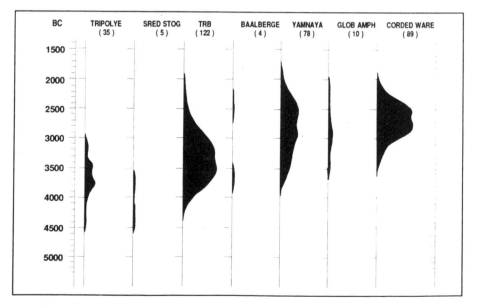

139 *Chronology of Corded Ware and the steppe cultures (number of dates in each sample indicated in parentheses).*

burial postures unknown in the Corded Ware horizon. While there may be some generic similarities, Kilian concluded that the specific differences do not support an historical connection between the two regions. For many years Alexander Häusler, an authority on the mortuary practice of both the Pontic-Caspian and the Corded Ware regions, has perennially campaigned against any possible association between them. He especially emphasizes that the ritual core of the Corded Ware burials involved depositing the deceased in the flexed position on his or her side, depending on sex. This signalling of the sexual dichotomy through burial posture is absent from the steppe region and, he argues, denies it any role in the formation of the Corded Ware horizon. He further emphasizes that the Corded Ware burial rite can be derived from local Central and North European cultures without recourse to steppe intrusions.

Objection to a Pontic origin for the Corded Ware horizon is not limited to the evidence for burials but extends throughout the range of arguments. Evzen Neustupný, for example, dismisses the entire concept of pastoral Corded Ware tribes as being incompatible with both the environment of Northern Europe and the archaeological evidence for agriculture in the Corded Ware culture. This, he argues, suggests a local evolution of the Corded Ware horizon from its earlier Neolithic and Eneolithic populations.

It should be emphasized that there is no widely accepted solution to the problem of Corded Ware origins. Ivan Artemenko recognizes the existence of at least four major camps: those who support a western origin between the Rhine and Vistula (such as Ulrich Fischer, Alexander Häusler and Karl Jazdzewski); a Vistula-Dnieper origin (Dmitry Kraynov, Raisa Denisova and Miroslav Buchvaldek); an origin in the forest-steppe zone of the Middle Dnieper region

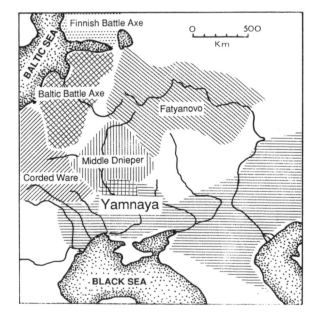

140 Corded Ware groups in Eastern Europe.

(Ivan Artemenko, I. K. Sveshnikov, V. P. Tretyakov, Sofia Berezanskaya, N. Bondar, and others); and a steppe origin (Gustav Rosenberg, P. V. Glob, Karl Struve, Marija Gimbutas, Aleksandr Bryusov and Valentin Danilenko). Anticipating the serious implications of granting to the Corded Ware culture an essentially local origin, we are impelled to survey all the possibilities that might indicate an historical link with the steppe.

We turn first to the Middle Dnieper culture, one of the local variants of the Corded Ware horizon, since it occupies the frontier between the Pontic and the rest of the Corded Ware horizon. The contact zone falls on the Middle Dnieper itself. Ivan Artemenko divides the Middle Dnieper culture, known from more than 200 sites, into three phases, the earliest of which is found in a number of graves located southwest of Kiev. As a rule, these burials were inserted into the kurgans of the local variant of the Yamnaya culture that had extended into the forest-steppe. They were accompanied by cord-ornamented pottery and perforated battle-axes. Artemenko has suggested that the origin of these burials is to be sought in the Sredny Stog, Yamnaya and Late Tripolye cultures. This phase is then followed by a middle period where the classic Corded Ware amphorae and beakers appear. Artemenko, and others, see in the Middle Dnieper culture the roots of some of the other local variants of the Corded Ware horizon in easternmost Europe, but no one seriously entertains the hypothesis that the Middle Dnieper culture is the earliest expression of the Corded Ware horizon, the one from which it later expanded westwards.

While the Corded Ware variant most proximate to the steppe cannot be seen as the point of origin for the Corded Ware culture, many archaeologists still envisage a major influential role here from the steppe cultures. One of the foremost authorities on the Corded Ware horizon, Miroslav Buchvaldek, has, on several recent occasions, addressed the problem of Corded Ware origins. He emphasizes the methodological problems of demonstrating whether the Corded Ware horizon was the product of an invasion or local development. According to both models, the number of sites belonging to either the intrusive culture or to the transitional phase between a former Neolithic culture and the subsequent Corded Ware horizon would be extremely small, a generation's worth of sites perhaps constituting no more than 5 per cent of the potential archaeological remains. The odds of discovering enough intrusive or transitional sites to establish a convincing pattern would consequently be extremely small.

Buchvaldek concentrates on the origins of the 'A' or 'common European' horizon of Corded Ware finds which embrace a series of axes, beakers and amphorae displaying remarkable similarities and which may be found from the Netherlands to the Ukraine. Those who support an indigenous development for this horizon make recourse to 'influences' spreading across Europe; Buchvaldek regards these as insufficient to explain the uniformity of the cultural phenomenon against the great variety of Europe's background cultures. The problem with an invasion, however, is also admitted – it requires a source, and there simply is not one that is particularly convincing. However,

Buchvaldek does note the similarities between the Yamnaya and Corded Ware cultures, such as tumulus, flexed supine burials, corded ornament, heavily pastoral component, absence of settlements, and several other items of grave accompaniment. He thus considers that the Corded Ware culture shows stronger ties with the Yamnaya culture than it exhibits with any other culture, though he admits that there are also striking differences between these two cultures. Also, parallels exist between the Corded Ware and the Tripolye, TRB, and Globular Amphora cultures. Buchvaldek opts for a migration or infiltration of small human groups from some region where all of these cultural influences or components may have come together. The actual location is uncertain and Buchvaldek expressly admits that it is on the basis of both 'intuition and hope' that he believes a home for the 'A' horizon may be found in the poorly known region between the Vistula and the Dnieper.

As the most superficial glance at a map will indicate, the Corded Ware horizon occupies essentially the same general territory as the preceding TRB culture. Where it exceeds the borders of the TRB, such as the Fatyanovo culture of the upper Volga, or the Baltic Haff culture, this is clearly a later intrusion outside the core area. For this reason, it is impossible to consider Corded Ware origins without taking into account the preceding TRB culture. This was by no means a uniform cultural entity that can easily be summarized with a few general statements. Burials, for example, ranged from simple, earthen flat graves to long barrows and megalithic tombs. Although this range was wide it can be argued that it offered a poor ancestry for the tumulus burials often encountered in the Corded Ware horizon; one variant of the TRB culture, however, proves the exception.

The Baalberge group is at present known from approximately 200 graves distributed in central Germany east to Bohemia. The ceramics accompanying the burials include characteristic TRB forms plus some vessels indicating more

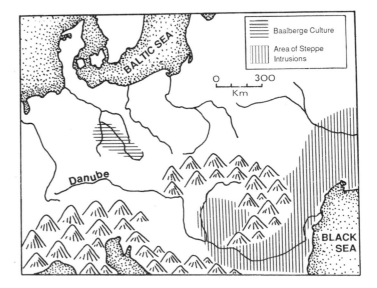

141   Baalberge and the steppe cultures.

easterly influences, such as the Bodrogkeresztur and Baden cultures. What is most important is that the Baalberge group often buried their dead in stone cists over which an earthen tumulus was erected. Those arguing for a local Corded Ware origin could point to the Baalberge group which provides a suitable ancestor for the Corded Ware grave structure plus distant ceramic prototypes for Corded Ware beakers and amphorae. On the other hand, some have argued that the Baalberge group was the result of steppe pastoralists who had proceeded along the Danube into central Germany where they effected the new burial rite. The difficulty in pursuing the latter model is that the nearest positively identified remains of steppe-like kurgans lie to the east of the Tisza river some 500 kilometres short of the territory in which the Baalberge group emerges. Unlike the Siberian steppe, this area is not a *terra incognita* within which we can optimistically hope for the discovery of classic steppe kurgan burials. Also, physical anthropology from the Baalberge graves offers no grounds for associating them with the more easterly Pontic intruders.

Another door we may try concerns the origins of the Globular Amphora culture. In her more recent publications on the expansions of the Pontic-Caspian tribes, Marija Gimbutas has regularly indicated that she believes the Globular Amphora culture to have been a major component in the creation of the Corded Ware horizon, a theory we encountered with Miroslav Buchvaldek.

Like the Corded Ware horizon, the Globular Amphora cultures emerged out of a TRB substrate. However, Gimbutas argues that upon this base was superimposed a ruling stratum from the Pontic region. The evidence, she argues, is to be found in the complete congruency of the burial rites of the two areas – stone cists, cromlechs, stelae, ritual burial of animals including horses, and the practice of suttee, executing the wife and possibly other members of the family on the death of the husband. To this we could add the occasional use of ochre and kurgans in the eastern region of the Globular Amphora culture. She compares the typical vessel of the culture, the globular pot with two to four small handles below the neck, with those from the Lower Mikhaylovka group. The Globular Amphora culture appears to have involved mixed agriculture; remains of cattle, sheep, pig and horse have been found on sites.

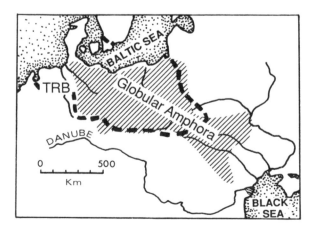

142 Generalized distribution of TRB (dotted line) and Globular Amphora (shaded area) cultures.

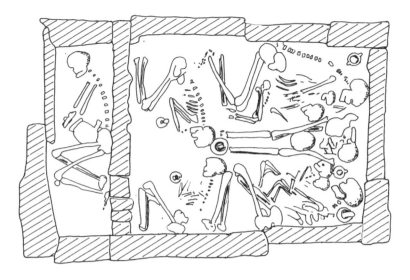

143, 144   Globular Amphora typical of those found in Globular Amphorae burials, such as this one at Voytsekhivka. The main burial is a central male flanked by two women, two children and two adolescents; another individual is buried in a smaller compartment.

Cartographically, there are difficulties in trying to sustain a steppe origin for the Globular Amphora culture, at least one that is confined to the comparisons cited by Gimbutas such as the stone cists and stelae of the Lower Mikhaylovka and more southerly steppe cultures. Again, we are speaking of a distance in the order of 500 kilometres between these two cultures. Moreover, Häusler observes that there are only two stelae in the Globular Amphora culture and that these are from northern Poland, while the ritual burial of animals, also cited by Gimbutas as evidence for steppe influence, was known already from the local TRB culture. Certainly such authorities as the Polish archaeologist Tadeusz Wislanski have generally opted for a Globular Amphora origin in the basins of the middle and lower Oder and Warta. In a recent review of Globular Amphora remains in the Ukraine, I. K. Sveshnikov favours a movement into the Ukraine from the west and does not even entertain the hypothesis of a steppe origin.

In order to attempt yet another link between Northern Europe and the steppe we need to recede still further in time. Alexander Kosko, for example, has recently argued that the steppe tribes, through both pressure and assimilation of their Tripolye neighbours, destroyed the traditional Dniester-Bug frontier that divided the North European cultures from the Pontic-Caspian. This is evidenced by the appearance of the Matwy group of the TRB culture, in the Vistula region, which shares a series of ceramic similarities with the later Tripolye culture. In short, Kosko is arguing for the creation of an interaction sphere that connected the Pontic with Northern Europe during the TRB culture, somewhat along the lines we have suggested between the Pontic and the Balkans-west Anatolia. The evidence for this, however, still seems to be extremely sparse.

Jan Lichardus has suggested that the steppe influences are to be found in the formation of the TRB culture itself. The earlier phase of the TRB culture, the B-phase, is linked to cultural impulses or immigrations from the Danubian region northwards, especially the Rössen culture (others would argue that the

Lengyel culture was the major donor). TRB ceramics, polished stone axes, burials in flexed position in flat graves are all products from the south. The slightly later TRB A horizon, however, he believes to be underivable from both the Danubian region and the local Ertebölle culture of Northern Europe. This horizon sees the introduction of extended burial, occasional use of ochre, knobbed hammer-axes, and several other features which Lichardus believes can only be derived from the east.

Lichardus resurrects an old theory, first suggested by the Danish archaeologist C. J. Becker, that the origin of the TRB culture may lie in the Ukraine. While the earlier theory has long been abandoned, Lichardus suggests that there is now sufficient evidence to revive it, since the Dnieper-Donets and Sredny Stog cultures do provide the most convenient source for what is new in TRB A. Here we find extended burials, use of ochre, similar orientation of burials and prototypes of the TRB A axes, as well as the early use of corded ornament on pottery. Wheeled vehicles are known both on the steppe and in the TRB culture. Of particular interest is the recent identification by Lichardus of a pair of late TRB antler psalia which are similar to those recovered in the Sredny Stog culture and elsewhere on the steppe. Lichardus has undertaken some experimental archaeology and has demonstrated that such devices serve admirably as cheekpieces for controlling horses. The evidence for domestic horse and horse-riding might, then, also link the two regions. The problem of route is resolved, according to Lichardus, by the fact that Dnieper-Donets sites are known to extend as far to the northwest as the Pripet. From there, mobile pastoralists, with horses and wagons, could push west to the Vistula and throughout Northern Europe. As TRB A is one of the major components of the Baalberge culture, we thus obtain a steppe presence throughout Northern and Central Europe that can also be ancestral to the Globular Amphora and Corded Ware horizons.

Opponents to Lichardus's theory assert that his model for an external origin for these TRB traits is unnecessary, unsupported by specific archaeological evidence and inherently unlikely. Brigitte Hulthen, for example, notes that we may derive the TRB ceramics from the previous local Ertebölle culture. Alexander Häusler argues that there was no difference between TRB B and TRB A burial rites, and that the extended position is precisely what one might have expected from a Neolithic culture whose substrate was the hunter–fishers of Northern Europe across which extended burial was the norm. The similarities between the Dnieper-Donets and TRB burials are largely generic to all of the sub-Neolithic populations of Northern Europe, from Scandinavia to the Urals. Furthermore, it is difficult to appeal to the cultural practices of two different cultures – Dnieper-Donets and Sredny Stog – in order to explain the intrusive element in the TRB culture. Sredny Stog sites are in no way proximate to the area in which the TRB culture appears, and the Dnieper-Donets sites along the Pripet have not been shown to provide suitable parallels for the TRB A horizon. Essentially, a number of German reviewers of Lichardus's work wonder whether an appeal to a migration of horse-mounted pastoralists from the steppe is either necessary or even plausible for Northern Europe. Moreover, Soviet archaeologists generally view the presence of the TRB culture in their own territory as an intrusion from the west rather than the reverse. Finally, Dmitry Telegin, the leading authority on both the Dnieper-Donets and Sredny Stog cultures, dismisses the thesis of a TRB origin from the Dnieper-Donets culture.

Lichardus's model is a variant of a broader explanation of the cultural change seen throughout both Northern and Central Europe in the Late Neolithic. Marija Gimbutas does not confine the effects of her 'first wave' of steppe pastoralists to Southeastern Europe. She argues that these intruders not only pushed local Balkan cultures westwards but also that they themselves passed further west along the Danube to stimulate the formation of 'kurganized' Late Neolithic cultures. Among these cultures Gimbutas lists the later Lengyel and Rössen cultures of Central Europe. This process of hybridization is set to the period about 4500 to 4000 BC. The evidence for 'kurganization', at least that published so far, would appear to be a series of very general cultural changes: reliance on stockbreeding rather than on agriculture; preference for defensive locations of sites, small settlements; solar symbolism on pottery; and the appearance of the horse. If we read between the lines, this case seems to suggest that the transformations seen across later Neolithic and Eneolithic communities in Central Europe were in the general direction of increasingly pastoral and aggressive tendencies in society, which could best be explained by the intrusion of pastoralists who took their ultimate origin from the steppe. Hence, defended sites from Cernavoda I in Romania west to the Rössen culture are all linked together as 'kurganized' cultures involving local populations and an intrusive, normally dominant, steppe element. If one were to accept this model, then we would be provided with steppe-based ancestors to the TRB culture as a whole (which, curiously enough, Gimbutas generally regards as the antithesis of the steppe cultures). The level of continuity that one encounters between the Linear Ware culture and the Rössen culture in, for example, settlement types and long houses, appears to be largely ignored, and where the argument concerns a steppe element, it seems mainly confined to very broad categories of cultural change, regularly regarded as the product of local processes rather than of foreign intruders. It is not that the model is wrong; there is just not enough evidence proposed to evaluate it seriously.

If we adopt the broad perspective and consider in general the formation of the large, cultural entities such as the Globular Amphora and Corded Ware horizons, we encounter the perennial problem of how such cultural entities might have come into existence. Invariably there are those who would support autochthonous development, with cultural convergence or 'peer-polity interactions' over a broad area to account for widescale cultural similarities. Others will generally opt for migrations that carry a similar culture over diverse substrates. Few would be so doctrinaire as to adhere only to the stadial development of local groups who just happen to share broad categories of ceramic types, decoration, weapons and burial rites over vast areas. Certainly the intrusive nature of Corded Ware in Upper Lusatia, the Baltic, the upper Volga and possibly Holland all require some external impulse if not actual population movements. On the other hand, even when one excludes these supposedly later peripheral areas, and pares down the size of Corded Ware distribution, it is still impossible to select confidently an area of origin.

We have now examined most proposals that attempt to give the steppe cultures a role in the cultural transformations of Central and Northern Europe. We have seen how they generally, if not universally, fail to present the type of primary evidence for migration that we have seen in the Balkans. On the other hand, much of the criticism levied at the steppe camp has concerned their failure to produce classic Pontic-Caspian burials west or north of the Tisza, and one must wonder whether this is necessary. The distance involved between the steppe and the putatively kurgan-dominated cultures of Central Europe is quite substantial, and the model for steppe intrusions does not require a single event-horizon of pristine horse-riding warriors ravaging the banks of the Danube. Progressive change as one moves from the steppe towards Central Europe is to be expected, and the failure of the Baalberge burials to mirror precisely the steppe kurgans of the Ukraine is not totally devastating to the theory of migrations. Similarly, aspects such as the sexual dichotomy in burial practice, advanced by Alexander Häusler as the 'ritual core' of the Corded Ware culture and hence a primary reason to exclude a steppe ancestry, is in turn dismissed by Nikolai Merpert as trivial compared with the more fundamental similarities between the two traditions.

Nevertheless, the archaeological evidence advanced for the origins of the Corded Ware horizon has, so far, failed to make a thoroughly convincing case for population movements or intrusions, the minimum requirement of our search for the trajectory of the earliest Indo-Europeans. In our evaluation of the archaeological evidence we are tied procedurally to assume local development unless demonstrated otherwise, and the case for intrusion simply is not strong enough. There is no question that a number of notable and quite knowledgeable archaeologists support the concept of some form of genetic relationship between the steppe and the Corded Ware horizon – either by simple intrusion or by some complex process of assimilation and convergence within the forest-steppe zone between the Dnieper and Vistula. They provide us with enough evidence to charge, but not enough to convict.

What, then, are the consequences of rejecting a Pontic presence in Central and Northern Europe during the Eneolithic? Both Lothar Kilian and Alexander Häusler have followed their rejection of Kurgan intrusions to its logical conclusion. If the Pontic-Caspian cultures cannot be derived from Northern and Central Europe, nor the latter from the former, then they must all be included within the Indo-European homeland. Since they admit of no Neolithic or Eneolithic relationship between the two major regions they must assume that it was during the Mesolithic or Palaeolithic that a vast linguistic continuum existed that connected the North Sea with the Volga-Ural. Out of this continuum there later evolved the Indo-European languages. If Proto-

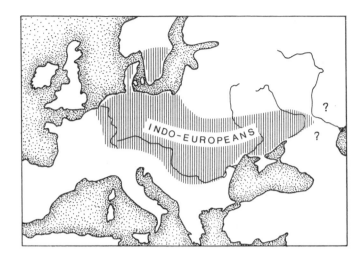

145   The Indo-European homeland according to Lothar Kilian.

Indo-European is defined in the strict sense to the period 4500–2500 BC, then TRB, Globular Amphora, Corded Ware, Sredny Stog, Yamnaya and the other steppe cultures should all be grouped together as Proto-Indo-European. This theory has wide currency though it is normally more implicitly maintained than explicitly developed. Many Soviet archaeologists also assign the Pontic-Caspian solely to the ancestors of the Indo-Iranian languages and assume that the other European languages, especially Baltic and Slavic, developed northwest of the Pontic from local cultures.

The models proposed by Kilian and Häusler seem to require a linguistic continuum some 2,000 to 3,000 kilometres long, during the Mesolithic or Palaeolithic. They postulate no archaeological phenomenon, not even a major lithic techno-complex, which might suggest that there was some form of historical interrelationship across this continuum. Even archaeologists such as Janusz and Stefan Koslowski, who frequently paint in the Palaeolithic and Mesolithic cultures of Europe with an exceedingly broad brush, do not propose some form of cultural entity that embraced this entire region. While it is true that an archaeological entity need not correlate with a linguistic one, how can one snatch at diverse archaeological cultures and merely assume that they all spoke related languages? We shall have to make a go at both evaluating this theory and defending it against our own objections.

First, it seems highly likely that an Indo-European homeland extending from the Rhine to the Dnieper or the Volga has certain problems of plausibility. Separated for thousands if not tens of thousands of years, the various bands of hunter-fishers distributed across this continuum would surely have evolved vastly different languages in terms of phonetics, grammar and vocabulary no matter what their original genetic relationship. Yet the model of such a homeland requires us to believe that they maintained an essentially unchanged phonetic or grammatical system up until about the fourth or third millennium BC, despite the fact that intense mutual interrelationships across this region are specifically denied by those who oppose a later Pontic-Caspian influence in

Northern and Central Europe. We are asked to believe that the ancestors of the Tocharians or Indians on the extreme east of this continuum shared the same vocabulary (including all those items that could not have entered the vocabulary prior to the Neolithic-Eneolithic), phonetic system and grammatical structure with the ancestors of the Germans and Celts who would have been situated somewhere on the western end of this continuum. All of this seems unlikely, and we need to emphasize again that linguists generally regard genetic relationships between languages spoken as long ago as the Mesolithic or Palaeolithic to be irretrievable because of the magnitude of linguistic change over many thousands of years. The result of expanding the Proto-Indo-Europeans across Mesolithic or Palaeolithic Europe sets the clock on linguistic change far earlier than is plausible.

One solution to our problem would be to abbreviate the size of this earlier territory and to seek some demonstrable connection between at least the Vistula and the Pontic-Caspian prior to the period we have argued for Kurgan expansions. Here we can return to Dmitry Telegin's proposal that the Dnieper-Donets culture can be included among a broad group of Vistula-Dnieper sub-Neolithic cultures. These would include the Narva, Valdai and Comb-pricked Ware cultures of Poland. It should be emphasized that Telegin himself does not associate these cultures with the Proto-Indo-Europeans (but rather with the ancestors of the Balts and Slavs), yet an historical association across the Vistula to the Dnieper during the Neolithic would provide an historical bridge between the two regions. With no specific archaeological justification this solution has been grasped, perhaps in desperation, by others who have also floundered on the uncertainty of the origins of the Corded Ware horizon. With cemeteries arguably related to the Dnieper-Donets culture appearing on the middle Volga, such as at Sezzhee, we might then argue for an expansion of this continuum from the Vistula to the Volga by the fifth millennium BC. This requires us to see the Dnieper-Donets culture as the dominant partner in the creation of the Pontic-Caspian steppe communities and its northwestern cousins as the primary substrate in the creation of the Globular Amphora and Corded Ware cultures.

Objections to this solution are several. Most, if not all, archaeologists engaged in the study of the Pontic-Caspian accept the hypothesis that the Dnieper-Donets culture was swallowed up, both in terms of culture and in terms of physical type, by other populations from the steppe. Although Telegin describes the Dnieper-Donets as a physical wedge driven from the north towards the steppe, he also indicates that it was assimilated by the Sredny Stog and Yamnaya cultures. Gimbutas specifically dismisses it as a local substrate assimilated by Indo-Europeans from the Volga-Ural region, a general course of development also accepted by other archaeologists. Moreover, we have the objections of Alexander Formozov who denies particularly close genetic relations with the northwest because Dnieper-Donets sites only expand in this direction in its latest phases. Similarly, V.P. Tretyakov emphasizes the independence of the Upper Dnieper Neolithic culture from the Dnieper-

Donets. Most importantly, the other cultures of Poland and the Baltic are sub-Neolithic and do not reveal the culture reconstructed for the Proto-Indo-Europeans until they have experienced the expansion of the Corded Ware horizon into their territory.

Another route out of this maze is the traditional fall-back position to the Linear Ware culture which does extend from the Rhine to the western Ukraine.[37] Its archaeological descendants – Rössen, *Stichbandkeramik* and Lengyel – occupied Central Europe and have often been credited as the external stimulus to the Neolithic economy of Northern Europe. Moreover, both the Linear Ware and Lengyel cultures penetrated into the northwestern region of the Ukraine along the upper tributaries of the Dniester. If the Linear Ware culture could be seen to have served as an integral component of Tripolye, we might then follow this linguistic vector as far east as the Dnieper. Here, even with good will, this theory begins to collapse, since we must also demonstrate an historical relationship between the Linear Ware and the steppe region where all the archaeological evidence denies any role to western intrusions during the Neolithic. Indeed, the entire trajectory of movement is in the opposite direction. Moreover, many would adhere to the hypothesis that the Linear Ware culture, at least in Central and Eastern Europe, was essentially a projection of Balkan populations into the Danube region which would then tie the Linear Ware culture to the same linguistic objections we have seen for Southeast Europe. It is no easier to derive the steppe cultures from Central Europe than it is to derive the North European cultures from the steppe.

Readers may feel that the author has betrayed them down an endless series of cul de sacs. Nevertheless, this is the current state of research into Indo-European origins and this seemed the best way to convey why the issue is by no means resolved. Ultimately, we have a remarkably unsatisfactory set of choices. We can accept a Pontic-Caspian homeland despite the fact that it still appears to be archaeologically undemonstrated, even under the most liberal canons of proof, in explaining the Indo-Europeans of Northern and Central Europe. Alternatively, we might wish to opt for a broader homeland between the Rhine and Volga during the Palaeolithic or Mesolithic which resolves the archaeological issues by fiat but appears to be linguistically implausible. Perhaps our only recourse is to return to our strict definition of the Proto-Indo-European homeland as where the Indo-European languages were spoken in the period 4500–2500 BC. By the end of this period it is reasonable to assume that they were spoken from the Rhine to beyond the Ural. How they achieved that position is still a problem.

The Process of expansion

As Ernst Pulgram observed thirty years ago, there are three ways by which we might imagine a language to expand: the migration of complete populations; infiltration of an area by small groups; or diffusion. As the last hypothesis has never been encountered, we assume that the borders of Proto-Indo-European or the individual Indo-European languages spread by migration or intrusion. We may suspect that the distinction between migration and intrusion is not particularly fundamental. Logistically, it is easier to move small numbers of people around rather than large numbers, but the traditional tendency to assure one's audience that you intend only small intrusions probably has more to do with the embarrassment one associates with long-ridiculed invasion hypotheses. We are always wary of suggesting models of expansion that will be caricaturized as hordes of frenzied Aryans bursting out of the Russian steppe and slashing their way into the comparative grammars of historical linguists. Similarly, we tend to shy away from making the Indo-Europeans anything but a numerical minority in their relations with the substrates which they eventually assimilated. On a broad scale this is probably correct, yet we have no reason to exclude the development of Indo-European majorities in many local situations that brought about the progressive assimilation of non-Indo-European-speaking neighbours. With these caveats behind us, we can turn to some possible models that might help to explain the incredibly successful expansion of the Indo-European languages.

It is reasonably certain that the process by which the Indo-European languages expanded was not uniform but rather dependent on particular circumstances. An expansion east of the Urals, for example, may have taken Indo-Europeans into steppe regions that were sparsely populated. Possessed with a more productive economy which was especially suited to the exploitation of the open steppe, the numbers of Indo-European speakers would predictably have swelled to become the dominant language(s) across the entire south Siberian steppe to the Yenisey. Local hunter-gathers could have been rapidly assimilated into the social organization of the Pontic-Caspian intruders.

When we turn to the spread of the Indo-European languages into areas where we find previously settled agricultural populations, we must seek other explanations for their expansion. These would include interactions with the proto-urban settlements of Central Asia, the substantial villages of the Tripolye and other Southeast European cultures. Here, within the context of overall regional settlement, it is likely that the natives were numerically superior. To explain how the Indo-European languages were ultimately adopted, we must return to first principles.

When two languages come into contact, people speaking one of them do not immediately abandon their own and adopt the language of the other. A prerequisite to language shift is societal bilingualism. This may remain quite stable over a long period but in the case of Indo-European expansions it was obviously a prelude to the adoption of Indo-European. We assume for the expansion of the Indo-European languages that native populations became bilingual for a time, speaking both their own language and adopting that of the intruder. Normally, social context determines which language is spoken. For example, natives might have spoken their own language at home but Indo-European in the market place or at ceremonial activities. If the intrusive language is employed in more and more different contexts, it will eventually lead to the total replacement, or language death as it is sometimes called, of the native language. In Western Europe we have witnessed Latin move from the vernacular to the language of the church and the learned classes to that of only the church, and now even that role has been greatly diminished. Languages upon the point of extinction are normally carried to the grave by the older members of the community when the younger members have failed to learn it. This process can happen within three generations. An immigrant family in Britain, for example, may speak exclusively Hindi while their children become bilingual. They in turn decide to raise their children exclusively in English. Within three generations grandparent and grandchild can no longer communicate. This process should have occurred across Eurasia wherever we find the expansion of the Indo-European languages.

It is clear, then, that the crux of the issue is bilingualism and how it was induced. Without state coercion, we do not imagine that second languages are forced upon people. Rather, bilingualism is induced when the context of speech requires the use of the new language if one wishes to obtain better access to goods, status, ritual or security. The success of Indo-European expansions should have been due to their ability to offer such advantages to the populations with whom they came into contact. There are several additional factors which may have favoured them in such contact situations.

Whatever side we view the Pontic-Caspian from, be it from the Volga-Ural region or the southwest corner of the Black Sea, we seem to encounter the more mobile economies of pastoralists. It is from these steppe regions that we trace Indo-European intruders into Asia and the Balkans. In both cases they eventually come into contact with stable village communities practising mixed agriculture. There is a considerable body of evidence concerning the nature of interrelationships between pastoralists and agriculturalists, especially in the Near East among both Iranian and Semitic-speaking populations. Pastoral economies display a potential for positive growth in that they are dependent on the natural productivity of the herd. Good years permit the growth of the herd which can be translated into both wealth and status, while bad years, caused by climate or disease, can be disastrous. Either way, the pastoral economy offers considerable opportunity for social mobility which is much more difficult for settled agriculturalists. In his examination of nomad-villager relationships in the Near East, Fredrik Barth observes that, in the long term, it is normally the pastoralists who are at an advantage in terms of exchange relations and capital accumulation, which ultimately leads to their dominance in local systems of stratification. In short, there will be a tactical advantage to mobile Indo-Europeans in their earliest expansions where they would have assumed positions of local dominance. As their mobility was greatly enhanced by the use of the horse, expanding their territorial movements over five times that of their pedestrian neighbours, they would also have had the opportunity to exploit and perhaps dominate larger political territories.

When we return to the archaeological evidence of Southeast Europe we encounter what V. Gordon Childe once termed the 'Late Neolithic Crisis'. He saw this reflected in the collapse of village settlement and the adoption of increasingly more pastoral modes of production. We have seen how Marija Gimbutas has attributed this structural change in society to the intrusion of Indo-Europeans whose presence, if not warlike activities, accounted for the collapse of the major Eneolithic cultures of Southeast Europe. Others have emphasized local processes to account for this collapse. Intensive agricultural productivity against a background of population growth might well have taken agriculture to its prehistoric limits and have required the adoption of pastoralism to maintain growth. Climatic change, especially associated with the shift from the Atlantic to the Sub-Boreal, has also long been regarded as an important factor. Graeme Barker has observed that the climatic change in the Balkans would have resulted in decreasing agricultural productivity, and an opening of the landscape, which would have been more suited to pastoralism than to agriculture. Certainly, in some pollen profiles from the region, we find a decrease in cereal pollen and a reforestation of the landscape contemporary with the intrusion of steppe pastoralists. Finally, technological developments associated with Andrew Sherratt's 'Secondary Products Revolution' would have been another contributory factor. Whatever the causes, we seem to find both the abandonment of earlier, stable communities and the reduction of the size of settlements with their subsequent dispersal. Jan Makkay, for example, notes that, in Hungary, the earlier Neolithic Tisza culture was represented by twenty-eight substantial sites. Later, in the Eneolithic, settlement was dispersed into about 243 small single-layer Tiszapolgar sites. Petre Roman and Sebastian Morintz have also shown how the structural reordering of Eneolithic society in Romania resulted in the collapse of former cultures and the appearance of scattered settlements on islands or in upland caves.

The various explanations for the changes in Southeast European Eneolithic society are all reasonably persuasive, and they may all have been important factors. The fourth millennium BC was a period of social fragmentation and apparently increasing pastoralism. Whether they induced these changes or, more probably, were coincidental with them, intrusive steppe populations may well have been at a social advantage with respect to the native cultures which were less easily able to adapt to new conditions.

In their interactions with the local populations, we should not immediately leap to simplistic (and typical) assumptions where superiority in mobility or weapons can be directly translated into linguistic dominance. Again, Fredrik Barth provides archaeologists with a cogent reminder that we need to look beyond apparent military advantages in determining the ultimate formation of super- and substrates. Barth examined the linguistic relations between the Pathans and Baluchi on the Afghan-Pakistan border. The Pathans were the more numerous, the wealthier, better armed, and even possessed a better military reputation. Nevertheless, it is the Baluchi who have been making the sustained linguistic assimilation of the Pathans. The Baluchi social structure is hierarchic and encourages vertical relationships between local leaders and clients. The various bands offer opportunities for social advancement within these hierarchies, and displaced Pathans in a frontier situation are attracted individually and in groups to join Baluchi communities. On the other hand, the more egalitarian society of the Pathans was ill-suited to absorb foreigners who could only enter it either in roles despised by the Pathans or by undertaking a more complicated process to being admitted as an equal in Pathan society. The nub of the issue here is not weapons, wealth or population size but the social permeability of the competing social organizations. As numerous historical instances testify, pastoral societies throughout the Eurasian steppe are typified by remarkable abilities to absorb disparate ethno-linguistic groups. Indo-European military institutions may have encouraged membership from local groups in the form of clientship which offered local populations greater advantages and social mobility. It is only possible to speculate about the nature of Eneolithic social structures in Southeast Europe. But with the traditional centripetal tendencies of settled agricultural societies, they may have been far less open to assimilating the mobile pastoralists who lived among them.

Towards the end of the fourth millennium BC the earlier processes of disintegration seem to have been reversed. We find the integration of former cultures into new groupings by which the Pontic, Balkans and northwest Anatolia appear all to be linked in terms of ceramics, metallurgy and architectural forms. This circum-Pontic interaction sphere now sees the emergence of citadels which may have served the centralizing tendencies of new élites. From our perspective, these could have continued the process of spreading the Indo-European languages where dependent populations were encouraged to learn the languages of the intruders in order to gain access to the products or services of the new élites, whom we may suppose spoke Indo-European languages.

These are only general and quite hypothetical models to suggest how the Indo-European languages may have expanded. We may conclude this section by laying to rest one fallacy that has often appeared in the past. A tendency to see the Indo-European languages as inherently those of the superstrate can be found widely in literature on the Indo-Europeans. This form of 'Aryan manifest destiny' ultimately calls into question the whole process of expansion. In any event, our prehistoric evidence suggests that Indo-Europeans did not always maintain their élite position. If they did penetrate the Caucasus, we know of no Indo-European language in the Kuro-Araxes region that survived into history. Similarly, the region of the Fatyanovo culture of the upper Volga, as well as other Corded Ware variants in the east Baltic, clearly succumbed to Finno-Ugric speakers. And, from our better-controlled historical evidence, we know that Indo-Europeans succumbed to the Hungarians in Europe, and we witness the lightning expansion of the Turks, largely at the expense of Indo-Europeans. Turkic speakers are probably to be credited with the linguistic death of Tocharian as well as with the assimilation of numerous Iranian speakers across the Asiatic steppe, and ultimately with the effective collapse of Greek as the major language of Anatolia. Indo-Europeans do not always win.

Recapitulation

After an extensive criticism of recent theories concerning the origin of the Indo-Europeans, Igor Diakonov concluded, 'Perhaps our readers will ask: "but what do you think actually happened?" If I knew, I would develop my own theory instead of criticizing somebody else's. However, if it is permitted to advance some hypotheses in this context, I will offer mine as well.' Diakonov then suggested a Southeast European homeland which is incompatible with the course of my own arguments. Nevertheless, some attempt at recapitulation is called for and it also provides a convenient opportunity to note particular problems and possibilities for future research.

Proto-Indo-European probably evolved out of the languages spoken by hunter-fishing communities in the Pontic-Caspian region. It is impossible to select which languages and what areas, though a linguistic continuum from the Dnieper east to the Volga would be possible. Settlement would have been confined primarily to the major river valleys and their tributaries, and this may have resulted in considerable linguistic ramification. But the introduction of stockbreeding, and the domestication of the horse, permitted the exploitation of the open steppe. With the subsequent development of wheeled vehicles in this area, highly mobile communities would have interacted regularly with the more sedentary river valley and forest-steppe communities. During the period to which we notionally assign Proto-Indo-European (4500–2500 BC), most of the Pontic-Caspian served as a vast interaction sphere. As Nikolai Merpert has observed concerning the social organization of the Yamnaya cultural area, the almost instantaneous spread of uniform burial rites over vast areas of the steppe suggests movements at the tribal level of society. Words would have passed freely between different dialects, and the later isoglosses which seem to leap geographical boundaries, such as Greek or German and Tocharian, may have been the result of these interactions. In addition, higher versus lower variants of Indo-European languages may have been spoken, which would further account for why some linguistic groups preserve certain words and others lack such reflexes. In the east, both Proto-Indo-Europeans and later ancestors of the Indo-Iranians were in contact with Finno-Ugric speakers. In the west, the shared agricultural vocabulary of the European languages may have developed along the middle Dnieper or in contact with the numerous Tripolyean settlements of the western Ukraine.

As the period 4500–2500 BC is an arbitrary segment of the linguistic processes of the Pontic-Caspian, it is difficult to pick and choose which cultures in this region might not have been Indo-European. Marija Gimbutas traditionally dismisses the Dnieper-Donets culture as genetically different from the Kurgan line of cultures since it practised a different economy, buried its dead in group pits and displayed a different, more massive, physical type. But since it flourished and died during the Proto-Indo-European period, and contributed to the formation of the Sredny Stog and possibly Samara cultures, it may well have been another component of the overall linguistic continuum which evolved into Proto–Indo-European. Similarly, we cannot isolate out languages which may have been associated with the Kemi Oba culture of the Crimea, or those that might have been connected with north Caucasian cultures, as non-Indo-European. The emphasis here is entirely on a territorial sphere of mutual interrelationships and that is the best we should ever hope for.

The eastern border of Proto-Indo-European is insecure, at least in the fifth and early fourth millennium BC. It may be that future work east of the Urals will uncover cultures genetically related to those of the Volga-Ural region, and that we will be impelled to extend our interaction sphere to the east. But, for the present, the archaeological picture suggests an expansion eastwards across the steppe and forest-steppe of western Siberia beginning in the late fourth millennium. Those who reached the far eastern periphery became the Afanasievo culture, and both their location and their isolation from other steppe tribes indicates that they were well positioned to become the ancestors of the Tocharians. What happened to the Afanasievans after the occupation of this region by the genetically unrelated Okunevo culture remains a mystery, but as they were replaced by a more northerly culture, a retreat southwards towards Chinese Turkestan would be a plausible solution.

After the expansion of Indo-Europeans to the Yenisey, the Indo-Iranian languages evolved, in the third millennium BC, in the broad expanse between at least the Volga and Kazakhstan. Out of this staging area there was a gradual drift southwards through the proto-urban communities of Central Asia. By the second millennium, Indo-Aryan was spoken by tribes south of the Caspian, and probably also in Afghanistan-north Pakistan from whence it ultimately pressed southwards into the Indus Valley. Concurrent with these developments, Iranian was evolving on the steppe and was then subsequently carried south into present-day Iran and Afghanistan, while the steppe itself was largely left to Eastern Iranian-speaking tribes. These expanded as far east as the Yenisey and westwards across the Pontic-Caspian where they have left us many of the names of the major rivers north of the Black Sea.

In bringing the Iranians into the Pontic region in comparatively recent times, I indicate that I do not share the opinion of many who have imagined that the Indo-Iranians dominated the entire Pontic-Caspian steppe from the Eneolithic period onwards. Rather, I prefer to see the Eneolithic cultures speaking largely undifferentiated (or at least anonymous) Indo-European, and that the Eneolithic expansions into the Balkans were carried out by linguistic ancestors of many of the European and Anatolian languages. Hence, the entire Pontic-Caspian steppe provided the environment for mutual interactions which would explain why we can isolate out Greek-Armenian-(possibly) Thracian-Iranian-Indic as an extensive continuum sharing a number of linguistic innovations. To place this continuum in the third millennium BC indicates that we must propel those Indo-Europeans ancestral to the Anatolian languages out of the Pontic-Caspian at an earlier date. A late fifth- or early fourth-millennium expansion is what we are looking for, and we have seen that there are two possibilities. There is disputable evidence for intrusions from the Pontic steppe into the Caucasus, and possibly eastern Anatolia, by the fourth millennium BC. If the evidence

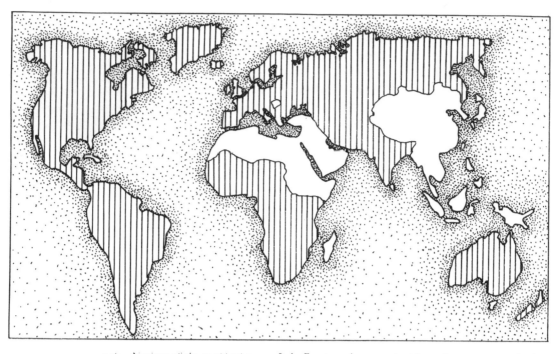

146   Nations of the world where an Indo-European language is either primary or recognized as an official language of state.

could be strengthened and traced westwards and southwards into areas where we have later record of Anatolian speakers, then it would provide a most plausible solution. For the present, however, the evidence for movements across Anatolia from the northwest appear somewhat more attractive. This would tie the Anatolian dialects to the Early Bronze Age cultures around Troy and, by extension, to the Balkan Danubian region. Hence, the earliest evidence for steppe intrusions in the Balkans, about 4000 BC, may have been associated with Indo-Europeans who carried their language into northwest Anatolia. Subsequent linguistic developments involving the ancestors of Greek, Armenian, Thracian, Phrygian, Illyrian and some of the Indo-European languages we later encounter in Italy followed on the continual movement of peoples from the steppe into Southeastern Europe throughout the fourth and into the third millennium BC.

When left with a choice between an archaeological model that is unconfirmed versus one that seems linguistically implausible, I would opt for the former hoping, like Miroslav Buchvaldek, that future evidence may rescue it. Hence, I would have to take it on intuition that some form of historical relationship between the Pontic and Central and Northern Europe will eventually be demonstrated, even if the evidence today is not convincing. Either way, it is most probable that the Corded Ware horizon provided the vector for a series of Indo-European languages that spread both to the west as far as Holland and east into the Baltic and upper Volga. Out of this later emerged possibly the Celtic and Italic, and more certainly the Germanic, Baltic and Slavic languages.

The expansion of the Indo-European languages was not completed by the Bronze or Iron Ages but has been an ongoing process which continues to the present. The rise of Europe and its colonial extensions into Africa, Australia and the New World carried English, Spanish, Portuguese and French into new lands where they are still assimilating the speakers of native languages. And in Asia, Russian is continuing to spread across the eastern territories of the Soviet Union. Over a period of 6,000 years we have witnessed the emergence and expansion of a language family until it embraces nearly half the population of this planet.

CHAPTER NINE

Epilogue

The ancestors of the Aryans cultivated wheat
when those of the brachycephalics were probably
still living like monkeys.

GEORGES VACHER DE LAPOUGE, 1899

The Aryan Myth

We cannot examine the legacy of the Indo-Europeans without first dispelling the spectre of the 'Aryan Myth'. The world is all too familiar with how the concept of racial supremacy was implemented by the National Socialists in Germany, and we would be quite mistaken to imagine that this grotesque obsession with the Indo-Europeans or, as they were then more popularly known, the Aryans, was merely the creation of a handful of Nazi fanatics. A fascination with the 'Aryans' was, in fact, very much part of the intellectual environment of the nineteenth and early twentieth centuries. We may dismiss Hitler's assertion that *only* Aryans were the 'founders of culture', but why should V. Gordon Childe have been compelled to find them 'fitted with exceptional mental endowments' and 'promoters of true progress'?

The blond, blue-eyed Aryan, fathered in Northern Europe, convinced of his superiority and obsessed with his racial purity, was the product of numerous intellectual currents of which the development of Indo-European linguistics was but one. Leon Poliakov has shown that the roots of this caricature reach back into the near-universal longing of the peoples of Europe to secure for themselves an illustrious ancestry. The Romans, of course, had sought theirs at Troy. By the Middle Ages the aristocracy of Spain were boasting of their superior Visigothic blood which set them both apart from and above their subjects, while the French endured chronic schizophrenia whether they were the linear descendants of Vercingetorix and his Gauls (Celts) or Charlemagne and his Franks (Germans). Some English, not content with their obviously mixed ancestry of Britons, Anglo-Saxons, Vikings and Normans, felt it necessary to drag a lost tribe of Israel to their shores to provide them with a still more ancient peerage. The Germans, on the other hand, saw their own history begin with those very expansions that provided the Visigoths, Franks and Anglo-Saxons – the illustrious ancestors – of their neighbours. When Tacitus maintained that the Germans were pure of blood, unmixed with other races and autochthonous, there was little reason to deny that their origins lay in Northern Europe. If the Church required a Biblical link, then Ashkenaz, a grandson of the prolific Japhet, could be found to trek his way to Northern Europe and establish the German people. But it was really pride in local origins that attracted the Germans, especially during the Reformation, when many found themselves pitted against what they despised as the weak, corrupt and foreign world of Rome. By the eighteenth and nineteenth centuries, the industrial and intellectual explosion of the Germanic-speaking lands further encouraged the belief in both German autochthony and the rising destiny of the north. Concurrent developments in physical anthropology and comparative linguistics helped to fuel this belief.

Coincidental with the rise of anthropology was the development of the concept of race. Western scholars, once they had isolated the different races of mankind, could hardly resist placing their own Caucasians at the top. Race was easily confused with ethnic group, nation and language. History was reduced to a succession of races, each holding power for a time before passing the baton on to a more energetic race. The busy seaports of England, Holland, Germany and Scandinavia, or the intellectual salons of London, Berlin and Vienna left little doubt in their own locales where that energetic race dwelt. The superiority of the north could even be measured by physical anthropologists who, by the nineteenth century, seemed to be ceaselessly measuring the cephalic index. Here they distinguished the dolichocephalic (long-headed) Nordics from their brachycephalic (broad-headed) neighbours to the south. Surprisingly enough, it was not until about 1870 that the blue-eyed blond, previously the caricature of the dreamy romantic, became the stereotype of the virile male. A superior Nordic physical type had been discovered by science; it remained for the philologists to provide him with an ancient and illustrious ethnic identity.

The discovery of the Indo-European language family did more than simply elucidate the historical relationship between many European and Asian languages. It severed once and for all the fantasy of deriving all languages from Hebrew, and by extension, Adam. The indivisibility of the human race was being destroyed not only by those who profited from exploiting different peoples, but by science itself. Following the West's discovery of the wealth of Indic and Iranian literature, European scholars looked beyond Eden to seek their own more illustrious forebears in Central Asia, Iran and India. Although Indo-European and Indo-Germanic had both been coined early in the nineteenth century, Max Müller, and other linguists, encouraged the use of Aryan to describe the ancient Indo-Europeans. Naturally, if these early Aryans were the ancestors of the Europeans, then they too must have been part of the superior white race.

A peculiar linguistic fallacy arose that provided further proof of Aryan superiority. Research into the essential structure of the world's languages revealed several basic types depending on how grammatical elements were indicated – inflected, agglutinative, and analytic. Although these were originally only typological classifications, many could not resist interpreting them as various stages in the evolution of language. A 'simple' word-based language (analytic) such as Chinese, for example, was placed on the bottom of the scale. Languages were then seen to develop to the agglutinative type (as in the Altaic and Uralic languages where separate endings are added to nouns) and, ultimately, to the inflected type, such as Indo-European. This suggested that the Indo-Europeans, or Aryans, having ascended the scale of linguistic evolution to its summit, spoke a more 'advanced' language than their neighbours. Canon Isaac Taylor, for example, once proposed the notion that the Indo-Europeans were essentially 'an improved race of Finns'.

But even if superiority of physical type, language, and culture were all being united under the name of Aryan, there was still one essential element missing – with the singular exception of Roger Latham's claim that the Indo-European homeland lay in Europe, the common opinion of most scholars prior to the later nineteenth century was that the Aryan homeland must lie in Asia. While no one doubted that the Aryans belonged to the white race, up until the end of the 1860s most believed that this race originally dwelt somewhere in the vicinity of the Hindu Kush or Himalayas. There was no reason to seek their home in Northern Europe.

It was in the 1860s that a number of scholars, particularly linguists, began to publish their doubts about an Asiatic homeland for the Indo-Europeans. Some of the reasons adduced, such as the Beech argument, have become part of the traditional stock of homeland research. But for our story it was the rise of physical anthropology that is most significant, since it eventually came to be applied to the problem of Indo-European origins. By 1870 Lazarus Geiger was supporting a homeland in Germany, employing the argument that the original Indo-Europeans must have been light-skinned blonds. But the man who first carried this theory into the widest arena was Theodor Poesche.

In 1878 Poesche surveyed the historical references to the various Indo-European peoples and assembled his evidence to demonstrate that they were regularly described as blue-eyed blonds. Even the brahmans of India were lighter than the lower castes – an observation made much earlier by Julius Klaproth, who had coined the term Indo-Germanic. From this one might conclude that the Aryans were originally light-skinned, fair-haired, blue-eyed and, in accordance with the anthropological evidence already adduced, dolichocephalic. Poesche then sought the centre of all of these characteristics and astoundingly enough concluded that the point where one might locate the highest incidence of albinism in Europe must have been the centre of the Aryan race. At last the Aryans had found a European homeland – in the Pripet marshes of Eastern Europe.

An Aryan homeland in the unhealthy environment of a swamp was hardly conducive to the development of the 'powerful, energetic blond race' or so Karl Penka argued in 1883. Rather, Penka pressed into service all the disciplines he could – archaeology, linguistics, anthropology and mythology – to demonstrate that the Aryans originated in southern Scandinavia. One of the arguments emphasized by Penka is still very current today. Denying any evidence in the archaeological record for major intrusions into Northern Europe, Penka concluded that the Aryans must have originated there and could not be derived from elsewhere. Penka's works, largely a series of polemics, were soon widely accepted. Noted anthropologists such as Rudolf Virchow and even Thomas Huxley not only concerned themselves with identifying the original Aryan race but also concurred that they were originally a race of 'blond dolichocephalics'. The great Indologist Max Müller, annoyed by the madness he had helped to create, blasted the anthropologists who spoke of an 'Aryan race, Aryan blood, Aryan eyes and hair' as a lunacy comparable to a linguist who spoke of 'a dolichocephalic dictionary or a brachycephalic grammar'. But it was too late: the Indo-Europeans and racism had become inseparable in the minds of many scholars. Although there would always be linguists and anthropologists to protest, the superiority of the ancient Aryan Nordic race had entered popular political culture.

The subsequent history of the Indo-European problem until the end of the Second World War was played out by several major camps. A European homeland was favoured by the great majority of scholars although there were always a few who would assert the ancient claims of Asia. Most arguments, however, were fought between those who supported a North European homeland (the German archaeologist Gustav Kossina and his followers, the linguist Herman Hirt, and many others) versus those who supported a steppe homeland, either European or Asian (Otto Schrader, Sigmund Feist, Alfons Nehring, Wilhelm Brandenstein, Wilhelm Koppers). Some scholars struggled to maintain a middle course, others provided comic relief. The American Charles Morris, for example, settled the earliest Aryans in the Caucasus where they not only perfected their language, but, in an instance of racial stereotyping that tells us far more about the author than the Indo-Europeans, they gained, according to Morris, their 'enthusiasm' from the darker races to their south. Cokamanya Bal Gangadhar Tilak provided the world with an entire monograph marshalling all the available mythological evidence to prove that the Aryan homeland was the North Pole.[38] This incredible theory gained at least one supporter when Georg Biedenkapp, flushed with enthusiasm for Tilak's hypothesis, produced his own book summarizing the Indian savant's work in German and added further evidence of his own. The Icelandic linguist Alexander Johannesson concocted another bizarre theory that related Indo-European roots to bird calls (Proto-Indo-European *ker- was imitative of a raven), grunts, and loud natural sounds which, according to him, could best be heard on the shores of the Baltic Sea.

The myth of Aryan supremacy, somewhat more evident in some pre-war anthropological journals than among the linguistic ones, was, in varying degrees, a widespread phenomenon until the consequences of its political expression made it anathema in the academic world. One hardly need emphasize that the implementation of Aryan supremacy by the Nazis was wholly inconsistent with Aryan as a linguistic term; Yiddish is as much an Indo-European language as any other German dialect, while Romany-speaking Gypsies had a far better claim to the title of Aryans than any North European. Thus, the myth of Aryan supremacy was neither a direct nor necessary consequence of the philological discoveries of the nineteenth century, but rather the misappropriation of a linguistic concept and its subsequent grafting onto an already existing framework of prejudices, speculations and political aspirations. The Indo-Europeans leave more than the legacy of Aryan supremacy.

The legacy

If the development of comparative philology played an unfortunate role in the creation of twentieth century racism, it should also be credited with providing the tools by which scholars were able to elucidate the cultural relationships and origins of the numerous non-Indo-European peoples of the world. The same techniques employed to compare the various lexical and grammatical items of the Indo-European languages were, and still are, equally applicable to the Algonquin, Altaic, Athapascan, Bantu, or indeed any other group of languages. Linguists, originally trained in the field of Indo-European, set out to establish the relationships between the other languages of the world, to reconstruct their proto-languages and investigate their origins.

When we turn to the actual achievements of the Proto-Indo-Europeans we find a rather different legacy from that of most ancient peoples. Unlike Samuel Kramer who can list the Sumerian 'firsts', there are few such achievements that we can credit to the Proto-Indo-Europeans. Recognizing this, and finding them so often in the position of destroyers of earlier cultures, V. Gordon Childe was thrown back to extolling their 'excellent language and the mentality it generated' while Albert Carnoy relished their expansive nature, their spontaneity, their creativity, their suppleness of spirit and a host of similar virtues. Why they should have been given such singular praise is unclear; can one be so perverse as to imagine the Chinese as uncreative, the Finns and Hungarians as mentally impoverished, or the Turks and Arabs as saddled with second class languages?

If we must have concrete legacies, then the best claim is that of horse domestication and the social consequences this revolution in transportation and warfare brought to the world. In addition, the Indo-Europeans are at least one of the candidates for the inventors of wheeled vehicles, although a number of non-Indo-European peoples have every bit as good a claim. But such instances of historical priority hardly constitute the type of legacy that persists uniquely among the Indo-Europeans.

Ideology is often regarded as the central core of culture and it is here that some would see the most striking evidence for the Indo-European legacy. We have already seen how the Dumézilian school not only acknowledges the genetic relationship of the Indo-European languages but also the persistence of an inherited ideology. The new comparative mythologists maintain that the trifunctional ideology of the Proto-Indo-Europeans permeates the religious texts of the ancient Indians and Iranians, emerges in the epic poetry and drama of the Greeks, hides behind the façade of history among the early Romans, and expresses itself in the prose tales of the medieval Germanic and Celtic peoples. Even with that overlay of Judeo-Christian ideology which characterizes

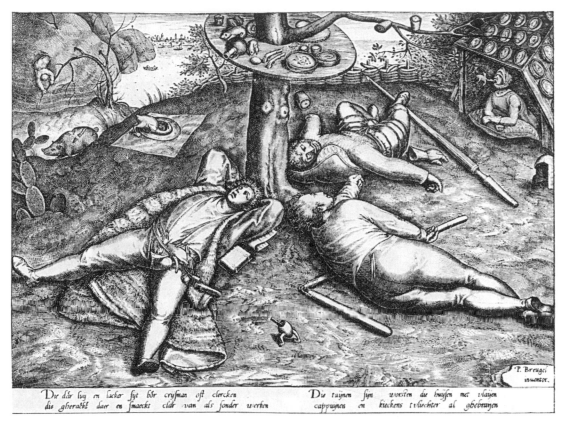

Die dar luy en lacker syt bor cryfman oft clercken
die gheraeckt daer en fmaeckt clar van als fonder werken

Die tuijnen syn worsten die huysen met vlayen
cappuynen en kieckens tvluchter al ghebrayen

147 The persistence of Indo-European tripartition? Peter Breugel's sixteenth-century 'Land of Cockayne' depicts the clerk, warrior and cultivator, the representatives of the three 'functions' of Indo-European society.

European culture, the Indo-European ideological structure still surfaces, as we see in the medieval tendency to equate the three sons of Noah – Japhet, Shem and Ham – with the three estates of society: nobles (warriors), clerks (priests), and serfs (cultivators). C. Scott Littleton has even suggested that this tripartite division of society extended unconsciously to the framers of the American Constitution, who, in dividing the totality of their state into three branches, were as much the heirs of their Proto-Indo-European ancestors as Zarathustra or the brahmans of ancient India.

It is natural to query whether social tripartition, and all of its attendant expressions in myth, literature, law, medicine, and folklore, is uniquely Indo-European. To many, the system proposed by Dumézil seems so natural as to be universal, and hardly the specific legacy of an Eneolithic people of Eastern Europe. Yet the 'new comparativists' argue that, even if such a system of priests, warriors and herder-cultivators seems natural, it is the treatment of this structure as a special class of concepts requiring and receiving almost endless elaboration in all spheres of cultural ideology and behaviour that makes it truly unique to the Indo-Europeans. Littleton has argued that similar methods applied to myths of other language groups would reveal other systems of ideology ranging from the seven-fold (astral) ideological paradigms of the Semites, to the four-fold (directional-based) systems of certain American Indian groups. Indeed, one may argue that tripartition itself need not result in the Indo-European system. Lawrence Krader, in his study of the non-Indo-European Buryat Mongols, observes that their 'triple division of the social world' is carried through into the spirit world and the three souls of men. The Buryat spirits are arranged according to the three different Buryat social classes, aristocrats, commoners and slaves, categories that are tripartite but not those of the Indo-Europeans.

Whether or not one is confident that such an ideological inheritance exists, the most secure legacy of the Indo-Europeans is surely to be found in the language spoken by over two billion people in the world. It is irrelevant whether we regard ourselves as Europeans, Asians, Africans, or Americans, we cannot escape this legacy if we speak an Indo-European language. We cannot ask questions of where, when, who or how, or answer them with our most basic pronouns, we cannot count, refer to the basic parts of our bodies, describe our environment, the heavens, basic animals or relatives, or express our most fundamental actions, without making frequent recourse to an inherited system of speech that our linguistic ancestors shared 6,000 years ago.

The common linguistic heritage of the Indo-Europeans was only discovered in the eighteenth century and it has seldom, if ever, impinged on the behaviour of the different Indo-Europeans. History provides little evidence that different Indo-European groups ever recognized their mutual kinship. If the ancient Greeks disparaged an Indian as a *barbaros*, the Indian dug into the same linguistic legacy to dismiss his non-Aryan neighbours with precisely the same word, *barbaras*. If kinship of the Indo-Europeans was overlooked in the past, it hardly needs emphasizing that it is absent today. In characteristic hyperbole, Hitler once wrote that the collapse of the Aryans would see the light of civilization extinguished in the world; given the distribution of nuclear arms on this planet, it is far more likely that it will be Indo-Europeans who will end it themselves. Yet we need not finish pessimistically, but rather hope to remind the great superpowers, that whatever their political differences, when they speak to one another, they do so in words that were once common when they shared the same language, the same home and the same beliefs.

Notes to the text

1 Jones had a number of predecessors (in addition to Parsons) who recognized the affinity of the languages of India and Iran with those of Europe. As early as 1583 Thomas Stevens, an English Jesuit working in India, wrote that 'many are the languages of these places. Their pronunciation is not disagreeable and their structure is allied to Greek and Latin'. Two years later an Italian merchant Fillipo Sasseti observed that there was much in common between Sanskrit and the European languages because in Sanskrit 'we can find many of our nouns, especially numbers: the 6, 7, 8, and 9, God, serpent, and others'. By the seventeenth century scholars were also accepting the similarities between Greek and German, and Franciscus Rapelengius argued for the association of German with Persian. The Dutch scholar, Marcus Boxhorn grouped Greek, Latin, German and Persian under the name of 'Scythian', a theory defended by no less a scholar than Leibnitz. Finally, in 1768 the Jesuit Coeurdoux derived Sanskrit, Latin, Greek, Slavonic, and the other languages of Europe from the language of Japhet (see Mukherjee, S. N., *Sir William Jones*, Cambridge 1968).

2 Both Rask and Bopp were required to labour against one of the last gasps of Goropianism when the great German Romanticist, Friedrich von Schlegel, published his *Über die Sprache und Weisheit der Indier* ('On the Language and Wisdom of the Indians', 1808) wherein he proposed that all of the Indo-European languages might be derived from Sanskrit itself. The fallacy was still very much alive in 1828 when Vans Kennedy published his *Researches into the Origin and Affinity of the Principal Languages of Europe and Asia*. Oddly enough, Kennedy dismissed the idea that Persian and the Celtic languages were related to the other Indo-European languages. Besides Thomas Young's introduction of the term Indo-European, mention should also be made of Julius Klaproth who coined 'Indo-Germanic', which is most often employed in German-speaking lands (indicating the extent of the language family from India to the Germanic speakers of the Atlantic). As we will see later, Aryan became a popular term for the Indo-Europeans in the later nineteenth and early twentieth centuries. In the first edition of the *Cambridge History of India*, P. Giles unsuccessfully attempted to introduce the term 'wiroi' for the Indo-Europeans, employing their own (reconstructed) word for 'the men'.

3 In this text, I employ a traditional system reconstructed for Proto-Indo-European that includes the vowels *a, e, i, o, u* (both long and short); the semivowels *y* and *w*; the nasals *m* and *n* and liquids *l* and *r*; the sibilant *s*; and a rich assortment of consonants that are arranged in the following triads: labials, *p b bh*; dentals, *t d dh*; velars, *k g gh*; palatals, *k̂ ĝ ĝh*; labio-velars, *kʷ gʷ gʷh*. In addition to these, there was the indeterminate vowel ə (schwa) which also functioned as a consonant (laryngeal). The existence of laryngeals was originally predicted on the basis of the internal structure of the Indo-European languages, and this was confirmed by the discovery of Hittite which yielded an h-like sound in the predicted position. The number of different types of laryngeals is still debated and several different systems of representation are employed by various linguists. Moreover, the past decade has seen major challenges to the traditional nineteenth-century reconstructed system (see Szemerenyi, O., 'Recent developments in Indo-European linguistics', *Transactions of the Philological Society* 1985: 1–71, for brief review). Purely in the interests of graphic simplicity, the more traditional reconstructions are employed in this work.

4 The personal names include those that are similar to names later attested by the Hittites themselves, for example, Sa-li-nu-ma- where Hittite *salli-* means 'great'. Some names such as Ta-ak-sa-nu-ma-an appear to be constructed from Indo-European roots (Hittite *taks-* 'make, build', Sanskrit *taksan* and Greek *tekton* 'carpenter').

5 The Hittites adopted the Hattic capital Hattusa and personal names, such as Hattusilis, from the Hattic population. Among the Hattic loan words in Hittite are words specifically associated with the palace polity of the Hatti, for example, throne, lord, queen mother, noble, and a whole series of names for officials and cult functionaries. Recognizable Hattic loan words pertaining to material culture include iron and some words for bread (Kammenhuber, A., 'Protohattisch-Hethitisches', *Münchener Studien zum Sprachwissenschaft* 14 (1959): 63–83.). It is generally assumed that the Hattic-Hittite bilingual ritual texts were necessary since, although the Hittites had apparently adopted the Hattic religion (and others as well), Hattic had gone out of use.

6 Archaic features of Hittite include laryngeals, r/n stem nouns, archaic pronomial forms, medio-passives; losses (or perhaps absences since a number of linguists would dispute that they ever developed in Hittite) include the feminine, the dual, the aorist, the optative. A number of the features absent from Hittite but which are reconstructed to Proto-Indo-European from other languages are also absent from Hattic. Hence a Hattic substrate has sometimes been credited as one of the major reasons for the restructuring of the Hittite language away from that evidenced by the other Indo-European languages.

7 G. Steiner (1981) has suggested that the Hittites were already well-settled in Kanes when the Assyrians arrived, and as the dominant population of one of the most important trading outposts their language served as a lingua franca across central Anatolia, coming to serve as the chancellery language of the Hatti. According to Steiner, the Hittites of the Old Kingdom were not primarily 'Hittites' but rather of Hattic stock which had adopted the new lingua franca.

8 The horse remains from the Late Eneolithic in eastern Anatolia are traditionally identified as wild individuals. S. Bökönyi, ('Horses and Sheep in East Europe in the Copper and Bronze Ages', in S. Skomal and E. Polome (eds), *Proto-Indo-European: The Archaeology of a Linguistic Problem*, Washington, D.C., 1987: 136–144), however, suggests that they were from domestic animals, and he associates them with the spread of domestic horses from the Pontic-Caspian region.

9 Linguistically, from what we can tell of Phrygian, it shares one apparent archaic feature (medio-passives in r) with Hittite and several other 'peripheral' dialects. It also shares the augment with Armenian, Greek, and Indo-Iranian, a putatively later feature assignable to the 'southern' dialects. This could suggest that Phrygian was earlier situated somewhere close to Anatolian to avoid later innovations and also close to the Greek-Armenian-Indo-Iranian chain of southern languages. Geographically, the southern Balkans or northwestern Anatolia should fit.

10 Regarding Armenian origins, Colin Renfrew (1987: 72) dismisses their traditional derivation from Southeast Europe as a product of the 'propensity to talk in terms of migrations', and argues that 'there is no very clear reason to link the Armenian language with western Anatolia or Thrace'. Renfrew fails to indicate that 1 Armenian cannot be derived directly from any of the adjacent Anatolian languages (which all lack common Proto-Indo-European features found in all the other Indo-European languages, including Armenian); and 2 Armenian shares major isoglosses that associate it most closely with Greek, and linguists generally require that the linguistic ancestors of the Armenians

and Greeks were either identical or in a close contact relation – Thrace or western Anatolia being the most economical explanations. Obviously, the Armenians could not have arrived in their historical seats without migrating since it was previously occupied by the non-Indo-European Urartians.

Renfrew takes some comfort from the fact that Gamkrelidze and Ivanov (1985) also place the Indo-European homeland in eastern Anatolia on linguistic grounds. While the two Soviet linguists do indeed place the homeland on the eastern Anatolia-Armenian plateau, they also accept the existence of a 'Greek-Armenian community' as an 'independent entity' and are consequently forced to send the Greeks migrating from eastern Anatolia (the reverse of the traditional model that has the Armenians migrate from the Balkans). Diakonov (1985) rightly finds this Greek migration across the face of the Anatolian languages quite incredible.

11 Renfrew (1987: 178–197) rejects as unproven the exclusion of an Indo-Aryan identity for the Indus Valley Civilization and proposes the hypothesis that the Indo-Aryan languages may have extended to west Pakistan with the spread of agriculture before 6000 BC. In this hypothesis, the Indo-Aryans, or at least their linguistic ancestors, were in the Indus region for thousands of years prior to the traditional interpretation of the linguistic data. He prudently labels this suggestion 'Hypothesis A' and also admits the possibility of the traditional model (Hypothesis B) discussed in this book. Other than the reasons cited in the main text there are other very serious grounds for rejecting Renfrew's Hypothesis A. A model that 'explains' the presence of the Indo-Aryans by referring them to the expansion of the Neolithic economy from the Zagros region around the seventh millennium BC ignores the close linguistic relationship between Indo-Iranian and Greek. In Renfrew's model, if the Indo-Iranians moved off to the east of what would become Anatolian, and the linguistic ancestors of the Greeks moved off to the west, there can be no intelligible explanation for how these different subgroups share so many isoglosses not found in Anatolian. It is curious that for someone who repeatedly adheres to Schmidt's 'wave model' as a key to explaining the relationships of the Indo-European languages, Renfrew pays no attention to the significance of the shared linguistic similarities (isogloss bundles) indicated by this model.

12 Here I follow Pedersen, Crossland, Adrados, Gamkrelidze and Ivanov, and others, who regard Tocharian as an archaic peripheral dialect. There are, however, many who would associate Tocharian much more closely with languages such as Germanic or Greek (*see* Adams, D. Q., 'The Position of Tocharian Among the Other Indo-European Languages', *Journal of the American Oriental Society* 104 (1984): 395–402 for the most recent review of this problem. Adams himself relates Tocharian closest to Germanic and sees no great difficulty getting them to their ultimate homes.)

13 Possible textual remains of a pre-Greek language are those commonly termed Eteo-Cretan, a small series of inscriptions dating from the seventh to the third centuries BC known from the island of Crete. They are written in the Greek script but are most certainly not Greek nor any other known language and may represent one or more of the pre-Indo-European languages of Greece.

14 Although these names have traditionally been interpreted as non-Indo-European, a number of linguists have proposed Indo-European etymologies, such as Achilleus (**Achi-lawos* 'one who causes distress to the army'). Indo-European etymologies for words such as *basileus* have been proposed by V. Georgiev, one of the main proponents of the Pelasgian theory.

15 Anna Morpurgo Davies carried out a cursory examination of the Greek vocabulary which revealed less than 40 per cent of the lexicon could be ascribed a transparent Indo-European etymology, 8 per cent had established non-Greek origins and about 52 per cent had no clear etymology (Davies 1986).

16 The Linear B script would render all of the following Greek words: *ago, akos, algos, argos, arkhon, askos*, only as *ako*, and it is up to the linguist to determine which, if any, of these words the Mycenaean text reflects. Moreover, the syllabic structure of Indo-European words, including Greek, tends to be closed, while the Linear A and B scripts indicate only open syllables. As for the linguistic identity of the earlier Linear A script we can say very little. There is sufficient similarity in signs between it and Linear B that a number of linguists are confident about assigning phonetic values to Linear A inscriptions. They have been variously translated as Greek, Anatolian and Semitic; none very convincingly.

17 The entire hypothesis of the *Nordwestblock* has recently been reviewed by W. Meid ('Hans Kuhns "Nordwestblock" – Hypothese', *Anzeiger d. österreichischen Akademie d. Wissenschaften* 121 (1984): 2–21) who, although critical of some specifics, indicates that there is sufficient evidence to accept the existence of a different language (from Celtic and Germanic) in Northwest Europe. Eric Hamp (1987, in Skomal and Polome) has been arguing for an apparently non-Indo-European substrate language in Northern and Central Europe on the basis of the non-Indo-European appearance of an entire series of words associated with pigs and pig-breeding that are found primarily in the Celtic and possibly the Germanic languages. The concept of relics of a non-Indo-European language has been explained by some as the linguistic residue of the earlier Neolithic settlers of this region.

18 Names common on Messapic inscriptions have been found on tombs in Albania (Toci, *Studia Albanica* 2 (1969): 163–85).

19 The model proposed by Renfrew envisages 'an Indo-European-speaking population in France and in Britain and in Ireland, and probably in much of Iberia also, by before 4000 BC.' Through the 'wave model' this area gradually emerges as Celtic speaking and regionalizes into its various Celtic dialects. This scheme for the origin of the Insular Celtic languages is, I believe, linguistically most unconvincing. The time depth for these Celtic evolutions seems to be totally incongruent with all our available linguistic data on the separation of the Celtic languages. Our earliest evidence of the Insular Celtic languages indicates that *1* they share common 'Late Bronze Age-Iron Age vocabulary' with each other and Continental Celtic, such as words for iron, lead, weapons, and chariot terminology, which seems to indicate little major dialectal separation from the time of their putative settlement (according to Renfrew) to the Late Bronze Age or Iron Age, that is about 3,000 years or more; *2* that the Celtic languages were extremely similar to one another when they first appear in written sources – a phenomenon best explained by a relatively recent divergence across Common Celtic; *3* that they began to undergo extreme restructuring during the first millennium AD – a process which may be due to internal forces but is certainly in conformity with one's expectation of a series of languages recently spread over linguistic groups speaking radically different languages on the periphery of Europe. For what it is worth, traditional Irish accounts of their own origins regularly placed them at the end of a series of migrations to Ireland, and they identified certain elements of Irish population as native in contrast to the Goidelic (Irish) speakers (cf. Greene 1983, Piggott 1983, Mallory 1984, and MacEoin 1986.)

20 Renfrew's (1987, 77–86, 103–104, 109–110), discussion of the use of linguistic palaeontology as a tool for reconstructing the culture of the Proto-Indo-Europeans would appear to discredit the entire method. His objections include the following:

1 A new invention such as the 'wheel' will often carry its original name as it is spread to other populations, so if we find this word among several languages it does not necessarily tell us much about their origins. The observation that a new invention might well diffuse with its name attached to it is quite true, and historical linguists frequently take advantage of such phenomena to elucidate the historical relations between peoples. For example, linguists know that in their early contacts with one another, the Latins borrowed a series of words relating to chariotry from their Celtic neighbours in northern Italy. Hence, Celtic *karros (Old Irish, Middle Welsh, Old Breton carr) was lent into Latin as carrus, a word that is clearly distinguished from the native Latin chariot word currus which is derived ultimately from the same Indo-European root. The word was then subsequently borrowed through Norman French (carre) into Middle English as carre, modern English car. The distinction between which words are inherited from an earlier linguistic stage, and which were borrowed later, is clearly traceable. When historical linguists reconstruct the wheel to Proto-Indo-European, they do so because its outcome in the various Indo-European languages conforms to the same rules as all other words reconstructed to Proto-Indo-European. That it may have been invented by the Sumerians and then borrowed by the Indo-Europeans is interesting but irrelevant since the word would still be reconstructible to that stage in the linguistic continuum that we would designate Proto-Indo-European. What is important is that we have no reason to believe that this or any of the other vehicle-related terms reconstructed to Proto-Indo-European were loan words passing from one differentiated group to another (see also note 25). I can hardly claim that there do not exist considerable difficulties in assessing the inherited versus the borrowed status of some words, especially when their phonetic shape does not result in markedly different outcomes in different Indo-European languages, but there are procedures by which one can make an intelligent evaluation of the data.

2 The meanings of words change such that we cannot be sure of the original meaning of words that we reconstruct. Any serious linguist engaged in cultural reconstruction does attempt to assemble as much data as possible to establish the most likely original meaning. Renfrew cites several rather muddled examples of how historical linguists may err in their reconstructions. He cites J. Fraser's observation that because we have words corresponding to our 'mead', and verbs in Greek and Sanskrit meaning 'to intoxicated', we cannot assume that the Indo-Europeans had an intoxicating drink. In actual fact, the root *medhu is attested in most 'branches' of Indo-European. In Celtic and Germanic it only means 'mead', in Indic and Baltic it means 'honey' or 'mead', in Avestan it means 'an alcoholic drink', in Greek it means 'wine', in Tocharian and Slavic it means 'honey'. We have verbal forms from the same root in several branches that indicate the meaning 'to be drunk'. We also have another word for honey that does not involve the meaning mead. What's the problem? Renfrew cites Fraser's *non sequitur* that because Slavic *pivo* 'beer' is cognate with Latin *bibere* 'to drink' this illustrates how commonly one may transfer the meaning 'drink' to an 'alcoholic drink'. If one were to attempt to reconstruct a Proto-Indo-European 'beer' on such evidence, there would be very good reason to object, however, this has absolutely nothing to do with the line of evidence that supports the existence of a Proto-Indo-European 'mead'. Other exam-

ples, similarly inappropriate or out of step with present thinking, are trotted out, the solidly reconstructed mixed with the debatable. He maintains that 'when we find words related to "birch" and "beech" in several Indo-European languages it does not follow that the common word in Proto-Indo-European from which they were descended had the same specific meaning'. The first word, birch, is attested as Proto-Indo-European *bhergo and has cognates in Slavic, Baltic, Italic, Germanic, Indic and Iranian. It means 'birch' in all these languages except Latin where it has been shifted to 'ash', plausibly enough because the birch is generally absent from the Mediterranean area. Furthermore, the root is paralleled by a verbal root meaning 'to shine, become white', again totally congruent with reconstructing the meaning as 'birch'. The original meaning of the beech word on the other hand, as the reader will see from the main text, is very much disputed and cannot be regarded as convincingly reconstructed to Proto-Indo-European. The lesson here, I believe, is not that the comparative method cannot be utilized to reconstruct past cultural items, that is, that the birch should be tossed onto the same bonfire as the ambiguous 'beech' word, but rather that linguists are required to exercise the same sort of judgment about their data as one would expect of an archaeologist. No linguist could pretend that all lexico-cultural reconstructions have been carried out with necessary rigour or that extremely naïve use has not been made of these reconstructions; however, historical linguists are not really so hopelessly lost as Renfrew's discussion seems to portray them (see Richard Diebold, 'Linguistic Ways to Prehistory', in Skomal and Polome, 1987: 19–71).

21 The Albanian evidence throws suspicion on reconstructing *bhagos as 'beech'. Although it is the most common deciduous tree in the Albanian forests, the Albanians employ the ash word (*ah* from *okso-*) to name the beech. If *bhagos originally meant 'beech' it is a bit difficult to understand why the Albanians applied the 'beech-word' to the chestnut-oak and then substituted the ash-word for the beech (Huld, M. E., *KZ* 95 (1981): 306).

22 In a recent re-examination of *uksan 'ox', Stefan Zimmer (*KZ* 1981, 84–91) emphasizes that this word, attested in Indo-Iranian, Tocharian, Germanic and Celtic, regularly indicates the castrated ox, which is further indication of its use as a draught animal.

23 Eric Hamp (*IF* 85 (1980), 35–42) has suggested that the word for dog was *pḱuon (*peḱ-ḱuon 'sheep-dog'?).

24 Szemerenyi (1977, 96–99) derives Proto-Indo-European *wiḱ which yields Indic *vis-* 'settlement, house, clan, tribe' etc. from a Proto-Indo-European verb *weik 'go, march', thus indicating that the word originally referred to a group on the move (cf. English *gang* from an obsolete verb *gang* 'to go') and was only later applied to the actual settlement of the clan.

25 Renfrew (1987, 86) dismisses the use of linguistic palaeontology to reconstruct such cultural items as wheeled vehicles for the Proto-Indo-Europeans. He writes: 'Certainly, the circumstance that the Sanskrit word for "chariot" *ratha*, is agreed by competent linguists to be cognate with the Latin for "wheel", *rota*, is interesting, and merits historical explanation. But that is a far cry from saying that the two cognate words tell us that some hypothetical Proto-Indo-Europeans used chariots with wheels (or indeed carts with wheels) in their original homeland.' The exclusion of such late cultural terms is necessary since Renfrew's hypothesis requires an expansion of the Indo-Europeans *c.* 3,000 years before our earliest evidence for wheeled vehicles. For the record, the *rota*- word cited above is attested in Indo-Iranian, Italic, Celtic, Baltic and Germanic. Another cognate word for wheel/wagon is known in Celtic, Germanic, Baltic, Slavic, Tocharian, Indo-Iranian, Greek and Phrygian. Yet a third is attested in Hittite and Tocharian. A word for the shaft or pole of a wagon is known in Hittite, Indic, Greek and Slavic. Harness is known in Hittite and Sanskrit. Axle is known in Indic, Greek, Latin, Celtic, Baltic, Slavic, Germanic and Tocharian. A fairly ubiquitous term for navel in the Indo-European languages is also frequently applied to the nave of a wheel. The word for yoke, normally associated with paired draught, is attested in Hittite, Indic, Greek, Latin, Germanic, Baltic, Slavic, Celtic, and Armenian. A verb indicating to ride or travel *by vehicle* is attested in Indic, Iranian, Greek, Italic, Baltic and Germanic. The reconstruction of wheeled vehicles to Proto-Indo-European is universally recognized by linguists and is not based, as Renfrew seems to imply, solely on a Sanskrit-Latin correspondence.

26 Friedrich (1966), Wordig (1970), and Gates (1971) all argue that Proto-Indo-European kinship was of the Omaha III type; Huld (1981) suggests that it was Omaha II or IV. Beekes (1976) maintains that there is no solid evidence for an Omaha-type kinship system in Proto-Indo-European. Similarly, Szemerenyi (1977) rejects the Omaha classification and, like Beekes, emphasizes the close role of ego with mother's brother (avunculate) without accepting the terminological identities, for example, FaFa-MoBr, postulated for the Omaha system. It is possible to assume confidently that the Proto-Indo-Europeans evidence a patrilineal system and that in the history of some subgroups there is evidence for a confusion of terms across generations, for example, FaFa and MoBr or SoSo with SiSo. Of the classic textbook kinship systems, the Indo-European languages suggest a system probably closer to Omaha than any other; however, it falls far short of replicating the classic Omaha system with its series of skewing, merging and half-sibling rules. Debate revolves particularly about the issue of whether this terminological mixing of generations in some Indo-European subgroups reveals traces of an original system which represents at least one set of characteristics (of a constellation of other features nowhere clearly argued) for an Omaha kinship type, or whether it represents later developments within the various Indo-European subgroups as their own kinship systems evolved to accommodate changing social relationships. It is useful to remember that other than an association with patrilineality (a feature which we could ascribe to Indo-European kinship without this debate), identifying one's kinship as Omaha does not appear to provide us with any further information about the Indo-Europeans.

27 Szemerenyi (1977, 125–149) provides a thorough summary of all the arguments concerning the word *arya-* and concludes that it is not even Indo-European but a Near Eastern, probably Ugaritic, loan word meaning 'kinsman, companion'.

28 Another approach to the dating of Proto-Indo-European is glottochronology (or lexicostatistics) which may be likened to the linguistic version of radiocarbon dating. It is based on the assumption that languages that once shared the same genetic ancestor will diverge from one another through the replacement of a basic vocabulary at a constant rate. A measurement of the shared or replaced words from a list of the basic vocabulary (usually a list of 100 or 200 words) is then computed into approximate calendar years. The technique, at least for determining the time depth of linguistic separations, has not been generally accepted by linguists and it has been challenged both on the basis of its theoretical premise (that languages experience a constant rate of vocabulary 'decay') and the very real

difficulties of its practical execution. When applied to the separation of the Indo-European languages from one another (see Swadesh, M., 'Unas Correlaciones de Arqueología y Linguistica', in P. Bosch Gimpera, *El Problema Indoeuropeo*, Mexico, 1960; also H. Wittman, *IF* 74 (1969): 1–10) the results normally suggest that the earliest divergences within the Indo-European family began about 4500–3500 BC. Many, if not most, linguists prefer to exercise their own intuitive sense of time reckoning for Proto-Indo-European based on the observed differences through time of historically attested dialects such as the Romance languages.

29 The r/n stems are heteroclitics, that is, the stem of the noun alters from an *r* in the nominative-accusative cases to an *n* in the other cases, for example, Hittite nominative *wader* 'water' but genitive *wedenas*. Traces of these are found in other Indo-European languages, such as Sanskrit *yakṛt* 'liver' but genitive *yaknas*, or Latin *iecur* but *iecinoris*. Normally, the other Indo-European languages levelled the paradigms off according to a single form, for example, Lithuanian *vasara* 'summer' but Old Church Slavonic *vesna* 'spring', from a Proto-Indo-European *wes-r/n-*. Only in Hittite were the r/n stem nouns still productive and not remnant archaisms.

30 I have intentionally omitted from the 'homeland' discussion all those hydronymic systems that embrace large portions of Europe as too suspect to warrant extended consideration in the main body of this text. These begin with Jan Rozwadowski's attempt in 1913 (*Rocznik Slawistyczny* 6: 39–73) to define an 'Old European' seat for the Indo-Europeans in Northern and Eastern Europe on the basis of the Indo-European etymologies for many of the major rivers in these regions. Perhaps the most famous 'system' was that of Hans Krahe's 'Alteuropäisch' (Old European) river names (see *Saeculum* 8 (1957): 1–16; also *Unsere Ältesten Flussnamen*, Wiesbaden) that spanned Europe from the Atlantic to the Baltic and were allegedly formed prior to the emergence of Celtic, Germanic, Italic, Venetic and Messapic at a time depth of approximately 1500 BC. W. P. Schmid (see *IF* 77 (1972): 1–18, and most recently in Skomal and Polome (1987)) has argued that these river names were established even earlier, prior to the differentiation of all the Indo-European languages, and that they could best be localized to the Baltic region. One of his 'proofs' for the Proto-Indo-European age of his names is that some can only be provided a meaning by appealing to words in individual Indo-European languages outside their area of occurrence, for example, Baltic river names such as *Indus*, *Indura*, *Indra* are only explainable by reference to Sanskrit *indu-* 'drops', therefore, Schmid argues that the river was named in the Baltic region before the divergence of the Indo-European languages. I find such conclusions remarkable since the Sanskrit word *indu-* 'drops' is described as 'without certain etymology' in the standard etymological dictionary of Sanskrit, and even where it is provided with an Indo-European etymology, such as Proto-Indo-European *oid-* 'swell', this would surely suggest an independent development in Indo-Aryan and there can be no claim to Proto-Indo-European status for such a river name. On the basis of such evidence I would have thought that the Baltic river names lacked any convincing etymology, and do not preserve a Proto-Indo-European word. The roots of many of Krahe's river names are often indistinctive (*ar-*, *is-*, *ver-*, *nar-*, *sal-*, and so on) and have also been employed to show the presence of non-Indo-Europeans in Iberia and even Dravidian speakers in Europe! Hans Kuhn (see *KZ* 71 (1954): 129–161; also *Anzeiger für Deutschen Altertum und Deutsche Literatur* 78 (1967): 1–22) who presented a detailed criticism of all this evidence, has himself introduced a second 'Old European' system of river names (see *Namn och Bygd* 59 (1971): 1–22). His alternative system is built of different elements from the first which supposedly represented the residue of non-Indo-European substrate names, especially in Northwest Europe, but extending all the way from Anatolia to Ireland. See D. P. Block, *Namn och Bygd* 59 (1971): 149–161, for a critical review of some of these ideas.

31 The place of the accent in the Indo-European languages may be fixed on a certain syllable, usually the first syllable in Germanic, Czech and Irish; the penultimate syllable in Polish and Latin; or it may be 'free' and move from one syllable to another depending on a given grammatical form, for example, Sanskrit, Lithuanian, some Slavic languages and Greek. The free accent is seen in the nominative, accusative and genitive forms for the word for 'foot' in Sanskrit and Greek:

	Sanskrit	Greek
nominative	pát	poús
accusative	pádam	póda
genitive	padás	podós

32 'Linguistic palaeontology' was first coined by Adolphe Pictet in 1859. His horrendously uncritical treatment of the lexical material (he assumed *a priori* that the homeland was in Bactria), plus many subsequent uncritical uses of the linguistic evidence, brought the name into disrepute. Other terms for describing the technique of reconstructing the proto-culture of a linguistic group through the comparative method include 'Wörter and Sachen' (words and things), 'lexico-cultural reconstruction' or, most recently, 'interpretive etymology'. See Diebold (1987) for a review of linguistic ways to prehistory. One should note that this technique has been widely applied outside Indo-European, for example, with Uralic, Semitic, Athapaskan and Algonquin.

33 See, for example, J. Jorgensen, *Salish Language and Culture: A Statistical Analysis of the Internal Relationships, History and Evolution*, The Hague, 1969. On a broader scale, a significant degree of correlation between major Amerindian groups and North American culture areas can be observed (see H. Driver, *Indians of North America*, 1969) although there are also major non-correlations, especially evident among linguistic groups that have spread over considerable distances, such as Athapascan, Uto-Aztecan.

34 Renfrew (1987) presents two models of Indo-Iranian origins. Model A derives them directly from the Neolithic populations of Western Asia while Model B takes them from the steppe (see note 11).

35 The economic foundations of the Seraglazovo culture remains problematic. There is some evidence for domestic animals in the Caspian depression and on the west bank of the Volga, however, an intensive survey on the east in the Volga-Ural interfluve has recently uncovered well-preserved settlements that yielded only wild faunas (Igor Vasiliev, personal communication).

36 The relationship between the Caspian and the Volga-Ural region is a perennial topic of debate among Soviet archaeologists. Witness most recently how G. Matyushin (in Zvelebil (1986): 133–150) links the southern Urals with the south Caspian by way of *1* their geometric lithic industry (Yangelsk culture of Urals; Belt, Hotu, Shanidar, Karim Shahir, Jarmo); *2* ovicaprids (most southern Ural Neolithic sites; north Mesopotamia, northern Iran); and *3* Mediterranean physical type (Mullino II in southern Urals; basic population known from

south Caspian). According to Matyushin all of these contacts long preceded the seventh millennium BC. E. Kuzmina (1986), however, rejects the derivation of the steppe economies from the south Caspian pointing out the unfavourable climatic conditions prevailing between the two zones, the absence of domestic livestock in the east Caspian Kelteminar culture which would have been contemporary with these supposed 'southern' impulses, and the meagre remains of ovicaprids in the frequently cited south Caspian sites such as Djebel Cave. Kuzmina assumes that the impulses producing the Neolithic economy were ultimately derived from the Balkan-Danubian region. I. Vasiliev (personal communication) has recently indicated that, although connections between the south Caspian and steppe region are not to be denied, the primary orientation of the populations north of the Caspian have been with the Caucasus and Pontic regions from the Mesolithic through to the Bronze Age.

37 J. Makkay (in Skomal and Polome (1987)) has recently offered a new defence of the LBK theory. He argues that it displays the necessary Neolithic economy, continuity over space and time suggesting a common language, correlation with the area of Old European hydronyms and avoidance of areas of suspected non-Indo-European substrates (Mediterranean, Atlantic Europe), is strategically situated to explain Indo-European expansions across the Alps into Italy, offers a donor region for the spread of Indo-European languages into Northern Europe (TRB), shows no evidence of having been invaded from elsewhere, and so on. He argues that the European and Asian (Indo-Iranian) languages had been separated before the Neolithic or at its very beginning because of the absence of agricultural terms in the Indo-Iranian languages. He draws the dividing line along the Dnieper and accepts those theories that derive domesticated animals in the steppe zone either from the Caucasus or the Caspian. The spread of Tocharian (with its centum relations in Europe) to Asia is regarded as a mystery. Specific objections to this theory include: *1* Indo-Iranian languages do reflect all the domestic livestock terms, names for secondary products and even words like 'plough' which are clearly associated with agriculture. *2* If the domestic animals entered the steppe from the Caucasus or the Caspian, why does Indo-Iranian share precisely the same terms with those attributed to the Balkan-Danubian zone? Makkay realizes rightly that we cannot project the Balkan-Danubian cultures east of the Dnieper to bring them into an historical relationship with the steppe peoples but he fails to generate an acceptable alternative that would explain the Indo-Iranians. A solution to the Indo-European homeland problem that cannot explain the Indo-Iranians is not a really viable solution.

38 Tilak's 'polar theory' for Aryan origins was not a bizarre quirk of a single individual but rather the culmination of an extremely long tradition of analysis of Indo-Aryan myth, for example, poems that indicate a home in the north where a day and a night lasted six months each, the Pole star rises to the zenith, and so on. A modern review of this 'northern cycle' of myths can be found in Bongard-Levin (1980) who argues that Indo-Aryan, Iranian and Scythian traditions (and by cultural contact also Greeks) all shared a common mythology of a northern mountainous land which, he argues, could only have been acquired in their prior common home on the Pontic-Caspian steppe.

Bibliography

A general reader wishing to acquire a more fundamental basis in the structure of the Indo-European languages might wish to consult Baldi, P., *An Introduction to the Indo-European Languages*, Carbondale, Ill., 1983, or Lockwood, W. B., *Indo-European Philology*, London, 1969. The standard general survey of the various Indo-European languages is Lockwood, W. B., *A Panorama of the Indo-European Languages*, London, 1972. There are two basic comparative Indo-European dictionaries: Buck, C. D., *A Comparative Dictionary of the Indo-European Languages*, Chicago, 1949, arranges the data by subject matter, while the basic tool of linguists is Pokorny, J., *Indo-Germanisches Etymologisches Wörterbuch*, Bern, 1959, which is arranged according to Proto-Indo-European root. There are a number of handbooks on Indo-European culture but the most extensive and still quite useful is Schrader, O. and A. Nehring, *Reallexikon der Indogermanischen Altertumskunde*, 2 vols, Berlin and Leipzig, 1917–1929. A good introduction to the ideas of Georges Dumézil and other comparative mythologists is Littleton, C. S., *The New Comparative Mythology*, Berkeley and Los Angeles, 1982. For a brief review of many of the theories concerning the Indo-European homeland see Mallory, J. P., 'A short history of the Indo-European problem', *JIES* 1 (1973): 21–65, while Scherer, A., *Die Urheimat der Indo-Germanen*, Darmstadt, 1968, offers a collection of previous works on the problem. An annual bibliography of all works related to the Indo-European languages (on the order of 2,000 entries per year!) is provided in the journal *Die Sprache*.

The references below were selected either on the basis of their fundamental importance in Indo-European studies or because they provided primary information utilized in preparing this book. In the interest of brevity, and excepting instances where authors are specifically mentioned in text, most basic conference proceedings and multi-authored collections, especially Russian and Ukrainian, are listed only by editor and title.

Abbreviations *CAH* – *Cambridge Ancient History*, *IF* – *Indogermanische Forschungen*, *JIES* – *Journal of Indo-European Studies*, *KZ* – *Zeitschrift für Vergleichende Sprachwissenschaft*, *SA* – *Sovetskaya Arkheologiya*

CHAPTER ONE

Anttila, R., *An Introduction to Historical and Comparative Linguistics*, New York, 1972.
Baldi, P., *An Introduction to the Indo-European Languages*, Carbondale, Ill., 1983.
Delbrück, B., *Introduction to the Study of Language*, Amsterdam, 1882.
Lockwood, W. B., *Indo-European Philology*, London, 1969.
——, *A Panorama of Indo-European Languages*, London, 1972.
Meillet, A., *Introduction à l'Étude Comparative des Langues Indo-Européennes*, Paris, 1922.
Pedersen, H., *The Discovery of Language*, Bloomington, Indiana, 1931.
Robins, R. H., *A Short History of Linguistics*, London, 1979.
Szemerenyi, O., *Einführung in die Vergleichende Sprachwissenschaft*, Darmstadt, 1970.
——, 'Recent Development in Indo-European Linguistics', in *Transactions of the Philological Society* (1985): 1–71.

CHAPTER TWO

Anatolia

Adrados, F., 'The Archaic Structure of Hittite: The Crux of the Problem', *JIES* 10 (1982): 1–35.
Carruba, O., 'Origini e Preistoria degli Indo-Europei d'Anatolia', *Revista di Filologia* 97 (1969): 1–30.
Crossland, R. A., 'Immigrants from the North', *CAH* 1/2 (1971): 824–876.
Friedrich, J. et al., *Altkleinasiatische Sprachen*, Leiden, 1969.
MacQueen, J., *The Hittites and Their Contemporaries in Asia Minor*, London, 1986.
Mellaart, J., 'Anatolia and the Indo-Europeans', *JIES* 9 (1981): 135–149.
Puhvel, J., 'Dialectal Aspects of the Anatolian Branch of Indo-European', in H. Birnbaum and J. Puhvel (eds), *Ancient Indo-European Dialects*, Berkeley, 1966: 235–247.
Singer, I., 'Hittites and Hattians in Anatolia at the Beginning of the Second Millennium BC', *JIES* 9 (1981): 119–134.
Steiner, G., 'The Role of the Hittites in Ancient Anatolia', *JIES* 9 (1981): 150–173.
Winn, M., 'Thoughts on the Question of Indo-European Movements in Anatolia and Iran', *JIES* 2 (1974): 117–142.
——, 'Burial Evidence and the Kurgan Culture in Eastern Anatolia *c*. 3000 BC: An Interpretation', *JIES* 9 (1981): 113–118.
Yakar, J., 'The Indo-Europeans and Their Impact on Anatolian Cultural Development', *JIES* 9 (1981): 94–112.

Phrygians

Barnett, R. D., 'Phrygia and the People of Anatolia in the Iron Age', *CAH* 2/2 (1975): 417–442.
Bittel, K., *Grundzüge der Vor- und Frühgeschichte Kleinasiens*, Tübingen, 1963.
Haas, O., *Die Phrygischen Sprachdenkmaler*, Sofia, 1966.

Armenians

Diakonov, I. M., *Predystoriya Armyanskogo Naroda*, Erevan, 1968.
——, 'Hurro-Urartian Borrowings in Old Armenian', *Journal of the American Oriental Society* 105 (1985): 597–603.
Greppin, J., 'Hittite-z(a), Armenian z-, and the Theory of Armeno-Hittite Loan Words', *JIES* 3 (1975): 87–94.

Indo-Iranian (*general*)

Asimov, M. S. et al. (eds), *Ethnic Problems of the History of Central Asia in the Early Period*, Moscow, 1981.
Bongard-Levin, G. M., *The Origin of Aryans*, New Delhi, 1980.
Grantovsky, E. A., '"Seraya keramika", "raspisnaya keramika" i indoirantsy', in Asimov et al. (eds), *Ethnic Problems of the History of Central Asia in the Early Period*, Moscow, 1981: 245–273.
Gupta, S. P., *Archaeology of Soviet Central Asia and the Indian Borderlands*, Delhi, 1979.
Jettmar, K., 'Die Steppenkulturen und die Indoiraner des Plateaus', *Irania Antiqua* 9 (1972): 65–93.
Kuzmina, E. E., 'O Nekotorykh Arkheologicheskikh Aspektakh Problemy Proiskhozhdeniya Indoirantsev', *Peredneaziatsky Sbornik* 4 (1986): 169–232.
Mandelshtam, A. M., *Pamyatniki Epokhi Bronzy v Yuzhnom Tadzhikstane*, Leningrad, 1968.
Masson, V. M. and V. Sarianidi, *Central Asia*, London and New York, 1972.

Mitanni

Ghirshman, R., *L'Iran et la Migration des Indo-Aryens et des Iraniens*, Leiden, 1977.
Littauer, M. A. and J. H. Crouwel, *Wheeled Vehicles and Ridden Animals in the Ancient Near East*, Leiden, 1979.
Mayrhofer, M., *Die Indo-Arier im Alten Vorderasien*,

Wiesbaden, 1966.
——, *Die Arier im Vorderen Orient-ein Mythos?*, Vienna, 1974.
Piggott, S., *The Earliest Wheeled Transport*, London, 1983.
Indo-Aryan
Allchin, B. and R., *The Rise of Civilization in India and Pakistan*, Cambridge, 1982.
Burrow, T., *The Sanskrit Language*, London, 1955.
——, 'The Proto-Indoaryans', *Journal of the Royal Asiatic Society* (1973): 123–140.
McAlpin, D., 'Proto-Elamo-Dravidian: The Evidence and its Implications', *Transactions of the American Philosophical Society* 71 (1981): pt. 3.
Iranian
Diakonov, I. M., 'Media', *Cambridge History of Iran* 2 (1985): 36–148.
Frye, R., *The History of Iran*, Munich, 1984.
Ghirshman, R., *L'Iran et la Migration des Indo-Aryens et des Iraniens*, Leiden, 1977.
Winn, M. M., 'Thoughts on the Question of Indo-European Movements in Anatolia and Iran', *JIES* 2 (1974): 117–142.
Young, T. C., 'The Iranian Migration into the Zagros', *Iran* 5 (1967): 11–34.
Tocharian
Heine-Geldern, R., 'Das Tocharerproblem und die Pontische Wanderung', *Saeculum* 2 (1951): 225–255.
Lane, G., 'On the Interrelationship of the Tocharian dialects', in H. Birnbaum and J. Puhvel (eds), *Ancient Indo-European Dialects*, 1966: 213–233.
——, 'Tocharian: Indo-European and non-Indo-European relationships', in G. Cardona (ed.) et al., *Indo-European and Indo-Europeans*, Philadelphia, 1970: 73–88.
Liu-Mau-Tsai, *Kutscha und seine Beziehungen zu China vom 2 Jh. bis zum 6 Jh. n. Ch.*, Wiesbaden, 1969.
Pulleybank, E., 'Chinese and Indo-Europeans', *Journal of the Royal Asiatic Society* (1966): 9–39.
——, 'The Chinese and their neighbors in prehistoric and early historic times', in D. Keightly (ed.), *The Origins of Chinese Civilizations*, Berkeley and London, 1983: 411–466.
CHAPTER THREE
Europeans (general)
Geipel, J., *The Europeans*, London, 1969.
Greeks
Arditis, Elly (ed.), *Acta of the 2nd International Colloquium of Aegean Prehistory: The first arrival of Indo-Europeans in Greece*, Athens, 1972.
Best, J. G. P. and Y. Yadin, *The arrival of the Greeks*, Amsterdam, 1973.
Cadogan, G., *The End of the Early Bronze Age in the Aegean*, Leiden, 1986.
Chadwick, J., 'The prehistory of the Greek language', *CAH* 2/2 (1975): 805–819.
Crossland, R. A. and A. Birchall (eds), *Bronze Age Migrations in the Aegean*, London, 1973.
Davies, A. M., 'The Linguistic Evidence', in G. Cadogan (ed.), *The End of the Early Bronze Age in the Aegean*, Leiden, 1986: 93–123.
Haley, J. and C. Blegen, 'The Coming of the Greeks', *American Journal of Archaeology* 32 (1928): 141–154.
Hammond, N. G. L., *Migrations and Invasions in Greece and Adjacent Areas*, Park Ridge, N. J., 1976.
Häusler A., 'Die Indoeuropäisierung Griechenlands nach

Aussage der Grab- und Bestattungssitten', *Slovenska Archeologia* 24–1 (1981): 59–66.
Hester, D. A., 'Pre-Greek Place Names in Greece and Asia Minor', *Revue Hittite et Asianique* 15 (1957): 107–119.
——, 'Pelasgian – A New Indo-European Language?', *Lingua* 13 (1964): 335–384.
——, 'Recent Developments in Mediterranean "Substrate" Studies', *Minos* 9 (1968): 219–235.
Hiller, S., 'Zur Frage der Griechischen Einwanderung', *Mitteil. d. österreich. Arbeitsgemeinschaft f. Ur- und Frühgeschichte* 32 (1982): 41–48.
——, 'Zur Ethnogenese der Griechen', *Symposium: Ethnogenese Europäischer Völker*, Mainz, 1982.
Hooker, J. T., 'The Coming of the Greeks', *Historia* 15 (1976): 129–145.
——, *Mycenaean Greece*, London, 1976.
Merlingen, W., 'Fair Play for "Pelasgian"', *Lingua* 18 (1967): 144–167.
Mylonas, G., 'The Luvian Invasions of Greece', *Hesperia* 31 (1962): 284–309.
Palmer, L. R., *The Greek Language*, London, 1980.
Rutter, J. B., *Ceramic change in the Aegean Early Bronze Age* (Occasional Paper No. 5, Institute of Archaeology, UCLA), Los Angeles, 1979.
——, 'The Gray-Burnished Pottery of the Early Helladic III Period: The Ancestry of Gray Minyan', *Hesperia* 52 (1983): 327–355.
Sakellariou, M. B., 'Linguistic and Ethnic Groups in Prehistoric Greece', in *History of the Hellenic World: Prehistory and Protohistory*, University Park, Penn. (1974): 364–389.
——, *Peuples Préhelléniques d'Origine Indo-Européenne*, Athens, 1977.
Van Royen, R. A. and B. H. Isaac, *The Arrival of the Greeks: The Evidence from the Settlements*, Amsterdam, 1979.
Thracians
Danov, C., *Althrakien*, Berlin and New York, 1976.
Detschew, D., *Die Thrakische Sprachreste*, Vienna, 1957.
Hoddinott, R. F., *The Thracians*, London, 1981.
Polome, E., 'Balkan Languages', *CAH* 3/1 (1982): 866–888.
Vulpe, R. (ed.) *Actes du IIe Congrès International de Thracologie*, 3 vols, Bucharest, 1980.
Illyrians
Katičić, R., *Ancient Languages of the Balkans*, The Hague-Paris, 1976.
Prendi, F., 'The Prehistory of Albania' *CAH* 3/1 (1982): 187–237.
Stipčević, A., *The Illyrians*, New Jersey, 1977.
Slavs
Baran, V. D. (ed.) *Problemy Etnogeneza Slavyan*, Kiev, 1978.
Birnbaum, H., 'The Original Homeland of the Slavs and the Problem of Early Slavic Linguistic Contacts', *JIES* 1 (1973): 407–421.
——, *Common Slavic*, Cambridge, Mass., 1975.
Chropovsky, B. (ed.), *Rapports du IIIe Congrès International d'Archéologie Slave*, 2 vols, Bratislava, 1979.
Gimbutas, M., *The Slavs*, London, 1971.
Rybakov, B. A., *Gerodotova Skifiya*, Moscow, 1979.
Sedov, V. V., *Proiskhozhdenie i Rannyaya Istoriya Slavyan*, Moscow, 1979.
Trubachev, O., 'Linguistics and Ethnogenesis of the Slavs', *JIES* 13 (1985): 203–256.
Werner, J., 'Zur Herkunft und Ausbreitung der Anten und

Sklavenen', in *Actes du VIIe Congrès International des Sciences Préhistoriques et Protohistoriques*, Belgrad, 1971: 243–252.

Balts

Gimbutas, M., *The Balts*, London, 1963.

Schmidt, W. P., Baltische Gewassernamen und das Vorgeschichtliche Europa, *IF* 77 (1972): 1–18.

Germans

Krüger, B., *Die Germanen*, 2 vols, Berlin, 1983.

Todd, M., *The Northern Barbarians 100 BC–AD 300*, London, 1975.

Italy

Barker, G., *Landscape and Society*, London, 1981.

Durante, M. 'Lingua e Dialetti dell'Italia Antica', in A. L. Prosdocimi (ed.), *Popoli e Civilta dell'Italia Antica*, vol. 6, Padua, 1978.

Pallottino, M., *The Etruscans*, London, 1975.

Poultney, J. W., 'The Language of the North Picene Inscriptions', *JIES* 7 (1979): 49–64.

Pulgram, E., *The Tongues of Italy*, Cambridge, Mass., 1958.

——, *Italic, Latin, Italian*, Heidelberg, 1978.

Ridgway, D. and F. (eds), *Italy before the Romans*, London, 1979.

Celts

Filip, J., *Celtic Civilization and its Heritage*, Prague, 1977.

Greene, D., 'The Coming of the Celts: The Linguistic Viewpoint', *Proc. VIth Internat. Congress of Celtic Studies*, Dublin, (1983): 131–137.

Harbison, P., 'The Coming of the Indo-Europeans to Ireland: An Archaeological Viewpoint', *JIES* 3 (1975): 101–119.

MacEoin, G., 'The Celticity of Celtic Ireland', in K. H. Schmidt (ed.), *Geschichte und Kultur der Kelten*, Heidelberg, 1986: 161–174.

Mallory, J. P., 'The Origins of the Irish', *Journal of Irish Archaeology* 2 (1984): 65–69.

Piggott, S., 'The Coming of the Celts: The Archaeological Argument', *Proc. VIth Internat. Congress of Celtic Studies*, Dublin (1983): 138–148.

Powell, T. G., *The Celts*, London and New York, 1980.

Savory, H. N., *Spain and Portugal*, London and New York, 1968.

Schmidt, K. H., *Die Festlandkeltischen Sprachen*, Innsbrucker Beiträge zur Sprachwissenschaft 18, 1977.

——, *Geschichte und Kultur der Kelten*, Heidelberg, 1986.

Untermann, J., *Monumenta Linguarum Hispanicarum*, Wiesbaden, 1975.

Wagner, H., 'The Origin of the Celts in the Light of Linguistic Geography', *Transactions of the Philological Society* (1969): 203–250.

CHAPTER FOUR

Indo-European culture (general)

Arntz, H. (ed.), *Germanen und Indogermanen: Volkstum, Sprache, Heimat, Kultur; Festschrift für Herman Hirt*, 2 vols, Heidelberg, 1936.

Benveniste, E., *Indo-European Language and Society*, Coral Gables, Florida, 1973.

Buck, C. D., *A Dictionary of the Principal Indo-European Languages*, Chicago, 1949.

Cardona, G., H. Hoenigswald and A. Senn (eds), *Indo-European and Indo-Europeans*, Philadelphia, 1970.

Carnoy, A., *Les Indo-Européens*, Brussels, Paris, 1921.

Crevatin, F., *Richerche di Antichita Indeuropee*, Trieste, 1979.

Devoto, G., *Origini Indeuropee*, Florence, 1962.

Feist, S., *Kultur, Ausbreitung und Herkunft der Indogermanen*, Berlin, 1913.

Gamkrelidze, T. V. and V. V. Ivanov, *Indoevropeysky Yazyk i Indoevropeytsy*, 2 vols, Tbilisi, 1984.

Georgiev, V., *Introduzione alla Storia delle Lingue Indeuropee*, Rome, 1966.

Hirt, H., *Die Indogermanen*, 2 vols, Strassburg, 1905–07.

Mallory, J. P., 'Time Perspective and Proto-Indo-European Culture', *World Archaeology* 8 (1976): 44–56.

Mayrhofer, M., W. Meid, B. Schlerath and R. Schmitt (eds), *Antiquitates Indogermanicae*, Innsbrucker Beiträge zur Sprachwissenschaft 12, 1974.

Pokorny, J., *Indogermanisches Etymologisches Wörterbuch*, Bern, 1959.

Polome, E. (ed.), *The Indo-Europeans in the Fourth and Third Millennia*, Ann Arbor, 1982.

Scherer, A., 'Hauptprobleme der Indogermanischen Altertumskunde (seit 1940)', *Kratylos* 1 (1956): 3–21.

——, 'Indogermanische Altertumskunde (seit 1956)', *Kratylos* 10 (1965): 1–24.

Schrader, O., *Prehistoric Antiquities of the Aryan Peoples*, London, 1890.

Schrader, O. and A. Nehring, *Reallexikon der Indogermanischen Altertumskunde*, 2 vols, Berlin, Leipzig, 1917–29.

Skomal, S. N. and E. Polome (eds), *Proto-Indo-European: The Archaeology of a Linguistic Problem*, Washington, D.C., 1987.

Environment and Material Culture

Adams, D. Q., 'Designations of the Cervidae in Proto-Indo-European', *JIES* 13 (1985): 269.

Barber, E. J. W., 'The PIE Notion of Cloth and Clothing', *JIES* 3 (1975): 294–320.

Diebold, R., 'Contribution to the Indo-European Salmon Problem', in W. Christie (ed.), *Current Progress in Historical Linguistics*, Amsterdam, 1976: 341–387.

——, *The Evolution of Indo-European Nomenclature for Salmonid Fish: The Case of 'Huchen'*, Washington, D.C., 1985.

Friedrich, P., *Proto-Indo-European Trees*, Chicago, 1970.

Hamp, E. P., 'Fish', *JIES* 1 (1973): 507–511.

Krogmann, W., 'Das Buchenargument', *KZ* 72 (1955): 1–29; 73 (1956): 1–25.

——, 'Das Lachsargument *KZ* 76 (1960): 161–178.

Maher, J. P., '*H₄ekmon: "(stone) axe" and "sky" in I-E/ Battle-axe Culture*', *JIES* 1 (1973): 441–462.

Mallory J. P., 'Indo-European and Kurgan Fauna I: Wild Mammals', *JIES* 10 (1982): 193–222.

——, 'Indo-European and Kurgan Fauna II: Fish', *JIES* 11 (1983): 263–279.

Kinship and Social System

Beekes, R., 'Uncle and Nephew', *JIES* 4 (1976): 43–63.

Bremmer, J., 'Avunculate and Fosterage', *JIES* 4 (1976): 65–78.

Friedrich, P., 'Proto-Indo-European Kinship', *Ethnology* 5 (1966): 1–36.

Gates, H., 'The Kinship Terminology of Homeric Greek', *International Journal of American Linguistics*, Memoir 27, 1971.

Huld, M., 'CuChulainn and his IE kin', *Zeitschrift für Celtische Philologie* 38 (1981): 238–241.

Scharfe, H., 'The Vedic Word for "King"', *Journal of the American Oriental Society* 105 (1985): 543–548.

Sihler, A., 'The Etymology of PIE *rēǵ- "king" etc.', *JIES* 5 (1977): 221–246.

Szemerényi, O., 'Studies in the Kinship Terminology of the Indo-European Languages', *Acta Iranica* 7 (1977): 1–240.

Wikander, S., *Der Arische Männerbund*, Lund, 1938.

Wordig, F., 'A Generative-Extensionist Analysis of the Proto-Indo-European Kinship System' (Ph.D. thesis, Xerox Microfilms), 1970.

Aryans

Dumézil, G., 'L'Ari et les Aryas', Appendix II of *Les Dieux Souverains des Indo-Européens*, Paris, 1977.

Thieme, P., *Der Fremdling im Rgveda*, Heidelberg, 1938.

Szemerényi, O., 'Studies in the Kinship Terminology of the Indo-European Languages', *Acta Iranica* 7 (1977): 1–240 (125–149).

CHAPTER FIVE

Dumézil, G., 'Dieux Cassites et Dieux Védiques à Propos d'un Bronze du Louristan', *Revue Hittite et Asianique* 11 (1950): 18–37.

——, *L'Idéologie Tripartie des Indo-Européens*, Brussels, 1958.

——, *Les Dieux Souverains des Indo-Européens*, Paris, 1977.

Grottanelli, C., 'Yoked Horses, Twins, and the Powerful Lady', *JIES* 14 (1986): 125–152.

Larson, G. J., C. S. Littleton and J. Puhvel (eds), *Myth in Indo-European Antiquity*, Berkeley and Los Angeles, 1974.

Lincoln, B., 'The Hellhound', *JIES* 7 (1979): 273–285.

——, *Priests, Warriors and Cattle*, Berkeley and Los Angeles, 1981.

Littleton, C. S., *The New Comparative Mythology*, Berkeley and Los Angeles, 1982.

Mallory, J. P., 'The Ritual Treatment of the Horse in the Early Kurgan Tradition', *JIES* 9 (1981): 205–226.

O'Brien, S., 'Indo-European Eschatology: A Model', *JIES* 4 (1976): 296–320.

Puhvel, J. (ed.), *Myth and Law Among the Indo-Europeans*, Berkeley and Los Angeles, 1970.

Puhvel, J., 'Aspects of Equine Functionality', in *Myth and Law*, 1970: 159–72.

——, 'Remus et frater', *History of Religions* 15 (1975): 146–157.

——, 'Victimal Hierarchies in Indo-European Animal Sacrifice, *American Journal of Philology* 99 (1978): 354–362.

CHAPTER SIX

Adrados, F. R., *Die Räumliche und Zeitliche Differenzierung des Indoeuropäischen im Lichte der Vor- und Frühgeschichte*, Innsbrucker Beiträge zur Sprachwissenschaft Nr. 27, 1982.

Barker, G., *Prehistoric Farming in Europe*, Cambridge, 1985.

Bosch-Gimpera, P., *Les Indo-européens: Problèmes Archéologiques*, Paris, 1961.

Childe, V. G., *The Aryans*, London, 1926.

Crossland, R. A., 'Immigrants from the North, *CAH* 1/2 (1971): 824–876.

Danilenko, V. N., *Eneolit Ukrainy*, Kiev, 1974.

Diakonov, I. M., 'On the Original Home of the Speakers of Indo-European', *JIES* 13 (1985): 92–174.

Dressler, W., 'Methodische Vorfragen bei der Bestimmung der "Urheimat"', *Die Sprache* 11 (1965): 25–60.

Gamkrelidze, T. and V. Ivanov, 'The Ancient Near East and the Indo-European Question [and] The Migration of Tribes Speaking Indo-European Dialects, *JIES* 13 (1985): 3–91.

Gimbutas, M., 'The Beginning of the Bronze Age in Europe and the Indo-Europeans: 3500–2500 BC', *JIES* 1 (1973): 163–214.

——, 'The First Wave of Eurasian Steppe Pastoralists into Copper Age Europe', *JIES* 5 (1977): 277–338.

——, 'The Kurgan Wave 2 (c. 3400–3200 BC) into Europe and the Following Transformation of Culture', *JIES* 8 (1980): 273–315.

——, 'Primary and Secondary Homeland of the Indo-Europeans', *JIES* 13 (1985): 185–202.

Gornung, B., *K Voprosu ob Obrazovaniy Indoevropeyskoy Obshchnosti*, Moscow, 1964.

Koppers, W. (ed.), *Indogermanen- und Germanenfrage; Neue Wege zu ihrer Lösung*, Salzburg and Leipzig, 1936.

Lamb, S., 'Linguistic Diversification and Extinction in North America', *XXXV Congreso Internacional de Americanistas*, 2 (1964): 457–464.

Mallory, J. P., 'A Short History of the Indo-European Problem', *JIES* 1 (1973): 21–65.

Mallory, J. P. and M. E. Huld, 'Proto-Indo-European "silver"', *KZ* 97 (1984): 1–12.

Meid, W., 'Probleme der Räumlichen und Zeitlichen Gliederung des Indo-Germanischen', in H. Rix (ed.), *Flexion und Wortbildung*, Wiesbaden, 1976: 204–218.

Meillet, A., *Les Dialects Indo-Européens*, Paris, 1922.

Pisani, V., *Indogermanisch und Europa*, Munich, 1974.

Porzig, W., *Die Gliederung des Indogermanischen Sprachgebiets*, Heidelberg, 1954.

Pulgram, E., 'On Prehistoric Linguistic Expansion', in M. Halle et al. (eds), *For Roman Jakobson*, The Hague, 1956: 411–417.

Renfrew, C., 'Problems in the General Correlation of Archaeological and Linguistic Strata in Prehistoric Greece: The Model of Autochthonous Origin', in R. A. Crossland and A. Birchall (eds), *Bronze Age Migrations in the Aegean*, London, 1973: 263–276.

——, *Archaeology and Language: The Puzzle of Indo-European Origins*, London, 1987.

Scherer, A. (ed.), *Die Urheimat der Indogermanen*, Darmstadt, 1968.

Schlerath, B., *Die Indogermanen. Das Problem der Expansion eines Volkes im Lichte seiner Sozialen Struktur*, Innsbrucker Beiträge zur Sprachwissenschaft 8, 1973.

Schmid, W. P., 'Baltische Gewässernamen und das Vorgeschichtliche Europa', *IF* 77 (1972): 1–18.

Thieme, P., *Die Heimat der Indogermanischen Grundsprache*, Wiesbaden, 1954.

Uralic

Burrow, T., *The Sanskrit Language*, London, 1955.

Collinder, B., 'Hat das Uralische Verwandte?', *Acta Universitatis Upsaliensis* 1 (1965): 4.

Hajdu, P., 'Über die Alten Siedlungsräume der Uralischen Sprachfamilie', *Acta Linguistica* 14 (1964): 47–83.

——, 'Finnougrische Urheimatforschung', *Ural-Altäische Jahrbücher* 41 (1969): 252–264.

Joki, A. J., *Uralier und Indogermanen*, Helsinki, 1973.

Toivonen, Y., 'Zur Frage der Finnisch-Ugrischen Urheimat', *Suomalais-Ugrilaisen Seuran Aikakauskirja* 56 (1952): 1–41.

Uesson, A-M., *On Linguistic Affinity: The Indo-Uralic Problem*, Malmo, 1970.

Vuorela, T., *The Finno-Ugric Peoples*, Bloomington, 1962.

Semitic

Bomhard, A., 'The "Indo-European-Semitic" Hypothesis

Re-examined', *JIES* 5 (1977): 55–99.

Brunner, L., *Die Gemeinsamen Wurzeln des Semitischen und Indogermanischen Wortschatzes*, Bern and Munich, 1969.

Diakonov, I. M., 'On the Original Home of the Speakers of Indo-European', *JIES* 13 (1985): 92–174.

Gamkrelidze, T. and V. Ivanov, 'The Ancient Near East and the Indo-European Question [and] The Migration of Tribes Speaking Indo-European Dialects', *JIES* 13 (1985): 3–91.

Hodge, C. T., 'Indo-Europeans in the Near East', *Anthropological Linguistics* 23 (1981): 227–244.

Levin, S., *The Indo-European and Semitic Languages*, Albany, New York, 1971.

Kartvelian

Gamkrelidze, T. and V. Ivanov, 'Kartvelian and Indo-European: A Typological Comparison of Reconstructed Linguistic Systems', in *To Honor Roman Jakobson, I* (1967): 707–717.

——, 'The Ancient Near East and the Indo-European Question [and] The Migration of Tribes Speaking Indo-European Dialects', *JIES* 13 (1985): 3–91.

Machavariani, G. I., 'On the Problem of Indo-European-Kartvelian (South Caucasian) Typological Parallels', in *Trudy VII Mezhdunarodnogo Kongressa Antropologicheskikh i Etnographicheskikh Nauk*, Moscow, 5, 1964: 658–661.

Wagner, H., 'The Origin of the Celts in the Light of Linguistic Geography, *Transactions of the Philological Society* (1969): 203–250.

CHAPTER SEVEN

Agapov, S. A., I. B. Vasiliev and V. I. Pestrikova, Khvalynsky mogilnik i ego mesto v eneolite Vostochnoy Evropy, in *Arkheologiya Vostochno-Evropeyskoy Lesostepi*, Voronezh, 1979: 36–63.

Alekseevka, I. L., Zhensky obraz v antropomorfnoy skulpture epokhi eneolita, in *Pamyatniki Drevnego Iskusstva Severo-Zapadnogo Prichernomorya*, Kiev, 1986: 43–50.

Anthony, D. W., 'The "Kurgan Culture": A Reconsideration', *Current Anthropology* 27 (1986): 291–313.

Artemenko, I. I. et al. (eds), *Problemy Epokhy Bronzy Yuga Vostochnoy Evropy*, Donetsk, 1979.

——, *Arkheologiya Ukrainskoy SSSR*, 3 vols, Kiev, 1985.

Basin, S. G et al. (eds), *Drevnyaya Istoriya Povolzhya*, Kuibyshev, 1979.

——, *Volgo-Uralskaya Step i Lesostep v Epokhu Rannego Metalla*, Kuybyshev, 1982.

Chernyakov, I. T. and N. M. Shmagliy, 'Derevyannye psalii yamnoy kultury', *Arkheologiya* 42 (1983): 10–16.

Chernykh, E. N., 'Metallurgical Provinces of the 5th-2nd Millennia in Eastern Europe in Relation to the Process of Indo-Europeanization', *JIES* 8 (1980): 317–336.

Formozov, A. A., *Kamenny Vek i Eneolit Prikubanya*, Moscow, 1965.

——, *Problemy Etnokulturnoy Istorii Kammenogo Veka na Territorii Evropeyskoy Chasty SSSR*, Moscow, 1977.

Futoryansky, L. I. et al. (eds), *Problemy Epokhi Eneolita Stepnoy i Lesostepnoy Polosy Vostochnoy Evropy*, Orenburg, 1980.

Häusler, A., 'Anthropomorphe Stelen des Eneolithikums im Nordpontischen Raum', *Wiss. Zeitschrift d. Martin-Luther Universität, Halle-Wittenburg* 15 (1966): 29–73.

——, *Die Gräber der Älteren Ockergrabkultur zwischen Ural und Dnepr*, Berlin, 1974.

——, *Die Gräber der Älteren Ockergrabkultur zwischen Dnepr und Karpaten*, Berlin, 1976.

——, 'Zur Altesten Geschichte von Rad und Wagen im Nordpontischen Raum', *Ethnographisch-Archaeologische Zeitschrift* 22 (1981): 581–647.

Krylova, L. P., 'Kernosovsky Idol (Stela)', in *Eneolit i Bronzovy Vek Ukrainy*, Kiev, 1976: 36–45.

Kuzmina, E. E., 'Kolesny transport i problema etnicheskoy i sotsialnoy istorii drevnego naseleniya Yuzhnorusskikh Stepey', *Vestnik Drevney Istorii*, 4 (1974): 68–87.

——, 'Rasprostranenie konevodstva i kulta konya u Iranoyazychnykh plemen Sredney Azii i drugikh narodov Starovogo Sveta', in *Srednyaya Aziya v Drevnosti i Srednevekove*, Moscow, 1977: 28–52.

Lagodovska, O. F., O. G. Shaposhnikova and M. L. Makarevych, *Mykhaylivske Poselennya*, Kiev, 1962.

Mallory, J. P., 'The Chronology of the Early Kurgan Tradition (Part 1), *JIES* 4 (1976): 257–294

——, 'The Chronology of the Early Kurgan Tradition (Part 2), *JIES* 5 (1977): 339–368.

——, 'The Ritual Treatment of the Horse in the Early Kurgan Tradition', *JIES* 9 (1981): 205–226.

Masson, V. M. and N. Ya. Merpert et al., *Eneolit SSSR*, Moscow, 1982.

Matyushin, G. Yu., *Eneolit Yuzhnogo Urala*, Moscow, 1982.

Medvedev, E. I. et al. (eds), *Problemy Arkheologii Povolzhya i Priuralya*, Kuibyshev, 1976.

Merpert, N. Ya., *Drevneyshie Skotovody Volzhsko-Uralskogo Mezhdurechya*, Moscow, 1974.

——, 'O plemenykh soyuzakh drevneyshikh skotovodov Vostochnoy Evropy', in *Problemy Sovetskoy Arkheologii*, Moscow, 1978: 55–63.

Potekhina, I. D., 'O nositelyakh kultury Sredny Stog II po antropologicheskim dannym', *SA* 1 (1983): 144–154.

Petrenko, A. G., *Drevnee i Srednevekovoe Zhivotnovodstvo Srednego Povolzhya i Preduralya*, Moscow, 1984.

Saygin, N. I. et al. (eds), *Problemy Epokhy Neolita Stepnoy i Lesostepnoy Zony Vostochnoy Evropy*, Orenburg, 1986.

Shilov, V. P., 'Modeli skotovodcheshikh khozyaystv stepnykh oblasty Evrazii v epokhu Eneolita i rannego Bronzovoga Veka', *SA*, 1 (1975): 5–16.

Shilov, Yu. A., 'Ostatki vozov v kurganakh yamnoy kultury Nizhnego Podneprovya', *Arkheologiya* 17 (1975): 53–61.

Telegin, D. Ya., 'Eneoliticheskie stely i pamyatniki nizhnemikhaylovskogo tipa', *Arkheologiya* 4 (1971): 3–17.

——, *Seredno-stogivska Kultura Epokhi Midi*, Kiev, 1973.

——, 'O neoliticheskikh pamyatnikakh Podonya i Stepnogo Povolzhya', *Arkheologiya* 36 (1981): 3–19.

——, *Mezolitychni Pamyatky Ukrainy*, Kiev, 1982.

——, *Dereivka*, BAR International Series 287, Oxford, 1986.

Telegin, D. Ya. and I Potekhnia, *Neolithic Cemeteries and Populations of the Dnieper Basin*, Oxford, 1987.

Vasiliev, I. B., *Eneolit Povolzhya*, Kuybishev, 1981.

Zvelebil, M. (ed.), *Hunters in Transition*, Cambridge, 1986.

CHAPTER EIGHT

Asia

Badetskaya, E. B., *Arkheologicheskie Pamyatniki v Stepyakh Srednego Eniseya*, Leningrad, 1986.

Chlenova, N. L., 'Arkheologicheskie materialy k voprosu ob irantsakh doskifskoy epokhi i indoirantsakh', *SA* 1 (1984): 88–103.

Gening, V., 'The Cemetry at Sintashta and the Early Indo-

Iranian Peoples', *JIES* 7 (1979): 1–29.

Gryaznov, M. P., *The Ancient Civilization of Southern Siberia*, New York, 1969.

Khlobystina, M. D., 'Drevneyshie mogilniki Gornogo Altaya', *SA* 1 (1975): 17–34.

Kiselev, S. V., *Drevnyaya Istoriya Yuzhnoy Sibiri*, Moscow, 1951.

Kuzmina, E. E., *Drevneyshie Skotovody ot Urala do Tyan-Shanya*, Frunze, 1986.

Potemkhina, T. M., *Bronzovy Vek Lesostepnogo Pritobolya*, Moscow, 1985.

Vinogradov, A., M. A. Itina and L. T. Yablonsky, *Drevneyshee Naselenie Nizovy Amudari*, Moscow, 1986.

Caucasus

Gimbutas, M., 'The Beginning of the Bronze Age in Europe and the Indo-Europeans: 3500–2500 BC', *JIES* 1 (1973): 163–214.

Kushnareva, K. Kh. and T. N. Chubinishvili, *Drevnie Kultury Yuzhnogo Kavkaza*, Leningrad, 1970.

Munchaev, R. M., *Kavkaz na Zare Bronzovogo Veka*, Moscow, 1975.

Southeast Europe

Chernyakov, I. T. and G. N. Toshchev, 'Kulturno-khronologicheskie osobennosti kurgannykh pogrebeniy epokhi Bronzy nizhnego Dunaya', in *Novye Materialy po Arkheologii Severo-zapadnogo Prichernomorya*, Kiev, 1985: 5–31.

Dinu, M., 'Quelques Considerations sur la Période de Transition du Néolithique à L'Age du Bronze sur le Territoire de la Moldavie', *Dacia* 12 (1968): 129–139.

Dodd-Opritescu, A., 'Les Éléments "Steppiques" dans L'Enéolithique de Transylvanie', *Dacia* 22 (1978): 87–97.

Ecsedy, I., *The People of the Pit-grave Kurgans in Eastern Hungary*, Budapest, 1979.

Garašanin, M., 'The Eneolithic Period in the Central Balkan Area', *CAH* 3/1 (1982): 136–162.

Georgiev, G., N. Ya. Merpert et al., *Ezero: Rannobronzovoto Selishche*, Sofia, 1979.

Jovanović, B., 'Some Elements of the Steppe Cultures in Yugoslavia', *JIES* 11 (1983): 31–43.

Kalicz, N., *Die Frühbronzezeit in Nordost-Ungarn*, Budapest, 1968.

Marinescu-Bilcu, S. et al., 'Contributions to the Ecology of Pre- and Proto-Historic Habitations at Tirpesti', *Dacia* 25 (1981): 7–31.

Merpert, N. Ya., 'Iz istorii drevneyamnykh plemen' in N. L. Chlenova (ed.) *Problemy Arkheologii Evrazii i Severnoy Ameriki*, Moscow, 1977: 68–80.

Morintz, S. and P. Roman, 'Aspekte des Ausgangs des Äneolithikums und der Übergangsstufe zur Bronzezeit im Raum der Niederdonau', *Dacia* 12 (1968): 45–128.

Necrasov, O., 'Physical Anthropological Characteristics of Skeletons from the Kurgan Graves in Romania', *JIES* 8 (1980): 337–343.

Nestor, I. and E. Zaharia, 'Sur la Période de Transition du Néolithique à L'Age du Bronze dans L'Aire des Civilisations de Cucuteni et de Gumelnita', *Dacia* 12 (1968): 17–43.

Roman, P., 'Strukturänderungen des Endäneolithikums im Donau-Karpaten-Raum', *Dacia* 15 (1971): 31–169.

Telegin, D. Ya., 'Über Kulturelle Kontakte zwischen der Neo-äneolithischen Bevölkerung des Nordpontischen Gebiets und der Balkan-Donauregion', in *Hügelbestattung in der Karpaten-Donau-Balkan-Zone während der Aneolithischen Periode*, Belgrade, 1986: 37–44.

Yarovoy, E. V., *Drevneyshie Skotovodcheskie Plemena Yugo-Zapada SSR*, Kishinev, 1985.

Zbenovich, V. G., *Pozdnetripolskie Plemena Severnogo Prichernomorya*, Kiev, 1974.

——, 'K probleme svyazey Tripolya s eneoliticheskimi kulturami Severnogo Prichernomorya', in *Eneolit i Bronzovy Vek Ukrainy*, Kiev, 1976: 57–68.

Northern and Central Europe

Bader, O. N., D. A. Kraynov and M. F. Kosarev (eds), *Epokha Bronzy Lesnoy Polosy SSSR*, Moscow, 1987.

Buchvaldek, M., 'Corded Pottery Complex in Central Europe', *JIES* 8 (1980): 393–406.

——, 'Zum Gemeineuropäischen Horizont der Schnurkeramik', *Praehistorische Zeitschrift* 61 (1986): 129–151.

——, 'Die Mitteleuropäische Schnurkeramik und das Nordliche Schwarzmeergebiet', *Pamatky Arkheologicke* 77 Pt. 2 (1986): 486–497.

Häusler, A., 'Zu den Beziehungen zwischen dem Nordpontischen Gebiet, Sudost- und Mitteleuropa im Neolithikum und in der frühen Bronzezeit und ihre Bedeutung fur das Indoeuropaische Problem', *Przeglad Archeologiczny* 29 (1981): 101–149.

——, 'Der Ursprung der Schnurkeramik nach Aussage der Grab- und Bestattungssitten', *Jahresschrift für Mitteldeutsche Vorgeschichte* 66 (1983): 9–30.

——, 'Kulturbeziehungen zwischen Ost- und Mitteleuropa in Neolithikum?', *Jahresschrift für Mitteldeutsche Vorgeschichte* 68 (1985): 21–74.

Kilian, L., *Zum Ursprung der Indogermanen*, Bonn, 1983.

Koško, A., 'On the Research of the Beginnings of the Parallel Developmental Ties of the Cultural Systems of the Boundary of Eastern and Western Europe', *Mémoires Archéologiques* (Lublin) (1985): 37–49.

Krzak, Z., 'Der Ursprung der Schnurkeramischen Kultur', *Germania* 59 (1981): 21–29.

Lichardus, J., *Rössen-Gatersleben-Baalberge*, Bonn, 1976.

——, 'Zur Funktion der Geweihspitzen des Types Ostorf,' *Germania* 58 (1980): 1–24.

Menk, R., 'A Synopsis of the Physical Anthropology of the Corded Ware Complex as the Background of the Expansion of the Kurgan Culture, *JIES* 8 (1980): 361–392.

Merpert, N. Ya., 'Drevneyamnaya kulturno-istoricheskaya oblast i voprosy formirovaniya kultur shnurovoy keramiki', in L. V. Koltsov et al. (eds), *Vostochnoy Evropa v Epokhu Kamnya i Bronzy*, Moscow, 1976: 103–127.

Neustupný, E., 'Economy of the Corded Ware Cultures', *Archeologicke Rozhledy* 21 (1969): 43–67.

Schwidetzky, I., 'The Influence of the Steppe People Based on the Physical Anthropological Data in Special Connection to the Corded Ware-Battle Axe Culture', *JIES* 8 (1980): 345–360.

Sulimirski, T., *Corded Ware and Globular Amphorae Northeast of the Carpathians*, London, 1968.

The process of expansion

Barth, F., *Process and Form in Social Life*, London, Boston, 1981.

——, *Features of Person and Society in Swat*, London, Boston, 1981.

Fasold, R., *The Sociolinguistics of Society*, Oxford, 1984.

Khazanov, A. M., *Nomads and the Outside World*, Cambridge, 1984.

Lefébure, C. (ed.), *Pastoral Production and Society*, Cambridge, 1979.

Sherratt, A., 'Plough and Pastoralism: Aspects of the Secondary Products Revolution', in I. Hodder, G. Isaac and N. Hammond (eds), *Pattern of the Past: Studies in Honour of David Clarke*, Cambridge, England, 1981: 261–305.

CHAPTER NINE

Krader, L., 'Buryat Religion and Society', *Southwestern Journal of Anthropology* 10 (1954): 322–351.

Littleton, C. S., *The New Comparative Mythology*, Berkeley and Los Angeles, 1982.

Mallory, J. P., 'A Short History of the Indo-European Problem', *JIES* 1 (1973): 21–65.

Poliakov, L., *The Aryan Myth*, London, 1974.

Sources of illustrations

Monochrome plates

1, 2 Hirmir Fotoarchiv. 3 Ankara Museum. Photo J. Powell. 4 Cincinnati Art Museum, No. 1957.29. 5 Original in State Hermitage, Leningrad. From electrotype in Victoria and Albert Museum, London. Photo P. Clayton. 6 Chester Museum. 7 British Museum, London. 8, 9 Musée Guimet, Paris. Photos Giraudon. 10 National Museum, Athens. Photo Hirmir. 11 National Museum, Athens. Photo J. Powell. 12 Archaeological Museum, Lovech. 13 A. Kastelić and the Archaeological Museum, Ljubljana. 14 Ashmolean Museum, Oxford. 15 Courtesy the Archaeological Institute of the Slovakian Academy of Sciences, Nitra. 16 Muzeum Archeolog znego w Poznaniu. 17 National Museum of Antiquities, Copenhagen. 18 Statens Historiska Museum, Stockholm. 19 Museo Civico, Bologna. From Kastelić, *Situla Art*. 20 National Museum, Copenhagen. 21, 23 Photos courtesy I. B. Vasiliev. 22, 26 Photos courtesy D. Telegin. 24, 25 Photos courtesy I. Potekhina. 27 Drawing by E. Brennan. 28 Magyar Nemzeti Múzeum, Budapest.

Line illustrations

Unless otherwise credited, line illustrations are courtesy the author. For full details of books see Bibliography. **Quotation** (p. 9): J. Parsons, *The Remains of Japhet*, London, 1767: iii. 2 After G. Rohlfs, *Romanische Sprachgeographie*, Munich, 1971: 279. 3, 4 After J. Parsons, *The Remains of Japhet*, London, 1767: 316–317; 340. Abridged and revised. 5 After E. Benveniste, 1973: 530–531, and revised, with permission of Faber and Faber Ltd. 6 W. P. Lehmann and L. Zgusta, 'Schleicher's Tale After a Century', in B. Brogyanyi (ed.), *Studies in Diachronic, Synchronic and Typological Linguistics: Festschrift for Oswald Szemerenyi*, Amsterdam, 1979: 455–466. 7 After H. Pedersen, 1931: 312. 8 After O. Schrader, 1890: 65. 9 After F. Adrados, *Die Räumliche und Zeitliche Differenizierung des Indoeuropäischen im Lichte der Vor- und Frühgeschichte* (= Innsbrucker Beiträge zur Sprachwissenschaft 27), 1982: 25, and slightly abridged. 10 After T. Gamkrelidze and Vy. Ivanov, 1984 vol. 1: 415. 11 After R. Anttila, 1972: 305, with permission of the author. 12 Excerpts from James Gordon, *The English Language*, New York, 1972: 157–158. **Quotation** (p. 24): Hans von Wolzogen, 1875. 'Der Ursitz der Indo-Germanen', *Zeitschrift für Völkerpsycholgie* 8, 1875: 2. 15, 16 Hattic text and Hurrian vocabulary from Friedrich J. et al., 1969: 458; 12, 16. 19 Texts from O. Haas, 1966: 66, 189. 20 Text and translation from W. B. Lockwood, 1972: 180. 21 After A. Jackson, *An Avestan Grammar*, Stuttgart, 1892: xxxi–xxxii. 22 After A. Meillet and M. Cohen, *Les Langues du Monde*, Paris, 1952: map XIa. 25 From German translation of A. Kammenhuber, *Hippologia Hethitica*, Wiesbaden, 1961: 54–55. 28 Adapted from S. P. Gupta, 1979: 241. 29 After B. and R. Allchin, 1982: 238. 31 After R. Kent, *Old Persian*, 1950: 146, with permission of the American Oriental Society, New Haven, Ct, USA. 32 After M. Winn, 1974: 127. 33 Text to Yasna 46 from H. Humbach, *Die Gathas des Zarathustra*, Heidelberg, 1959: 148; translation from J. Duchesne-Guillemin. *The Hymns of Zarathustra*, London, 1952: 75, with permission of John Murray Ltd. 34–35 After A. Mandelshtam, 1968: 15, 27. 36 Text from W. Thomas, 'Ein Tocharischer Liebesbrief', *KZ* 71, 1954: 78–80. 39 Location of languages after I. Diakonov, 1968. **Quotation** (p. 66): W. Ripley, *The Races of Europe*, London, 1900: 453. 40 After J. T. Hooker, *Linear B: An Introduction*, Bristol, 1980: 104–105. 41 Translation from J. T. Hooker. 1976: 12, with permission of Routledge and Kegan Paul Ltd. 42 Adapted from N. G. L. Hammond, 1976: 132. 43 After S. Hiller, 'Zur Frage . . .', 1982: tafel 1. 44 Poem by D. Agolli in M. Gёrecaliu, Q. Haxhihasani and J. Panajoti (eds), *Cёshtje tё Folklorit Shqiptar I*, Tirana 1982: 358. 45 Map after A.

Stipčević, 1977: 32; quote from *Appian's Roman History*, vol. 2, 55–57, translated by Horace White, Loeb Classical Library no. 3, with permission of Heinemann Ltd, London. 46 Texts from W. B. Lockwood, 1972: 165–171. 48, 50 After V. Sedov, 1979: 20; 79. 49 After V. Baran, 1978: 18. 51–53 After B. Rybakov, 1979: 201; 197; 207. 54 After M. Gimbutas, 1963: 30. 55 From S. Chatterji, *Baltic and Aryan*, Simla, 1968: 159–160, with permission of the Indian Institute of Advanced Study. 58 Adapted from B. Kruger, 1983, vol. 1: 96–97, 384–385. 59 After E. Pulgram, 1958: 198, with minor additions. 60 G. and L. Bonfante, *The Etruscan Language*, Manchester, 1983. 61 Translation by J. Poultney, *The Bronze Tablets of Iguvium*, 1959: 158, with the permission of the American Philological Association. 62 After E. Pulgram, 1978: 66–68, with permission of C. Winter Universitätsverlag; and M. E. Huld, pers. com. 63 Text from J. Poultney, 1979: 50. 64 From E. Pulgram, 1978: 53, with permission of C. Winter Verlag. 66 After M. Gimbutas, 1973: 195. 69 After M. Szabo, *The Celtic Heritage in Hungary*, Budapest, 1971: 8. 70 After J. Untermann, 1975: 108. **Quotation** (p. 110): M. Haas, *The Prehistory of Languages*, The Hague, 1969: 32. 73 Drawn from information in F. Wordig, 1970. **Quotation** (p. 128): P. Thieme, 'The Comparative Method for Reconstruction in Linguistics', in D. Hymes (ed.), *Language in Culture and Society*, New York, 1964: 593. 74–77 After R. Dussaud, 'Anciens Bronzes du Louristan et Cultes Iraniens', *Syria* 26 (1947): 213. Redrawn by E. Brennan. 78–79 After B. Lincoln, 1981: 114, 160. **Quotations** (p. 143): A. Sayce, *An Introduction to the Science of Language*, London, 1880: 121. A. Sayce, *An Introduction to the Science of Language*, London, 1880: 121. A. Sayce, 'The Aryan Problem – Fifty Years Later', *Antiquity* 1, 1927: 204–215. 81 After D. Pitcher, *An Historical Geography of the Ottoman Empire*, Leiden, 1972: maps I–IV. 82 See ref. ill. 22: map vii. 84 After P. Friedrich, 1970: 113, with addition. 85 After M. Gimbutas, 1977: 331, and amended by Gimbutas 1985. **Quotation** (p. 186): B. Lincoln, 1981: 181. 86–88 After I. Artemenko et al., 1985: vol. 1, 112, 136. 90, 92 After V. Masson, N. Merpert et al., 1982: 101; 287. 91, 93 After Artemenko et al., 1985: 204. 94 After D. Telegin, *Dereivka*, Oxford, 1986: 7. 95 Courtesy of D. Ya. Telegin. 96–99 After D. Telegin, 1973: 138, 88, 73, 111. 100–106 After Artemenko et al., 1985: 314, 314, 312, 282, 333, 326, 326. 107 After R. Munchaev, 1975: 150. 110–111 After I. Vasiliev, 1981: 122–123. 108 After I. Vasiliev and G. Matveeva, *U Istokov Istorii Samarskogo Povolzhya*, Kuybishev, 1986: 39. 112 After I. Vasiliev, 1974: 153. 113 After O. Lagodovska, O. Shaposhnikova, and M. Markarevic. 1962: 66. 114 After Yu. Shilov, 'Ostatki vozov . . .', 1975: 54. 115 After I. Chernyakov and N. Shmagliy, 1983: 13. 116–118 After Artemenko et al., 1985: 341, 343, 343. 119 After A. Häusler, 1966: 64. 120 After I. Alekseevka, 1986: 45. 121 After Häusler, 1966: 64. 122 See ref. ill. 108: 39. **Quotation** (p. 222): R. von Ihering, *The Evolution of the Aryan*, London, 1897: 5. 123–124 After E. Badetskaya, 1986: 20, 21. 126 Adapted from N. Chlenova, 1984: 100–101. 128 After K. Kushnareva and T. Chubinishvili, 1970: 60–61. 129 After Gimbutas, 1977: 315. 131 After Masson and Merpert et al., 1982: 300. 132–134 After Artemenko et al., 1985: 250. 136 After I. Chernyakov and G. Toshchev, 1985: 8. 137 After I. Ecsedy, 1979: 29. 138 Adapted from M. Buchvaldek and D. Koutecky, *Vikletice*, Prague, 1970: 105. 140 After O. Bader et al., 1987: 61. 144 After T. Sulimirski, *Prehistoric Russia*, London, 1970: 163. 143 After Artemenko et al., 1985: 288. 145 After L. Kilian, 1983. **Quotation** (p. 266): G. Vacher de Lapouge, *L'Aryen, Son Role Social*, Paris, 1899: 372–373, quoted in L. Poliakov, *The Aryan Myth*, London, 1974: 270. 147 From H. Klein, *Graphic Worlds of Peter Breugel the Elder*, New York, 1963: 151, with kind permission of Dover Publications, New York.

Acknowledgments

I would like to acknowledge the questionable honour bestowed upon me by the late Glyn Daniel who convinced me that I should tackle a subject wherein I would not only be able to run afoul of almost every regional specialist in archaeology from Ireland to China but also wander outside my own discipline and subject myself to the criticism of my colleagues in linguistics, mythology and anthropology. Except for a career in politics, one seldom gets the opportunity to offend so many people at once.

Preparation of this book was greatly facilitated by the British Council and the Academies of Science of both the USSR and the Ukrainian SSR. I would like to thank especially Nikolai Merpert (Moscow) and Dmitry Telegin and all his associates in the Institute of Archaeology (Kiev) for their generous assistance and hospitality. In addition, I would like to thank Igor Vasiliev (Kuibyshev) for reading a portion of the manuscript and supplying me with several illustrations; Alexander Häusler (Berlin-Halle) for over a decade of book and article exchanges which has made it possible for me to obtain numerous works I would otherwise have been unable to consult. The production of maps and figures was greatly facilitated by the assistance of Paul Campbell and Evelyn Cooper of December Publications, Belfast, and Emma Brown, Queen's University, who prepared most of the illustrations. I would thank Louise Porter of the

Queen's secretarial centre who endured several drafts of the text, Barrie Hartwell of the Archaeology Department for photographic assistance, R. B. Warner of the Ulster Museum who permitted me access to his programme for graphically representing radiocarbon dates, J. B. Rutter (Dartmouth) who provided valuable comments on my treatment of Greek origins, and Stuart Piggott who read through the entire text. I owe a special debt to M. E. Huld (California State University, Los Angeles) who read the first eight chapters making many valuable comments and preserving me from numerous linguistic errors. None of these is responsible for any infelicities of fact or interpretation that I may have stubbornly or unwittingly persisted in, nor are any of those who originally instructed me in the languages, mythology and archaeology of the Indo-Europeans, among whom I would mention Raimo Antilla, Ken Chapman, P. K. Ford, Hans-Peter Schmidt, C. Scott Littleton, Jaan Puhvel, J. Caerwyn Williams, Lilli Kaelas and most especially Marija Gimbutas – who if not entirely in agreement with my conclusions might at least draw some amusement that I have at last overcome my disdain for intuition. Finally, very special thanks to my wife Eimear for both her assistance and patience which saw me through to the end of this book.

Index